William Anderson Scott

The Christ of the Apostles' Creed

The Voice of the Church Against Arianism, Strauss and Renan

William Anderson Scott

The Christ of the Apostles' Creed
The Voice of the Church Against Arianism, Strauss and Renan

ISBN/EAN: 9783337028138

Printed in Europe, USA, Canada, Australia, Japan

Cover: Foto ©ninafisch / pixelio.de

More available books at **www.hansebooks.com**

THE CHRIST OF THE APOSTLES' CREED:

THE VOICE OF THE CHURCH AGAINST ARIANISM, STRAUSS AND RENAN,

WITH AN APPENDIX.

Τί ὑμῖν δοκεῖ περὶ τοῦ Χριστοῦ; τίνος υἱός ἐστι;
MATT. XXII. 42.

"The LORD of hosts hath walked
This world of man: the one Almighty sent
His everlasting Son to wear the flesh,
And glorify this mortal human shape."—MILMAN.

BY
REV. W. A. SCOTT, D. D.,
PASTOR OF THE 42D STREET PRESBYTERIAN CHURCH.

NEW YORK:
ANSON D. F. RANDOLPH,
770 BROADWAY.
1867.

Entered according to Act of Congress, in the year 1867,

BY REV. W. A. SCOTT, D. D.,

In the Clerk's Office of the District Court of the United States for the Southern District of New York.

MCCREA AND MILLER,
Stereotypers.

THE APOSTLES' CREED.

I Believe

in God the Father Almighty, maker of heaven and earth;

and I Believe

in Jesus Christ his only Son, our Lord;

Who was conceived by the Holy Ghost, born of the Virgin Mary;

Suffered under Pontius Pilate, was crucified, dead, and buried;

He descended into hell;

The third day he rose again from the dead;

He ascended into heaven, and sitteth on the right hand of God the Father Almighty;

From thence he shall come to judge the quick and the dead.

I believe in the Holy Ghost; The Holy Catholic Church; The Communion of Saints; The forgiveness of sins, The resurrection of the body, and the life everlasting. Amen.

PREFACE.

NEVER since the foundation of the world was there so much learning and human intellect employed on Pilate's question: "What shall I then do with Jesus which is called Christ?" as at this moment. But if this was a grave and solemn question with the Roman Procurator and the Jewish people more than eighteen hundred years ago, it is not less important now. The knightly Roman Governor and both Jews and Gentiles made great mistakes in answering this question. Barabbas was released and Jesus was crucified. But when the Lord of glory was slain with wicked hands, this question did not cease to agitate the minds of both Jews and Gentiles. Nor has it ever been entirely at rest from that day to this; but at no time, nor in any generation since Jesus was born, has this question excited as much interest as it does now, throughout the civilized world. For nearly fifty years the leading Reviews of Europe have been heavy with elaborate Articles on lives of the Lord Jesus. Such publications are almost endless, and their names legion.

In Great Britain and Germany and France, and perhaps even in our country, theological and metaphysical subjects are among the most popular topics of discussion. The public mind is greatly exercised on matters of the most solemn importance concerning Christ, the Church, and Christianity. "Tracts for the Times," "Essays and Reviews," and "Replies;" and Renan, Newman, Pusey, and "Ecce Homo," are rivals for popularity with the latest sensational novels. Nor is this to be regretted. For although the results are not always such as are to be desired, yet the mental excitement manifested on such questions is far more hopeful than indifference or stupidity. Amid the awful tendency of modern times to a gross materialism, we hail this intellectual activity as a good omen. All light, it is true, is not saving, yet saving grace always enters the soul by light. And besides, this intense interest on such subjects is in itself altogether justifiable. For if Christianity is any thing, it is every thing. And as Scherer most feelingly admits, a religion that is not positive is nothing at all.* And any proper idea of the Christian religion without some knowledge of the person and character of its Founder, is impossible. There have been many controversies in the Christian world on minor points, concerning which different branches of the Catholic Church took their position, and in process of time have modified or changed their grounds. But from Simon

---

* Mélanges d'histoire religieuse ; pp. 250–254.

Magus and Cerinthus to Theodore Parker and Renan, the question, "What think ye of Christ? Whose Son is He?" has been a vital one. Faith in the Incarnation, the personal history, real death, and Resurrection of Jesus Christ is the fundamental article of Christianity, and without this belief the Church could have had no existence. Is this belief correct? Does it rest on the truth, or is it a misbelief? A *conspectus* of the theological and critical literature of the age would lead us to think that this, beyond all comparison, is the most absorbing question of our times. Perhaps one reason for this is, that there is more critical learning set free from other pursuits, and at leisure to be employed on such investigations, than ever before. Our scholars are now better acquainted with the languages and dialects cognate to the Hebrew. We know more of the habits and feelings of Oriental life. We can perhaps better apprehend the modes of thought common to our Lord's followers in His day, and hence we are brought more closely into sympathy with Him, and our desire is therefore stronger to know more fully the particulars of His human life. Nor is it possible for us to conceive of a greater subject, or one that should more earnestly employ our noblest energies than to apprehend the true God, whom to know aright, and his son Jesus Christ, is life eternal.

CHRIST OF THE APOSTLES' CREED! And why not? According to Pearson, there are twelve articles in this Creed, half of which are concerning Christ; or, if we count the lines composing it as printed in our Catechism, nine out of the fourteen are taken up in defining and expressing what we are to believe concerning God's only Son, Jesus Christ our Lord. And in the Nicene and the so-called Athanasian Creed, quite as much prominence is given to explaining what we are to believe concerning Christ. Only ignorance or prejudice can say the Apostles' Creed is not our Creed. The Apostles' Creed is common to all believers in Christ. It no more belongs to prelatical and papal communions than does the Bible, or than Christ himself. All branches of the one great holy Catholic Church claiming to hold evangelical or orthodox doctrines, believe in the Apostles' Creed as fully as they do in the Ten Commandments, the Lord's Prayer, or the Sermon on the Mount. It is a part of their symbols and is taught in their families and in their schools. They do not hold that the Creed was given in its present form by inspiration, as the holy Scriptures were, but that it embodies the fundamental doctrines of the Gospel, as believed and preached by the Apostles.* And if in some quarters there are signs of unduly exalting the rites and formularies of Christianity, or even a tendency in some prelatical zones towards Rome, there are, on the other hand, evidences of a deep and earnest awakening, as we believe, to the great doc-

---

* The purpose of this volume does not require a critical history of the Apostles' Creed, but a brief review of false doctrines put forth in the early ages, which this Creed was intended to deny and confute, as well as some remarks on the use of Creeds, and the Council of Nice, may be found in our Appendix.

trines of the Cross, indicated by an increasing desire, in many non-prelatical communions, to make more prominent the doctrines of their ancient symbols, and to adhere more steadfastly to such a platform as the Apostles' Creed. This, with an out-pouring of the Holy Spirit, is all we conceive to be necessary for the latter day glory.

The occasion of the following Discourses is easily described. In the midst of other excitements and a different style of preaching, the author felt a very great desire to hold up "the central figure of the universe" more prominently before the minds of his hearers. In casting around for a plan, he thought to make Witsius on the Creed the foundation of a series of Discourses on Christ, but he soon became convinced it would not be expedient to follow this great author as closely as he had intended to do; he therefore determined to adopt a plan of his own, more fitted, according to his judgment, to the necessities of the times. Accordingly, he applied himself to the study of Lightfoot, Baronius, Barrow, Hooker, Bingham, Lardner, Leland, Charnock, Bates, Leighton, Ridgely, Dwight, Hill, Dick, Calvin, and Hey, with a free use of lexicons and commentators on the points under examination. As, however, I did not find any one of these authors, great and learned as they are, altogether such as I thought just the kind of book I should like to put at this time into the hands of my congregation, I have attempted to interest them in the following discourses. *I swear by no man's words*, nor do I profess wholly to adopt any of the authors referred to in this volume; but I wish here to acknowledge the value I set upon and the use I have made of Witsius' "Dissertations on the Apostles' Creed;" Burnet's and also Rev. E. Harold Browne's "Exposition of the Thirty-nine Articles;" Suicer de Symb.; Bull Def. Fid. Nic.; Pearson's "'Great' Exposition of the Creed;" Bishop Forbes' "Explanation of the Nicene Creed;" and Harvey's "History and Theology of the Three Creeds."

Although freely using these authors, I have followed my own plan, and endeavored to present THE CHRIST OF THE APOSTLES as the great Saviour of the world. And I hope I shall not be considered rash and presumptuous for venturing to preach and publish Discourses on subjects so profound and so mysterious, because so many other authors of the highest culture and finest intellectual powers have already put forth their best efforts in the same direction. It has seemed to me the specialities of the times laid this duty on me, at least as far as my own congregation was concerned. It is indeed not easy for us to realize the debt we owe to the able and learned defenders of our holy faith in past ages; and after all the slurs at, and attacks made upon our Creeds, on account of their stiffness, dry logic, and artificial and professional definitions, I am more than ever convinced that we are in greater need of an exact theology than at any time since the days of the Apostles. It is one of the many evidences of God's care over His Church, that He has raised up from age to age men qualified by learning and grace to explain, defend, and propagate the great doctrines of the Cross, which have been most surely believed by the Church of God from the beginning. And as it has been, so we believe it will be. And as every age has its own characteristics, and calls for its own authors, so every man has his own anointing (*charisma*), and is called to do his own work in his own day, and to do it well and quickly, and with all his might, for the night of death cometh speedily, when no man can work. As the only way to get darkness out is to let light in, so my great desire in these Discourses has not been so much to find out novelties or to expose false doctrines in detail, as to explain the truth according to the Divine Word, and with the light of the interpretation put upon it in past ages by some of the ablest and most pious scholars, and thus to guide the mind to a well-grounded faith in the "Redeemer of God's elect." For if Christ be formed in our hearts the hope of glory, then we are not so easily led astray by false doctrines. If the mind is full of the light of truth, error cannot enter.

If this volume should find its way into the hands of the learned critic, I beg he will remember that these Discourses are not sermons, but rather historical and expository *Dissertations*, delivered before large assemblies, consisting of persons of all ages and classes and conditions in life; and being continued from week to week, some repetition was occasionally necessary, as also frequent amplifications and explanations that would not have been required before a body of theological students. And they are now published as nearly as possible just as they were delivered, and at the desire of many who were interested in them as they fell from their author's lips. If otherwise qualified, it is well known that the absorbing cares and labors and sympathies of a city Pastor in our times do not allow leisure and strength for the pursuits of literature as he might desire. But God does not require every thing from any one man.

I beg also to invite the attention of kind readers, especially of liberally educated young men, to the "Aspect of Modern Thought concerning Christ," as seen in our examination of the theories of Strauss and Renan, in the Appendix to this volume. It is also hoped that the brief review of the early heresies and philosophical opinions advanced in the early ages concerning Christ, and the notice of the Arian controversy, as given in the Appendix, will be acceptable to the reader, and increase his interest in these Discourses. The volumes which I have ventured heretofore to offer to the public, have been chiefly historical expositions of Biblical characters, and designed mainly for the young. In this one, my earnest wish is to promote the sincere, intelligent, and humble belief of the Truth concerning Christ, and especially to present Him as He has been believed on in the world and received up into glory, an Almighty Saviour.

NEW YORK, *February*, 1867.

CONTENTS.

I.

BELIEVING IN THE NAME OF JESUS.

PAGE

The Great Miracle—*Dean Stanley.*—The only Rule of Faith—The NAME JESUS, its Etymology and Signification—Strong Attachment of early Christians to the Person and Name of Jesus—Bernard's Hymn 17–32

II.

BELIEVING ON THE NAME CHRIST.

Use of Creeds—Paul's Style of Preaching—The Faith of the ancient Jewish Church—*Cyril* on the Name CHRIST—Why Jesus is called Christ—Anointing—*Hooker* and *Leighton.*—Why we profess to believe this Article...33–43

III.

CHRIST GOD'S SON AND OUR LORD.

Respect for the Proper Titles of Persons—St. Peter's Confession of Christ the True Faith—Mystery on such a Subject as the Persons of the Godhead—Jesus is God and Lord—*Gregory Nazianzen, Theodoret.*—Our Covenant a Sacramental Oath—Quotations from *Cleanthes, Epictetus,* and *Seneca.*...49–67

IV.

JESUS "CONCEIVED" AND "BORN OF THE VIRGIN MARY."

Disbelief—"Needle-Guns" now wanted—"A Restatement of Doctrines—Testimony of the Creeds—*Athanasius.*—The Incarnation—Our "Goel"—*Leighton.*.....................................68–84

V.

CHRIST SUFFERED UNDER PONTIUS PILATE.

Rabbinical Invention about *two* Messiahs—Pontius Pilate and his Official Report to Rome—The Article of the Creed abundantly sustained....85–101

VI.

JESUS CHRIST WAS CRUCIFIED.

King *Clovis*—The Bearing of this Article—The History of the Cross—The Empress Helena—Death by Crucifixion described—This Doctrine fundamental—Christ's Trophies still hanging on the Cross as his Great Triumphal Arch..102–123

VII.

GOD'S ONLY SON OUR "DEAD CHRIST."

Christ Suffering an exact Fulfilment of the Prophecies of the Jewish Church concerning the Messiah—The Specialities of this Article of the Creed confuting *Mohammed* and early Heretics—Our Lord's real Death, and why—Benefits—*Luther* on Willingness to die....................124–143

VIII.

OUR LORD CHRIST BURIED.

Invited to Jesus' Funeral—The Hebrew Belief—Christianity teaches Respect for the Dead and their Bodies—The Prophecies fulfilled in a Roman Death and a Jewish Burial—Our Lord's Pall-bearers—Why Jesus was buried—Uses of this Article.....................................144–168

IX.

"HE DESCENDED INTO HELL."

Unsatisfactory State of this Article—Its History—Use of Abstracts—*Calvin*, *Dr. A. Alexander*, Reformed Dutch Church—History of Terms, *Sheol*, *Hades*, *Hell*—Theory of Witsius, Calvin, and others rejected—What the *Descent into Hell* means...169–193

X.

"HELL" NOT GEHENNA NOR PURGATORY.

Sheol and *Hades* among the Fathers—Peter's Argument—Dr. Barrow on *Sheol*—The Scriptures know nothing of Christ in Gehenna, nor of a *Limbus Patrum*..194–223

XI.

CHRIST ROSE THE THIRD DAY.

Christ's Resurrection a Vital Doctrine—Witnesses and Proofs—Jewish Burial and Tomb—Why Jesus was so long Buried 224–248

XII.

THE RESURRECTION HISTORICALLY DEMONSTRATED.

Not incredible—Narratives not Fictions—The Witnesses—The *Marys*—The Evidences as a Whole—Benefits of this Doctrine 249–273

XIII.

CHRIST ASCENDED INTO HEAVEN.

Historic Notice of Ascension Day—*Place* from which He Ascended—Sacred Associations with Nature—*Time* of the Ascension—The Fact itself and the Proofs—With what Body He Ascended—Why He Ascended, and the Benefits 274–295

XIV.

"AND SITTETH ON THE RIGHT HAND OF GOD."

Our Lord's "Session" at the Right Hand of God—Heaven of Heavens—*Sir William Rowan Hamilton's* Suggestion that our Lord was Ten Days in Ascending—Equality with the Father—The Place of Honor—*Sitting* and *Standing*—Why He sitteth at the Right Hand of God 296–313

XV.

CHRIST COMING TO THE LAST JUDGMENT.

History of this Article, and its Points concerning the Coming of Christ in the Last Judgment—Paul on Eternal Judgment—The Doctrine as set forth in the *Confession of Faith*—*Place* and *Time* of the Last Judgment—JESUS CHRIST the Judge, his Qualifications for this Office—*Augustine*.—Proofs of God's Love 314–337

XVI.

CHRIST JUDGING THE WORLD.

Christ is the Final Judge of Quick and Dead—The Day is fixed—It follows the General Resurrection—Premonitions and Moral Proofs of the Judgment—Unfinished Problems—Awful Splendor of the Day—The Parties

Judged—Sins of the Godly—Our Responsibilities in View of the Last
Judgment 338–357

XVII.

RULES OF CHRIST'S FINAL JUDGMENT.

"Orations" on the Last Judgment—*Dr. Watts* on "According to their Works." Distinct separate Destinies—Proceedings public—Eternity unchangeable follows—The terrible Individuality of the Last Day—Doctrines and Lessons from the Day of Final Judgment 358–381

The Appendix, page 383.

For chief things in the Appendix, see Contents to Appendix, page 431.

I.

BELIEVING IN THE NAME OF JESUS.

"And this is His commandment, that we should believe on the name of His Son Jesus Christ, and love one another, as He gave us commandment."—1 JOHN iii. 23.

JESUS CHRIST is "the greatest miracle of history." He is himself the strongest "testimony to Christianity." And man himself is the most complete proof that he needs Christ. Human history is an illuminated pictorial series demonstrating man's need of a Saviour, just such as the Gospel makes known to us. "For after that in the wisdom of God the world by wisdom knew not God, it pleased God by the foolishness of preaching to save them that believe." "But of him are ye in Christ Jesus, who of God is made unto us wisdom, and righteousness, and sanctification, and redemption: That according as it is written, He that glorieth, let him glory in the Lord." 1 Cor. i. 21, 30, 31. "When the fulness of the time was come, God sent forth his Son, made of a woman, made under the law, to redeem them that were under the law." Gal. iv. 4, 5.

DEAN STANLEY well says: "First and above all, stand those great moral doctrines of the Gospel, to which the highest place has been assigned, beyond dispute, in the Gospel itself. But, next after these, ecclesiastical history teaches us that the most vital, the most comprehensive, the most fruitful has been, and is still—not the supremacy of the Bible, or the authority of its several books; not the power of the Pope or of the Church; not the sacraments, not original sin, not predestination, not justification, but the doctrine of the Incarnation."* Now, if I am not mistaken in my reading of Dean Stanley's various works, there is in them a decided tendency to Broad Churchism, and perhaps to Monotheism or Sabellianism, with which I cannot sympathize. I say this, however, in no invidious sense. What I wish here to say is mainly this, that I am not willing to be held responsible for the opinions or views of any author, however learned or great his reputation, whom I quote, except as far as I expressly adopt them. I acknowledge no king in Zion but the LORD JESUS, and no Rule of Faith but the HOLY SCRIPTURES. Nor do I wish here to dogmatize in any unfriendly manner on the great question of the relative importance of the doctrines taught in the Word of God. It is not for me to settle the proportion or quantity of the doctrines of Revelation necessary to salvation, but in this case, as I understand the Dean, we have the truth, the great truth. For whatever may be said of the point of a standing or falling church, our holy religion, from beginning to end, depends upon the Incarnation. This certainly was included in the Apostle's direction: "Believe on the Lord Jesus Christ, and thou shalt be saved." God the Father Almighty is known to us by His two great works of creation and redemption. The Gospel of St. John opens with a solemn declaration that the Son of God is the author of both these works. "In

---

* Lecture V., on Eastern Church.

the beginning was the Word, and the Word was with God, and the Word was God." "All things were made by Him. And the Word was made flesh and dwelt among us, and we beheld His glory, the glory as of the only begotten of the Father, full of grace and truth." It is impossible by any fair interpretation of these verses to deny that the Word means Jesus the Son of God. "The Word was God," and "all things were made" by the same Word, and this same "Word was made flesh." The author of creation is God the Son, and the same is the author of the work of redemption. As creatures and subjects of moral government, therefore, we have a deep concern in apprehending the true character of the Son of God, for He is our Creator and our final Judge. But it is still more important for us as sinners to apprehend the mercy of God in Christ, and receive Him as our Saviour. The work of redemption at once implies our ruin and misery, and declares the necessity for the Son of God becoming our Mediator. As sin has separated us from God, and as the very idea of religion implies our reconciliation to God, so there is no religion without faith. For whosoever cometh to God must believe that He is, and that He is what He reveals Himself to be in his Word. There is no reconciling the sinner with God—no coming of the sinner to God—no receiving of the sinner by God—without a Mediator. This Mediator is God's only Son, Jesus Christ our Lord. There is for us as sinners no such a thing as truly believing in God the Father, but by believing in Jesus Christ His Son. "No man comes unto the Father but by me."

It is true, there is a place for repentance and prayers and a new obedience; but nothing brings us to God except faith in Jesus. Nothing washes away our sins but the blood of the Lamb of God. We cannot worship

God but through Christ. We cannot see God but in Christ, nor can God look on us in love but as He sees us in Christ. There is then a specialty in our professing *to believe in Jesus Christ* that we must not overlook.

1. In our text, the sum of our duty is declared to be to believe on the Name of the Son of God, and to love one another as He hath commanded us. This is the commandment of God Himself. In other Scriptures we are taught that we must worship the Son as we worship the Father—honor Him as we honor the Father—and we are commanded to *hear* Him rather than Moses or Elias, and we are taught to ascribe the names, works, titles, and perfections to Him that we find given to God in the Scriptures. But here a positive command from God is given *to believe in the Name*—that is, in the Person, character, and mission of His Son Jesus Christ.

2. As a commandment of God, the text not only implies duty on our part, but grace from God. "Faith in Jesus Christ is a saving grace alone, whereby we receive and rest upon Him for salvation, as He is offered to us in the Gospel." The gift is grace, and the exercise of it is God working in us. It is God's commandment that we should believe on his Son. So Jesus commanded the man at the pool of Bethesda to rise and walk, and enabled him to obey. The same is true of the man with a withered hand. The command was accompanied with the gift of power to obey.

3. Note also that we have clear illustrations from the Scriptures that *Duty and Grace* are joined together. "Work out your own salvation with fear and trembling; For it is God which worketh in you both to will and to do of his good pleasure." Phil. ii. 12, 13. In the text

the command of faith and the command of love are linked and knit together, as if the weight of our salvation hung equally and alike upon both; as without faith it is impossible to please God, so it is equally impossible to please Him without love. No duty will profit without faith, and no faith will profit without love. As whatever is not of faith is sin, so whatever duty we perform without love to our fellow-men and towards God is not accepted of God. If I give all my goods to feed the poor, and have not love, I am nothing. See *Burkitt*.

The specialty of the text, then, is, that God commands us by the Gospel to believe in His Son Jesus Christ—to come to Him pleading His name and merits, that we may obtain the forgiveness of sin and the blessings of salvation; and that for His sake, and after His example, we should love one another, and be liberal and self-denying and charitable, even as Christ himself hath loved us and given Himself for us. It is this that makes a Christian a follower of the Lord Jesus, a child of God, an heir of glory.

My principal purpose for the present, however, in reference to the text, is to offer some remarks on believing in JESUS, or rather on JESUS as the object of belief. Faith, belief, and the authority of the Divine command and the reasons for obedience, cannot be here dwelt upon. The second Article of our Creed is, "And (I believe) in Jesus Christ, His only Son our Lord." Here are three leading subjects: 1st. The double name given to our Lord; 2d. His relation to the Father is declared: *His only Son;* 3d. His dominion over us, and our submission to Him as our Sovereign Lord. Or perhaps I should be more easily understood if I said, we have here *four* titles ascribed to our Lord:

I. His proper name, JESUS, which like other Bible names is also significant, and in his case truly significant, of his character and work.

II. We have the name of his office, CHRIST.

III. His nature—HE IS GOD'S ONLY SON.

IV. His dignity—OUR LORD.

I limit myself this evening to the Name Jesus: "And this is his commandment, that we should believe on the Name of his Son Jesus Christ.'

Then let us attend to the Name, and see how its meaning is realized.

I. The *Name* of a person, according to the usage of Holy Scripture, signifies the person himself, his authority, and all that is implied in or expressed by his titles. And so far are our Lord's names and titles from being insignificant, that it is boldly affirmed by our best scholars that the name of JESUS is possessed of a dignity and meaning superior to all the other names ascribed to him, or even of God the Father, and that it is for this reason it is said, "His name is above every name, and that at it every knee shall bow, and every tongue confess that He is Lord."

It is not considered that the double name *Jesus Christ* is to be reckoned as a proper and surname. This designation is not like Simon, with the surname Peter, or John, whose surname is Mark, but like John the Baptist; that is, a proper name with an official title. JESUS was his proper name, and CHRIST his official title. The learned have also called our attention to the fact that one of these names is Hebrew and the other Greek, and that these names are intended to signify that the Son of God is a Saviour alike to Jews and Gentiles,—a light to lighten the Gentiles and the glory of his people Israel. Perhaps, too, the first name is Hebrew and the other Greek, to show that salvation is of the Jews—to the Jew first, and also to the Greek. Salvation is of the Jews, as a fountain or reservoir, until the time appointed of the Father; then it overflowed. As in baptism, the second place is assigned to the Son, so the same order is followed in the Creed. And as, in declaring our belief "in God the Father Almighty, Maker of heaven and earth," we acknowledge His attributes of power and majesty, so also by believing in Jesus Christ we accept of his miraculous history, and believe in his whole life, sufferings, and work, from his birth to his coming in glory as the Judge of quick and dead. Nor is it without reason that the name JESUS CHRIST is made a part of this Article of the Creed. Particular significancy is attached to the name. Twice do we find the angel referring to it. Speaking to Joseph, he said, "She shall bring forth a son, and thou shalt call his name JESUS; for He shall save his people from their sins." And on another occasion, the angel said to the Virgin Mother, "Behold, thou shalt conceive in thy womb and bring forth a son, and shalt call his name JESUS. He shall be great, and shall be called the Son of the Highest; and the Lord God shall give unto him the throne of his father David." The NAME, then, was intended to be significant. Its etymology admits of a twofold analysis. One is intimated by the first angelic announcement, which is a direct interpretation of the name, "for He shall save his people from their sins." This may be understood as from the Hebrew Hiphil infinitive *Hosheang* (הוֹשִׁיעַ) as an abstract term, SALVATION, or as the concrete, SAVIOUR. The meaning, then, is, "He is salvation," that is, "He shall save."

The other etymology attaches the name Je Hovah to the name Jesus by the use of the letter J, as the pronominal prefix: "*He* shall save," in which case J represents the abbreviated form *Jeho*, which occurs several times in the Bible, as in *Jeho*-ram, *Jeho*shaphat, &c. This interpretation is also according to the very order of the words in the Nicene Creed. Closely after the Eternal Word is declared to be God of God, it is added: "Who for us men, and for our salvation, came down from heaven, and was incarnate by the Holy Ghost of the Virgin Mary." That is, as his name intimates, He is "Jesus, Jehovah, Salvation."

The angelic announcement of the name JESUS, then, was exceedingly emphatic. "Jehovah shall save." "Thou shalt call his name Jesus; He shall be great, and shall be called the Son of the Highest—to give the knowledge of salvation unto his people by the remission of their sins." Luke i. 33–77. According to our understanding, then, of the angelic announcement, JESUS is only an abbreviation of the two names of JEHOVAH JOSHUAH, that is, Jehovah, Salvation.* The Hebrews were familiar with this combination. Thus in Exo. xiv. 13: "Fear not, stand still, and see the salvation of the LORD." Here the Hebrew words are *Jehovah Joshuah*, and the very same form occurs in 2 Chron. xx. 17. Nor is this interpretation set aside by saying that our name JESUS is Greek-Latin, for it is confessedly the Greek rendering of the Hebrew Jeshua or Joshua, just as we have Ose for Hosea, Messias for Messiah, Esaias for Isaiah, Zecharias for Zachariah. Nor is this view interfered with by the fact that the name Joshua or Jeshu was common among the Jews.

---

* See Harvey on the Creed, 1 vol., p. 165 *et seq.* Also Witsius.

The first individual having this name may be regarded as typifying the Son of God. Joshua, you know, was the leader of the chosen people into the Land of Promise, which was a type of the rest that remaineth for the people of God in heaven. Even some of those writers who have wished to get rid of a Hebrew etymology for the name JESUS, seek to derive it from a Greek word having the same signification, for example, *ιω*, making its future *ιασω*, and thence *ιασους*, and by changing alpha into eta, *Ιησους*, Jesus, meaning *one who heals*. The great Witsius on this subject gives a remarkable quotation from *Rabbi Hakkados* in support of Theophylact's declaration, that "the name JESUS is not Greek, but Hebrew," which is this: "Because Messiah shall save mankind, He will be called Jeshua. But the people of another nation, who shall embrace his religion, will call him JESUS; and, therefore, you find this name JESU pointed out in Gen. xlix. 10. For the first letters of the Hebrew words for *until Shiloh come*, form the name ישו JESU."

The name, then, may have belonged to Joshua, and still its full signification have been reserved for Christ Jesus. In its fullest sense the name JESUS means JEHOVAH—SALVATION. That is, in Himself He is God, and in relation to us, He is the salvation of God—He is God our Saviour. I have said that Jesus is the Greek for the Hebrew of Joshua, and that the name was not an uncommon one among the Jews in Apostolic times. See Acts xiii. 6; Col. iv. 11; Heb. iv. 8. Still there is no room for any confusion or uncertainty as to the name applied to our Lord. It was assigned to him *twice* before his birth, and was given to him, according to Hebrew usage, when he was dedicated to God. For when "eight days were accomplished for the circumcising of the child, his name was called Jesus, which was so named of the angel before he was conceived in the womb." Luke ii. 21.

He was also distinguished from others bearing the same name by the place of his residence, and by his reputed father's name. Thus he was called "Jesus of Nazareth," "Jesus the son of Joseph;" and in process of time, "Jesus Christ," and then "the Lord Jesus Christ." The general meaning, then, of our Lord's proper name is Deliverer, Saviour, or, more strictly in accordance with Hebrew idiom, JEHOVAH OUR SALVATION, or JEHOVAH THE SAVIOUR.

Eusebius says, "the name Jesus translated into the Greek language signifies the salvation of God—that is, the salvation of JEHOVAH." And this interpretation is supported by Hebrew usage. Joshua, who was a type of our Saviour, was first called *Hoshea;* but Moses prefixed the letter Jod, and changed it into *Jehoshua*, Joshua. The reason for this is thought to have been threefold:

1. By this prefix a more certain assurance was given to Joshua himself that JEHOVAH would be with him in the conquest. The prefix united his name with God's, and then it meant: *He shall save.*

2. The people, perceiving that God had thus joined his own name with that of their leader, were more willing to obey, and more courageous and hopeful.

3. Moses, being a prophet, foresaw that Joshua was a type of the coming Messiah, and therefore attached this sacred prefix to his name. Nor is it altogether unworthy of notice, that the name thus composed contains all the letters of the name Jehovah, the true God.

II. In the second place, when we profess our faith, and say, *I believe in Jesus*, that He is Christ, the only

Son of God, our Lord, how are we to understand that the name JESUS fulfils its signification?

When the angel announced that his name shall be called "*Jesus,*" he added, "for he shall save his people from their sins." *Save* not by setting up a temporal kingdom—*Save* not by merely setting a virtuous example—*Save* not by merely explaining the doctrines of the Gospel, not merely by working stupendous miracles and dying a martyr for the truth. He shall *save* not simply by rising from the dead, and opening up the way to immortality and everlasting glory, but He shall save his people from their sins by offering himself once for all a sacrifice to satisfy Divine Justice and reconcile them to God. "But this man, after he had offered one sacrifice for sins, for ever sat down on the right hand of God. For by one offering he hath perfected for ever them that are sanctified—for having himself purged our sins, sat down," &c. See Heb. i. 3; x. 12, 14. To understand, therefore, the name, Jesus, a Saviour, we must remember—

I. Our state by nature—dead in trespasses and in sins. Children of disobedience and of wrath—sinners, poor and blind and miserable. And then—

II. That Jesus *procures and applies* to us a real, spiritual and eternal salvation. But what is salvation? What is it to be saved? Is it not freedom from evil and a participation in all good? Is it not deliverance from *sin*, which is the greatest of all evils—redemption from *sin*, its curse, pollution, dominion, and damning power? Sin was so prominently in the mind of the angel as the sum of all misery that he speaks of no other evil. As if he meant to say, Jesus saves his people from all real evils in saving them from their sins. And that this is the true view of sin, we have only to reflect that it is the abominable thing that God hates. Its *odiousness* lies in its being the very work, image, and chief delight of the devil, whose works Jesus came to destroy.

It is an extremely vile kind of pollution, which infects the soul. It is a tyrannizing domination that binds around our limbs and our very souls the heaviest and most galling chains. And it taints the conscience with a sense of guilt, which is a heavy punishment. It is guilt that makes an accusing conscience—and awakens a certain fearful looking for of judgment and fiery indignation, which shall devour the adversary. Sin is the fountain-head of all misery; hence if it is put away, if we are saved from sin, we are saved from all real evil. There is only one thing therefore to be afraid of, and that is sin—only one thing to desire, and that is to be saved from our sins—for that implies God's favor, which is heaven and eternal salvation. "Blessed is the man whose transgression is forgiven."

By all this, however, I must not be understood to mean that there is not something positive in our salvation. We are not only redeemed *from sin*, but redeemed *to righteousness and true holiness forever*. Not only saved from sin, but saved to heavenly bliss. Salvation is not all a negative. A state of happiness is deliverance from evil into a state of good. Darkness is dispelled by light, but light itself is a reality; nakedness is remedied by clothing, and poverty is removed by abundance: so sin is taken away in respect to its *guilt* by our propitiation, the Lamb of God, and in regard to its pollution and dominion by the renewing of the heart and the indwelling of the Holy Spirit.

In order, then, to our salvation by Jesus, we must have justification of life, true holiness, and communion with God; and this brings peace of conscience, and lastly the enjoyment of God in glory. This is the salvation of JEHOVAH JESUS, which He has provided, purchased, and applies to all who believe in Him.

And this He did by taking upon himself our guilt. For, being God-man, he could bear the weight, and give ample satisfaction to Divine Justice for our sins. For Christ hath redeemed us from the curse of the law, being made a curse for us. By his obedience righteousness comes upon all men to justification of life, and grace reigns through righteousness unto eternal life. Hence the Apostle is able to say, "God is in Christ, reconciling the world unto himself, not imputing their trespasses unto them."

This salvation is applied, as our theologians say, *initially* in this life, and *perfectly* in the world to come. Believers have the first-fruits here, and the full harvest in the future life. "He that believeth on the Son hath everlasting life, and is saved by hope." JESUS lives now as the Intercessor with the Father. By His Spirit in the ministry of His Word, He calls, invites, and draws to himself His people. They are born again, are penitent, regenerated, and believing, and made heirs of glory. And at death He receives the soul immediately into His kingdom above.

JESUS fulfils the meaning of His Name, then, by procuring salvation for His people and applying it to them. But to receive this salvation, we must receive Him. This is the "commandment of God, that we should believe on the name of His Son Jesus Christ." There is but one God, and one Mediator between God and man, the man Christ Jesus. Nor is there any other Mediator. There is no other Saviour. "Him hath God exalted with his right hand to be a Prince and a Saviour." "For God hath highly exalted him, and given him a name which is above every name: that at the name of Jesus every knee shall bow, of things in heaven, and things in earth, and things under the earth." Phil. ii. 9, 10.

In the person of Jesus Christ we have the God-man. God the Son is here, and man is here, with a reasonable soul and a true human body, and thus God and man meet. This is proof of man's restoration to the image in which he was created. And this is proof also that there is a God, a truly living personal God, in contradistinction to the dead god of deism, the far-off indifferent god of heathenism, or the impersonal force or power, or *natura naturans*, of unbelieving Science and of German transcendentalism, or pantheism, which is atheism. The necessities of my nature are such that God must come down to me, or I can never glorify and enjoy him. He must take pity on me, and, self-moved, come down to me and seek me, or I can never go up to Him. The cravings and aspirings of the great universal heart of suffering humanity plead for just such a Jehovah Jesus as is our Lord Christ. The poor heathen could not live without gods, but while they made their heroes gods, they remained themselves as base as their vilest gods. But Christianity reveals God to us, and reveals His Son Jesus Christ in us, that we may become partakers of His nature and live with Him forever.

Since, then, such is the precious import of the Name of Jesus, ought we not seriously to ask ourselves, Do we really "believe in Jesus Christ, His only Son, our Lord?"

It is not enough that we have heard of Him, and can tell who is the *Redeemer of God's elect*. It is not enough that we have never formally renounced Him. We must believe that Jesus is Christ, and believe this with the heart unto righteousness. Do you really know the meaning of the Name, the precious Name Jesus? If so, you know there is no other name to be compared with it. As the sun in the firmament darkens all the stars, so the glory of Christ's sufficiency, as seen by the eye of an appropriating faith, eclipses the lustre of all other objects. As salvation is found in Jesus alone, what are honors and riches without Him? If you are a merchant, and all your property is on board a ship, would you not feel anxious about bringing it safely into port? How much more anxious should you be to come to Jesus and lay up your salvation in Him. It is wonderful how strongly many of the early Christians expressed their affection for Jesus. In the first ages of the Church, Christians seem to have had such a believing, loving soul—such strong affection for the person of Jesus, that no other creed or profession was needed. It was enough to know Jesus. Many of them, like *Bernard* in his celebrated Hymn to the Lord Jesus, could say:—

"Most blessed Jesus, dearest friend,
Hope of my longing, panting mind,
I seek Thee with my tears and sighs,
To Thee my soul lifts up her cries.
O Jesus, cordial to the heart,
Who light and life dost still impart,
A living fountain, full and fresh,
Surpassing every joy and wish.
When on my heart Thou'rt pleased to shine,
My soul is cheered with truth divine;
All I contemn but things above;
My bosom glows with heavenly love.
Jesus, my chief and lasting Good,
My Saviour, strength, and precious food,
Thy presence grant, Thy glory show,
Thy boundless love cause me to know."

O everlasting Truth, Incarnate Wisdom of the Father, hear us when we call upon Thee. Prostrate in spirit at the footstool of Thy Majesty, we adore Thine infinite perfections, rendering all glory and benediction to Thee. We come to Thee in search of Thine Own Self, the Eternal Verity, to catch a ray from Thee, the light of the world; to walk in Thee, who art the Way; to live in Thee, who art the Life. Open Thou our hearts, to attend to that which Thou hast revealed of Thyself, of Thine Everlasting Father, and Thy Blessed Spirit. And as by Thine Incarnation new light has come to us, lighten Thou our eyes, that we may see Thee, and let memory, will, and understanding, all bow down before Thee, that Thou mayest be all in all.* Amen.

---

* Slightly altered from Bishop Forbes.

II.

BELIEVING ON THE NAME CHRIST.

"And Paul, as his manner was, went in unto them, and three Sabbath-days reasoned with them out of the Scriptures, opening and alleging, that Christ must needs have suffered, and risen again from the dead; and that this JESUS, whom I preach unto you, is CHRIST." "And testified to the Jews that Jesus was Christ" .... "showing by the Scriptures that Jesus was Christ."—ACTS xvii. 2, 3; xviii. 5, 28.

THE only authority we acknowledge in matters of faith is the Word of God. The authority of Creeds and Articles and Confessions of Faith is derived from Holy Scripture alone. And the best guides for the interpretation of them are, *First*, the natural, literal, grammatical meaning of their text.

Secondly, a knowledge of the controversies prevailing at the time these creeds and confessions were drawn up, and which made it necessary to have such articulated formularies of faith.

Thirdly, the doctrines of the primitive Church which it was the intention of these formularies to embody, defend, and follow.

Fourthly, the writings and known opinions of the eminent men who drew up these formularies, or who adopted and defended them. We all believe that all synods, and associations, and convocations, and councils, and assemblies, and Popes, and Bishops may err, and have erred, and that the only infallible rule of Faith and Life is the Word of God given by Inspiration. And we believe that the authority of the Holy Scripture for which it ought to be believed and obeyed dependeth not upon the testimony of any man, or church, or assembly, but wholly upon God, who is Truth itself, and the author thereof. We receive the Bible, therefore, as our infallible Rule, and it alone and only, because it is the Word of God.

"The infallible rule of interpretation of Scripture, is the Scripture itself; and therefore, when there is a question about the true and full sense of any Scripture (which is not manifold, but one), it may be searched and known by other places that speak more clearly.

"The Supreme Judge, by which all controversies of religion are to be determined, and all decrees of councils, opinions of ancient writers, doctrines of men, and private spirits, are to be examined, and in whose sentence we are to rest, can be no other but the Holy Spirit speaking in the Scripture.

"The whole counsel of God, concerning all things necessary for His own glory, man's salvation, faith, and life, is either expressly set down in Scripture, or by good and necessary consequence may be deduced from Scripture: unto which nothing at any time is to be added, whether by new revelations of the Spirit or traditions of men."—*Conf. Faith,* chap. i. secs. 2, 4, 9, 10.

It is plain, then, that in using the Catechism, the Ten Commandments, the Creed, and Articles of Faith, we do not mean to substitute them for the Word of God. They are only helps—they are nothing except they are supported by and are according to the Holy Scriptures.

We are told in our text what was Paul's manner. *Three Sabbath-days* he went into the synagogues, to their religious meetings, where their sacred Scriptures were read and explained, and prayer was made; and there he offered salvation first to the Jews, "opening and alleging that Jesus is Christ."

His method seems to have been to prove to the Jews, by collating their own Scriptures—by citations from them, *first*, that the Messiah they were looking for was to be *a suffering* Messiah, and that it was spiritual blessings, and not temporal, they were to receive from Him—that the Messiah promised was not to be a great hero, like David, to deliver them from the Roman yoke, but a *suffering Prince*, who was to save them from sin. Then, *secondly*, he applied these citations to Jesus of Nazareth, and by appealing to the well-known and admitted facts of his life, he showed that all their own Scriptures were fulfilled in him, and therefore "this Jesus, whom I preach unto you, is THE CHRIST."

And as he did at Thessalonica, so also we find him doing at Corinth, where "he reasoned in the synagogues every Sabbath, and persuaded the Jews and the Greeks, and was pressed in the spirit, and testified to the Jews that Jesus was *the Christ.*" And so did Apollos also: "For he mightily convinced the Jews, and that publicly, showing by the Scriptures that Jesus was THE CHRIST."

1. Then these passages prove that it was a custom of the Jews to allow liberty of speech in their synagogues, after the reading of the Scripture lessons, to men of reputed learning, or such as might be supposed able to say something for edification, although they might not be

priests. So Jesus at Nazareth, who was not a Levite, and Paul and Apollos in the Acts of the Apostles.

2. Here is proof that the Jews in the days of the Apostles had, and acknowledged their Holy Scriptures as divinely inspired.

3. That they believed their Scriptures taught them to expect a Messiah.

4. That the material facts in the life of Jesus of Nazareth, as then publicly stated by the Apostles and early disciples, were admitted to be true. In rejecting Him as the Messiah, they did not deny the truth of his personal history as related by his followers. We have here proof

5. Also that *expository preaching* was the style mainly adopted by our Lord and his Apostles. Apollos was eloquent and learned, and pre-eminently "mighty in the Scriptures," but he used all his eloquence and knowledge of the Scriptures to convince the Jews that Jesus *is the Christ*. And so Paul employed himself with all his might in opening up and showing from the Old Testament that Jesus, whom he preached, was *the Christ*. Note

6. It is said, they *reasoned, testified, persuaded, convinced*. They did not show any edict from king or emperor. They had no commission from Cæsar to persecute, imprison, or burn those who would not believe. They *reasoned, testified, convinced*, and *persuaded*, by pouring light into the mind ; by discoursing first from the received Scriptures, and then by applying these Scriptures to the facts of our Lord's life. They *reasoned* with vehemence of spirit and earnestness of affection, as well as with great judgment, and an abundant use of learning and common sense. *They* believed, and therefore they spoke, and they

spoke as they believed, and their words were from their hearts. They loved the souls of men, and they were on fire for the glory of God. If their sermons were printed in the old style, they would be full of italics—quotations from the Bible. Their grand point was to demonstrate everywhere that Jesus of Nazareth, whom they preached, was the long-expected Messiah. They aimed to gain this demonstration by producing the prophecies of the Old Testament, and applying them, and comparing them with what Jesus had done and suffered, and by urging what had taken place after his death, in proof that He was what He claimed to be. His resurrection, ascension, the descent of the Holy Ghost, the miracles wrought by the Apostles, and the success of their preaching, they alleged were proofs of his Messiahship. It was thus they sought to convince the people that Jesus is the Christ. And oh, if all who have been and are called Christ's ministers, had only kept closely to their commission, and preached the Gospel, and nothing but the Gospel, as Paul did, it is our solemn conviction the whole world would have been converted to Christ long ago.

In the discourse last Sabbath evening on the Name Jesus, it was shown that it was not without a purpose that the form of words, *believe on the Name of His Son Jesus Christ, was used* by the Apostle. 1 John iii. 23. The names of the Son of God are significant and precious. The name JESUS being the abbreviation of JEHOVAH JOSHUA, Jehovah our Saviour, or the Salvation of Jehovah, was expressly given to our Lord by the Angel, while the other appellation, CHRIST, expresses His functions. It is to the second name, CHRIST, given to our Lord in the second Article of the Creed, that I now invite your prayerful attention.

While the name JESUS occurs about seven hundred

times in the four Gospels to designate our Redeemer, the name CHRIST, by itself, is used about sixty times in the Gospels and in the Acts, and two hundred and forty times in the Epistles and the Book of Revelation. The name JESUS was our Lord's proper human name, and the name CHRIST expresses his official title. The form JESUS CHRIST is found, I believe, but five times in the Gospels and one hundred and sixty times in the Epistles, and the opposite collocation, *Christ Jesus*, is not found in the Gospels at all, but occurs quite frequently in the Epistles. It was to be expected that in the course of time the proper human name JESUS would be absorbed in the official designation—CHRIST. And as the Evangelists give us *memoirs* of our Lord, describing his human life—that is, his life and acts as He appeared in the world as a man, so they generally call him JESUS; and, as in the Epistles, the object is to show the great work He accomplished by his life and death, so He is generally designated by his official name, CHRIST. Christ is His hypostatical name, indicating His two natures in one person. He is called Christ, says Cyril, "not because He was anointed by human hands, but because he was from eternity consecrated by the Father to be an High Priest over men." And not a Priest only, but a Prophet and a King. "He anointed himself as God, anointing his body with his own Deity, and being anointed as man." And hence we may see why it is said in the Holy Scriptures that Jesus was anointed with the Holy Ghost; namely, because the work whereby the Son of God became the Son of man is ascribed to the power of the Holy Spirit. He was conceived by the Holy Ghost. His unction (anointing) was that of the Deity on the humanity, as some of the ancients have expressed it.

Our Lord's proper human name, then, is Jesus, and

his official title is Christ, which also expresses his person, human and Divine. And the way his double name and his title are used throughout the New Testament, is a proof both of the intelligence and honesty of the sacred writers, and proves also their faith in his Supreme Divinity, as well as in his real humanity. As the name *Christ* is his official title, it should be preceded by the definite article in the text. Thus: "This Jesus whom I preach unto you is *the* Christ," and he "testified to the Jews that Jesus was *the* Christ." That is, Paul proclaimed, and proved mainly out of their own Scriptures, that Jesus was the Messiah promised to their fathers. And so also when our Lord himself says: "It is life eternal to know the only true God, and Jesus Christ whom He has sent," He means that he was to be received as the Messiah—that they must believe that He, Jesus, was THE CHRIST. Jesus the Christ is to be taken, then, in the same way that we understand John the Baptist or the Baptizer—that is, Jesus is the Messiah, who is called CHRIST because he is God's Anointed One as *Prophet, Priest,* and *King.* The Messiah is spoken of in the Old Testament as *The Anointed,* especially by David and Isaiah. And Daniel uses the appellation, "the anointed One," with express reference to the Great Deliverer, and calls him THE PRINCE, and the High Priest, and the expiator of guilt. ix. 24, 26. When Jesus was born, the common appellations by which the Great Deliverer of Israel was spoken of were these two: *He who is to come,* and *the Messiah who is called Christ.*

To believe, then, that Jesus is the Christ, means: *First,* that He is the Deliverer promised under the name of Messiah, the anointed One, the Holy One of God, in the Old Testament, and that all that is said of this Deliverer or Saviour in the Old Testament Scriptures, under this or any other name, is true of Him. *Secondly*, to believe that Jesus is the Christ, and that all that is said concerning the Messiah of the Old Testament is true of Him, requires us to receive Him distinctly as fulfilling the offices of *The Anointed One:* namely, as our Prophet, Priest, and King, and that He is supreme and absolute in all these offices. He is the divinely *appointed, qualified, commissioned,* and *accredited* Saviour of sinners. "His name shall be called Jesus, for He shall save his people from their sins." Every one, therefore, who understandingly and sincerely unites in saying, "And I believe in Jesus Christ," confesses to the belief that Jesus is the true and only Messiah, "the Redeemer of God's elect." This confession distinguishes us as Christians from Pagans and Mohammedans, and from all deists and atheists. And also from the Jews, for *I believe in Jesus Christ* means that I believe the Messiah who was promised to the patriarchs *has come*—the prophecies *are already* fulfilled, and fulfilled in Jesus of Nazareth. I therefore believe He is the Messiah. I believe that a promise was made to our first parents, repeated, enlarged, and renewed afterwards in many ways, but specially to Abraham, and foretold by the prophets, *that a Divine man, the God-man, was to come, who should be the Messiah,* and redeem his people; and I believe that Jesus, who was born of the Blessed Virgin Mary in the days of Herod, is that true Messiah, so long and so often promised. *And I believe* not only that He fulfils all the signification of his angel-selected and announced name JESUS, "for He shall save his people from their sins," but I also believe that Jesus is the Christ, the Messiah, *anointed* to three special offices, belonging to Him as the Mediator between God and man—that He executes his office as "a Prophet in revealing to us, by His Word and Spirit, the will of God for our salvation," and the office of a priest in his once offering up himself a sacrifice to satisfy Divine Justice, and reconcile us to God, and in making continual intercession for us; and "the office of a king in subduing us to himself, in ruling and defending us, and in restraining and conquering all his and our enemies;" and that as my Prophet, Priest, and King, He will at last confer actual, perfect, and eternal happiness upon me, and all who believe in Him. And I believe all this, because it is according to His Holy Word, and because the unction by which He became and was proved to be the true Messiah, was not only typified by the material anointing with the holy oil, but was according to the fore-ordination of the Father, by the Spirit of God, which He received as the Head, and conveys to all his members, who are in Him as the branches are in the vine—Christ is their life. "Who is He then that condemneth? It is Christ that died, yea rather that is risen again, who is even at the right hand of God; who also maketh intercession for us." All this is the true meaning of "And I believe in Jesus Christ."

I. What, then, is the signification of the name CHRIST? As *Jesus* is the Greek for the Hebrew *Joshua*, so Christ is the Greek equivalent for the Hebrew MESSIAH, or, as it is written in the New Testament, MESSIAS. You may remember that the woman of Samaria said: "I know that Messias cometh which is called Christ." And Andrew said to his brother Simon, "We have found the Messias, which is, being interpreted, the Christ." The signification of both names is the same, namely, *the anointed*. And as Paul and the most of the Apostles, if not all of them, used the Greek language in writing, so they used the Greek name *Christ* for Messiah, and the same was retained in the Latin language by simply rendering it into Latin letters, *Christus*, which is the original of our English name.

II. Why is our Lord Jesus THE ANOINTED ONE? The answer to this question carries us back to the custom of anointing as we find it in the law and among the Patriarchs. With them, whatever was set apart to holy or religious uses, or specific offices, was anointed with oil, under the notion that such an anointing was an ordination or official setting apart to the service of God. Thus Jacob poured oil on the top of the pillar. And Moses anointed the tabernacle and all the vessels, and this anointing was their dedication. And so the High Priest was invested with his office by the use of the holy anointing oil. When Jesus therefore is called Messiah, Christ, the meaning is, that He is THE ANOINTED ONE, who fulfils all these types under the law. Now it is plain there was a general expectation that such a person as Christ was to come.

The woman of Samaria said: "I know that Messias cometh."

The Jews acknowledged that our Lord's name was Jesus, but "agreed that if any man did confess that He was CHRIST, he should be put out of the synagogue." Jo. ix. 22. "And all men mused in their hearts of John the Baptist, whether he were the *Christ*, or not," and when Jesus taught in the Temple, those who doubted as to his character and claims said: "When *Christ* cometh, no man knoweth whence He is," and those who believed said, "When *Christ* cometh, will He do more miracles than these which this man doeth?" From these passages it is plain that both parties, those who believed in Jesus and those who did not believe, agreed that a Messiah was to come. And this expectation was built on the promises made to the fathers; and as they understood the promises and the prophecies, Christ was to be the Anointed One, and the *time* for his coming was at hand, if not actually fulfilled. The line of argument to prove that *Jesus* of Nazareth is Messiah is on this wise: Because in Him all that is promised or foretold of the Messiah, as to *descent, family, place and time* of coming, is minutely fulfilled. Jesus was born and lived and died before the Jewish people were dispersed or were wholly deprived of a national polity, and while the second Temple was standing, and sacrifices were still continued, and the tribes and their genealogies were still distinctly preserved. The prophecies as to the *time, place,* and *manner of his birth* not only all meet in Him, but meet in no one else. He is therefore THE CHRIST. And besides, Jesus taught what the Messiah was to teach, wrought such miracles as the Messiah was to work, and suffered and accomplished all that the Messiah was to suffer and obtain. All that John the Baptist foretold of Jesus he had learned to expect of the Messiah, nor did Jesus fail to fulfil every thing he had promised concerning Him. And His Apostles went everywhere preaching and proving out of the Scriptures that Jesus is Messiah. In a word, it is proved that Jesus came into the world at the time the Messiah was to come—that he was born of the very family, in the very place, and at the very time, and after the same manner, that the prophets had foretold of the Messiah, and that these predictions were never fulfilled in any one before His coming, nor have they been fulfilled in any one since. We conclude, therefore, that Jesus is the Messiah. Moreover, He taught the great truths, wrought the very miracles, suffered the very indignities, and received such glory, as the prophets said the Messiah was to teach, and which he was to do and suffer and receive. We conclude, therefore, that it is our duty to believe that Jesus is Christ, the promised Messiah.

III. *How* and *when* did Jesus become the Messiah, Jehovah's anointed One?

It is well known that great use was made in ancient

times of anointings of various kinds, and for many purposes. The *general meaning of the act was to designate, set apart, consecrate, and qualify.* Thus, Cyrus is called God's anointed, because God had consecrated him to the work of releasing the Jews from their captivity in Babylon. And so also, but in a far higher sense, Jesus is called Jehovah's anointed One in the second Psalm, and in other Scriptures. And hence also in the Bible, *anoint, anointed,* and *anointing,* are employed in a variety of forms to illustrate the sanctifying influences of divine grace upon the soul.

At least three significant kinds of anointing are found in the Scriptures:

1. One for health and cleanliness, as for sundry diseases, and under this head we perhaps should class the anointing of the dead body. 2. Anointing of guests and strangers, as when the woman who was a sinner washed Jesus' feet. Among the Egyptians this was the ordinary method of making a guest feel his welcome. 3. The great anointing, however, was for the consecration and inauguration of a person to some part of divine service—thus the designating to the service of God, or to a holy use, the vessels of the tabernacle and the priests, and subsequently kings and prophets. Proof is abundant from the monuments that this custom prevailed in Egypt as well as among the Jews. It was the usual way of investiture into any sacred office among the ancients. The appellation, then, belongs to our Lord in a pre-eminent degree. *First,* He was anointed by His Father's designation—being pre-ordained to his work; *secondly,* He was anointed typically in the Jewish priests and kings and prophets. The proof that they were anointed and were types of the Messiah is so well known, that no citations or illustrations are needed. And as the Messiah unites the func-

tions of Prophet, Priest, and King, so *typically* He was anointed, and so pre-eminently anointed as combining all in one, that his name expressed his official title—THE ANOINTED ONE. Jesus was anointed typically to the prophetical office, and to the priestly office and the kingly office in all the prophets, priests, and kings that God gave to his people in their typical economy.

And *thirdly*, JESUS was actually anointed with the Holy Spirit. He fulfilled all righteousness, was circumcised, and was baptized with water. And the Holy Spirit descended upon him at his baptism. Isaiah had foretold this, saying: "The Spirit of the Lord is upon me, because the Lord God hath *anointed* me to preach good tidings unto the meek; He hath sent me to bind up the brokenhearted, to proclaim liberty to the captives, and the opening of the prison to them who are bound; to proclaim the acceptable year of the Lord, and the day of vengeance of our God; to comfort all that mourn; to appoint unto them that mourn in Zion, to give unto them beauty for ashes, the oil of joy for mourning, the garment of praise for the spirit of heaviness; that they might be called trees of righteousness, the planting of the Lord, that He might be glorified." Isaiah lxi. This prophecy Jesus explained and applied to himself in the synagogue of Nazareth. And St. Peter tells us that "God anointed Jesus of Nazareth with the Holy Ghost and with power."

As to the question, When did Jesus become "The Anointed One?" it must be remembered that the whole work of Redemption was decreed in the Eternal Mind from all eternity. Our salvation by the work of God's dear Son is not, therefore, any "after-thought" of the Almighty, by which to "mend" or repair his works of creation that had been marred by Satan. In the Divine Mind, God's Son was contemplated as incarnate and crucified from all eternity. The actual incarnation was when the Word was made flesh—when the two natures, "the Godhead and the manhood, without confusion of substance," were inseparably united in one Divine Person, whom we know as Christ. The great *Hooker* says, Jesus "took the very first element of our nature, before it was come to have any personal subsistence, and the flesh and the conjunction of the flesh with God began both at one instant; his making, and taking to himself our flesh was one act, so that in Christ there is no personal subsistence but one, and that from everlasting."

In the incarnation of the Son of God his glory was put into the form and habit of our flesh, so that the Apostle says, "We beheld His glory, the glory as of the only-begotten of the Father." It was this taking of manhood into God, when the Word was made flesh, that the Apostle Paul speaks of as the mystery of godliness: "God manifest in the flesh." It is quite enough, then, for our purpose in this discussion, to say, first, that Jesus was anointed of God, when, in the *Divine purposes*, "He was set up from everlasting." "He was foreordained before the foundation of the world." He was sent from the Father. He came from God, appointed to this work. *Secondly*, He was anointed *typically* under the Old Testament. *Thirdly*, He was anointed *actually* with the Holy Ghost. And his anointing was *accredited* by his miracles, and by the outpouring of his Spirit in conversions, and the building up of his kingdom.

For the Redemption of sinners by the Messiah consisting in their deliverance from a state of sin and death, and in bringing them into a state of righteousness and eternal life, it was necessary that He should offer a sacrifice propitiatory, and hence it was necessary that Messiah should be a PRIEST. And as deliverance from sin could not be obtained without the revealing of God's will to us concerning our salvation, so there was a necessity that the Messiah should be a prophet. And as the salvation of sinners implies their translation from a state of darkness into the light of God's kingdom—from the kingdom of Satan into the kingdom of heaven, and this requires the authority and power of a king—even of the Son of God, who was manifested that He might destroy the works of the devil—our Redeemer must therefore be a king. And thus we see that in every particular Jesus has the *unction*, the threefold anointing, and is indeed the Anointed One, our Saviour.

"Jesus Christ is our anointed Saviour, anointed to be our King, our great High Priest, and our Prophet, and in all those our Saviour; our Prophet, to teach the way of salvation; our Priest, to purchase it for us; and our King, to lead and protect us in the way and bring us safe to the end of it. A name full of sweetness and comfort. It is a rich ointment, and in the real and true preaching of the Gospel it is an ointment poured forth, diffusing its fragrant smell for believing souls."—*Leighton*.

Finally, we should believe and profess this article, 1st. Because *unless Jesus is Christ we have no Saviour.* If He is not the Prophet of God, He could not reveal the way of salvation; nor could He work out salvation for us, if He is not a Priest; nor could He confer salvation upon us, unless he is a king. But we have proved that Jesus is the Messiah who was to come, and that he was anointed to all the offices of a Prophet, Priest, and King. We therefore have boldness to enter into the holiest by the blood of Jesus; and having such a High Priest over the house of God, we may draw near with a true heart, in full assurance of faith. Heb. x. 19.

2. We must profess this article, and prove by our lives that it is true, or we practically say Jesus is not the Messiah. "For whosoever believeth that Jesus is Christ, is born of God." And again saith St. John, "Who is a liar, but he that denieth that Jesus is the Christ? This man is the antichrist, as denying the Father and the Son." "He that believeth and is baptized shall be saved." Whosoever believeth shall be saved.

Christ died for us that we should live to Him. He bought us with a price. We are therefore not our own, but must glorify God in our bodies and in our spirits, which are God's.

3. This profession of faith must be an individual, personal one. "*I believe* in Jesus Christ." We must receive him as the Redeemer of God's elect—as our Prophet, Priest, and King. It cannot be done by proxy.

Whence is our name *Christians?* Are we not so called after CHRIST? Have we then His spirit? Do we rejoice at this name as the early Christians did? When it was given to them it was a name of reproach, but they loved it, and they suffered all manner of persecution and death for His sake. "Let every one then that nameth the name of Christ depart from iniquity." Christ was the Anointed One, a Prophet, a Priest, and a King. Are we, like Him, consecrated to God? Do we teach the way of salvation, and offer ourselves a living sacrifice to God, and labor and pray for the coming of His Kingdom? If we are really Christians, then we have an *unction* from Him, for God hath established and anointed us in Christ to be Kings and Priests unto Him. What think ye then of Christ? Dost thou believe on the Son of God? O that every one of you may be able to say, *Lord*, I believe; help Thou mine unbelief. Amen.

III.

JESUS CHRIST GOD'S SON AND OUR LORD.

"But these things are written, that ye might believe that Jesus is the Christ, the Son of God; and that believing ye might have life through his name."—JOHN xx. 31.

It is properly considered a part of a good education to acquire the habit of addressing every one by his proper titles, giving honor to whom honor is due, and reverence to whom reverence is due.

This is clearly the teaching of the Bible. And St. Paul recognized it when he said, in relation to his reproof of Ananias, "I wist not, brethren, that he was the high priest: for it is written, Thou shalt not speak evil of the ruler of thy people." Acts xxiii. 5.

We are ready to form our estimate of a person's bringing up, character, refinement, and politeness, by his tone of voice and the style he uses in addressing his neighbor. His culture and acquaintance with good society are at once recognized by the grace with which he makes his salutations. Nor is this inconsistent with common sense, or in any way forbidden by the Gospel. *Christianity* is not a crusade against good manners; nor is it built upon the ruins of civilization and of the Fine Arts. Ancient history, and the monuments of the early ages of the Church, prove that no man was more honest and polite than Abraham the friend of God, and the Father of the faithful; and no people were more considerate in showing marks of respect where they were due, and could not be construed into, or be mistaken for, marks of homage to idols, than the primitive Christians. But, if I am not mistaken, our times are distinguished for two grave errors, the prevailing of which proves that our Christianity, in at least two particulars, is not equal to that of the first ages of the Church, namely: *First,* We are deficient in respect for aged persons, and we do not give honor where honor is due, to our teachers, magistrates, and parents. Irreverence, and a want of obedience and humility before superiors, are prominent faults among us. And the fruits of such things in childhood and youth are nothing but evil to the Church and to society. And, *secondly,* There is in our day a sad, a very sad want of reverence for the name of God, and especially for the NAME of Jesus CHRIST. The early Christians were so full of love for the name and character of Jesus, that they had very little need for any other Creed, or Confession, or Articles of Faith, than the mere name of their Redeemer. To be called a Christian in honor of Christ, although the name was then one of reproach, and subjected them to the severest persecution, was their highest honor and greatest delight. But so much are we given to things gross, earthly, and temporal—so great is our idolatry for human intellect, and its developments and creations, progress and material achievements, that but few seem to be aware of the deadly heresy that is destroying the life of our Christianity. Nothing is more clearly proven by the present age of the world, and the present state of Christendom, than this: namely, that the advance of the physical sciences, increased wealth from the wonderful aids of science in using the elements, and the products of the earth, is not true piety; it is not even morality. The printing-press, the public schools, the telegraph and railways, steamships, oil-wells, and gold-mines, are intended for good, but they are not THE ONLY GOOD; they may be so used as not to be good at all. They are not of themselves sufficient to make men decent and moral and happy, much less pious.

The politeness and mental activity and scientific culture of France were never greater than when she abolished Christianity and drenched her soil in blood. You may depend upon it, mental culture, public education, commercial prosperity, and material wealth, may be very far from morality and true piety. However much we may insist on good works, and admire every thing that is lovely and refined, still the amenities and elegancies of society are not always evidences of pure morals, nor is mere morality the same thing as grace. We may have even the form of godliness, and yet be without its power. And when we see from the Holy Scriptures on the one hand, that God's only-begotten Son has a name that is above every name, and excels all mankind in glory, and that there is nothing in the universe to be compared to Him, and that consequently we owe Him the deepest reverence, the profoundest homage, the most ardent love, and that it should be our greatest delight to confess His name; and then, on the other hand, call to mind the fact, that we have many schools of philosophy and theology, representing colleges and universities in all parts of Christendom, that agree scarcely in any thing else except as Herod and Pilate agreed—to condemn Jesus of Nazareth—either by denying His personal existence, or His divinity, or atonement, or the influence of His Holy Spirit;—when we see that Strauss, and Renan, and such writers, are the most popular of our day; and when we find so little reverence for the Son of God in many of the books used in our Christian families and societies, then we are filled with shame, and are obliged to confess that our type of religion falls far below that of the martyrs, and confessors, and covenanters of old. We seem to forget that it is the will of God the Father "that all men should honor the Son, even as they honor the Father." "No man can say that Jesus Christ is Lord, but by the Holy Ghost." We seem to forget that "whosoever shall confess that Jesus is the Son of God, God dwelleth in him, and he in God, and whosoever denieth the Son, the same hath not the Father." We read that when many disciples went back, and walked no more with Jesus, He said unto the twelve: "Will ye also go away?" And then Simon Peter nobly answered, saying: "Lord, to whom shall we go? Thou hast the words of eternal life. And we believe and are sure that Thou art that Christ, the Son of the living God." John vi. 66-69.

Here Peter declares that (1.) Jesus is Christ—*that Christ*, meaning the Christ promised in the Old Testament as the Messiah to come, and (2.) that the promised Messiah who is called Christ was the *Son of God*, and therefore (3.) he called him LORD. And so in Matth. xvi. 16, 17, when Peter said, "Thou art the Christ, the Son of the living God," Jesus not only acknowledged the truth of his profession, but added: "Blessed art thou, Simon Bar-jona:' for flesh and blood hath not revealed it unto thee, but my Father which is in heaven."

And as on the Day of Pentecost, so everywhere and always the burden of the preaching of the Apostles was to prove that Jesus of Nazareth was the Christ the Son of God, risen from the dead and exalted to reign both *as Lord and Christ*. So the Ethiopian converted said:

"See, here is water; what doth hinder me to be baptized?" And Philip said, "If thou believest with all thine heart, thou mayest." And he answered and said, "I believe that Jesus Christ is the Son of God." And so Philip preached in Samaria, and so Paul preached, from his first sermon in Damascus to his last one from the block on which he was beheaded in Rome, saying, Jesus is Christ the Son of God. Acts viii. 35, 37; and ix. 20.

It would perhaps surprise many of you if you were to look out the passages of Holy Scripture that speak of Jesus as Christ the Son of God, and make faith in Him as such the only condition of salvation. You remember that the second article of our Creed on which we are speaking says: "And I believe in Jesus Christ, His only Son, our Lord." We have already spoken of the name Jesus, and also of His official title, Christ. It remains therefore for us now to dwell on the other two titles in the article: *His only Son, our Lord*, which declare His relation to the Father and His relation to us. And here,

I. It is reasonable, if our holy religion be what we believe and say it is—a revelation from God, the Infinite, to us His finite creatures, that there should be mystery in it—and there must be, until the finite can comprehend the Infinite, which is clearly impossible. Jesus Christ and the Holy Spirit are not known from the works of creation. All we know of them is from Revelation. The Doctrine of the Trinity no man can know unless it is revealed, and no mortal can fully comprehend it even when it is revealed. A *fact* or doctrine may be declared, and the manner or nature of it still be incomprehensible. We believe many things as facts which we cannot explain. The mystery of the Incarnation, the miraculous birth of Jesus, and of his relation to the Father Almighty—a relation expressed by the words,

"His Son," "His only Son"—"His only-begotten Son" —"His eternal Son," I believe, because I find it declared in Revelation, and I believe it on the simple direct authority of God Himself, which is to me the highest possible authority, and to believe which I consider the highest act of reason and common sense; but, at the same time, I candidly and boldly confess I do not comprehend this doctrine. And although I do not know that I have a correct understanding at all of what is meant when I say, *I believe that Jesus Christ is the Son of God,* His only-begotten and eternal Son, still I do honestly and firmly believe it, and I have good and sufficient grounds to believe it, for Jesus Christ Himself so says of Himself. He declared that He was the Son of God, therefore I believe He is. The Father himself proclaimed by a voice from Heaven that Jesus was His Son, and the Holy Spirit proved that Jesus was the Son of God, as the voice from Heaven proclaimed Him to be, by descending upon Him. I see no way to escape from the necessity of believing that Jesus Christ is the Son of God, but by rejecting the authority of the Holy Scriptures, for certainly they do represent it to be the sum of our Confession of Faith in relation to Jesus Christ, to believe and profess that *He is the Son of God.* And this is precisely what our opponents have done and are doing directly and indirectly; namely, rejecting, undermining, weakening, or overthrowing the authority of the Holy Scriptures.

I candidly confess, I do not understand the use of many words found in our theological literature. Some terms and phrases are used I could wish altogether omitted. Nor do I think it wise and best for us to indulge our curiosity in speculations on the miraculous conception of Jesus. The history of the Church is full of the proceedings of councils and of the writings of learned men, endeavoring to explain the miraculous birth of Jesus and his Divinity, but all is of very little use. I understand that the Gospel requires me to believe that Jesus of Nazareth is *the Christ*, the Son of God, and that he is God, and I believe just what the Holy Scriptures teach. And by the terms, *Son*, His *only Son*, *begotten*, and *only-begotten*, I understand that Jesus the Christ came from God the Father, as a Mediator—that the term Son denotes *proceeding* from the Father, sent by the Father, and yet equality with the Father, both as to Nature and the Degree of it. According to the Scriptures, the term father is applied to God expressing personal agency, intellect, devising, loving, and sending his Son; while the term Son denotes coming in obedience to the will of God, and is used in reference especially to his making known to us the will of God, revealing the knowledge of God to us for our salvation. And for this reason He is called The Word, as words, language, and speech are the means of communicating ideas to and among men. And so also named Jesus, for He shall save his people, and Christ with reference to his official titles as Mediator, the Anointed One, prophet, priest, and king. And the Holy Spirit makes us holy by applying to us the merits of Christ—the benefits purchased for us by his death: namely, enlightening us in the knowledge of Christ, renewing our hearts, and working in us the fruits of the Spirit, which are love, joy, peace, and charity—making intercession in us, and preparing us for the inheritance of the saints in light—dwelling in us, that we may be meet to dwell with God. This is the reason the term *holy* is made a prominent prefix to the third person of the Trinity.

II. The texts just cited, and they are only a specimen of many more of a like nature, prove that JESUS CHRIST is THE SON OF GOD in a sense higher than any creature. Angels are sons of God, but Jesus Christ is more excellent, not only as to the degree, but also in the kind of his nature, than they. When our Lord told the Jews that He was the Son of God, they inferred that He made himself equal with God. And if this inference was not correct, surely He would have protested, and told them that they were doing him injustice—that it was a calumny to charge him with claiming to be equal with God, when He had not done so. If He were a mere man, or creature, however high, He would certainly have vindicated himself from the charge of blasphemy in claiming to be the Son of God, and therefore *equal* with God. As our Lord allowed them to put this interpretation on his words, it must have been correct. That was what he meant. John v. 18. He did not seek his own glory, but the glory of the Father who sent him, and as the Father was to be honored in His Son, He taught them, in claiming to be the Son of God, that He possessed the same nature, essence, power, and dignity that belonged to the Father. "The Name of God is in him." The same titles, attributes, works, and worship that are proper for the Father are, according to the Scriptures, to be given to the Son. "He is the brightness of the Father's glory and the express image of his person." He is the light of Light, and the life of the world. "We beheld his glory, the glory as of the only-begotten of the Father." "Christ Jesus, being in the form of God, thought it not robbery to be equal with God. * * Wherefore God hath exalted him * * that every tongue should confess that Jesus Christ is Lord, to the glory of God the Father." Phil. ii. 5–11, inclusive.

III. The relation of Jesus Christ to God the Father denoted by the words, HIS ONLY SON, not only gives him pre-eminence over all creatures. but equality with, *iden-*

tity as God Jehovah himself. Jesus Christ is not only superior to all creatures, but is in all respects like and equal to God, and one with Him. "There is but one only living and true God; but in the unity of the Godhead there be three persons, of one substance, power, and eternity: God the Father, God the Son, and God the Holy Ghost."—*Conf. Faith,* chap. ii. " And these three are one God, the same in substance, equal in power and glory." See also I. and II. of the XXXIX. Articles, and *Conf. Faith*, chap. viii. The same point is made in the Epistle to the Hebrews. The great proposition of that epistle, according to Schœtgen, *is that Jesus of Nazareth is God*, and one of the arguments is that He is superior to angels, and therefore, as according to old Hebrew theology, whoever was superior to the angels was God, for they believed angels were so near to God, that there could be no higher creature. As Jesus was higher than the angels, who were the highest creatures, He was God.

IV. In professing our belief in Jesus Christ, God's only Son, we say also that He is OUR LORD.

The Names GOD and LORD both signify the Divine Nature without distinction of persons, but the words Father, Son, and Holy Ghost indicate a separate personality. This is according to Theodoret, and seems to us to be well expressed. It is well understood that among the Jews the word Lord was used for God. They held the name Jehovah in such reverence, that instead of pronouncing it, they used the equivalent term Adonai, Lord. " So the Father is Lord, the Son is Lord, and the Holy Ghost is Lord. And yet there are not three Lords, but one Lord."* We are not baptized into three names,

---

*Bishop Forbes, Nicene Creed, pp. 115–117.

but in one Name. "Baptizing them in the name of the Father and of the Son and of the Holy Ghost." *One Name, One God, but three persons.* Gregory Nazianzen says: "Define our pious faith, teaching that we acknowledge one unbegotten God, that is the Father, and one begotten Son, that is the Son, who indeed is called God when He is spoken of by Himself, but who is termed Lord when He is mentioned with the Father. The first term is given to Him on account of His Nature, the latter on account of there being one principle in the Deity [μοναρχία]." Examples could be given also from the Scriptures of the term Lord being applied to the third person as well as to the second person in the Trinity. 1 Cor. viii. 6; xii. 3. We are not, then, without Apostolic authority to apply the term *Lord* pre-eminently to Jesus. This term is generally attributed to the second person of the Trinity. And for this and in so doing we have strong historic testimony for our faith to rest upon. The term is given to Jesus by the Apostles, who were Jews, and were accustomed to use that term as convertible with the term God, and as the equivalent of Jehovah. It is applied in the Apostles' Creed to Jesus, and so also in the Nicene-Constantinople Creed. And thus we have historic annals bringing to us from the very days of the Apostles themselves the proof that there was such a person as Jesus of Nazareth, who claimed to be the Son of God, and called himself Lord, and was received and believed in as such then, and has been ever since to our day. Whatever we may claim for the supernatural in our holy religion, it starts with historical facts, and we cannot know what it is until we believe them. It is not in any wise derogatory to the divinity of our faith that it receives aid from the facts of history, just as any other system does.

Our theologians attempt to make the clause of the

Creed under consideration emphatic by telling us that Jesus is OUR LORD *essentially*, because He is God, and *vicariously* because, according to the designation of the Father, He became incarnate, and to Him as such was given all power in heaven and earth, and all things were put under His feet, and He was exalted as Head over all things to the Church. It is in proof quite sufficient for us, then, that He is *our Lord :—First*, That He called himself Lord. His disciples called him *Lord—the " Lord from Heaven "—" My Lord and my God."* And every tongue is bound to confess that Jesus Christ is Lord, to the glory of God the Father. *Secondly*, The old versions, the Fathers, and ecclesiastical historians from the earliest ages gave the name *Lord* to Christ. *Thirdly*, The name Jesus, it has been shown, is the abbreviation of the two Hebrew words JEHOVAH JOSHUA, meaning Jehovah Saviour, or Salvation. He then is our Lord. *Fourthly*, Jesus is assuredly both LORD and CHRIST, because as God's Son He was *designated, appointed, sent forth, qualified*, and *accredited* as His *Anointed One*, to execute the threefold offices of a Prophet, Priest, and King. It is only in this view, I can understand the Scriptures that speak of the Father's eternal Decree, and of believers as the Father's gift to his Son, and of the Son's purchase of them with a price, and of the Son's actual dominion over them, possession of them, and reigning in them— as by His effectual calling, and delivering them from this present evil world, bringing them to himself and purifying them as a peculiar people. And hence, David before his Incarnation called him *Lord* (See Acts ii. 35, 6), and his Apostles and disciples and followers ever since have called him Lord, and every creature at the final *judgment* and *forever* afterwards shall acknowledge that of truth He is *Lord, to the glory of God the Father.*

My dear brethren, no presentation of Jesus Christ as the *only-begotten Son of God* can suffice, unless we contemplate his relation to us as the Son of God, as well as his relation to the Father. It is only then that the sovereign love of God the Father presents itself to our view. It was when we were enemies, God loved us and gave His Son for us. We who are by nature the children of wrath, and of disobedience, and of our Father the Devil, are exalted through him to be the sons of God. He gave his only-begotten and well-beloved Son to die on the cross, that we may be conformed to his image, that He might be the *first-born among many brethren*. So amazing is his grace that the Lord Jesus is not ashamed to call us brethren. How amazing, how astonishing, that He who, being in the form of God, and who thought it not robbery to be equal with God, made himself of no reputation, but took upon him the form of a servant—in the likeness of sinful flesh— God manifest in the flesh—and that He hath exalted us at the same time to the greatest height of dignity of which we are capable, by giving us the glory which the Father gave Him, and by making us partakers of the Divine nature. Brethren, God's dear Son has neither *sold* his birthright as Esau did, nor *forfeited* it like Reuben, nor lost his kingdom like Saul, by disobedience. Nor has he *resigned* His offices as *The Anointed One*. He executes them to-day, and as our High Priest, Prophet, and King reigns to make us joint heirs with Him in his glory.

V. Why, then, do we insist on professing our faith in this Article of our Creed?

I. We should believe all this Article of our Faith, not only because it contains the doctrine which, according to the Holy Scriptures, is unto salvation, but also because *it is the articulated voice of the pious in all ages*. It is the voice of the Church coming down to us from Eden. It is the voice of Abel, of Enoch, of Noah, Abraham, and Moses. It is the voice of the prophets and of the Apostles, and of the Church in all ages, that Jesus is the Christ, the Son of God, and our Lord. It is the *united* voice of all Christendom, Roman, Greek, Anglican, and American —of all the house of Israel on earth or in heaven, that God hath made that same Jesus who was crucified, both LORD and CHRIST. It is pleasant and full of comfort to think that the Church in heaven and on earth agree in this Article, to think how many millions have professed their faith saying, And I believe in Jesus Christ, His only Son our Lord, and are now in the New Jerusalem.

II. We must profess this Article, *in order to our renouncing the jurisdiction, reign, and dominion of Christ's enemy, Satan, whose works He came expressly to destroy*. It is not merely in the pious romances and legends of the Church, but it is a blessed reality, that the Name Jesus has power over Satan and all his legions. Satan is the prince of the power of the air. He rules in the children of disobedience. He is the god of this world. His subjects are the slaves of sin and the flesh. To belong to Christ, then, we must renounce the world, the flesh, and the devil. There are but two kingdoms— the kingdom of God, and the kingdom of the devil. There are but two masters, nor can we serve them both at the same time. We must make a choice. Whoever belongs to Christ does not belong to Satan. He is rescued from his tyranny. He is translated from his kingdom. He is delivered from this present evil world. He has learned that the friendship of this world is enmity with God. He is dead to sin, through the death of Christ. It is not, then, as a mere empty or unmeaning form of words, that in baptism, or confirmation of your baptismal vows, when you publicly professed your faith in Jesus, that you renounce the world, the flesh, and the devil. I find in Witsius* a copy of a pathetic address delivered by a pastor in the earlier days of Christianity to young persons at baptism, an abstract of which seems to me worth reading to you. It shows the earnestness of the pious servant of Christ, and illustrates the custom of our own days. "You intend," said he to the young persons presenting themselves to be baptized, "you intend this day to show the hand-writing of your faith to Christ. Your conscience will be the pen, ink, and paper; your tongue, the form. Attend, then, to the manner in which you subscribe this profession. Men that are about to die make a testament, and appoint another to inherit their possessions. To-morrow night you, too, are going to die to sin; and now your renunciation is a testament; you make the devil the heir of your sins, and you leave them to him as an inheritance. If any of you, then, retains in his mind any thing which belongs to the devil, let him renounce it as one that is about to die, who is no longer master of his own possessions. Let none amongst you, therefore, retain in his heart any thing that pertains to the devil. Cast in the devil's face all the remainders of filthiness and wickedness, and be joined to Christ. The whole transaction in which you are now engaged is awful and tremendous. All the powers of heaven are present in this place; the angels and archangels, though invisible, are recording your words; the cherubim and seraphim are bending from heaven to receive your engagements and present them to the Lord, that the angels may all rejoice over the penitent." It is well to note the solemn, devout, and pious manner in which it was usual in ancient times

---

* Witsius on the Creed, 1 vol. p. 361.

for persons on becoming communicants to renounce Satan and all his works, and all his service, and all his angels, and all his pomp, and to join themselves to the Lord Christ, and to his service forever.

III. We must, then, believe this Article, and acknowledge our belief of it, in order that we may truly and really become the subjects of our Lord Jesus Christ.

How can we acknowledge that we are His, and not our own, except by receiving Him as He is offered to us? *Abel* confessed Him when by faith he offered a more excellent sacrifice than Cain. *Moses* did the same when he preferred the reproaches of Christ to the glory of Egypt. And so DANIEL confessed his faith in Christ in Babylon. *He is thy Lord,* saith the Psalmist, *and worship thou him.*

IV. Do we really believe in Jesus Christ, His only Son, our *Lord,* then we *must obey Him as our Sovereign.* If we profess to call Him Lord, and yet do not obey His precepts, then our profession is false and hypocritical. " Why call ye me, Lord, Lord, and do not the things which I say?" "If ye love me, ye will keep my commandments."

If a centurion's authority over his soldiers and servants is such that he secures prompt obedience, saying to one go, and he goeth, and to another come, and he cometh; how much more supreme is the authority of Him who reigns at the right hand of the Almighty, both as LORD and CHRIST? I have often wondered at and admired the address of Socrates to God, saying, "Whatever place or rank thou mayest assign me, I would die a thousand deaths rather than abandon it." (Arrian. lib. iii. cap. 24.) And so said *Epictetus:* "The life of every man is a military service,—both long and diversified. Thou must act the part of a soldier, and perform without reserve whatever thy supreme commander may require, even anticipating, if possible, his will." It is even supposed by some of our great scholars that our name *Sacrament*, for the Lord's Supper, is borrowed from the oath of a soldier to his general—*Sacramentum*—by which he bound himself to follow his general's standard and obey his orders. Do you not remember David's heroes? They heard the king express a wish that some one would give him water to drink from the well of Bethlehem, which was before the gate, and immediately they broke through the warrior host of the Philistines, and drew water out of that well, and brought it to David. Oh, is there any one of us willing to do so arduous, so perilous, so glorious a service to please God? Can we say of the trials and sorrows and labors of this life, as Paul did—"None of these things move me, neither count I my life dear to myself, so that I might finish my course with joy, and the ministry which I have received of the LORD JESUS." Acts xx. 24. [See these quotations in Witsius.]

V. Do we really *believe in Jesus Christ His only Son, our Lord?* Then we cheerfully submit to be disposed of by Him as our true and only Sovereign. If He is our Lord, then we are his property, and there is no one to hinder Him from doing what He will with his own. "Nay, but, O man, who art thou that repliest against God? Shall the thing formed say to him that formed it, Why hast thou made me thus? Hath not the potter power over the clay?" Strive to remember, dear brethren, in your heavy losses and bereavements and afflictions, the noble examples of cheerful submission set us by Aaron and Moses, Eli and David. Besides, it is not only *wicked*, but it is in *vain* to contend with the Providence of the Almighty. It is *wicked*, for to set up our judgment in opposition to God's, is to asperse his government, and say we know better than He does, or we are better than He is. It is wicked and vain. "Let the potsherd strive with the potsherds of the earth; woe unto him that striveth with his Maker."

And *Job* says, "I know that Thou canst do every thing, that no thought can be withholden from Thee. Nothing is too hard for Thee." Although, then, you fret and vex your soul, yet you cannot change or control the ways of Providence; but by submitting, acquiescing, you can make them all subservient to your happiness. Even the heathen teach us, as I have just said, that it is the part of every good man to receive the will of the gods as best, and to follow their appointment without murmuring. Very few Christian poets have surpassed the following lines from *Cleanthes*, which I copy from Witsius:

> "Father of all! Great Ruler of the sky!
> Thy power I own, thy wisdom still descry.
> Whate'er the paths through which thou'rt pleased to lead,
> With joy I follow, and obey with speed.
> Were I to fret, and act a wayward part,
> Follow I must, though with an aching heart.
> Fate leads the willing, drags the unwilling soul;
> Tranquil, the good; the bad, compelled to howl."

Epictetus, the philosopher, furnishes us also with a beautiful paragraph on this point:

"I have surrendered my inclination to God. Is it His will that I should be sick of a fever? Then it is my will also. Is it His will I should give my attention to any thing? It is my will too. Is it His will I should earnestly desire any thing? Then I do earnestly desire it. Is it His will I should obtain the possession of any thing? Then I am so inclined. Is it His will that I should not obtain it? Neither is it mine."

Surely it is enough to say with *Seneca*, "A man should be pleased with whatever pleases God." "To a good man there is nothing evil, either living or dying. What then shall I think when God does not afford me the means of subsistence, or the power to live? What else, but that as a good commander he sounds a retreat for me? I submit, I follow, commending my Leader, and praising his works. I came into the world when it seemed good to him, and now I retire when He pleases; and while I lived, this was my employment, to praise Him alone or with many, rendering thanks to God for all things, blaming nothing whatever that is done by Him."

Have we received Christ as our Lord? Are we happy in the thought that He is supreme, commanding and disposing of all things? Can we say cheerfully with our Hymn—

> "He that formed me in the womb,
> He shall guide me to the tomb;
> All my times shall ever be
> Ordered by his wise decree.
> Times of illness, times of health,
> Times of penury and wealth,
> Times of trial and of grief,
> Times of triumph and relief,
> Times the tempter's power to prove,
> Times to taste a Saviour's love;
> *All* must come, and last, and end
> As shall please my Heavenly Friend.
> Thee at all times will I bless;
> Having thee, I all possess;
> How can I bereaved be,
> Since I cannot part with thee?"

And are we striving to be conformed to His will, who said: "Not my will, but thine be done," that we may know the power of his resurrection and be conformed to his death? Then we have the blessed hope that we shall be raised in the resurrection of the last day, and our bodies be made like unto his own glorious body. Cheerfully therefore and with courage let us fight on, and faithfully perform all our duties, and suffer, all the evils our heavenly Father sees best to send upon us.

> "Trials must and will befall;
>   But with humble faith to see
> LOVE inscribed upon them all,
>   This is happiness to me.
> God, in Israel, sows the seeds
>   Of affliction, pain, and toil;
> Trials make the promise sweet;
>   Trials give new life to prayer;
> Trials bring me to his feet,
>   Lay me low, and keep me there."

IV.

JESUS "CONCEIVED" AND "BORN OF THE VIRGIN MARY."

"And the Word was God. . . . And the Word was made flesh, and dwelt among us."—JOHN i. 1-14; with 1 JOHN iv. 2, and 1 TIM. iii. 16.

THE FORMS of modern DISBELIEF, which are both widespread and exceedingly dangerous, are in many points widely different from the unbelief of the last century. In many ways they are peculiar, and differ from and are more subtle than the forms of unbelief that have existed at any time, or through any of the ages since Christ and his Apostles. A general resemblance may indeed be traced through them all from age to age, but each age has its peculiarities. The prevailing *forms of unbelief* in our day are exceedingly subtle. Great modesty is professed. And the highest mental culture, and the most intense admiration for the works of the Creator, and for the Fine Arts as expressive of the Godlike in man, are made the glosses under which the Personality of God, and the existence and character of His Son Jesus Christ are denied or undermined. The character of the attack agreed upon by the enemies of Revelation is changed. There is, then, in some measure, a necessity for " *a restatement* of Christian doctrines," and a new line of defense. Many of the old arguments, like the arms and artillery of a past age, fail to meet the necessities of our times. We now want *needle-guns.* A very large portion of what is called the evangelical Christian literature of our day is useless— irrelevant to the new issues. Its uselessness is owing to the crudeness of the thoughts, and the want of elegance, elevation, and refinement in its literary style. If I am not greatly mistaken, this is generally admitted by our best scholars and our most pious men, and that, too, in regard to a great many publications found in our Sabbath-Schools and popular religious societies. The necessity that certainly in some measure exists for "a *restatement* of Christian doctrines," does not, then, arise from any new revelations made to us, nor from any progress or improvement in the doctrines of Revelation, but is owing chiefly to the style in which these doctrines have been set forth, and to the kaleidoscope views of error that are filling the land. Its *Protean* forms require manifold answers. Nor are we without fear or some suspicion that "a restatement of Christian doctrines" does not always mean a new statement of old Christian doctrines, but a new statement of *new* doctrines under the cover of restating the old. It is apparent to all, that in some cases we have old and familiar phrases employed in an entirely different sense from that in which they were used when they first became precious to the people of God. Nor are we without evidence that zeal for new forms of doctrine, a restatement of the orthodox faith, is sometimes a wish to get rid of old doctrines altogether.

Ever since the *fourth* century, at least, our Creed has been received as the Apostles' Creed, to distinguish it from the Athanasian, Nicene, or other formularies. By calling it the Apostles' Creed is not meant that it was composed, or adopted by the Apostles just as we have it; but that it embodies and sets forth the doctrines which the Apostles believed and preached. It is true that the whole of the Christian religion is comprehended in two parts:—*what* we are to believe, and how we are to *live* in order to be saved. These two parts are the mystery of the Truth, and the mystery of Godliness or Piety. And the only rule or standard for both is the Word of God contained in the Scriptures of the Old and New Testaments. These Scriptures teach in a way very different from all the systems of philosophers. They do not arrange their doctrines into any regular system, according to the precepts of any human school, ancient or modern, Oriental or Western. As chemistry, geology, or astronomy exists in its elements in nature, but is not set before us in orders and classes until Science has worked out its discoveries, so it was only when the first teachers of Christianity found it necessary for the instruction of the young and of heathen converts, that they arranged the principal doctrines of the Bible under heads and into classes. The followers of Jesus Christ at first required no other Creed, Confession of Faith, Articles or Catechism, than simply to receive Him as He was preached to them, believe on his Name, and live so as to explain and recommend their religion by their temper and conduct. It is also to be remembered that the *Apostles' Creed* is received by the whole Christian world; with small exceptions, and without serious dissension we may add, it is properly explained in the Nicene Creed, and is embodied in almost all the doctrinal statements of Christians everywhere, and so has been from the earliest ages.

The texts of Holy Scripture just read, seem to me to require but little analysis, defence, or explanation. It is true that some have denied that the first chapter of John, and the sixteenth verse of the third chapter of 1 Timothy, are a part of the inspired writings. But the reasons given for rejecting these portions from the New Testament are not satisfactory. As to the first chapter of John, they are absolutely worthless, and cannot be entertained. As to the sixteenth verse from the third chapter of 1 Timothy, I think it only necessary to say that I use it in connection with the other texts, because I regard it as genuine, and because, if it were not, it most happily expresses the doctrine of the Incarnation as taught everywhere in the Holy Scriptures. The doctrine of the Trinity or of the Incarnation does not depend on any one text of Scripture. I am willing to rest the defence and explanation of these great mysteries on the Word of God as a whole. While, therefore, I do not regard the sixteenth verse of 1 Timothy, third chapter, as of doubtful authority, still I rest more upon the testimony of the inspired writers as a whole, than upon any one text. And surely it were difficult, perhaps impossible, to find anywhere else words more happily chosen and better put together to express our views of the great mystery of the Incarnation. "God was manifest in the flesh." Jesus Christ, God's only Son our Lord, is *Emmanuel—God with us*. The Incarnation as set forth in the Apostles' Creed was the first great truth elaborated and defined by the scientific thought and classic culture of the early Church, and it seems to us impossible to improve it. Perhaps this is one of the reasons why the thought and strength of Christendom are now absorbed on the Person of Christ.

It is true that I am ready to believe any doctrine upon the authority of God, whether it is set forth in one or many texts. One word from God is sufficient. One text clearly interpreted is quite and altogether sufficient—just as one demonstration in mathematics is as good as a thousand. The great doctrines of the Gospel, however, are not tied to any one text, nor dependent on any peculiar line of interpretation. They beam from the whole volume of Revelation, as light does from the whole heavens when the sun appears.

It must be remembered also, as I have endeavored before to impress upon your minds—that MYSTERY belongs to true religion, for it is a communication from the Infinite to the finite—and that *a fact* or *a doctrine* may be revealed, and yet *its mode* of existence not be comprehended. The existence of a thing is apart from our comprehension of its existence. There is a God, but no creature can fully apprehend the nature or existence of God. The miraculous conception and nativity of Jesus Christ I believe, because the Word of God says so. The whole Incarnation is a mystery. I believe the facts stated, but I do not understand, nor am I able to explain them fully. Nor have I any ear for, nor patience with, the spurious Gospels that crowded the early ages of the Church, and have come even to our own times, concerning the birth, infancy, and youth of Jesus. I regard them as the tales of inconsiderate writers—mere fables or monkish legends, although such men as Baronius and Xavier have given some of them the sanction of their great names. Again : I wish to say that on these subjects I know nothing beyond the testimony of the Holy Scriptures. I have no explanation to give except what it has seemed good to the Holy Ghost to reveal to us, saying : "A Virgin shall conceive and bear a son, who shall be the son of the Highest, the Mighty God, the Everlasting Father, the Prince of Peace," and "the Holy Ghost shall come upon thee, and the power of the Highest shall overshadow thee," and accordingly "she was found with child of the Holy Ghost." "He was conceived by the Holy Ghost and born of the Virgin Mary."

The *third* Article of the Creed, as embodying and setting forth the meaning of the texts quoted concerning the mystery of the Incarnation, presents us two main parts, namely :

I. The SUBJECT of the Incarnation ; and

II. The FACT AND MODE THEREOF.

I. The subject : *Who* is it that was conceived and born ? The relative refers to its antecedent in the second Article, which is—"and in Jesus Christ His only Son our Lord ;" and the *third* is : "Who was conceived by the Holy Ghost, born of the Virgin Mary." This Article does not say that the Father or the Holy Spirit was born of the Virgin Mary ; but it does say, Jesus Christ, God's only Son our Lord, was *conceived and born*.

When Paul says, "Without controversy, great is the mystery of godliness: God was manifest in the flesh, justified in the spirit, seen of angels, preached unto the Gentiles, believed on in the world, received up into glory," he gives us the whole Gospel.

Here I understand, 1. "Without controversy" to mean, it cannot be disputed that in revealed religion there are mysteries, especially that such facts as he immediately alludes to are undeniable as facts, and yet sublimely mysterious.

2. GOD in this passage is the Creator of all things. And,

3. *Godliness* here denotes the substance of all revealed religion. The doctrines therefore stated in the 16th verse of this third chapter of 1 Timothy, are identical with the whole tenor of the Gospel, and the very same that we find in the first chapter of John. It is admitted that Jesus Christ

is called THE WORD, and that the Word was with God in the beginning, and the *Word was God.* [2-5 verses.]

The term WORD represents also the intimate relation of the Son with the Father. As reason dwells in man, so the Word dwells in God; and as the Word goes forth from the heart and lips of man, so the Word is sent forth from God the Father. (See p. 65, Dr. Browne.)

It is equally clear that THE WORD of the first verse, and of which the following verses are adjuncts descriptive of the Word, and THE WORD of the 14th verse, are one and the same. "*And the Word* was made flesh, and dwelt among us." *What* or *who* then was it that was made—not simply was, but *was made flesh?* "Without controversy," may I not say the antecedent here is THE WORD which was in the beginning with God and was God, of which the Apostle says, "All things were made by him?" [2-5, verses.] "God was manifest in the flesh."

Was made flesh—became man, not by bringing humanity from Heaven, nor by transmuting Divinity into human nature, but by being born of a woman, deriving from her his humanity. Perhaps the language of the original creation will assist our apprehension of this clause. God made man's body out of the dust of the ground, and then breathed into his nostrils the breath of life, and man became—*was made*—a living soul; for so the Apostle explains: The first man, Adam, was made a living soul. Man became *a living soul*, not by casting off the nature and qualities of dust. The created elements of dust still remained—dust he still is and to dust must return—but he became a living soul by receiving a soul from the Almighty. After the same manner, perhaps, we may compare the Incarnation with the creation, and say, so *the Word was made* flesh; not ceasing to be God or man, but became God-man—IMMANUEL, God with us. So the Council of Ephesus (A. D. 431) decided against the Nestorians, decreeing that "Christ was but one Person, in whom two natures are intimately united but not confounded." And so also the Council of Chalcedon (A. D. 451) condemned the doctrine of the transubstantiation of the human nature of Christ into the Divine, as held by Eutychus. They decreed that the two distinct natures of Christ "are united in one Person, without any change, mixture, or confusion."

When one Apostle says, "God was manifest in the flesh"—and another says, "And the WORD was made flesh and dwelt among us, *full of grace and truth*," we are to understand God in human nature, which human nature was composed of a true body and a rational soul, which means, as old *Athanasius* expressed it, that God "appropriated to himself a human body as an instrument personally united to him," and with whose eyes God might look on us and see mankind, with whose ears He might hear, and with whose hands He might act, and with whose feet He might walk among His people, and in which he might both suffer and be glorified, and both die and revive and rise from the dead; so that on account of the very intimate union of human nature with God the Son, the actions performed by Him are really and truly the actions of God, and the blood he shed is the blood of God, and of Him might be justly said: "Lo! this is our God, we have waited for Him, and He will save us: this is JEHOVAH, we have waited for him, we will be glad and rejoice in his salvation." Isa. xxv. 9. This is the glory of the Lord revealed, which the Apostle John says we beheld, "the glory as of the only-begotten of the Father, full of grace and truth." There are many lines of argumentation that might be pursued to prove the truth of this Article: such as 1. The general and essential agreement of all orthodox creeds: Heidelberg, Westminster, Church of England. It is a noteworthy fact, that the miraculous proofs of our Lord's nativity and life were so manifest in the earliest ages of the Church, that the reality of his human nature was called in question by errorists long before His Divinity was impugned.

2. The prevailing idea of the heathen concerning the communication of the gods with men. Rude and civilized nations have believed that the divinities descended to earth, assumed human forms, and mingled with men, and did and had to do with human beings just as they have with one another. The gods in heathen fables are often made a great convenience when paternity was wanting for a child.

3. There was an outstanding promise from the earliest time that God would walk in the midst of his people.

4. *Symbols* of the old dispensation taught the same thing. I cannot dwell on these. Are they not found in the books?

Then without allowing our curiosity to carry us into mysteries which it is not becoming in us to profane, we may say that the reason why the Lord Jesus is called the WORD is that it has pleased the Father to make known to us the revelations of His grace through His Son. Language, words, speech is the vehicle, the channel for conveying thought—making known our wishes. So it is only through His Son that the will of God is made known to us for our salvation. Even the patriarchs and prophets spake by the Spirit of Christ. They were illuminated by His Spirit. He is the only High Priest and Prophet of God. And as *the Word* was the Creator of the world in the very beginning, so it was worthy of the Divine Method that the way of salvation should be revealed by the WORD, and that the heart should be created anew by the very same power that created all things. Nor is it unworthy of being remembered that it is the work of Him who is God's only Son to make us the sons of God, even all who believe on His name—that He who is himself the express image of the Father and the brightness of his glory should restore us to the image of God in which we were created. And hence as this is done by His Spirit, whose office it is to make us holy by renewing the heart, and applying the benefits of his redemption, so the Spirit is called the Holy Spirit.

II. As to the FACT AND MODE of God manifesting himself in the flesh, we are to receive the words *conceived* and *born* in their full force. The Gnostics, the Docetæ, and the Manichæans taught that Jesus did not actually take, but only assumed the appearance of a man. This opinion prevailed generally for a time among several Oriental and Judaizing sects. This and similar errors are found floating along the current of theological controversy in the early ages, and connected with the Apollinarians, Nestorians, Eutychians, and Monothelists. It was to meet and refute such heathenish conceits or Jewish fancies, the Church put forth and adhered so firmly to the terms of our Creed: "The Word was made flesh." Jesus was truly man—not a phantom or spectre, but was born of his mother as other children, and grew in stature and in wisdom just as John the Baptist did. He had all the essential parts of a human being, mind, soul, body, and affections, and was subject to thirst, hunger, fatigue, sorrow, and tears, just as we are, excepting our sense of guilt or sin. He came eating and drinking, and was found in fashion as a man. He was perfect man because, according to the Scriptures, he had a human body and a human soul, both subject to human conditions and invested with human attributes. His human body took its substance from his mother; he was born, grew, and was liable to hunger, pain, weariness, bleeding, and wounds and laceration. He had flesh and blood, and bones, and nerves, and was crucified, dead and buried, as if he were only a man; and yet He was God.

First. "God was manifest in the flesh." "The Word was made flesh," not by any *change* of Divinity into humanity. This is impossible, for it is essential to the Divine nature that it should be unchangeable. Nor, *secondly*, Was there any *confusing, compounding*, or *confounding* of two natures into one; for in Jesus Christ we have two distinct natures, each having its own distinct properties, and yet but one person.

Nor, *thirdly*, Was this union of these two natures for a few years only. It remains forever. In Phil. ii. 7, we are expressly told that the Son of God took upon himself the form of a servant and was made in the likeness of men. By *the form* of a servant we are given to understand his debased condition. His human nature was in the state or debasement of a servant, and his humanity was real. Being in the form of God—equal with God—God himself. Heb. ii. 14.

And, *fourthly*, In the mother of our Lord, *all the requirements* of the prophecies and promises concerning the Messiah are fully satisfied. He was to be of the seed of Eve and of the seed of Abraham, of the nation of Israel, of the tribe of Judah, of the house of David, and to be born in Bethlehem, and of a virgin. And every one of these requirements is fully met in the history of the miraculous conception and birth of Jesus of Nazareth.

Born of the Virgin Mary asserts then that she was his mother—that his human nature was not brought down from heaven, but was taken from her substance, just as John the Baptist was born of his mother. He "was made of a woman." He was "the fruit of Mary's womb, and the seed of the woman." The blessed Virgin is expressly called his mother, and is so recognized by Him and by his disciples. The expression then that Christ *descended from heaven* does not belong to his human nature, but to Him as the Son of God. By this expression I understand simply what the Apostles say: "God was manifest in the flesh." "The Word was made flesh." It is worse than blasphemy to seek any explanation of our Lord's descent from heaven in the dew of the eternal Godhead, or of celestial, starry, or elementary matter becoming refined, and producing as a result the child Jesus. Errorists have shown themselves exceedingly ingenious in devices to get rid of the simple truth of our inspired record, but still it remains true, that Jesus Christ, God's only Son, our Lord, was conceived by the Holy Ghost in the womb of the Virgin Mary, and born of her at the stated time and in the usual way, and yet without sin, so that He did really come in the flesh, was the Son of man, as well as the Son of God.

The wording of this Article concerning the Incarnation is very important. "The Son of God took man's nature in the womb of the blessed Virgin, of her substance; so that two whole and perfect natures, that is to say, the godhead and manhood, were joined together in one Person, never to be divided, whereof is one Christ, very God and very man."

What, then, are the benefits, or as Witsius denominates them, *the fruits* of the Truth of this Article to us? The *Heidelberg* catechism answers, that Christ is "our Mediator; and with his innocence and perfect holiness covers in the sight of God my sins, wherein I was conceived and brought forth."

There are three points in this Article:—1. Jesus Christ was *born of a Virgin by the power of the Holy Ghost.* 2. He was taken from among his brethren as one of them; and, 3. He was truly *man* as well as really God. And the *first*, that he was born of a Virgin, shows that He was not under the curse that fell upon Adam on his own account. He was not represented in Adam's covenant, and consequently not liable to the imputation of Adam's guilt. He did not exist in Adam, when Adam sinned; for He was not born by virtue of the ordinary law of generation descending from Adam, nor as a fruit of the Divine command given to Adam before the fall, which said, "Be fruitful and multiply." On the contrary, Jesus Christ was born in the fulfilment of the new promise in the covenant made after the fall, in which He is denominated "the seed of the woman," and appointed the second Adam, the Head and representative of the new creation to proceed from the woman. [See this subject presented at length in Witsius, vol. ii., p. 29, &c.] This immaculate conception and birth of our Lord establishes the original purity of his human nature. He was holy, harmless, without sin of any kind, except as He bore our sins as our propitiation. And this view of our Lord's human nature is important, for it gives Him the right and ability to suffer for us as our Surety, since He was under no obligations to suffer for himself; and it also is intended as *a cover* for our original sin, in which we are conceived and born. As our *Surety* His righteousness is perfect in every thing the law could demand of us. For our sake, therefore, He was conceived and born without sin, in order that His original righteousness might cover our original sin, and supply our want of original righteousness. When we say that Christ is thus made of God to us righteousness, and that by *putting on Christ* we are covered, and are one with Him, and thus saved from original as well as actual sin, we do not mean that the life and sufferings and death of Christ were not also necessary. By no means. His great redemption work consists in and of all his life and death.—His entire righteousness, original and actual, active and passive.

And as to the other two points, *that Jesus Christ was man, and taken from his brethren* to represent them, we may consider them together. They are in fact inseparable, and are supported by the same texts of Scripture. "There is," says Paul, "one Mediator between God and men, the man Christ Jesus." And as the one only Mediator, He combined in himself the two natures between which He was to mediate. He was the Son of GOD —was GOD; and he was the Son of man—was man. He could therefore lay his hands upon both and make them *to be at one*—make an atonement—"satisfy divine justice and reconcile us to God."

And still more, as our SURETY, He had to perform all the law *required* of us, and endure all the law *demanded* of us; and as the law is very extensive and searching in its demands of us, reaching the body, the soul, and the spirit, both as to its requirements and its threatenings, so Jesus was made of a woman, and made under the law, that human nature in Him, subject to the law, could magnify it and make it honorable, fulfil all righteousness in body and soul, and that He by his death might taste death for all, and deliver his people from the power of death. And hence He is our GOEL, REDEEMER. "For he who sanctifieth and they who are sanctified should be all of one blood, that they might call each other brethren." "Wherefore it behoved him in all things to be made like unto his brethren." "For verily He took not on him the nature of angels, [He undertook not the redemption of angels,] but He took on him the seed of Abraham."

You remember that the Hebrew GOEL, REDEEMER, was to be the nearest of kin that was capable of the functions pertaining to the Goel. And it was his duty to redeem the inheritance of his kinsman that had been sold or alienated ; and to recover his kinsman's freedom if he had become a captive, or was in bondage for debt ; and to avenge his blood, if murdered ; and *fourthly*, to marry the wife of his deceased kinsman to raise up seed to him, that his family might not become extinct in Israel.

It is not strange, therefore, that the Prophets who flourished after Moses should speak of the coming Messiah as the great GOEL, REDEEMER, KINSMAN, for all things that the law required in the GOEL are found united in Christ. *First*. By his meritorious righteousness He has redeemed our forfeited inheritance, and makes "Paradise Regained" more glorious than the "Paradise Lost." *Secondly*. He delivers us from the captivity of Satan and the power of sin. *Thirdly*. He takes vengeance on our enemies, the devil and his allies, and all our sins. The Son of God was manifested to destroy the works of the devil. *Fourthly*. By redeeming us from the guilt, and power, and pollution, and dominion of sin, He gives us power to become the sons of God, even to as many as believe on his Name. Thus he saves and redeems by price and by power.

In conclusion, let us learn especially,

I. That Jesus Christ, God's only Son our Lord, is the *one and only Mediator between God and men*. It is only when, and as we see the glory of God in Christ, that the conscience oppressed with the load of guilt finds peace. God's method of justifying and saving sinners is wisdom beyond the grasp of any creature. How astonishing the love, how sublime the plan, that God's Eternal Son should be born of a woman and become a man to redeem them that are under the law, who should believe on his name, and accept Him as their surety. Having both the natures of the parties at variance which He was to reconcile, He could do justice to both. God and man meet in Christ, and man who was at enmity with God is reconciled to God, and taken into his close embrace. It is there and thus the treaty of peace was begun and concluded. "Had God and man treated anywhere but in the person of Christ, a peace had never been concluded, yea, it had broke up at first; but being in Him, it could not fail, for in him they were already one, One person, so there they could not but agree : 'God was in Christ, reconciling the world to himself.'"—*Leighton*. Dear hearer, do not these mysteries satisfy your soul, thirsting after salvation? Is not this the only way of reconciliation worthy the perfections of God and safe for man? Are not these some of the awful mysteries of the Gospel, which eye hath not seen, nor ear heard, and which have not entered into the heart of man; which were kept secret since the world began, but now are made manifest, and by the Scriptures of the prophets, according to the commandment of the Everlasting God, are made known to all nations for the obedience of faith? Rom. xvi. 25, 26.

II. *Should we not feel the strongest love for Christ, seeing that He has so loved us?* Angels are superior to us, but when angels sinned, they were left without a Goel—left to suffer the punishment due to their transgressions. Christ took not upon himself the nature of angels, but our nature. He came down to us in the likeness of men—became man. The Lord of glory did not empty himself, did not veil the rays of ineffable majesty, to become one of the cherubim or seraphim, or a companion with the highest orders of angelic hosts in their government of worlds—not to be born a monarch, and sit on a throne, but to be born of a woman in a stable—born to suffer and to die, that we might live. "In all things he was made like unto us, that he might be a merciful and faithful High Priest, in things pertaining to God, to make reconciliation for the sins of the people."

III. Forget not, dear brethren, one thing more: *He who was conceived of the Holy Ghost and born of the Virgin Mary* must be formed in our hearts, the hope of glory. He must live in our hearts, and be nourished there, and grow up there, until by His dwelling in us, we attain unto the measure of the stature of the fulness of Christ. We are not Christ's unless we have His spirit. Are we Christ's? Do we really belong to him? Angels, you know, announced his birth, saying: "Glory to God in the highest, peace on earth, good-will toward men." *Have we peace with God?* Can we and do we truly say: We adore Thee—we worship Thee—we acknowledge Thee as our God and Saviour—we expect salvation from Thee? May the whole world unite with us in knowing, acknowledging, and praising Thee, to whom be glory, with the Father and the Eternal Spirit, as it was in the beginning, is now, and ever shall be, world without end. Amen.

V.

CHRIST "SUFFERED UNDER PONTIUS PILATE."

"Thus it is written, and thus it behooved Christ to suffer."—LUKE xxiv. 46. "But those things, which God before had shewed by the mouth of all his prophets, that Christ should suffer, he hath so fulfilled."—ACTS iii. 18, together with chapter liii. of ISAIAH.

I HAVE not time this evening, nor do I consider it at all necessary, in such a presence as this, to analyze or to present a synopsis of the texts of Holy Scripture read in order to show that they teach that *Jesus Christ suffered under Pontius Pilate*, nor is it my purpose now to speak of the application of the fifty-third chapter of Isaiah to the Messiah. It is confessed by the most ancient Jewish authorities that this prophecy does relate to the Messiah. And so plainly does it suit the character of Jesus, that it has long been contended by some Jewish Rabbis that *two* Messiahs are promised in their sacred books, one to redeem and suffer, and another to reign as a glorious Prince. A sufficient answer to this is, that such an interpretation of the old Hebrew Scriptures is clearly an invention, for the purpose of getting rid of the testimony of the sacred writers to Jesus as the promised Messiah. We are not able to find a syllable in support of it from the beginning of Genesis to the end of the book of Revelation. Moses and the Prophets, and the Psalms, know nothing of *two* Messiahs, but they do speak of *one* Messiah who was both to suffer and die and to triumph, to be humbled and to be exalted, to be clothed with humanity, and yet to wear the robe of immortality and of ineffable majesty. There is no trace of any expectation of *two* Messiahs among the Jews before the coming of Christ. This interpretation was not thought of until it became a necessary invention to weaken or destroy the proof that Jesus was the Messiah, by showing that all the requirements of the old Jewish Church were fulfilled in Him.

The fourth Article of the Apostles' Creed is: "Suffered under Pontius Pilate, was crucified, dead and buried." We do not find both expressions, "suffered" and "was crucified," in some of the old Creeds, but only *was crucified under Pontius Pilate*. The sense is not changed by the omission, but I prefer both expressions just as we have them, and, by divine assistance, I hope to show that both are true, and that both are important terms in our holy religion. I confine myself, for the present, to the first clause: "Suffered under Pontius Pilate." Common ecclesiastical usage appropriates the word *Passion* to the sufferings of our Lord at and during his crucifixion, as in Acts i. 3: "To whom also he showed himself alive after his *passion*"—his suffering—preeminently, his sufferings at the close of his life.

I. Then let us look a little at the heathen judge under whom our Lord suffered.

First. PONTIUS PILATE is named in this Article of the Creed, not because he was in any way able to impart value to our Lord's sufferings; but it was well to identify historically the period of our Lord's sufferings and death. The Evangelists had told us of the epoch of his birth, so also it was desirable to fix that of his death. There are historic periods connected with historic names in the Roman Empire. And such simple references to easily identified persons are strong collateral proof of the truthfulness and authority of our sacred writers. If they had not been honest, straightforward men, never suspecting that any one would ever doubt their veracity, we cannot think they would have dared to commit themselves to dates, names, and events, as they have done.

The CREED, in saying that Jesus *suffered under Pontius Pilate*, fixes the date of his crucifixion, and enables us to examine the events of the Gospel by the light of the profane history of the same times, in the same century. *Luke* tells us that Pontius Pilate was governor of Judea when John the Baptist came preaching in the wilderness, and we know from Roman history that this was true; and we know also that Pilate was removed from office just before the death of the Emperor Tiberius, and after he had held his government ten years. And it is also in evidence that it was the custom for all Roman governors to make reports from their government to the Emperor, and for these reports to be kept on file at Rome. And no doubt Pilate made a report to his imperial master at Rome concerning the life and trial and death of Jesus of Nazareth, and accordingly *Justin Martyr*, in his defence of Christianity, or *Apology*, as it was called in his day, written in the early part of the second century, boldly appeals to the "Record of the Acts of Pontius Pilate," on file in Rome, for the truth of the facts concerning Jesus as given by our Evangelists. *Tertullian* also, from the early age of the Church, and in fact, I believe, the volume of evidence from the Fathers and the first ages of the Church, is decidedly in favor of the Acts of Pilate as a well-known and existing record, on file in Rome, of Pilate's government in the second century.

And you are all aware, I presume, that there is a passage in *Josephus* that speaks of Christ as an extraordinary person who appeared at this time in Judea; but as it is alleged that this passage is an interpolation, and does not belong to the original text, I do not insist upon it. I am not willing to decide dogmatically that the passage in Josephus is spurious, but we do not need any doubtful authority. We have direct testimony from the "Annals of Tacitus," which cannot be impeached, that "Nero persecuted with exquisite torments a sect of men commonly called *Christians*,—so called from CHRISTUS, who in the reign of Tiberius was executed under Pontius Pilate, the Procurator of Judea." Testimony of this sort might be greatly multiplied, but it cannot be necessary.

Secondly. It is a fact, then, in the next place, that Roman history acquaints us with the state of Judea as a Roman province under just such a government as is implied in our narrative. The Jews were then under the Roman yoke, a foreign, heathen, hated government. *Pontius Pilate* was a Roman knight, and the Roman governor of Judea under the Emperor Tiberius. The sceptre had actually departed from Judah. The appointed time for Messiah's advent had expired. The Jews themselves bore witness to their own degradation, when they said to Pilate, "It is not lawful for us to put any man to death;" and confirmed it by saying: "We have no king but Cæsar." It is not material to determine *how* the Jews had lost this power of life and death. It is sufficient to prove that such was the fact at this time, and that it was also a fact that the Procurators had the power of life and death, which is well attested by the history of the administrations of the provinces of the Roman empire, that of Judea included, and to prove also that Jesus suffered under Pontius Pilate. Now, let it be noted that prophecy required, if Jesus of Nazareth were the true Messiah, that he should be taken *from prison and from judgment*—that is, from confinement and guards, and from the place of judgment; and that at this judgment-seat his innocence should be established. Accordingly, after all the base arts employed to condemn our Lord, after a strict investigation, and protracted discussion, the perfect innocence of Jesus is fully recognized by his judge, and *five times* declared by him. And I need not here say that "the whole concern of our salvation turns upon this hinge;" namely, that Jesus Christ was innocent, and was condemned and suffered not for sins of his own, but for us. Pilate acted unjustly in condemning Jesus to gratify the clamors of the mob—condemning a person whom he himself had acquitted; but this acquittal is a precious testimony to us. "Then was the chastisement of our peace upon him, and with his stripes we are healed."

Again, *Thirdly*. As the promised Messiah was to be a Saviour for Gentiles as well as Jews—all nations were to be blessed in Abraham's seed—so it was right for him, in suffering "*for all, to suffer from all.*" "For of a truth, [Acts iv. 27] against thy holy child Jesus, whom thou hast anointed, both Herod and Pontius Pilate with the Gentiles and the people of Israel were gathered together."

Again, *Fourthly*. Nailing to the cross was a Roman punishment—unusual among the Jews. If Jesus had been put to death by a Hebrew judge, he would have been *stoned*, according to the laws of the Jews; but as he was condemned under a Gentile governor, he was *crucified*, and the Scriptures were fulfilled.

Again, *Fifthly*. It is in evidence abundantly from profane history, that Pontius Pilate was a man of just such a *temper and disposition* as we should expect him to be, from his picture drawn for us by the Evangelists.

Philo says he "was a man of an inflexible and severe disposition, charged with accepting bribes, with acts of injustice, rapacity, violence, and oppression, with the frequent murders of persons uncondemned, and, in fine, with the most insatiable and savage cruelty." And surely it required such a man ;—a man of such barbarous character only could have pursued so cruel, inconsistent, and vacillating a course as he did in condemning Jesus. We may add, however, before we leave him, that his wickedness was no gain to him. He was punished for his crimes in various ways. First he was reprimanded, then deposed by the Goveror-General of Syria, and at last sent to Rome, to plead his cause in person before the Emperor, but failed in his defence, and was condemned to perpetual exile in Gaul, and there he was so tormented by his own conscience, and by persecution, that he laid violent hands on himself. "Thus," as Bishop *Ado*, in his *Chronicles* of Vienne, the place where Pontius Pilate died, says, "seeking in death a speedy release from a train of protracted calamities." I might add here that this kind of testimony could be rolled up almost indefinitely, and that there is no conflicting evidence—there is not a syllable of counter or impeaching testimony. Therefore, when we say *suffered under Pontius Pilate*, our Creed is in harmony, *first*, with historic, with known and acknowledged historic personal verities belonging to the life and times of Jesus of Nazareth, the Son of God.

Secondly, it coincides with *prophecy*—in this, *first*, Shiloh could not come until the sceptre had departed from

Judah, which was not true until after the death of Herod the Great. *Secondly*, according to the Psalmist, Christ the Lord's anointed was to suffer not only from the Jews, but also from the Gentiles: "Why do the heathen rage, and the people imagine a vain thing? The kings of the earth set themselves, and the rulers take counsel together against the Lord and his anointed." And so our Lord himself predicted. "The Son of man shall be betrayed unto the chief priests, and unto the scribes, and they shall condemn him to death, and shall deliver him to the Gentiles to mock, and to scourge, and to crucify him."

II. Let us inquire, in the second place: WHO "suffered under Pontius Pilate?" Answer: It was Jesus Christ, God's only Son, our Lord, who was conceived by the Holy Ghost, and born of the Virgin Mary—Christ the Mediator, the God-man, who suffered in his whole person. The whole man, body and soul, owed obedience to the law of God. The whole man, therefore, was liable to punishment. It was necessary then for Christ, as our representative and *surety*, to suffer in his whole person, both in soul and body, that He might satisfy Divine Justice in all its claims upon man, by sustaining the punishment due to sin, expiating human guilt, and glorifying God in both the body and soul of human nature. Guilt lay on man; both his body and soul were therefore to suffer,— both were contaminated with sin, and all his faculties impaired by sin. The whole man must suffer. Heidelberg Catechism well says, "The words, *He suffered*, mean that all the time Jesus Christ lived on earth, but especially at the end of his life, He sustained, in body and soul, the wrath of God against the sins of all mankind; that so, by his passion, as the only propitiatory sacrifice, he might redeem our body and soul from everlasting damnation, and obtain for us the favor of God, righteousness, and eternal life."

III. *In what sense did Divinity suffer in the person of Christ?* In itself the Godhead suffered nothing; but Divinity afforded strength to the suffering humanity of the Mediator. So great was the weight of the curse upon sin that human nature could not have endured it without support.

Again, the indwelling of Divinity imparted value and worth to the sufferings of the Messiah Christ. It is in reference to such an indwelling that the Apostle refers in Col. ii. 9, when, in speaking of Jesus Christ, he says, "In whom dwelleth all the fulness of the Godhead bodily." *Bodily* here is emphatic. Christ dwells in true believers *mystically*, and is present in the elements of the sacrament *symbolically*, and is said to have dwelt *figuratively* and *typically* in the Ark, in the Temple; but here it is said, all the fulness of the Godhead dwelleth *bodily* in Christ. *Bodily*, that is, *really and personally*: as the body is opposed to the shadow, and means the reality, and designates a person. The merits of the sufferings of Christ are often described as flowing not from the length of time he suffered, nor from the intensity of his sufferings, but from the dignity of the sufferer. Apostles tell us, "God hath purchased the Church with his own blood"—"the Lord of glory was crucified"—"Christ through the Eternal Spirit offered up himself unto God"— that "the blood of Jesus Christ, the Son of God, cleanseth us from all sin." The boundless value, the infinite worth of the God-man is derived from the Dignity of His person—"all the fulness of the Godhead dwelleth in him bodily."

IV. WHAT did Christ suffer under Pontius Pilate? Answer: He suffered the wrath of God against us. He endured the penalty of the law of God. He satisfied Divine Justice by the sacrifice of Himself, so that, as the lamb of God, he taketh away the sin of the world.

As God is holy and just and good, He hates sin. "Thou art not a God that hath pleasure in wickedness. Thou hatest all workers of iniquity. Evil shall not dwell with Thee; the foolish shall not stand in Thy sight; Thou shalt destroy them that speak leasing." "And the wrath of God is revealed from heaven against all ungodliness and unrighteousness of men." Here the wrath, and the revelation of the righteous judgment of God, are joined together by the Apostle. Now as God is a holy God, He will not forgive transgression and sin, and will by no means clear the guilty, unless there is satisfaction rendered—His law magnified and honored. And this is just what Christ does by His righteousness, obedience, and suffering. God vindicates His holiness and makes manifest His displeasure against sin in three ways. 1. He punishes sin in the believer's Surety. He is the propitiation for our sins. 2. He punishes believers themselves at the same time that He forgives them. Ps. xcix. 8. 3. Sinners impenitent and unbelieving, rejecting Christ, are made to suffer under the guilt of unpardoned sin. "It therefore became Him, for whom are all things, and by whom are all things, in bringing many sons unto glory, to make the captain of their salvation perfect through sufferings." Heb. ii. 10. And in Romans iii. 25, 26: "Whom God hath set forth to be a propitiation through faith in His blood, to declare His righteousness—that He might be just, and the justifier of him that believeth in Jesus"—"who is the end of the law for righteousness to every one that believeth."

The purpose therefore of his sufferings is to be learned from the history of our sin and misery.

"By one man sin entered into the world, and death by sin, and so death passed upon all men, for that all have sinned." The sentence on all men, therefore, is death : "For in the day thou eatest thereof, thou shalt surely die." It is true our first parents did not die, that is, their mortal life did not end the moment they sinned, but they did at once begin to die. The sentence began to be executed. They became mortal—liable to sickness, and fell under the sentence of death, which is only delayed in its execution ; and they died spiritually, and so became subject to eternal death. And this is precisely our situation. Now the purpose of Christ's sufferings and death is to redeem us. "The righteousness of God, which is by faith unto all and upon all them that believe, being justified freely by His grace through the redemption that is in Christ Jesus ; whom God hath set forth to be a propitiation, through faith in His blood, to declare, I say, at this time His righteousness for the remission of sins that are past, through the forbearance of God ; to declare, I say, at this time his righteousness : that he might be just and the justifier of him which believeth in Jesus."

The cause of our Lord's sufferings, therefore, is not to be found in any shortcomings of His own, but in *his substitution* for His people ; that is, the wrath of God was laid on Him for the punishment of our sins. It is in this sense we understand the Prophet, saying : "We did esteem him stricken, smitten of God, and afflicted—*wounded* for our transgressions, *bruised* for our iniquities —*despised* and *rejected* of men ; a man of sorrows and acquainted with grief. Surely He hath borne our griefs and carried our sorrows. He was oppressed and He was afflicted. It pleased the LORD to bruise Him and to make His soul an offering for sin. Therefore he shall divide the spoil with the strong; because He hath poured out His soul unto death; and he bare the sin of many, and made intercession for the transgressors."

V. *What constituted the sufferings of Christ?* His sufferings began with his human life, and ended with it on the cross. For man's sake the ground was cursed. In sorrow we eat of it all the days of our life. As Christ suffered for us as our Surety, bearing the form of a servant, and appearing in the likeness of sinful flesh, so the sufferings of his whole life are to be taken into the account and collected into one amount and laid upon Him. *Think* of his sufferings in *volunteering* to come and die for us, when He emptied himself of the glory which He had with the Father before the world was. Then think of his *infancy*, his *circumcision, flight* into Egypt, the journey through the desert, and the murder of the children of Bethlehem. Think of his *private life* as the son of the carpenter Joseph, to whom he was in subjection till he was of age. Think of his *public life*, his baptism, temptation, toil, preaching, travelling, working miracles, and how He was persecuted, misrepresented—his life hunted by the Scribes and Pharisees, and betrayed, deserted, apprehended, and crucified! And shall we visit with Him the garden of Gethsemane, after eating the last Passover and the last supper with his disciples? Think of his anguish and sorrow when betrayed and forsaken, insulted and mocked. Think what He suffered from the Jews when He was falsely accused, unjustly condemned, cruelly derided, thrice denied by Peter. Think how He suffered in the judgment hall of Pilate and before Herod, and was condemned and the robber Barabbas preferred before him; and how He was torn with cruel scourges, crowned with thorns, clothed in robes of mock royalty, and hung on the cross! And when we consider also that all these sufferings He took voluntarily upon himself—that He knew them all beforehand—the bitter dregs of the cup He anticipated from the beginning; and then consider how repulsive sin, and the odious sufferings of guilt, must have been to a nature so pure and sensitive as was the Holy Sinless One, and surely we are ready to exclaim:

> "O how He loved us! O amazing love!
> O for this love let rocks and hills
>   Their lasting silence break;
> And all harmonious human tongues
>   The Saviour's praises speak."

As to the *duration* of our Lord's sufferings it is not necessary to enlarge. His whole human life was, like ours a long mortal disease, a continual death. From his conception he was stricken, smitten of God and afflicted. The shadows of the cross began to fall upon his manger cradle. For us He was presented at the Temple and circumcised, and for us He was baptized, and was tempted in the wilderness; nor did He cease His sufferings until He gave up the ghost on the cross.

I do not seek here, my brethren, any novelties, or claim any originality, as if we had made new discoveries in theology. I am only trying to present you with as clear an exhibition of the truths believed from the beginning as I can. And according to my view, an abstract of the argument for the truth of this Article of our Creed would run in this line; namely,

1. We have historic evidence in support of the fact alleged, both from the Evangelists and from cotemporary and subsequent profane history. The existence of the

Christian Church itself, from the period of the crucifixion to this moment, and such an existence and such a history as it is, is no mean evidence—but in fact a living miracle of the truth of the Gospel history, embracing the miraculous birth and supernatural sufferings of Jesus of Nazareth. You must remember here that our Lord's enemies as well as his friends confessed and believed in the fact of his suffering under Pontius Pilate, and that his enemies alleged this fact as a reason for *not* believing in him. They rejected Him because it was true He suffered under Pontius Pilate.

2. There is a natural, or very wide spread notion, that suffering either procures by merit or purchase, or is in some other way efficiently connected with, the pardon of sin. It is not material now to speak of the origin of this opinion. It is quite sufficient that it prevails and has prevailed—namely, that the suffering of victims, animals sacrificed, for example, was in some way effective towards the pardon of the sins of the persons who offered them. If Jesus Christ then has made an atonement for sin, He must have suffered.

3. All our ideas of the perfections of GOD demand satisfaction to His justice before there can be pardon offered to the sinner. It is the voice of all heaven, earth, and hell, that there can be no remission of sins without the shedding of blood. Blood cannot be shed without suffering. It behooved Christ therefore to suffer under Pontius Pilate.

4. The promises and prophecies of the Old Testament concerning the Messiah to come represent Him as a suffering Messiah. The seed of the woman was to bruise the serpent's head, but the serpent was to *bruise his heel*—and so in the Psalms and in the Prophets.

5. Jesus Christ *foretold* his own sufferings—making the revelation of them to his disciples stronger and clearer as they became able to bear it, and as the time approached for Him to suffer and die. He was a true prophet; his predictions were fulfilled.

6. Then, in the next place, we have the testimony of the Evangelists, supported by profane historians, that Jesus did suffer under Pontius Pilate.

7. Jesus, after his resurrection, speaks of his sufferings—shows his wounds—and his Apostles and the early Christians all thus believed, preached, and testified, and many of them died as martyrs to their faith—martyrs for the truth of what they saw and heard.

8. *The miracles* of the day of Pentecost, of the planting of the Church in the first ages, and the success of the Gospel in the world, and the second coming of the Lord Jesus and his judgment of the world—all imply the truth that He suffered under Pontius Pilate, but is now ascended and reigning at the right hand of the Father as Lord and Christ. The truth of this Article then rests partly on historical documents and partly on theological reasons. The historic evidence is overwhelming. It is as strong as it can be made. And besides, all the theological reasons that require satisfaction to be made to the justice of God in order that sin may be pardoned, require also that Jesus as our Mediator should suffer for us. All the Scriptures that speak of Him as a High Priest to make an atonement for sin, or as being a propitiation for us, imply of necessity *His suffering* before, during, and leading to his death as an atonement.

And if still it be asked, *Why did Christ suffer under Pontius Pilate?* our answer is, "to satisfy Divine Justice and reconcile us to God." He expiated our guilt. He evinced his love to the Father and to us, by bearing the wrath of God due to us on account of our sins. When we were enemies we were reconciled to God by the death of his Son. All things are of God, who hath reconciled us to himself by Jesus Christ. "God was in Christ reconciling the world unto himself, not imputing their trespasses unto them."

"It hath pleased the Father,—having made peace through the blood of his cross, by him to reconcile all things to himself."* These texts must now suffice as specimens of what the sacred writers teach on this subject. It is true that in the Scriptures reconciliation is ascribed to God the Father, as He loves us and determines to give His Son to die for us, and also to *the Son*, as he obeys the Father, and renders satisfaction, and intercedes for us and in us, and believers are said to reconcile themselves to God by receiving Jesus Christ as he is offered in the Gospel.

Again, all the rites, types, and texts that speak of and set forth Jesus Christ as the *propitiation*, *the propitiatory* in his blood, are in proof of Christ's sufferings to take away sin. The essential idea of atonement is covering in order to an agreement, or *an at-one-ment*. The covering of the Ark of the covenant was called the *Mercy-Seat—first*, because it covered the law, and, *secondly*, because it offered mercy to the believer. And hence Christ is himself our *Mercy-Seat*. He covers our sins with his own perfect righteousness, so that they may not condemn us in the sight of God. He sprinkles us with his blood. And

---

* Rom. v. 10; 2 Cor. v. 18, 19; Col. i. 19, 20.

he erects a throne of grace, on which God sits to hear our prayers, and grant us pardon and eternal life.

Finally, WHAT BENEFIT do we derive from the sufferings of Christ under Pontius Pilate ? What are the results ? Our standards generally sum up saving knowledge as consisting of a knowledge of our misery, deliverance from it, and gratitude for this deliverance. See Rom. vii. 24, 25.

The sufferings of Jesus are a picture of our misery from the evil of sin. All this He suffered for our sins. How awful their demerits, when such punishment was endured by God's own Son on their account! If such things were done in the green tree, what shall be done in the dry ?

How should we hate sin? It was the sole cause of the sorrows of our Lord. It is said, you know [see Witsius], and correctly, that by the shadow projected from the pyramids, we may estimate their height. So it is by Christ's death and Christ's sacrifice we should estimate the evil of sin ; and by what sin is, we may estimate the length, and depth, and breadth, and height of the atonement through which we may obtain forgiveness. It was our sins that crucified Jesus, the Lord of glory. Neither Judas, nor the Scribes, nor the chief priests and rulers of the people, nor the Jewish populace, nor Herod, nor Pontius Pilate could have done any thing against the Son of God; neither scourges nor thorns nor nails would have been prepared to torment him ; nor would the prince of darkness have attacked him with all his forces —unless He had taken upon Himself our sins, which could not be expiated in any other way. Whatever then our Lord dislikes, let us abstain from. What He commands, let us do. Let us take up our cross and cheerfully follow Him. He has set us an example. "The chafe comes not by wearing chains, but *feeling* them." There are many great truths which are lost amid the noise and glittering mazes of the world. It is only among the iron facts of life we are able to grind them out. To know what poverty is, we must taste it—we must try its temptations, grudges, and gnawing shame—we must freeze with it, test its sleepless hunger—our own crippled backs must ache over the same long furrows, or bend over the same straight benches. It is on this principle our great High Priest is able to succor us when tried. "He knows what sore temptations mean. He has felt the same."

"—How was He,
The Blessed One, made perfect? Why, by grief—
The fellowship of voluntary grief—
He read the tear-stained book of human souls—"

He poured out his soul unto death for us. He carried our griefs—bore our sins. Let us love Him—believe in Him—live and die for Him And to Him be all the glory, world without end. Amen.

VI.

JESUS CHRIST WAS CRUCIFIED.

"When the morning was come, all the chief priests and elders of the people took counsel against Jesus to put him to death.

"And when they had bound him, they led *him* away, and delivered him to Pontius Pilate the governor.

"And Jesus stood before the governor: and the governor asked him, saying, Art thou the King of the Jews? And Jesus said unto him, Thou sayest.

"And when he was accused of the chief priests and elders, he answered nothing.

"Then saith Pilate unto him, Hearest thou not how many things they witness against thee?

"And he answered him to never a word; insomuch that the governor marvelled greatly.

"Pilate saith unto them, What shall I do then with Jesus which is called Christ? *They* all say unto him, Let him be crucified.

"And the governor said, Why, what evil hath he done? But they cried out the more, saying, Let him be crucified.

"When Pilate saw that he could prevail nothing, but *that* rather a tumult was made, he took water, and washed *his* hands before the multitude, saying, I am innocent of the blood of this just person: see ye *to it.*

"Then answered all the people and said, His blood *be* on us, and on our children.

"Then released he Barabbas unto them: and when he had scourged Jesus, he delivered *him* to be crucified.

"Then the soldiers of the governor took Jesus into the common hall, and gathered unto him the whole band *of soldiers.*

"And they stripped him, and put on him a scarlet robe.

"And when they had platted a crown of thorns, they put it upon his head, and a reed in his right hand: and they bowed the knee before him, and mocked him, saying, Hail, King of the Jews!

"And they spit upon him, and took the reed and smote him on the head.

"And after that they had mocked him, they took the robe off from him, and put his own raiment on him, and led him away to crucify *him*.

"And as they came out, they found a man of Cyrene, Simon by name: him they compelled to bear his cross.

"And when they were come unto a place called Golgotha, that is to say, a place of a skull,

"They gave him vinegar to drink mingled with gall: and when he had tasted *thereof*, he would not drink.

"And they crucified him, and parted his garments, casting lots: that it might be fulfilled which was spoken by the prophet; They parted my garments among them, and upon my vesture did they cast lots. And sitting down they watched him there; and set up over his head his accusation, THIS IS JESUS THE KING OF THE JEWS."—Matt. xxvii. 1, 2, 11–14 and 22–37.

IT is written of Clovis, the first king of France, that when he heard the Bishop of Rheims read an account of the crucifixion of our Lord, he exclaimed, laying his hand on his sword: "Had I been there with my trusty Franks, I should soon have dispatched that impious rabble." Nor is it improbable that there are many now who are more ready to draw their swords for the name of Jesus, than they are willing to live for Him and love their fellow-men for His sake. It is desirable for us to have as noble a feeling for and sympathy with our Lord as the founder of the Frank monarchy, while at the same time we should evince it in some more Christian-like way. "They mourn the dead aright, who live as they would have us do."

St. Paul, in his Epistle to the Philippians, says he counted all things but loss for the excellency of the knowledge of Christ Jesus, and that I might "know him," says he, "and the power of his resurrection and the fellowship of his sufferings, being made conformable unto his death;

if by any means I might attain unto the resurrection of the dead."

In considering the question of our Lord's sufferings under Pontius Pilate, it was found that *historically* the evidence was as complete as it could be in the nature of the case—that there is no counter testimony, no conflicting or contradictory evidence—not a syllable. "The matter of fact concerning the death of Christ," says Bishop Burnet, "is denied by no Christian." Even the early and the best informed Jews, and all the early opponents of Christianity, acknowledged the personal existence and the main facts in the life of Jesus of Nazareth, as related by our Evangelists. Severus, Celsus, Porphyry and Julian, and Gibbon did not deny the substantial facts reported in the evangelical memoirs of Jesus. They endeavored to explain them, however, in such a way as to take from him his true character. His manner of life, His sufferings and death on the cross, were not only acknowledged by them, but used as an argument against his claims as the Messiah. His followers were bitterly reproached with his sufferings and the ignominy of his cross; and yet we know historically that they gloried in it. They did not deny, nor seek to cover up and hide from public view, the sufferings and death of Jesus Christ on the cross. They avowed their belief in Him because He "suffered under Pontius Pilate, was crucified, dead and buried." Paul, you remember, tells Felix and Festus and Agrippa that these things were not done in a corner. He appeals in his discourses to the facts of Jesus' life and death as well known and uncontradicted. And you remember his determination not "to know any thing among the Corinthians save Jesus Christ and Him crucified." THE CROSS OF CHRIST, in his estimation, was the centre and sum of all true religion.

"The foundation of foundations and the pillar of sacred wisdom."

The last chapters of the four Gospels give us so plain and full an account of our Lord's sufferings and death as scarcely to require a word of comment. The details are familiar to you all, and yet they cannot fail always to be deeply interesting to you. The *reality* of our Lord's sufferings and death is proven by the prophecies and types of the Old Testament, by his own predictions concerning Himself, and by the preaching, letters, and discourses of the Apostles, and by all the theological reasonings that require an atonement such as we understand Christ to have made in order to the forgiveness of sin. This Article of the Creed was intended, as indeed were all the other Articles, to meet and deny heretical opinions, or false doctrines, that began to spread in the Church even in the first ages. As some denied that Jesus had really come in the flesh—that is, denied the reality of his human nature, so they denied the reality of his sufferings and death.

It is a distinctive statement in our Creed that Jesus Christ, who was conceived by the Holy Ghost in the womb of the Virgin Mary, and born of her, and who suffered under Pontius Pilate, *was also crucified, dead and buried*, for the following reasons:

First. A theory known as the *Sabellian* had been put forth, declaring that the sufferings of our Lord Jesus were the sufferings of the Father Almighty. In Church history this is known as *Patripassianism*. The zeal of the followers of Sabellius was so great for the unity of the Godhead, as they understood it, that they contended there is but one person in the Godhead, and consequently that it was the Father himself who was born of the virgin and suffered on the cross. They believed the [ουσια] *substance* of the Godhead was the sole property of the Father, and the other two persons of the Adorable Trinity were only influences or energies embodied and sent forth from him. It is to meet this view that the *Catechism* says, "There is but one only, the living and true God;" but that "There are three persons in the Godhead; the Father, the Son, and the Holy Ghost; and these three are one God, the same in substance, equal in power and glory." And for the same purpose the Creed affirms, it was God's only Son, Jesus Christ our Lord, who suffered, was crucified, dead and buried.

Again, *Secondly*. This distinct affirmation is made to deny the doctrine of Basilides and his followers. Basilides was a disciple of Simon Magus, and lived in the second century, and taught in Egypt and Persia. He said that our Lord suffered only in semblance and not in reality—that it was really Simon the Cyrenian, who had been compelled to bear his cross, that was crucified in his stead. A small sect called *Docetæ* also maintained this opinion. This was also in part the views of the Gnostics. Mohammed also, in the Koran, says that at the last hour of his sufferings Jesus was withdrawn and caught up to heaven, and a Jew was crucified in his stead. For such a corruption of the true history, there is of course no shadow of proof. No authority is even offered. It was a mere idle assertion. Still it was thought desirable to preserve, in a well-selected and guarded form of words, what the Church believed on so important a point. For surely no part of the Gospel history is written more plainly than the account of our Lord's sufferings and death. For the Divine Word endured all things in the flesh, His Divinity not suffering, but giving support and worth to the sufferings He endured. For in the one

Christ, who was God and man,—truly man, and yet the fulness of the Godhead dwelling in him bodily,—while that which was born of the woman was born to suffer and did suffer, yet it was impossible for the Godhead himself to suffer. Hence we may say, God suffered in the flesh, God redeemed us; and the blood of Jesus, God's only Son, may be called the blood of God, shed for us; but we may not and do not say the Ineffable Godhead suffered in the flesh, or through the flesh.*

In order that we may have this subject before us as clearly as possible, I propose to consider, I. The meaning of the affirmation made in the Creed—*was crucified.*

And here, *First.* It is not necessary to prove that the literal or material wooden cross did not exist before the death of Christ. It is a mistake to contend, as some do, that the cross is original with Christianity. Crucifixion, or death on a cross, as a punishment for alleged offences, was not Jewish at all, but a Roman—a heathen one, and not peculiar to the Romans. It was practised among the Hindoos, as a punishment for theft, from the earliest period of their history; and is found also in the remotest times among the Scythians, Persians, Syrians, Egyptians, Greeks, and African tribes, and is still in use among the Mohammedans, and I think also among the Chinese, who do not, however, nail the sufferer, but tie him to the cross to be tortured to death, or killed in some other way.†

Secondly. We find three terms in use among the Romans by which *crucifixion* as a punishment was expressed: namely, *Patibulum, Furca,* and *Crux.* These terms are sometimes distinguished by good Latin writers, and some-

---

* See Forbes on the Nicene Creed, pp. 220, 221.
† See word *Crucifixion* in Encyclopædia Britan. 8th ed.

times employed indiscriminately. *Patibulum* was the cross with one beam bifurcating, resembling our capital letter Y, and probably has its name from its two spreading branches or horns—*patientes*, the lying open of the horns, from *patere*, to stretch apart. And hence the same kind of a cross was called *Furca* from its resemblance to a fork, an instrument familiar in husbandry. *Constantine* the Great introduced the new *Patibulum*, that is, the gibbet or our gallows, on which the malefactor was strangled and not nailed to the wood. The form of this new *Patibulum* was that of the Greek capital letter Pi, or nearly like our capital H. The reason for changing the old *Patibulum* into the new, given by Constantine, was, that it was not becoming for a Christian government to continue the punishment of the cross, in the same form at least as it was anciently used by the Pagan Romans. The more common term was *Crux*, which is our English Cross, the form of which was not always the same. Sometimes it was like the capital letter X, consisting of two beams crossing each other in the middle. This is a very ancient form, and is called *Saint Andrew's Cross*, from a tradition that he was crucified on a cross of this kind. The other and more frequent form made use of resembles our capital letter T, the erect or middle beam rising, however, a little above the cross-beam. On some of the crosses of this kind there was also a central bracket or projection to assist in keeping the body from falling from the upright beam. It is no doubt in allusion to this that the Latin poet *Mæcenas* is quoted, saying:—

> "Whate'er th' events that may betide,
> Don't fail for me this to provide;
> Even though I share the dreadful lot,
> On the sharp cross to sit, and rot."

All crosses were not exactly of the same size. The

higher the cross the greater the infamy, or supposed atrocity of the crime punished. Accordingly *Suetonius* tells us of the mockery of *Galba*, who, when a poor victim cried out for relief, protesting that he was a Roman citizen, and appealed to the laws for protection, the Emperor mocked him by pretending that his punishment should be mitigated by putting him on a much higher cross, and also by painting it white. Ordinarily, however, crosses were not high, for the sufferers were generally fastened to them without ladders, and in many cases it is historically in evidence that the dogs and jackals and wolves tore out and devoured the entrails of persons crucified as they hung on the cross. This also is proven from what *Suetonius* says of Nero, who was certainly as near an impersonation of the fiend of hell as we can find in history. The Roman historian says that Nero bound a number of young men and girls naked to crosses, and then clothed himself in the skin of a wild beast, and came rushing out upon them from a cave, and acted upon them all the fury of a devouring beast. This implies that their bodies, as they were fastened to the cross, must have been within a short distance of the ground, probably within about four feet of the ground. There was also a piece of wood usually on the centre of the transverse beam, to which was attached a statement of the crime for which the person on the cross was put to death. So you remember our Lord's accusation was set upon his head: "This is the King of the Jews."

The Greek term used in the history of our Lord's crucifixion is not definite as to the form of the cross. It simply denotes a beam or stake of wood used for crucifying. But the general belief is that it was the ordinary Roman cross, which was in form like our capital letter T, the upright beam being longer, and extending below the line and above the transverse beam. Pictures, monuments, coins, allusions in the early Fathers, especially Tertullian, and history, prove, I think, quite conclusively that this was the form of our Lord's cross. The history of the pious labors of the Empress Helena, mother of Constantine, to find the true cross, and how she succeeded, is it not written in the books at great length? I hope, however, I may say without irreverence, that I do not attach any importance to the story of the finding of the true cross on which our Saviour was crucified by the mother of Constantine. The learned are divided as to the facts of the life of the Empress Helena, and generally consider the story of the finding of the cross an invention, and of no consequence. The only remark I have to make concerning it, at present, is this; as the dead body was granted to Joseph of Arimathea, it is probable the disciples could have had the cross also, and would have taken it with them from Jerusalem to Pella, when they fled, according to the warning given them by our Lord, from the horrors of the siege by the Romans. If they did not take it with them, it was because they did not consider the mere wood on which He was crucified as of any consequence. And if they did take it with them, it would hardly be found in Jerusalem again in the time of Constantine. The material cross is certainly of no advantage to the Church. It is not the wood of the true cross, but Him who died on it we worship. It is faith in, and love to, and service for Him who was crucified that avails for salvation.

II. From these short notices of the history of crucifying, as a punishment for alleged crimes, I proceed in the SECOND place to speak briefly of the *Mode of Crucifixion*, as in use among the Romans at the time of our Saviour's death.

The Mode of Crucifixion deserves our attention in several particulars. *Three* things were customary before fastening the person to the cross: *beating*, compelling the person to be crucified *to carry* his own cross, and *stripping* him of his clothes. The order for capital punishment among the Romans in our Lord's day was in these terms: "Go, sergeant, bind the hands, beat, muffle up the head, hang on the ignominious tree;" or thus: "Sergeant, take away, strip, beat, chastise, execute all the law on this person." Accordingly *Livy* says: "Being scourged, they were fastened to the cross." And *Josephus* says, at the destruction of Jerusalem, "the Jews were, in the first place, whipped and tortured" with all sorts of stripes, and then crucified. It is even said they ceased to crucify because they could get no more wood for crosses.

The books prove to us that *the whipping* or *beating* was done sometimes with rods, and sometimes with whips having sharpened birds' claws and small bones or pieces of lead attached to the lashes or ends of the whips. This beating was sometimes inflicted on the road to the place of execution, and was often so severe that the sufferer perished under it before reaching the place for the crucifixion. Sometimes it was done at a post before starting to the place of crucifixion. This *scourging* was one of the kinds of suffering which our Lord endured. St. Matthew says: "And when he had scourged Jesus, he delivered him to be crucified." So also says *St. Mark*, and *St. John* says the scourging was inflicted by Pilate for the purpose of appeasing, if possible, the fury of the Jews, hoping, as is said by *St. Luke*, that having chastised him, the Jews would consent to let him go. Pilate's weakness and his desire to let Jesus go is seen, *first*, in this—that he is convinced that Jesus is innocent, and so repeatedly declares. *Secondly.* He hoped that the sight of Jesus severely scourged would melt the enraged Jews, so that they would no longer demand his crucifixion; and then, *Thirdly,* if his policy did not succeed, and he was compelled on expediency to yield Jesus to the populace to be crucified, then the Roman law would be observed in first scourging him.

The *second* thing done, according to Roman custom, to a person about to be crucified, was to compel him to carry his cross to the place of execution. They did not carry the condemned to the fields or to the prison-yard in a wagon, as we do, to be executed, but required the malefactor to carry his cross to the place where he was to die. This was a part of his punishment, and formed a part of his shame and disgrace. *Plutarch* alludes to this in his Discourse "on the slowness of the Divine Vengeance," saying, as the malefactor carries forth his cross on his body, so every one by his wickedness is the author of his own calamities, and produces out of his own bowels his own sorrows.

Accordingly our Evangelists tell us Jesus *bore his cross* until exhausted, when Simon the Cyrenian was compelled to help him. This help seems to have been granted him, however, more from cruelty than out of pity. They were afraid lest he should faint and die by the way, and they should thereby lose the satisfaction of seeing Him expire on the cross.

Again, *Thirdly.* It was a Roman custom to crucify malefactors *naked*—they stripped off their clothes. The wording of the law required the condemned to die on the cross "as naked as he was born." The testimony on this subject is very full; and I need not stop to show

how all these particulars are found in the history of our Lord's crucifixion.

III. *The Crucifixion itself.* It is evident, I think, that the cross was usually planted in the ground, and raised before the body was fastened to it. This explains the forms of expression which we find so often: "To ascend the cross;" "to mount the cross;" "to climb the cross;" "to be lifted up on the cross."

The instruments with which the body was fastened to the cross were cords or nails, generally rugged nails, such as we usually call spikes, used for the purpose not only of fixing and holding the body, but also to increase the suffering. The hands were first bound with cords, beginning with the right hand, and the nails driven through the palm of the hand, or the wrist, and then the feet were stretched out and transfixed in the same manner—sometimes crossed, so that the same spike transfixed both, and sometimes with a distinct spike to each foot, and sometimes only tied across.

Much ingenuity was exercised in making the *position* of the body of the criminal as painful as possible. The most usual posture was with the arms extended at right angles from the body, as nearly as possible, with the feet hanging down in front of the upright beam. Sometimes the posture was inverted, and the head was downwards towards the earth, as Seneca expressed it. It is said St. Peter was crucified in this posture, at his own request, because, he said, he was not worthy to die in the same way his Lord had suffered.

Revilings were common after the body was fastened to the cross. Dying on the cross was full of pain and shame. Death was brought on by various causes. Sometimes it was occasioned by the loss of blood gradually flowing from the wounds made by the nails and by the scourging; sometimes the unfortunate sufferers would live long enough on the cross to die by hunger and thirst, or to be devoured by birds or beasts, and sometimes they were killed by being pierced with a sword or a spear, and sometimes burned with fire. Instances of all these kinds are easily found in history. The Evangelists tell us that the legs of the thieves were broken, and Christ's body was pierced. All the particulars required in the Roman crucifixion are found in the history of our Lord's death. He was *beaten, made to carry his cross* without the gates, and *was stripped* of his clothing. He was lifted up on the cross, and subjected to the bitter revilings of Jews and Gentiles, and the soldiers mocked him, coming to him and offering him vinegar, and the customary guard was also there,—"the soldiers sitting watched him there."

DEATH on the cross was distinguished as the most *painful* and the most ignominious kind of punishment. Anciently, it was only the meanest and the most abandoned persons that were condemned to die on the cross. Robbers, assassins, and slaves guilty of the worst offences—"monsters in human shape," as Witsius says, "only were candidates for the detested cross." Before a Roman citizen could be subjected to this punishment, he had to be degraded by servile stripes and deprived of the rights of a freeman, just as a priest or ecclesiastic in Papal countries must be *unfrocked* before the civil law can punish him. *Crucifying* was synonymous with the severest suffering—our word *excruciating* is derived from it. And *Cicero* in his impeachment of Verres, who had crucified a Roman citizen, says that "crucifixion was the most cruel and terrible of all punishments, such as no man should ever see, or hear, or think of." And

Horace more than once speaks of the severity of the punishment of whipping and scourging among the Romans: "To be cut by the terrible whip and to be whipped to death." And when we apprehend the fact that there are many nerves and tendons in the hands and feet, and consider that the wounds from the scourging were left open, and the action of the air, wind, and sunshine on such fresh open wounds, and then remember the transfixing of the feet and the nailing of the hands with rugged spikes, and that the weight of the body was chiefly sustained on these open and distended wounds in the expanded limbs, and, still more, that the blood under such circumstances was forced in an unnatural quantity on the brain and stomach, then we may perhaps begin to have some idea of the painfulness, the awful painfulness of death by crucifixion.

Even in the law of Moses it is said: He that is hanged is *accursed, a curse of God*, which St. Paul applies to Jesus. Deut. xxi. 22, 23, quoted Gal. iii. 13. Here it may be proper to remark, that although crucifixion was not a *Jewish* mode of punishment, yet the Jews were in the habit of hanging the dead body on a gibbet or gallows. This I illustrated to some length in my Lectures on Esther, in the death and disgrace of Haman. Ordinarily the Jews put to death either by stoning, burning, or strangling, or with the sword or battle-axe. And after death, in order to let the people see that the offender was really dead, his body was exposed by hanging on a gallows. Why, then, was peculiar infamy attached *to hanging on the cross?* May we say with *Witsius* that God was pleased thus to brand this kind of punishment with peculiar infamy, because the sin of our first parents had relation to *a tree?* Is every one hanged *a curse, accursed of God,* to remind us of the fatal tree where the Divine wrath was first kindled against our race? And is it for this reason that the Cross has become the symbol of our deliverance from the curse? Moses' law did not mean that the simple hanging on the cross of the body of a person, guilty or innocent, penitent or impenitent, necessarily excluded him altogether from the mercy of God, but it did signify, and was a memorial of the fact, that the only hope of mankind escaping from the curse of the sin that was committed by disobedience in eating of the forbidden fruit of a tree, rested in the sufferings of God's own Son on the Cross, who would come and die in the fulness of time to redeem us from the curse of the law. "Christ hath redeemed us from the curse of the law, being made a curse for us; for it is written, Cursed is every one that hangeth on a tree."—*St. Paul.* To hang on a tree among the Jews was *literal*, as it is now in rude and lawless districts, as the branches of trees were used for gibbets or a gallows; and as wood is part of a tree, so the beams or stake used for crucifying was also called a tree.

The curse of *hanging* on the tree, in Paul's mind, was emphatic, for it was a painful death, a shameful death, a lingering death, amid the jibes and scoffs of the profane, and such a death as only the lowest and the vilest could suffer among the Romans.

I believe that Jesus Christ, God's only Son, *was crucified and dead*, because this is implied in all the types that speak of Him as a sacrifice. It was thus He finished the work committed to him. He laid down his life for his sheep. He laid it down voluntarily, and he did it *piously*, offering up prayers and supplications, and with perfect peace and composure committing his soul to his Father. "Father, into thy hands I commend my spirit." The Paschal Lamb, Isaac, and the Jewish altars, all preached this doctrine. The reasons, then, why our Lord was put to death on the cross, may be stated in this way :—

1. It was predicted the Messiah should so suffer ; the types proclaimed the same thing ; He himself foretold his own sufferings, including crucifixion.

2. Man's first disobedience, "that brought death into the world and all our woe," was about a tree. And it pleased God that the atonement by which pardoned sinners may regain Paradise should be finished on a tree.

3. As Jesus was the Mediator, the Messiah for Gentiles as well as for Jews, so it was requisite He should die under Jewish as well as Gentile law. But how could this be brought about? There were only four methods known to the Mosaic law for capital punishment, namely : *first, slaying* with the sword, but this involved no disgrace ; *secondly, stoning*, but this would break his bones, which was not to be done to the Messiah ; *thirdly, burning*, but this could not be done, for then the flesh of the great Paschal Lamb would not have remained to be the food of his people ; *fourthly, strangulation*, but then this would have rendered his flesh unclean. How, *then, was Jesus* to die? The accusation against him under the Jewish law was blasphemy, because He made himself equal to God by calling himself the Son of God. The punishment for this was death by stoning. But they had not the power to put any one to death according to Jewish law. This indictment, therefore, fails, and the offence made available was a political one, that he claimed to be a king, and was therefore Cæsar's enemy and rival. The superscription over his head on the cross proves that the procuring cause of his death, according to the judgment rendered against him, was that he claimed to be *the king*

of the Jews. On this charge he was condemned to suffer *Roman* punishment, which was to be crucified. And this kind of a death meets all the prophecies concerning the sufferings of the Messiah. It was necessary He should die from the shedding of his blood, and that He should die in a conspicuous and open manner; and that his sufferings should be with such agony, and under such shame as would properly express the wrath of God against sin; and that He should die on a tree, as one under the curse of God. All these requisites are found in his crucifixion, and found only there.

In bringing this discourse to a conclusion, I wish, my dear hearers, to say:

I. I have not, and do not consider it important to dwell on the explanation and proofs of this article of our holy religion, because I suppose that any of you are in danger of believing *Sabellius*, the Egyptian philosopher of the third century, or of following Basilides, the disciple of Simon Magus, or that you are about to adopt the Koran; but I am aware that while the forms of error are changed, that their *restatements* are quite as dangerous as the old ones, and often much more so, because the restatement embodies all the essential error of the old one, but in a more subtle and plausible form. I believe that the Son of God, having taken man's nature, "truly suffered, was crucified, dead and buried, to reconcile His Father to us, and to be a sacrifice, not only for original guilt, but also for actual sins of men." Here is a great vital purpose in view. I do not see any way to be saved unless this Article is true. I know the Deist, the Socinian, and all who deny the Divinity of our Lord, think but little of this Article. Those who deny that there is any necessity for a propitiatory sacrifice, or that God had need to be reconciled to man, may adopt the opinions of the *Docetæ* or of the

Koran, and deny that our *Lord truly suffered and was really crucified.* It may content them to say that as it was man who was at enmity with God, and not God with man, that Jesus had only to come and set an example, and call men to repentance, and then be recalled to heaven without really suffering and dying. This would be more consistent in our humble opinion than to hold to the reality of his death, and yet deny that his blood was shed for the remission of sins, and in order to appease the wrath of God. We can see no way to save sinners but by reconciling the justice of God with his mercy. Justice calls for wrath on the sinner; Mercy pleads for pardon. To reconcile *Justice* and *Mercy*, to punish sin and yet forgive, the sinner being penitent and believing, God was pleased to ordain the sacrifice of His Son; and in order to this He sent His Son, made of a woman and under the law, conceived of the Holy Ghost, born of the Virgin Mary, and suffered under Pontius Pilate.

And in support of this view you will remember many passages of Scripture that speak expressely of reconciling God to us. For example, 2 Cor. v. 19.

You know, also, that there are many texts that tell us of the wrath of God against sinful men, illustrated by the expulsion from Eden, by the flood, the destruction of the cities of the Plain, the Canaanites and the history of the Jews, and in fact of all ancient nations.

And the same thing is proven expressly and distinctly by the Jewish sacrifices. It is not necessary for my argument to prove, as I believe, that sacrifice was at first and originally a divinely instituted rite, for even if it were devised in the first instance by man, still, as sacrifices were sanctioned by the Almighty and made a type of Christ, so the purpose of sacrifices remains unchanged, and that purpose certainly was to deliver *from the wrath of God.* There was and there is an opinion; almost or quite universal, that in some way sacrifices could and did turn away the wrath of God. The Passover was expressly appointed and made to represent the turning away of the wrath of God from the Israelites when it fell heavily upon the Egyptians. And then we find in the books of Moses the most minute and painful directions for those who have sinned as to how they may offer a sacrifice that shall avail as an atonement for their sins. Whether it was a priest, a prince, or any one of the people, he was to bring a victim, confess his sins upon its head, and then slay it as a *sin-offering.* The same thing is illustrated in the services appointed for the day of expiation, when the high priest made an atonement first for himself, and then for the people; and also of the scape-goat, which was offered at the same time, the sins of the people were confessed on his head. Now the Jews looked on these sacrifices as strictly propitiatory. And the heathen made the same confession of faith by their sacrifices; and especially in times of peculiar danger, when they went so far as to resort to human sacrifices, hoping to propitiate the gods by the noblest victims. And as the terms used by the sacred writers to describe the death of Christ are taken from the Jewish sacrifices, these sacrifices must have been types of the death of Christ, and his death must therefore be regarded as propitiatory. He was led as a lamb to *the slaughter. He is called the Lamb of God—the Lamb slain—a Lamb without blemish and spot.* And the Epistle to the Hebrews expressly compares the priesthood of Aaron with that of Christ, and explains that whereas the Aaronic priest offered the blood of bulls and goats, which could not take away sin, that, on the other hand, Christ offered not the blood of others but, his own blood— offered himself to bear the sins of many; and so put away sin by the sacrifice of Himself. Under the law, without the shedding of blood there was no remission, and so it is under the Gospel; but here it is the blood of God's dear Son that cleanseth us from all sin.

II. It should be observed that our Lord's sufferings on the Cross were attended with some notable advantages: namely, it was *public*—everybody knew of his crucifixion; and as he was three hours on the cross, there was sufficient time to take note of his sufferings and death, and so also there was time and opportunity for him to show his pity upon the penitent malefactor at His side, and to manifest his heavenly disposition, and pour forth His fervent prayer for His murderers, and commend his spirit to his Father. It thus pleased God, by his Providence, so to order the crucifixion that the course and manner of our Lord's death might be conspicuous, and every reasonable excuse for unbelief concerning it be taken away. St. Paul declared before King Agrippa that the main facts of the Gospel were open and known to all the world. *These things were not done in a corner*, or secretly. And our Lord himself boldly declared to His accusers: I spoke freely to you and to the world. I taught publicly in your synagogues and in the Temple, and in secret have I done nothing. And as He had lived and taught, so He died. As Moses lifted up the serpent in the wilderness on a pole in a conspicuous place, so was the Son of Man lifted up on the Cross, that He might draw all men unto Him, and that whosoever believeth on Him, thus crucified, should be saved.

III. Nor, *thirdly*, is it improper to say that *his posture* on the cross *was emblematic of the design of his death*—signifying his Infinite Love. His arms were extended signifying the comprehensiveness of his love, embracing all mankind, and showing how earnestly He sought and entreated them to be reconciled to God. The Cross was as it were his pulpit, from which, by his streaming blood and expiring groans when He gave up his spirit, He calls men to repentance, and preaches free grace and offers remission of sins. Nor was there ever a throne that taught such humility blended with the most exalted dignity as the Cross of Jesus. On the Cross, He was encircled with rays of infinite glory, yet suffering the acutest pain, the most awful agony and the deepest shame on our account. But it was then as a glorious conqueror, having spoiled *principalities and powers*,—the powers of hell, of darkness, sin, and death,—He made a show of them, openly triumphing over them upon His Cross. Never was there such a triumphal column as the Cross. Never were such trophies hung on any triumphal arch as those of Jesus when He hung on the tree. There *the world*, with all its counterfeit pleasures and bewitching charms, was held up defaced and worthless. Henceforth the believer says, the *world is crucified to me*, *and I am crucified to the world*. And here too our *sins* are exposed as His trophies. They are abolished in His flesh and slain upon His Cross, so that the handwriting of ordinances that condemned us was nailed to His Cross, and our bonds cancelled and our debts paid.

And so the old grim monster, "the terror of kings and King of Terrors," *Death* itself, hangs gasping and dying on His Cross. Here we see Death with its sting plucked out and all its terrors quelled, and the grave no longer claiming the victory.

It is thus we may understand St. Paul's words: *conformable* to his death—planted together with him in the likeness of his death—crucified together with Christ;

having our old man crucified together with him, that the body of sin may be destroyed, so that we may no longer serve sin—for they that are Christ's have crucified the flesh with the passions and lusts thereof.

I know not where to find any thing equal to *the word of the Cross*, which *is the power of God to salvation*, for exciting us to our duty. Does it not inflame our hearts with love to think of our Lord's cruel sufferings for us? How He was despised, and endured the shame and the pain of the Cross! What should we not be willing to endure and do for Him, who died for us? What greater encouragement can we have to hope for mercy from God than this, that He spared not His own Son, but delivered Him up to the sufferings of such a death for us? How can we have higher evidence of God's love towards us than this? Is it not the heart of God we see yearning over us in the dying agonies of His Son on the Cross?

How great a horror should sin excite in us, seeing that it was for sin Jesus thus died! How much should we love Him who voluntarily yielded himself to such a death for us! With what readiness should we give up the world and devote ourselves to His service! With what patience should we bear suffering and affliction, bereavement and pain, seeing he has suffered for us, and endured far more than we are capable of feeling! And with what confidence should we accept of the offer of mercy! seeing that it hath pleased God to bruise Him and put Him to grief in our stead! Oh! how earnestly should we flee to the Refuge set before us by His atonement! And surely, if we neglect so great a salvation there will be no escape for us. But if we come unto Him, He will in no wise cast us out.

VII.

GOD'S ONLY SON OUR "DEAD CHRIST."

THE evening of last Lord's Day we contemplated CHRIST AS CRUCIFIED on a Roman cross under sentence of Pontius Pilate, the Roman governor. This evening, if the Lord will, we are called to behold CHRIST DEAD. "And at the ninth hour Jesus cried with a loud voice, saying, Eloi, Eloi, lama sabachthani? which is being interpreted, My God, my God, why hast thou forsaken me? And Jesus cried with a loud voice, and gave up the ghost." In Mark xv. 38, 39 ; Matth. xxvii. 50–57 ; Luke xxiii. 46 ; John xix. 30–42.

To say that these passages of the sacred writers concerning the last hours of Jesus can be explained away, so as not to mean that Jesus really died on the Cross, is to say they have no meaning at all. I hope you will here observe, (1.) *The promises and prophecies* of the Old Testament, the rites, and types, and sacrifices of the Mosaic dispensation, contemplate and require that the Messiah should *suffer*, be *crucified*, and *die* from crucifixion on the Cross. (2.) The Evangelists give us a narrative of events leading to his crucifixion, and of the results that followed ; and, (3.) This narrative has been received by all Christians from the time the records were made—which was soon after the events occurred—to this day as a true history. It is in evidence also, (4.) That our history contains an account of things that were most surely believed at the time they are alleged to have taken place, both by friends and enemies. Our Lord's enemies believed that He really died on the Cross, and his friends and followers were so certain of the reality of his death, that they prepared him for his burial, and did actually lay him in a tomb. The truth of this clause of this Article in our Creed is believed by us, then, (1.) Because the other Articles being proved to be true, this one is true also. (2.) It is believed distinctly on account of the tradition of the Church concerning His death both before and subsequent to the crucifixion. (3.) The direct testimony of the narratives. (4.) All the theological arguments that call for the death of the sacrifice offered for sin, and the shedding of blood in order to the remission of sins, call for the death of Christ as our Mediator.

We have considered the sufferings of our Lord. We have witnessed his passion and crucifixion. We have seen the man Christ Jesus after a night of misery and insult; buffeted before the priests; mocked in royal array before Herod; scourged and crowned with thorns by Pilate; betrayed by one of his Apostles and forsaken by them all, and his precious body nailed to the cross. *Behold the man!* "Is it nothing to you, all ye that pass by? Behold, and see if there be any sorrow like unto my sorrow, which is done unto me, wherewith the LORD hath afflicted me in the day of his fierce anger?" But God has mercifully put it beyond the power of the body to endure the extremity of mortal agony for any great length of time, for when the forces of nature are spent, life ceases in death. This law obtained with Jesus. And if any other proof could be wanting for the reality of his death, it is given in his pierced side, when from his heart there came out a mingled flow of blood and water. This is of itself, without the torturing, the scourging, and crowning with thorns, and the nailing to the cross, quite sufficient to cause his death. And when this witness of blood was given, it was accompanied with such phenomena, that the Centurion cried out, "Truly this was the Son of God." The words of our Creed, *suffered under Pontius Pilate, was crucified, dead and buried*, may seem a useless repetition, and accordingly in some of the ancient copies this Article was expressed by the single phrase, *was crucified under Pontius Pilate*. And this does indeed comprehend all; still there was a purpose, and an important one, to be served by retaining the four terms, *suffered, was crucified, dead* and *buried*. Each one of these terms disclaimed and rejected from the faith of the Church some erroneous conceit or false doctrine concerning the sufferings and death of Christ, and by using them all in the order of the Article, we have a more full and clear statement, affirming the *reality* of his sufferings, and setting forth *the manner* and *main circumstances* and *complete effect* of his sufferings, which ended in his death on the cross and actual burial in the tomb of Joseph of Arimathea. It is a possible supposition in such cases, that, even after crucifixion was commenced, the sufferer might be taken down and live. Such cases are on record in the books. Our Lord's persecutors, in their cruel mockery, spoke of his saving others, now let him save himself by coming down from the cross. But in his case it is plain nothing of the kind was done. Our Lord remained on the cross, and his sufferings continued till they terminated in death. And our surgeons and medical men will all tell you that the wound from the Roman spear in his side would have produced certain death, if there had been no other cause.

Under Pontius Pilate does not exclude his sufferings

before nor after his arraignment at Pilate's judgment bar—does not deny his sufferings in the garden, and before Herod, and on the way to Calvary, and on the cross. *Suffered under Pontius Pilate*—ἐπὶ Ποντίου Πιλάτου—is intended to express what He underwent in the way of judicial process, his arrest and arraignment, his sentence from Pilate—that He was treated, prosecuted, condemned and put to death, professedly, according to law as a malefactor. It embraces all the infirmities which He bore for our sake, from his manger-cradle to his last moment on the cross—all the discomforts and sufferings of his infancy, youth, and manhood, of his private and public life—all the pains and sorrows that He underwent and endured in the course of his ministry, and chiefly just previous to his death. *Under Pontius Pilate* designates the consummation of the judicial process. All before was leading to this, and all after was the effect of his condemnation by the Roman governor, who scourged him and delivered him to be crucified. *Suffered*, then, is to be taken in the sense of *was punished as a malefactor*, and so were fulfilled the Scriptures which foretold that Christ should thus suffer. *He was stricken* and *smitten* of God for us. God made him sin for us—a propitiation—a sacrifice—made *Him*, His only Son our Lord, who knew no sin—who was perfectly innocent and free from all sin—*made Him sin for us*. That is, He was treated as a malefactor in our place, and bore the wrath of God against sin, that we might be made the righteousness of God in him. He was numbered among the transgressors.

But while *suffered under Pontius Pilate* affirms the punishment of death under a professed legal process, inflicted upon him as a condemned malefactor, it remained still to describe *the nature, and exact kind and manner* of that suffering, which, according to the Scriptures, had to be most painful and covered with ignominy. Hence, the expressions *was crucified and dead* were added. It is true, we might suppose *was crucified* included suffering, for crucifying was the most *excruciating* kind of suffering, and also that *was crucified* would mean also that he really died. But it has already been shown, *first*, that Sabellius held that it was the Father Almighty that suffered and was crucified, and, therefore, the Creed and Catechism affirmed it was Jesus Christ, God's only Son, who suffered and was crucified. And, *secondly*, that the Docetæ and Basilides, and such like errorists, said that Jesus did not really suffer, but only seemed to suffer.

And *Apollinaris* conceived the monstrous notion that Christ had no human soul, but that the place of the proper human soul in his body was occupied by his Divinity. Consequently, he denied the possibility of Christ's true and natural death. For if He had no proper soul in union with the body, of course there could be no death, for there could be no separation of body and soul, as when we die. And, *thirdly*, Mohammed and others said it was Simon the Cyrenian, and not Jesus Christ at all, that "suffered, was crucified, dead and buried."

The affirmation, therefore, is emphatic, *Jesus Christ suffered under Pontius Pilate*—so suffered that He was crucified even unto death, and that He did actually die, and was buried as *a dead man*, his body being treated as that of any other dead man. Our Catechism asks: "Wherein did Christ's humiliation consist?"

"*Ans.* Christ's humiliation consisted in his being born, and that in a low condition, made under the law, undergoing the miseries of this life, the wrath of God, and the cursed death of the cross; in being buried, and continuing under the power of death for a time." The

Heidelberg Catechism asks: "Why was it necessary for Christ to humble himself, even unto death?"

"*Ans.* Because, with respect to the justice and truth of God, satisfaction for our sins could not be made otherwise than by the death of the Son of God."

I thought last Sabbath evening that I should be able to treat of both terms, *dead* and *buried*, this evening, but find now that I shall be obliged to postpone Our Lord's Burial to the next Sabbath evening.

To assist your memory, I propose the following order in the remarks which I hope now to make on *Christ as dead on the Cross:* namely,

I. Of *the nature of his death.*

II. Why, or how, and for what reasons it came to pass that Jesus did die on the Cross. The necessity of his humiliation unto death.

III. And *thirdly*, but briefly, the ends aimed at and accomplished by his death.

IV. And *lastly*, something as to the benefits secured to us by his death.

I. *In what did Christ's death consist? What was its nature?* The Article declares, *first*, the *fact and quality* of Our Lord's sufferings. He was dealt with as a malefactor by the Roman governor, Pontius Pilate; and, *secondly*, He was crucified, which explains *the manner* of his sufferings, fulfilling exactly all the requisites of the Scriptures; and, *thirdly*, it affirms the result or end of his sufferings on the cross—He was dead. His sufferings were completed only when, and not until, he gave up the ghost. He lost, or rather laid down his life by the sufferings He endured when He died on the Cross.

Plain, however, as the narrative of our Lord's sufferings and death is, I confess I am not altogether surprised at the weakness that would seek for some interpretation that would relieve the sacred writers from affirming the literal, actual death of the Son of God. Were not the heart-sorrows of His life enough to satisfy the wrath of God against sin? If Enoch and Elijah were translated to heaven without tasting death, how is it that God's own dear Son must pass through the mortal agony of actual death? There certainly must have been some great cause why the Lord Jesus humbled himself unto death. And so indeed there was. The law of God said, "The soul that sinneth, it shall die." "Without the shedding of blood, there is no remission of sins." Man is a sinner, and must therefore die, or an able, accepted substitute must die for him. Mere suffering, wrung from the heart, mere agony of the body and soul, however severe, and long continued, is not enough unless it end in actual death. *Death is the penalty.* Not mere suffering, however exalted the sufferer, or however severe, can meet the requirements of the law. No seeming death, no deep trance, no syncope from which the sufferer may be recovered will meet the case. The law calls for blood—for life. The law is earnest, specific, distinct. It demands blood, and that the blood be so shed as to produce actual death; the law calls for suffering, to be endured with agony and under shame, and to be continued till death actually takes place on the accursed tree. So it was with the Hebrew sacrifices. The Paschal Lamb really died—was truly slain. At the very hour, or at least at the same great Jewish Festival, at which Jesus was crucified, thousands of Hebrew lambs were recently slain or dying. The death of their great antitype was as real.

Again, the Son of God took on Himself human nature, became truly man, was born, and breathed, and lived in this world just as a true and proper man—as John the Baptist did; and one of the chief ends for which He became man was, that He might die. For this end He came into the world. *Wherein, then, did his death consist?* I answer, Jesus died when and just as a man dies when his soul leaves his body. His human nature it was that suffered and died; and his human nature was perfect. As his Divine nature was not changed or confused with his human nature when He became man, so neither did his human nature cease to be human nature when it was taken by his Godhead. It was his manhood that was crucified, was dead and buried. His death did not, therefore, consist of the separation of his Divinity from either his body or his soul. If this were so, then it was not the Son of God that died, but the Son of Mary. Then Christ would be divided into *two* separate persons, and the mystery and the blessing of the Incarnation would be lost. But we believe "the eternal Son of God became man, and so was, and continueth to be, God and man in two distinct natures, and yet inseparable in one person forever. When Jesus said, "*It is finished*, and gave up the ghost," the meaning is not that his Godhead disconnected itself from his humanity. His human nature was, and is, and will ever remain absolutely perfect. "Christ, the Son of God, became man by taking to himself a true body and a reasonable soul, being conceived by the power of the Holy Ghost, in the womb of the Virgin Mary, and born of her, yet without sin." Catech., 22 Ques. After Jesus expired, his body was there before the eyes of the beholders, just as the body of your friend is before you on the bed after the breath has left it, and you are closing the eyes. This was the DEAD CHRIST of our sculptors and painters. His holy head was slightly drooped; his gentle and loving eyes were softly closed; his blessed heart was still; his wounds ceased to drop the clotting blood; his body is still suspended by the rugged nails; but the long agony is over. "He has lived our life to its last pang. His soul has gone out of the torn and mangled body. Jesus of Nazareth is dead."* The death of Christ must be as complete a dissolution of his soul and body as was that of Adam, and of every one of Adam's race at death. Accordingly the record is emphatic. *Jesus breathed out his spirit and gave up the ghost.* But who can tell what death is? Who knows what life is? Now the term *dead*, applied to Jesus Christ, must comprehend and mean all that death physical means when applied to any mortal man. When our first parents sinned, they died a spiritual death—fell from original righteousness and lost communion with God—and in this state of spiritual death we are all born and continue until we are regenerated, and if not regenerated or born again, this spiritual death ends in death eternal, which is also called the *second death*—which is an endless separation of the soul from the presence of God and the joys of heaven. In the word *dead*, as applied to Jesus Christ, there is, then, no reference to spiritual or eternal death, as just described. It belongs exclusively to his body. It means his true and proper death, not differing in any way from that *temporal death* which all of our race must undergo. Jesus Christ actually died just such a death as you and I must go through in meeting the appointment of our Creator, who has appointed

---

* See Bethune.

unto all men once to die—we must needs die, and are as water spilt upon the ground that cannot be gathered up again. What man is he that liveth, and shall not see death? Shall he deliver his soul from the hand of the grave? The awful sentence on Adam was in these words: "In the sweat of thy face shalt thou eat bread, till thou return unto the ground: for out of it wast thou taken: for dust thou art, and unto dust shalt thou return." Gen. iii. 19. And accordingly, dying is described as returning home, for at death the body, which is dust, returns to the earth as it was; and the spirit returns to God who gave it. Ecc. xii. 7. Death, in the light of these texts, is a returning of man to original principles. It is a ceasing of the vital functions of the body. It is no longer capable of motion, appetite, or passion. There remains in it neither perception nor sense. There are the hands and arms, but they are crossed over the body, cold, stiff, motionless. There are the eyes, but they see not. There the lips once so fervid and eloquent, but now mute as marble. The chest and lungs, once heaving with rushing blood and deep emotions, are as lifeless as the tombstone. There has been a sad dissolution of partnership between the body and the soul. This separation is so complete that it looks as if the body were the cage, and the soul a winged inhabitant who had just fled away—as if the body were a temple, and the soul a Divinity that dwelt in it, but had departed from it. And this dissolution between the body and the soul produces fatal effects upon the body. For death is a breaking of the link that unites the body and the soul together, and when this link is broken the body is nothing but dust. Now, in the history of the crucifying of our Lord, we have such *antecedents* and such signs *following* as plainly imply the reality of his dying. In this history, we see what would produce death in any of his followers—

exactly what did produce death in nearly every one of his Apostles. There is the same extreme anguish, the same tearing and gashing and rending of his flesh, the same effusion of blood, and the same breathing out of the breath of life, that there would have been, if it had been St. Peter or St. Paul who was crucified. The Scriptures speak of his *being slain, cut off, taken away, destroyed, slaughtered, sacrificed, crucified,* and these terms mean, when applied to the Son of God, just what they express when used in describing the violence done to a prophet, an apostle, or any other martyr. And He was judged to be dead by the same signs that would lead to such a conclusion in any other similar case. Thus the soldiers judged him to be dead—*seeing him already dead, they did not break his legs,* and both friends and enemies concur in the judgment of the soldiers. His enemies *exult* over him dead, and his friends and followers *mourn* him as really dead, and think of nothing more than of giving him a proper burial. And accordingly, the very terms used by the Evangelists express precisely the real nature of his death. St. Mark says, *He expired, He breathed out his soul or his last breath.* St. Matthew says, *He let go his spirit, or gave up the ghost;* and St. John says, *He delivered up his spirit into the hands of God;* and St. Luke describes the same thing by repeating the words of Jesus: "*Father, into thy hands I commend, or commit my spirit.*" And in proof of the same thing, we may call to mind his own words, saying, *I lay down my life, I give my life a ransom.* And accordingly, on the Mount of Transfiguration, Moses and Elias spake to him of his *decease,* which he should accomplish at Jerusalem. Again and again, and by various figures and terms, did He foretell to his disciples his sufferings and the kind of death He was to die. "And when Jesus knew that his time was come, that he should depart from this world."

Wherever his going out of the world or leaving his disciples, or his dying is spoken of, the idea is that He would die just as one of them would die : His soul would leave his body, and the ordinary signs would be found on his body, and he would be judged to be dead, just as one of them would be.

Shall we say with Peter and Paul, that death is a *dissolving of our earthly house*, or the *laying of it down*, or *putting off our tabernacle?* Shall we say it is going abroad, away and out of the world, being absent from the body—a going hence, the way of all the earth, a being seen no more among men ; a resting from one's labors ; a falling on sleep ; sleeping with one's fathers ; gathered to our people ; being added to our fathers, or *a going over to the majority ;* being taken or cut off from the land of the living ; going down into the pit ; to the house appointed for all living ; making our bed in darkness, or a lying down, or resting, or sleeping in the dust ? In a word, we find no phrase in philosophy, poetry; or Scripture, by which human death is expressed, that does not apply to our Lord's death. I believe, therefore, with the Creed, in Jesus Christ, who suffered, was crucified, dead and buried—that his death was a true and proper death—just such a real separating of his soul and body as takes place when one of us dies.

In the death of Christ, who is the second man, the Lord from heaven, we have *first*, then, just such a death as was pronounced against Adam, the first man. Christ, as our substitute, surrendered himself to the whole of the death which lay upon Adam, as the effect of the Divine wrath for his sin. And surely this is love beyond degree—love transcending reason's grasp, and almost paralyzes faith itself—that He who restored so many diseased persons and raised the dead, and who is the author of life and immortality, should himself submit to death. And that He should die for the expiation of our sins; for He "made his soul an offering for sin, to finish the transgression, to make an end of sin, to make reconciliation for iniquity, and to bring in everlasting righteousness." "As it is appointed unto men once to die, so also Christ was once offered to bear," to take upon himself, and thus to take away, "the sins of many."

Again, *secondly. In Christ's death, we have him witnessing to the whole of the New Covenant.* "The Old Testament was confirmed by the blood of victims sprinkled on the altar, the book of the Covenant, and the people. Ex. xxiv. 6–8; Heb. ix. 18, 19. But as the New Testament far excels the Old, it was proper that it should be ratified by much nobler blood, even by the blood of the Son of God, dying as a testator for the confirmation of his testament."—[See *Witsius* on this head.] He died to make the promises of the New Testament sure and irrevocable. In Him as a faithful and true witness all the promises of God are yea and amen. As *a prophet he preached* unto us a new and better covenant, which was established upon better promises, and was ratified with his blood, and hence He himself calls his blood "the blood of the New Testament," and where a testament is, there must also of necessity be the death of the testator. His death, therefore, was necessary for the fulfilment and confirmation of his prophetical office.

And, *thirdly.* The same thing is true of his *priestly office.* "For every high priest taken from among men, is ordained for men in things pertaining to God, that he may offer both gifts and sacrifices for sins." But Christ had no other sacrifice to offer than himself. Therefore He made his soul an offering unto death for sin. As our Passover, Christ must be slain for us. We were sold under sin, and nothing but the life's blood of Him who would redeem us could purchase our ransom. We could not be redeemed "with corruptible things, as silver and gold, but only with the precious blood of Christ, as of a lamb without blemish and without spot." "We, who were sometimes alienated and enemies, were reconciled to God by the death of his Son." "Yet now hath He reconciled us in the body of his flesh through death."

And again, *fourthly*. It was necessary for Christ to die to complete His kingly office, and exalt His regal dignity.

II. *Why was it necessary for Christ to humble himself even unto death? or How did it come to pass that God's only Son, so holy and sinless, died such a death as this?*

I answer, *first*. It was according to the determinate counsel and foreknowledge of God. It was not by chance or a casual event, or a suddenly devised expediency, that the Son of God was delivered up to be crucified and slain by wicked hands, but by the eternal decree of God. Hence, although Herod and Pilate, Jews and Gentiles conspired together to crucify the Lord of glory, God's innocent Son, yet He was a Lamb slain from the foundation of the world.

Secondly. It was by his *own free consent* that He was crucified to death. He yielded himself voluntarily. He laid down his life for his sheep. Hence it is said the Church is *purchased with his blood*. "When thou shalt make his soul an offering, thou shalt see thy seed and prolong thy days, and the pleasure of the Lord shall prosper in thy hand; thou shalt see of the travail of thy soul, and be satisfied." And so the Apostle tells us Jesus, for the suffering of death, was crowned with glory and honor—that He, pouring out his soul unto death, received from his Father a portion with the great—that He being obedient to the death, God exalted him, and gave him a name above all names. Isa. liii.; Heb. x. and ii. And in regard to all typical persons and rites in the old Dispensation, especially the paschal lamb, St. Peter says expressly those things which God before had shewed by the mouth of all his prophets, that Christ should suffer, He hath so fulfilled; and so the risen Saviour said, O fools and slow of heart to believe all that the prophets have spoken: ought not Christ according to their predictions to have suffered these things, and so to enter into his glory? It was thus the Spirit of Christ which was in the prophets testified beforehand of his sufferings.

And, *thirdly*. As Christ was ordained to death from eternity by the appointment of the Father, and by His own free choice, and was so set forth by the types and in the prophecies, *so also He was instrumentally and judicially and actually put to death in his proper person under Pontius Pilate*. A special Providence so directed that the treachery of Judas and the conspiracy of the Jewish rulers and the concurrence of Pilate and Herod should bring about His death in exact fulfilment of the Scriptures. And this moreover, we are told, was done without destroying the free agency of those who executed our Lord. They did it all with *wicked hands*. Judas was covetous, the rulers were blind with envy and rage, and the governor was fickle and selfish, yet it was Jehovah who laid upon Him the iniquities of us all: He was stricken, smitten, afflicted of God. It was the Lord of Glory, the Prince of Life who was thus treated. "Ye denied," says Peter, "Ye denied the Holy One and the

Just One; Ye slew the Prince of Life, ye crucified the Lord of Glory."

III. *Why did Christ thus die? What ends did He accomplish by humiliating Himself unto death?*

Answer. *First.* He fulfilled the Father's purpose, and finished the work and mission on which He was sent into this world. He came from the glory of eternity which He had with the Father before the world was—from the bosom of his Father to do His will—to reveal His love to us, and to die that God might be just and yet the justifier of them that believe in Jesus. It pleased Jehovah to *bruise* him for us. This command to lay his life down, says He, I received of my Father. And the cup which my Father hath given me, shall I not drink it? No one taketh my life from me, but I lay it down of myself; I have power to lay it down, and have power to take it again. The blood which I shed is my flesh, which I will give for the life of the world. The Son of Man came to give his life a ransom for many.

Secondly. By dying He illustrated the perfections of God in harmony and manifested the Divine Glory. On the cross we have a demonstration of His righteousness (Rom. iii. 25).

Thirdly. Hereby Christ also acquired a right to universal dominion and eternal glory. For to this end Christ died, that He might be Lord of the dead and living. The Prince of our Salvation was made perfect through suffering. For the joy that was set before Him He endured the Cross; He was obedient unto death—therefore God hath highly exalted him, that at the name of Jesus every knee should bow, of things in heaven and things in earth, and things under the earth; and that every tongue should confess that Jesus Christ is Lord, to the glory of God the Father. Phil. ii.

Fourthly. He died on the Cross to redeem us by being made a curse for us. "Being justified by His blood, we shall be saved by Him from wrath. For if, being enemies, we were reconciled to God by the death of His Son, much more shall we be saved by His life." But now once in the end of the world, as the Apostle in the Hebrews saith, hath He, Christ, appeared—that is, in the end of the old Dispensation, He hath appeared to the putting away, the expiating, the abolishing of sin, the procuring of pardon for sin by the sacrifice of himself. "For the blood of Christ the Son of God cleanseth us from all sin." "He gave himself for us that He might deliver us from this present evil world, and redeem us from all iniquity, and purify unto himself a peculiar people, zealous of good works. He loved us, and hath washed us from our sins in his own blood."

I have but little time left for practical inferences from this great and awful theme. But surely you are already prepared to admit—I. that we should love Him who hath loved us, and given himself for us. And surely we should exercise repentance toward God and faith in His Son, seeing that He did not spare His own Son, but delivered him up to death for us all—and having done this, made the greatest possible gift: how shall He not with Him also freely give us all things?

II. *Christ's death is to be regarded as the death of Death.* Heb. ii. 14, 15.

When the sorrows of death compassed, Him and the sorrows of hell, as the Psalmist expresses it, compassed Him about, then Death came upon Him to swallow him up; but Death himself was swallowed up by the dying

Redeemer in a perfect and complete victory. CHRIST abolished death—rendered it feeble and without effect; so that the believer's death is not to be regarded as the punishment of sin, but as the termination of sin, and the end of all his sorrows, and the entrance into life eternal.

"Since, then, Christ died for us, why must we also die?"

"*Ans.* Our death is not a satisfaction for our sins; but only an abolishing of sin and a passage to eternal life." Heidelberg Catechism.

> "Death, we confess, retains its name;
> Its fatal sting it cannot claim.
> The Christian finds this last of foes
> Ordained to give him sweet repose."

I have selected from one of *Luther's* letters a few striking sentences on this subject, in his own peculiar style. "Our enemies often threaten us with death. But if they were as much distinguished for wisdom as they surpass every one in folly, they ought really to threaten us with life. A truly ridiculous sort of terror, as if they could deter Christ and His people from their purpose by the fear of death; for Christians are the conquerors of death through Christ, who vanquished and triumphed over the King of Terrors, and showed himself alive as a trophy of his victory to his disciples. Those men, in reality, discover the same egregious madness, as if I should intend to intimidate a person by bringing forth his horse saddled and bridled, that he might take a ride." Rather, since the world and sorrow and sin and Satan press us so hardly, we would say, Make haste, O death, and let my last day on earth soon come to end my sins, and usher me to my home with Jesus. Nor, III. is it improper for us *to make the death of Jesus an example*, for from Him we learn, 1. To do with all our might the work given us to do by our Heavenly Father, and not be impatient to rest from toil, or to win the prize, till our work is all done, and done successfully.

2. Like our Lord, as the decisive hour approaches we should endeavor so to disengage ourselves from domestic concerns and secular affairs, that we may be ready to depart promptly and go willingly whenever Jesus calls.

3. We may humbly imitate Him, committing our departing soul to God. Stephen did this under a shower of stones. This may be done even when there is not left power to utter words. And,

4. We should die believing that He is the resurrection and the life—in the hope of a blessed resurrection at the last day.

O my beloved brethren, what a sight is a dead Christ! The amazement of heaven, the terror of hell—the wonder of the beholding universe! Dead from suffering the wrath of God due to us—upon both his body and his soul,—the death-punishment which in fact makes the hell of the lost in the world of woe, except a feeling of conscious personal guilt. When He bowed His head and said, "It is finished," He bore the pang of the curse and drank the cup of wrath, and the Father accepted His atonement for His people. If, then, Jesus our Lord, who thus gave himself for us, is with us in the toils, sorrows, and temptations of life, we need not fear that He will forsake us when the last enemy approaches. Through the whole way of the dark valley, in the fearful mystery of death, He will be with us, and comfort us.

> "Jesus can make a dying bed
> Feel soft as downy pillows are,
> While on His breast I lean my head,
> And breathe my life out sweetly there."

But, my dear hearers, let me beg you not to forget that the precious benefits of Christ's death are offered to you upon the condition that you accept them. They are not absolute and without conditions. Our Lord established a covenant and fulfilled His engagements with His Father for all that will come to God through Him. He invites, He draws, He calls, and whosoever will may come. Whosoever believeth and is baptized shall be saved, but he that believeth not shall be damned. We must accept salvation as it is offered to us in the Gospel, or we have no share in it.

VIII.

OUR LORD CHRIST BURIED.

"And when they had fulfilled all that was written of him, they took him down from the tree, and laid him in a sepulchre."—ACTS xiii. 29.

THE way in which our text was fulfilled is described by the Evangelists. Let us read their record from St. Matt. xxvii. 57–66, and St. John xix. 31–42.

Last Sabbath evening, following the order of the words in the fourth Article of our Creed, we were witnesses of our Lord's death. We are now to attend his funeral and burial: such a funeral as never was since graves were first digged, or tombs first cut out of the rocks, nor ever will be again till tombs and graves are no more. The Evangelists tell us of *the preparation* made for the funeral, both as to the body of our Lord and as to the tomb to receive it. And then they tell us who were the *bearers* of the sacred body, and their attendants, and as to how the funeral was conducted. The funeral was public, solemn, and decent. There was no pomp or empty show; no hypocrisy in tears or outcries; no hired mourners; but there were melting hearts and flowing eyes over his tomb. There was deep, unutterable feeling in the breasts of those who laid Jesus in Joseph's tomb.

In many of the ancient Creeds, the two particulars, "buried," and "descended into hell," are joined together as one Article; or else the latter phrase, "He descended into hell," was wholly omitted; or, if inserted, was regarded as the substance of the former, and stood in its room. But, for quite sufficient reasons, I prefer the whole Article as we have it: "Suffered under Pontius Pilate, was crucified, dead and buried." It is necessary for us now, however, to consider these two particulars separately. "He descended into hell," according to Bishop Pearson, belongs to the *fifth Article* of the Creed, and should be taken together with the words, "third day He rose again from the dead."

One purpose, at least, is secured by the use of all these words: "Buried; He descended into hell:"—namely, we have a wonderful fulness, distinctness, and security for every thing mentioned in the Scriptures concerning our Lord's person and sufferings, concerning his arrest, arraignment, and treatment by Pilate and Herod, and of his conduct on the cross, his actual death and burial, and how He was employed while his body lay in the tomb: all these particulars are comprehended in the scope of the Article professed as a part of our faith; and when we remember how many spurious gospels were afloat in the early ages of the Church, and how many crude notions were in the minds of philosophic Gentile converts, we are not at all surprised that the ancient formulas of the Faith of the Church should be so full and particular about so many of the incidents of our Lord's last hours, and burial and resurrection. Our Creed specially makes mention of our Lord's burial to oppose the erroneous views of Simon Magus and the Docetæ, or Phantasiasts, as they were called, who denied the reality of our Lord's human nature, and said that He had no true body, and did not therefore really suffer, but only *seemed* to do so; that all the history is unreal—a mere appearance. We know that such errors began even in the lifetime of the Apostles themselves, as we learn from 1 John iv. 1-3: "Beloved, believe not every spirit, but try the spirits whether they are of God; because many false prophets are gone out into the world. Hereby know ye the Spirit of God: every spirit that confesseth that Jesus Christ is come in the flesh, is of God: and every spirit that confesseth not that Jesus Christ is come in the flesh, is not of God: and this is that spirit of antichrist, whereof ye have heard that it should come; and even now already is it in the world."

In the previous discourses, I have attempted to prove that the DIVINITY and the HUMANITY of our Lord were not confused or mingled, but each perfect in its own nature, and so remained, and is so still, and yet constituting one person forever; and that the perfect humanity of our Lord consisted of "a true body and a reasonable soul," and that his dying was, like the death of Adam or of St. Paul, the separation of his "reasonable soul" from his "true body;"—that the death of the Son of God did not consist in His Divinity freeing itself from and leaving his humanity, but in the dissolution of his soul from his body. And from this it follows, that his burial was the sepulture of his dead body, according to the custom of his countrymen at the time.

The reality of our Lord's death is clearly demonstrated by the actual commitment of his body to the grave, and is acknowledged by the Apostles in their discourses and epistles. *St. Paul*, in 1 Cor. xv., declares that the burial of our Lord was one among the other great Articles of our holy religion, which he was accustomed to preach as a matter of faith. His words here are so remarkable, I beg you will especially notice them. Please to read with me from 1 Cor. chapter xv., beginning with the first verse, and onward to the end of the fourth verse:

"Moreover, brethren, I declare unto you the Gospel which I preached unto you, which also ye have received, and wherein ye stand:

2. "By which also ye are saved, if ye keep in memory what I preached unto you, unless ye have believed in vain.

3. "For I delivered unto you first of all, that which I also received, how that Christ died for our sins according to the Scriptures.

4. "And that he was buried, and that he rose again the third day according to the Scriptures."

In maintaining the proposition of this Article of our Creed, that *Christ was buried*, I desire to call your attention:—

To the fact that *the burial of Jesus of Nazareth, crucified under Pontius Pilate*, was in exact fulfilment of the Holy Scriptures concerning the Messiah. This will be sufficiently proven from two things: *First*, that according to Jewish prophecies and types, the promised Messiah was to be *buried;* and, *secondly*, according to our sacred records, Jesus was buried precisely in the way the long promised Messiah was to be buried, and therefore our Jesus of Nazareth is the Messiah, the Christ of God, the Saviour of sinners. These points are after Pearson's manner.

I. *The Jewish Messiah was to be buried.*

As kindness to the aged and unfortunate distinguishes Christianity from Paganism, so does the respect shown in the burial of the pious dead. It was urged by the Emperor *Julian* the Apostate, that one of the great inducements held out to the heathen to turn Christians was the care that would be taken of them at death, and the funeral solemnities with which they would be honored. It is true the early Christians not only showed becoming honor at their funerals to their dead, because the majority of them at first were Jews, and as such they had been carefully educated in such a custom; but also, perhaps, as a mark of peculiar affection to the faithful, as one with them in Christ, and in the hope of the resurrection of the dead. As the Gospel in India changes the funeral pile of the widow into decent mourning, so Christianity taught the heathen from the beginning to bury the dead, while remembering their virtues, in hope of life and immortality. Thus we read that when *Ananias* died, though he died for his sin, yet they "wound him up, and carried him out, and buried him." And when *Stephen* was stoned, "devout men carried him to his burial, and made great lamentation over him;" and when *Dorcas* died, "they washed her, and laid her in an upper chamber," to get her ready for her burial. *Burying* the body is moreover eminently proper among Christians with respect to their bodies, which are "temples of the Holy Ghost," and are purchased by Christ as well as their souls. The bodies of believers are therefore at the resurrection to be made like unto his own glorious body. Surely, then, it is becoming for them to be laid in the wardrobe of the grave with such solemnity and propriety as if we expected them to come forth at last to an immortal and glorious life.

It is therefore an error of the great historian *Tacitus*, to say as he does, that the Jewish custom of burying the bodies of their dead, instead of burning them, as the Romans did, was borrowed by them from Egypt. In this the Jews did not differ from the Romans more than they did from the Greeks, for the Greeks also burned the bodies of the dead. And if we must say the Jews borrowed the custom from any other nation, it was rather from the Persians than from the Egyptians, for they had the custom before they went down to Egypt at all. The oldest and the most beautiful fragment of history on the subject is Abraham's purchase of a burying-place of the children of Heth, in which to bury his dead out of his sight.

The rites of burial were almost universally granted among the Jews, both as to funeral ceremonies and a place for interment. The place of burial was not always the same. It seems never to have been particularly determined. For we find their graves upon the highway or in their gardens [2 Kings xxi. 18, 26], and upon the mountains, and in the towns and in the country. The general custom, however, was, and it is still the custom in the East, and in some measure throughout Christendom, to have the graveyard outside of the town, on a hill-side, not very far from the gate. And though at first the Greeks and Romans made their temples repositories for their dead, in later ages they buried the dead without their cities, and chiefly by the highways.

In proof that the Hebrew Church believed that the promised Messiah was to be *buried*, let us consider:—

1. That all among the Jews who admitted that the Messiah was to suffer and die, believed that he was also to be *buried*. For this was the custom of the Jewish

people. And the proof of this is so abundant, there can be no need of specifications beyond the general statements just made concerning Jewish funeral rites and burying-places. Every one who reads the history of the Jews, knows how often there is mention made of the sepulchres of their fathers. The care of their own poor, the education of their children, and the respectful and proper burying of their dead, have always been *specialties* of the Hebrew race. It is also in evidence, that among them public criminals who were executed were not buried in their fathers' graves, but in sepulchres appointed for them by the civil authorities, or obtained for them by their friends. If our Lord's body had not been claimed by his friends, he would have been buried in the common place for executed persons, and then we should not have had such clear evidences of his identity in the resurrection. It was also usual for the instrument which was used in the punishment to be buried with them. And if I attached any importance to the story of the finding of the true cross by the Empress Helena in the holy sepulchre in Jerusalem, I would urge this latter statement as a proof of its truth; I have, however, before stated, that I concur altogether in the judgment of many eminent men, who regard the whole story as an invention, and to be ranked with pious frauds. It was, however, in exact conformity with the doctrines, sentiments, and customs of both the Jewish and Christian Church to show respect to the dead, and for our Lord's friends to give him precisely such a burial as our Evangelists say they did.

2. The 53d chapter of *Isaiah* is full of expressions setting forth the sufferings and death of the Messiah. Let us turn to this chapter. I must for the present rest on the authorities ancient and modern, Jewish and Christian,

who admit that this prophecy relates to the Messiah. Read verses 2-9.

Here it is to be noted—He was not only "stricken, smitten, afflicted of God, wounded, bruised, chastised, covered with stripes, oppressed, and carried as a lamb to the slaughter, and taken from prison, but he was *cut off out of the land of the living: for the transgression of my people* was he stricken. And *he made his grave with the wicked, and with the rich in his death;* because he had done no violence, neither was there any deceit in his mouth." Here, then, it is affirmed of the Messiah that He should be remarkable in his sufferings—that they were to end in his death, and that He was to be buried. And he made his grave with the wicked—that is, as Bishop Lowth translates it, *his grave was appointed for him*—by his persecutors—*with the wicked*. It was their design to throw him into the common grave of malefactors, without any mark of respect, or means of future identification. And even if Lowth's rendering be not received, still the Scriptures cannot be broken. *His grave was with the wicked* in this respect: the garden of Joseph of Arimathea was near Golgotha, which was pre-eminently the place of the wicked; and He was also surrounded and guarded by heathen soldiers, and by a most ungodly Jewish mob. Verily his grave was among the wicked.

3. The words of the Psalmist are prophetic of the Messiah, saying: "My flesh shall rest in hope, for thou wilt not leave my soul in hell, neither wilt thou suffer thine Holy One to see corruption." xvi. 9, 10.

As this passage from the Psalms is expressly quoted and made the subject of comment and argument by the Apostle Peter, let us turn to the second chapter of the

Acts of the Apostles, where Peter is explaining and defending the conduct of the Apostles filled with the Holy Ghost against the charge of drunkenness, as alleged against them by the vain and mocking Jews on the day of Pentecost. "But Peter, standing up," &c. [Please read verses 14–36.]

This discourse of Peter is full, clear, powerful. It proves the Jews had the book of Joel and the Psalms, and that the Psalms were ascribed to David—that Joel and David foretold Gospel times, and David expressly predicted the death and burial, and yet not the corruption of the flesh of the Messiah in the grave. These allegations could not be applied to David. His flesh did see corruption. The moth and the worm did have power over him, and over every one else that has been buried except Jesus. "Therefore let all the house of Israel know assuredly, that God hath made that same Jesus, whom ye crucified, both Lord and Christ." ver. 36.

4. The only other passage I have time to refer to is Matt. xii. 40, where our Lord says: "For as Jonas was three days and three nights in the whale's belly,"—[and here note, *whale* means any great fish, the term in the original not being definite as our English name *whale* is], "so shall the Son of man be three days and three nights in the heart of the earth." This must mean his burial in the grave. Our Lord meant to say, I will fulfil this type of myself. And so He did most accurately—for he was laid in the tomb.

Secondly. We are now prepared for the statement, that *our Jesus of Nazareth*, whom we most surely believe to be the true Messiah, *was buried in the very way the Jew-*

ish writers foretold that their Messiah would be buried. And this was done, too, contrary to all ordinary or mere human expectations in the case. As our Lord was crucified on a Roman cross, and by virtue of Roman law, it was to be expected his body would be left to share the fate of the bodies of other malefactors, and have been given to the fowls of the air or to the beasts of the fields. Both *Horace* and *Juvenal*, as well as other writers, tell us this often happened to the bodies of persons who were executed on the cross. Sometimes the dead bodies were exposed in the wind and weather until the flesh was consumed, and a mere skeleton was left. Classical authors abound in descriptions of cases verifying each of the foregoing statements. It is also in evidence that among the Romans, a guard was usually stationed around the cross, lest a pitying hand should take the body from the accursed tree, and cover it with earth.*

First. Remember here, that it was under the authority of Roman law that Jesus was crucified. His body, therefore, on the cross, is under the custody of a Roman guard. Accordingly, we find a centurion in command at the crucifixion,† with Roman soldiers, watching Jesus. And as soon as Jesus is dead, this officer reports the fact to Governor Pilate; but the watch still remain. How, then, is Jesus to have a grave with the rich? Who is to provide a tomb? How is his blessed body to be obtained and laid in it? Here again, as so often before, we find the wrath of man made to praise God. They who had petitioned for his death, *who* had always met Pilate's affirmations of Jesus' innocence, and willingness to show

---

* See authorities in Pearson, pp. 322, 323, 324.

† See author's "Centurions of the Gospel"—second edition now in press, by the same publisher.

him mercy, with the cry of, "*Crucify Him! crucify Him!*" now intercede that his dead body may be taken down from the cross and buried. They make no scruple to have the innocent Jesus crucified, yet they were very zealous for some of their laws. Their prejudices were so bitter and their bigotry so malignant, they thought themselves serving God by slaying his dear Son, and yet they must have the law kept that required the dead bodies of executed malefactors to be buried before or by the going down of the sun of the same day of the execution. Thus they understood the words of Moses, in Deut. xxi. 22, 23, saying: "If a man have committed a sin worthy of death, and he be put to death, and thou hang him on a tree; his body shall not remain all night upon the tree, but thou shalt in any wise bury him that day." Accordingly, under this general law, and the more especially in this case, because the next day was *an high day*, that is, one of the Sabbaths, of which there were three in a year, which was called the Sabbath of the holy convocation, "the Jews besought Pilate that their legs might be broken, and that they might be taken away." John xix. 31.

According to Lactantius, it was a kind of *coup de grâce*, and often done to criminals on the cross, to break their legs, that they might the sooner be put out of pain. The Jews, in our Lord's case, did not ask it to be done for this reason, but to hasten his death by increasing his sufferings.

The day of preparation is a well-established fact in Jewish history. In Josephus we have a copy of an edict of the Emperor Augustus in favor of the Jews, which says: "No one shall be obliged to give bail or surety on the Sabbath day, nor on the preparation before it after the ninth hour." The Sabbath began at the ninth hour, that is, at 3 o'clock the preceding evening. Lightfoot, with many others, thinks it was called "a high day"—

1. Because it was the Sabbath.

2. It was the day on which all the people presented themselves in the temple, according to the word of the Lord in Exo. xxiii. 17.

3. It was the day on which the *sheaf* of the first-fruits was offered, according to Lev. xxiii. 10, 11. And in this case it is also probable the Passover fell on that Sabbath. It was with great emphasis therefore a *high day*. For upon this day this year it happened that three or four solemnities fell together.

Secondly. You will bear in mind, brethren, that as the Jews had not the power of life and death in their hands at this time, so, although they instigated, conspired for, and procured his death, yet he was put to death by *Roman* authority, and that his body was still in the hands of the Romans; yet by Roman custom it was left to the option of the magistrate to do, or allow to be done, what might seem good to him with the bodies of executed malefactors. Pilate had power to dispose of the body, of Jesus as he pleased. He could have had it burned, according to Roman custom, or he could have caused it to remain on the cross to be consumed. But the disposing of the body was not a matter that gave him any anxiety. It was required of him that, in his report to the emperor at Rome, he should acquaint his imperial master with the fact, that such a person as Jesus of Nazareth was crucified on the charge that he claimed to be the king of the Jews; but no report about his body or about his peculiar Jewish notions was required. And as Pilate had no personal ill-will against Jesus, and delivered him to be crucified wholly to please the Jews, so he had no motives to gratify in refusing the request that his body might be taken down from the cross in order to its burial. But still, we are trembling as we see the three bodies taken down from their crosses, lest the Scriptures are now to be broken. Is He to make his grave with the same wicked persons with whom he died? For these two thieves crucified with Him, one on his right hand and the other on his left, the Jewish authorities have already provided the appointed or usual burial-place. Are they going to carry our Lord's body away with them? Is there no help for it? Will no one come to the rescue? How can we hope for any one having wealth and influence now to come forward, and profess respect for the dead Christ? Is there any one who will be bolder for Him now that He is dead, than while he was yet alive? What says the record? "There came a rich man named Joseph, a counsellor: and he was a good man, and a just:

51 "(The same had not consented to the counsel and deed of them:) he was of Arimathea, a city of the Jews; who also himself waited for the kingdom of God.

52 "This man went unto Pilate, and begged the body of Jesus.

53 "And he took it down, and wrapped it in linen, and laid it in a sepulchre that was hewn in stone, wherein never man before was laid."

II. This brings me, in the next place, to the BURIAL ITSELF.

We have had a Roman death. Jesus was treated as

a malefactor under judicial process and was crucified, and so met in His suffering and death every requirement of Jewish prophecy concerning the promised Messiah; but if the prophecies required a *Roman* malefactor's death, they quite as certainly call for a *Hebrew* burial, and just such a burial we have in every particular. Our Lord's body was disposed of neither according to Roman or Jewish custom, but precisely as the Prophets had said the body of the suffering and dying Messiah would be disposed off. You have seen how the body was obtained. Let us now see how it was prepared for the grave; how the tomb is prepared for it, and the persons who actually fulfilled the Scriptures by burying Him.

First. In a Hebrew burial, linen clothes and precious spices were used, varying in quality and quantity according to the wealth of the parties. You have not forgotten, that *a woman having* an alabaster box of ointment of spikenard, very precious, once came to Jesus, and brake the box, and poured it on His head; and that Jesus then said, "She is come beforehand to anoint my body to the burying." Mark xiv. 3-8. And when Christ was risen, "Mary Magdalene and the other Mary brought the spices which they had prepared, that they might come and anoint Him." Mark xv. 1. Luke xxiv. 1.

Wrapped it in a linen cloth. Such cloths were then common, and so were precious spices. Embalming, it is well known, was common in Egypt, as we know from its monuments and mummies, and from the Bible history of Jacob and Joseph. Jewish embalming differed in some respects from that of Egypt, and as it was with the Egyptians, so it probably was with the Jews, their earlier embalming was more costly than in later times. Still the *hundred pounds' weight* of the Evangelist is not too much. For, (1.) the fact itself of such a quantity being used is not incredible. Nicodemus and Joseph of Arimathea were men of large wealth. And it was proper for them to give some expression of their respect for the dead, by the value, of the precious spices used for his burial. Nor, (2.) is collateral history wanting to confirm our narrative. Even in 2 Chron. xvi. 14, we find that such a quantity of spices was used that they formed *a bed* on which the dead body was laid. "They laid King Asa in the bed, which was filled with sweet odors and spices." And, according to Josephus, at the funeral of Herod *five hundred* servants bearing aromatics were employed, and *Onkelos* used 80 lbs. Tyrian weight of the most precious spices at the funeral of Rabbi Gamaliel Senex.*

Our Lord's body was wrapt in the linen cloth with a mixture of myrrh and aloes, but this was all done in great haste—an imperfect embalming. The time was too short to perfect it, the Sabbath was approaching. Hence the pious women prepared themselves for a second embalming as soon as the Sabbath should be past.

Thus we see how the spices and linen clothes of Nicodemus were used in wrapping the body of Jesus, just as had been done to his friend Lazarus of Bethany, who, when Jesus called him, "came forth bound hand and foot with grave-clothes, and his face was bound about with a napkin." John xi. 44. And so when "Peter went into the sepulchre, and saw the linen clothes lie, and the napkin, that was about his head, not lying with the linen clothes, but wrapped together in a place by itself." John xx. 6, 7. See Pearson on Creed, p. 326.

See Witsius, vol. ii. pp. 121-2.

Secondly. Observe, that as our Lord's dear body was carefully prepared for his burying, according to Hebrew custom, so also a sepulchre meeting the requirements of our prophecies was also punctually prepared. "And when Joseph had taken the body of Jesus. he wrapped it in a clean linen cloth, and laid it in his own new tomb, which he had hewn out in the rock : and he rolled a great stone to the door of the sepulchre, and departed." Matthew xxvii. 59, 60, with Mark xv. "For in the place where he was crucified, there was a garden, and in the garden a new sepulchre, wherein never man was laid, which Joseph had hewn out of a rock for his own tomb : there laid they Jesus, and rolled a great stone to the door of the sepulchre."

Thirdly. The bearers and attendants, or the persons who fulfilled the Scriptures by burying our Lord.

The history shows that both our Lord's *friends* and *enemies* agreed in begging for his body, but from very different motives. It was of no consequence to Pilate to distinguish between the friends and enemies of Jesus. Their different motives in asking to have his body removed were nothing to him. All he cared to know was the fact that he was really dead, and that the crucifixion had taken place according to Roman usage, so that his report of the case to Rome would not bring him into trouble. The persons begging for Jesus' body were in his sight Jews, simply *Jews.* Among them, first in application were our Lord's implacable enemies, who desired that his body should be taken down from the accursed tree, not out of any respect to Him or sympathy for his friends, but for fear the land should be defiled ; and they were the more importunate because of the approach of a high Sabbath day. Nor is it improbable that their consciences began to sting them for what they had done, and that they were therefore anxious to remove their victim out of their sight by removing it away from public view.

And now just at this time, when our Lord's enemies are asking for his dead body, and Pilate has made himself sure that He is really dead, and shows a willingness to consign the bodies of the malefactors to Jewish treatment, a rich man, an honorable counsellor, that is, a member of the Sanhedrim, and Nicodemus, also a member of the Great Sanhedrim, supported by a company of pious women, beg that, as Jesus' friends, they may have the custody of his dear body. Their object is to show respect and to bury it. Our Lord's enemies, being satisfied that He was really dead, have no zeal for his body, except to avoid breaking the law by its remaining on the Cross; they therefore relinquish it, and the more readily because no doubt Pilate preferred to accommodate parties so honorable, influential, and wealthy as Nicodemus and Joseph of Arimathea, and such a company of women. They beheld the crucifixion afar off. The soldiers and the crowd of surging people keep them at a considerable distance; but still they showed more courage and greater affection for Jesus than his disciples, did who had vowed they would rather die with him than forsake him.

Joseph of Arimathea was a rich man, a good and just man, and an honorable counsellor. He was a man of high rank and respectability. He belonged to Rama in the tribe of Benjamin, but his residence was now in the City of Jerusalem. Nicodemus was also a member of the Sanhedrim—the same who came to Jesus by night, and who believed upon Him, but did not confess Him openly during his lifetime, for fear of the Jews, who said that whoever did confess him should be a cast-out.

A Divine Providence is seen in the character of these men. The Apostles could not so properly ask permission to bury their Master, lest the Priests and Pharisees, who fabricated the story about the stealing away of his body, should have alleged he had never been buried at all. It was well, just, and proper that such men as these—men of culture and social position, rank, and wealth, should get possession of the body and give it an honorable burial.

III. *Why was Christ buried?* Seeing He was so soon to rise from the dead, why was there any funeral at all? Our answer is—

1. To fulfil the types and prophecies, and to prove that Jesus was the true Messiah.

2. To prove thereby that he really was dead,—that there could not be any mistake about it. Nor can any more vital reason than this be given, for on the reality of his death depends the perfection of his sacrifice as our Priest, and the fact of his resurrection. The truth of Christianity depends upon the reality of Christ's death, burial, and resurrection. If these are not facts, just as our Creed affirms, and as the Scriptures teach, then we are yet in our sins. These are the most important subjects we can possibly think of, or devote our attention to. Since so much depends on his death, if we may so speak, abundant proof of it should be given, and this proof should be as convincing, clear, and powerful as it can be in the nature of the case, and the nature of the human mind considered. And such, we maintain, is the evidence before us of the death and burial of Jesus Christ. He

bowed his head and gave up the ghost. His enemies exult; his friends mourn. Both are convinced he is really dead. The Roman soldier makes it doubly certain by an awful cut in his side, that brings out both blood and water. And here also, note how Providence protects the Scriptures, and turns their fulfilment so pointedly on Jesus. He was to be *pierced*, and not *a bone of him was to be broken;* and an ignorant Roman soldier, unbidden, fulfils both requirements. The soldier is sent to break his bones, but he disobeys his commander—and does what he was not sent to do. And yet both his disobedience of his lieutenant, and his voluntary piercing of the dead body of Jesus, were necessary to prove that He was the Messiah. A simple and direct proof of the reality of his death is therefore given in his burial.

3. Such a distinct statement of our Lord's burial assists us to comprehend more clearly his *Hypostatical or Personal* union: His two natures in one person. His death did not consist in the separation of his Divinity from his humanity, but in the dissolution of his soul from his body, so that it was the true and proper body of the Son of God that was laid in the tomb.

4. Christ's burial has its place and influence in our *Lord's great work of redemption.* His estate of humiliation was completed by being brought to the dust of death. The English Litany well says: "We invoke Him, by the mystery of Thy Holy Incarnation, by Thy holy nativity and circumcision, by Thy Cross and Passion, by Thy precious death and burial." And although I am not ready to believe that every act of Jesus has a sacramental influence in our salvation, still I think Augustine's words on this point are worthy of attention. "Whatever," says he, "was done on the Cross of Christ, at his

burial, at His rising the third day, at His ascension into heaven, and sitting at the right hand of God, were so done that mystically, not in words only, but in actions, the Christian life here below is depicted. For we that are Christ's, 'have crucified the flesh with the affections and lusts.' 'If ye then be risen with Christ, seek those things which are above, where Christ sitteth at the right hand of God.'"

5. The distinction of the parties who honored our Saviour by burying him, and the *new* tomb, and the place where it was, and its being a tomb hewn out of the living rock, in which no man had ever been laid, all contributed to make our Lord's death more widely known at the time, and more fully to demonstrate the truth of his resurrection, as stated by his friends.

6. Again, Christ's burial is specific and emphatic, in order that correct, sweet, and proper thoughts may be connected with our meditations upon the grave. Archbishop *Leighton* expresses this reason somewhat in this way: For the further assurance of his death, and the glory of his resurrection, as likewise to commend the grave itself to us, as now a very sweet resting-place, He hath warmed the cold bed of the grave to a Christian, so that he need not fear to lie down in it, nor doubt but that he shall rise again from it, after our Lord's example.

When He was laid in the tomb, He went to conquer Death in his own dominion—as if by man's sin death was an enthroned dragon, and the grave was his den—a loathsome place of indescribable terror; but our Lord went into it, grappled with him there, overcomes him, and so conquers that henceforth he is not an enemy, but a benefactor to all Christ's friends—a mere door-keeper to open the way for them to glory, or to provide for them a bed to rest on. When believers die, they do but go into Christ's bed, where he lay before them. Accordingly, St. Stephen's death is described as a falling on sleep, and the grave was known among the early Christians as a resting-place. Indeed, our name Cemetery is the Greek word for a resting-place, or a place to sleep in and be refreshed—in which to wake up and go forth to a more vigorous and happy life.

IV. THE PRACTICAL USES of this part of the Article are easily stated.

I. The narrative of our Lord's burial is full of instruction. It gives us distinct information as to the certainty of his death. Pilate would not allow Joseph to take possession of our Lord's body till after he had made careful inquiry respecting his death, and was well certified of the fact. Mark xv. 44, 45. Nor was it *enemies* that buried Jesus, who might have been so anxious to get rid of a disagreeable job, that they would not hesitate to lay him in the sepulchre half alive. It was *his friends* who had charge of his body and directed his burial, and we are sure they were well satisfied that there was no longer a breath of life in him. He was really dead; and his literal burial was necessary to complete his humiliation. It was thus that He descended into the lower parts of the earth.

II. The burial of our Lord is a clear and certain proof that his work of expiation has been thoroughly performed and the curse abolished by His death. In his humiliation He endured the wrath of God due to us for our sins. As the hanging on the tree fulfilled the curse, so the burial of the body denoted that the curse was exhausted. The penalty could not go beyond death. Our Lord's sleep, therefore, in the tomb was sweet to him. He then rested from his labors, that had been indeed great and long in their accomplishment, but were now thoroughly and well done. The law called for the shedding of blood, and blood has been shed. The law called for the death of the sinner; and here is the death of his voluntary, able, and accepted surety. And in our surety's burial our sins were buried. They are removed from God's sight, and covered over, so that we are justified by believing in Him.

III. And, *thirdly*, by his burial we have assurance also of complete *sanctification*. It was our old nature that He took on him, out of the flesh and blood of the blessed Virgin Mary, and it was in this nature He "suffered, was crucified, dead and buried." By his death He broke the tyranny of sin, by which the devil held us captive; and when He was laid in the grave, He buried the mortal flesh that He might raise it in newness of life unto eternal blessedness. This is the Christian's true and only life—to be dead with Christ and buried with Him, and risen with Him to the life of God—a life with Christ in God.

It was thus that He pursued Death to the remotest and strongest corner of his dark castle, and, conquering him in his own fortress, sanctified the grave, so that it becomes, like Esther's spice-baths, a resting-place for our bodies, until they are called forth to be perfumed and anointed, and we awake to behold God's face in righteousness, and to be satisfied with his likeness.

IV. Here is, therefore, an illustration of our Lord's *complete sympathy with his people*. As the Father hath loved Him, so He loves them, and He not only gave his life, but also his death for them. There is no kind of trial nor form of suffering through which they are called to pass, that He has not passed through himself on his way to victory and glory. "In that He himself hath suffered, being tempted, He is able to succor them that are tempted." Here, then, dear child of God, only be careful·to remember your glorious Leader;—tempted, weak, afflicted, mourning, remember how your blessed Lord endured for your sake. Only imitate Him—receive the cup your Heavenly Father gives you; and when you come to pass into the dark shadow of death, go as your Lord did, commending your soul to God, and say, O death, where is thy sting? O grave, where is thy victory? Thanks be to God, which giveth us the victory through our Lord Jesus Christ.

V. The example of Joseph of Arimathea and Nicodemus, and the pious women who showed their veneration for the *dead Christ*, should quicken our faith and zeal, and increase our love. We may not be able, like Constantine, to build a cathedral in honor of his tomb, nor to burn incense and costly spices in our places of worship in memory of his embalming—such service He has not asked from us; but He does require our hearts and our lives. The most costly spices and the most magnificent temples are not as precious in his sight as faith, love, and charity. I do not, however, envy the man so devoid of the religion of places as to have no emotions on visiting the reputed tomb of Jesus. It is of very little consequence whether the holy sepulchre is the precise tomb, or covers the exact spot where Jesus was buried. It stands for that sacred place. And as we do not worship the material wooden cross, but Him who died on the cross, so we do not worship the marble tomb in the church of the Holy Sepulchre, but Him who was crucified, dead and buried, as our Mediator, and of whose burial this is the local commemoration. Nor need we go as pilgrims to the Holy Land in order to receive the benefits of our Lord's death and burial. From the history before us, we have such an account as to put us into living communion with Him whom these weeping women and their rich friends buried in Joseph's tomb in the garden. "By virtue of the sacrifice of Christ on the cross, our old man is crucified, dead and buried with him, that so the corrupt inclinations of the flesh may no more reign in us; but that we may offer ourselves unto him a sacrifice of thanksgiving." *Heidelberg Catechism.*

But oh! my brethren, it were a vain and useless thing for us merely to investigate the historical accuracy of the narrative, of our Lord's sufferings and death, and to take our views of Calvary just as we do of any other mere historical place. Is there not something exceedingly precious in the blood of Christ? Are we not closely related to Him who was crucified, dead and buried? Was he not God-man, our Mediator, and did He not die, and was He not buried *for us?* Truly may we say, all other miracles grow dim before the Cross. The Cross shines all others into shade and darkness. What in all the universe is of equal value with the blood of the Son of God? Well may we say (as a great French preacher does), "Ye other miracles, wrought in favor of our souls! ye astonishing prodigies that confirm the Gospel! ye great and terrible signs of the second coming of the Son of God! vanish all of you before the Cross! This glorious light makes your glimmering vanish; and after my imagination is filled with the tremendous dignity of this sacrifice, I can see nothing great besides."

But what is the sepulchre to the ungodly? It is darkness, and worms, and corruption, and the doorway to hell. The grave is a terrible place to them who are out of Christ. Death, in respect to them, is but the arresting sergeant of the Judge. The grave is but a prison to keep their bodies in, to secure them against the great day of trial. If the grave is but a perfumed bed for the saints to rest on until they are called to see the King in His beauty, and enter into His kingdom, so it is only a dark and loathsome dungeon for the wicked till they are called to hear their doom, and go to their awful execution.

"The hour is coming, and now is, when the dead shall hear the voice of the Son of God: and they that hear shall live. Marvel not at this: for the hour is coming, in the which all that are in the graves shall hear his voice, and shall come forth: they that have done good, unto the resurrection of life; and they that have done evil, unto the resurrection of damnation."—John v. 25-29.

IX.

"HE DESCENDED INTO HELL."

It is my purpose now, if the Lord be pleased to continue his blessing upon us, to ask your attention to the first part of the *fifth Article* of our Creed just recited: "*He*," that is, "Jesus Christ, God's only Son, our Lord, who was conceived by the Holy Ghost, born of the Virgin Mary, suffered under Pontius Pilate, was crucified, dead and buried: *He descended into hell.*" I do not, as is my custom, name any text of holy Scripture this evening, because I cannot find one that teaches what these words of the Creed are generally supposed to mean, if they are received in their popular or usual sense. Even *St. Paul's* language in Ephesians, about Christ's descending, do not affirm that *He descended* after his death *into hell*. Nor does *St. Peter* say in his sermon on the day of Pentecost that Jesus *descended into hell*. He says that the 16th Psalm is a prophecy of the resurrection of Christ, and proves that Jesus of Nazareth is the Christ, the true Messiah. And it is candid also, to admit, that the words of the Psalmist applied to Jesus: "Thou wilt not leave my soul in hell," do imply that in some sense He was in hell, for if He was not *left in hell*, He must once have been there. There is a sense, then, in which the Creed does affirm that Christ descended into hell. What is this sense, and is it true? Is it according to the Scriptures? As the words: "He descended into hell," are not found in the Bible applied to Messiah, who is called Christ, in the sense attached to them by the Church of Rome, it is important for us to ascertain, if possible, the sense in which this Article is to be received as containing the truth of God. The meaning of the word *hell*, and of *descended*, will come more appropriately under discussion in another place, and an examination of those passages of Scripture which it is alleged teach the literal, local descent of Christ into hell, and so authorize the doctrine of Purgatory and its kindred errors, I must reserve for the next Discourse.

It is not surprising this Article of our Creed should have attracted great attention and given rise to much learned discussion, and yet, perhaps, there never was a time when it was more worthy of attention than the present. The current of religious thought in our day is so spasmodic and unsettled, that a subject of this nature receives, perhaps, greater attention because it is obscure, and the terms in which the doctrine is taught are harsh and repulsive. And, besides, important doctrines are supposed to depend upon the interpretation of this Article. In a general way, we may say the Church of Rome, the Lutheran Church, and a portion of the High Church party of England are arranged on one side in the discussion, and almost all other branches of the Church are on the other side. The most learned men, and men of the greatest intellect and culture of the last generation and of the present, have given their profoundest investigations to this subject.

In the works of Barrow and Lightfoot, Pearson and Burnet, Witsius and Harold Browne, and the late Archbishop Whately, we have learned, able, and exhaustive dissertations on this Article or kindred topics. Almost every actual or possible side of the questions involved is presented, and yet, after one has toiled through them all, it is very much to be doubted whether he is really any wiser, or any better satisfied, than he was when he began his investigations. All learning is not wisdom. Nor are we all able for all things. One of the great Calvin's best sayings is, that "God has not given it to any one man to know all the truth." On many subjects, as if to mock the pride of human intellect, it is still true that *ignorance is bliss*. The indefinite and unsatisfactory results of the learning, time, and talents that have been spent on this subject may be accounted for, perhaps, by remembering that great and good men are not always free from bigotry and prejudice. Their investigations are often carried on to support certain dogmas of faith or peculiar views, and every thing is seen with that coloring on it which favors them. The great authors I have named, and many others might be added, scarcely agree on the leading points of this Article, and yet they do not so differ as to materially affect a single doctrine or precept of the Gospel which is in order to salvation. Again, a great difficulty in all discussions of this kind is to determine the meaning of the terms used in presenting the doctrine, and its explanation; and in this particular case the difficulty is increased, from the fact that the terms used are taken from four different languages embracing in their range of historic signification a period of, let us say, three or four thousand years; and these terms are used, moreover, in different senses in our historic documents even in the same age, and greatly modified in their meaning by the subjects to which they are applied, and their adjuncts. And let it also be distinctly kept in mind, that we are not obliged to believe any doctrine or Article of faith simply because it is in the Catechism, Creed, Confession, or Thirty-nine Articles, but because it is taught in the Word of God. And if there is any doctrine in our *formularies* that is contrary to the Word of God, I do not and will not believe it—though all the patriarchs and czars of Russia, and all the emperors, popes, and councils and convocations and assemblies on earth should affirm it.

In order to be brief and as easily understood as I can in my presentation of such a subject, the following method is proposed : namely,

I. A condensed history of the Article.

II. Endeavor to ascertain historically, and from the Scriptures, the meaning of the terms used.

III. Examine briefly some of the passages of Scripture alleged to teach the literal, local descent of Christ into hell, and which are thus perverted to the support of the doctrine of Purgatory, and kindred follies which are subversive of salvation by grace. This last head must, however, lie over altogether, for the evening of next Lord's day.

I. Then let us attempt a condensed notice of the history of the Article itself. The words : "He descended into hell," do not appear to have had a place in the most ancient Creeds, either private or public, and consequently their authority and meaning have been much disputed in ancient times among the Fathers, just as they are now among learned men. It may not be for our edification in this presence, to attempt an exhaustive review of the opinions and explanations that have been given of it. And in view of the confusing and unsatisfactory nature of the results obtained by those who have engaged so laboriously and so learnedly in the investigations of this Article, I have often been ready to wish that our Creed, like that of Nice, had omitted the words altogether, or that some Scriptural and definite interpretation had been affixed to them. Still, I do not feel myself at liberty to pass over these words altogether, however difficult they may be, or however unsuccessful I may be in presenting my thoughts concerning them, because they occur in the symbolic books of all Christendom, and are taught by the catechisms in our schools and in our families by every Church of the Reformation as well as by the Church of Rome. Formerly it was the custom, in all the Reformed churches, for their ministers to read the Scriptures regularly and in course, and to explain the Catechism systematically and regularly before their congregations on the Lord's day. And to aid them in this method of instruction, and so secure an intelligent acquaintance of the people with the Articles of our holy religion, and promote as far as possible a uniform and Scriptural exposition of God's truth, summaries of Christian doctrine—epitomes or heads of our great common faith—were drawn up and printed for the use of ministers. Numerous works of this kind were published in Holland and in Great Britain. The late Dr. A. Alexander, of Princeton, N. J., prepared a synopsis of Bible Truth, or of Christian doctrines of this character; and in former years, and in fact until quite a recent period, the greatest theologians and the men of most mind and culture employed themselves a great deal in preparing catechisms and abstracts of Bible truth for the young.

"The Institutes of Christian Doctrines," by the "great theologian," John Calvin, were prepared professedly as a Commentary on the Apostles' Creed.

Many of our best bodies of Divinity, or treatises on Theology, have been written on and according to the order and arrangement of the Catechism, or, more briefly, of the Apostles' Creed. Originally it was made the duty of our brethren, the Pastors of the Reformed Dutch Church, to go through the exposition of the Catechism containing our Creed *once every year*, each of the fifty-two Sabbaths having such a part assigned to it as would enable them to accomplish it in the year; but this has been changed so as to require the Pastors of the Dutch Church in America to complete this exposition only once every four years, so that now a lecture of this kind about once a month is substituted for one every Sabbath. Still this is better, far better, than the total neglect of such lectures by perhaps all the other churches. Once a month is better than not at all. How far the preaching of the fundamental doctrines of the Gospel has been discontinued—to what extent the regular systematic teaching of the doctrines of the Bible, as presented in our Catechism, and authorized by the standards of the Church, has been neglected—and how far this neglect has led to the apostasy of the times, to the decay of family religion and the prevailing of false doctrines, you have as good an opportunity to judge as I have. And while I assume not to be a monitor to my brethren, nor will I bring any railing accusations against them, I must say, that it seems to me the root of all the calamities of the times, and the fruitful source of the prevailing irreligion and infidelity and awful extravagance and licentiousness of our day, is in a great measure owing to the decline of fundamental religious truth—the Truth of God's Word; and this decline among the people is in a great measure to be laid to the charge of the ministers who have ceased to preach it.

As to the Article: "*He descended into hell*," we have no knowledge of any writer before *Ruffin*, in the beginning of the fifth century, who speaks of it as a part of the Creed of Christians. He tells us it was neither in the symbol of the Church of Rome, nor in the symbols of any of the Oriental churches before his day; but says he found these words: *He descended into hell*, in the symbol of the Church at Aquileia, a large city in the northern part of Italy, immediately following, as in our Creed, the words, *was dead and buried*. The words as he gives them are: *Descendit ad inferna*, which he says are borrowed from St. Paul's Epistle to the Ephesians. But *Ruffin* himself explains Paul and the Creed as speaking of Christ's *burial*.

It is confidently affirmed, by men qualified to make such an affirmation, that there is no mention of such a doctrine as that *Christ descended into hell*, in the sense put upon these words by the Church of Rome, by any of the Fathers or Councils of the Church for at least four hundred years after Christ. Although Irenæus, Tertullian, Clement and Origen, Ambrose and Augustine,* seem to have believed in an intermediate kind of state into which our Lord descended,—which they speak of as the invisible state, where men are after death, and concerning which they seem neither to have held nor to have been able to give any very definite expressions,—still, they know nothing of any draught or copy of the Apostles' Creed that contains the words: *He descended into hell*.

The first place, then, we find these words, or their fair equivalent, in use as a part of the Creed of the Church was at Aquileia, about four hundred years after Christ, After this, but whether before the beginning of the eighth

---

* Augustine even went so far as to say that nobody but an unbeliever could deny the *descent of Christ into hell*. But he gives no proof from Scripture nor from ancient Creeds of the doctrine. Nor does he explain the sense he attached to these words. *What did he mean by them?*

century we cannot say, this Article was inserted in the Creed of the Church of Rome, where it remains to this day, and is acknowledged as a part of the Apostles' Creed, adopted by all our churches. The Church of England at the Reformation received three Creeds, in two of which this Article is contained. These three Creeds are the Apostles' Creed, the Nicene, and the so-called Athanasian. The Article is in the Apostles' Creed as received by the Church of England, and in the Creed of Athanasius, also received by that Church, but is not in the Nicene or the Constantinople Creeds. In the service of the Protestant Episcopal Church in the United States there are two Creeds, the Apostles' Creed and the Nicene Creed, as modified by the Fathers of Constantinople. The words, *He descended into hell*, are not in this Creed. And in the Book of Common Prayer, before the Apostles' Creed, are these words of direction: "Then shall be said the Apostles' Creed, minister and people standing. And any churches may omit the words: He descended into hell, or may, instead of them, use the words: *He went into the place of departed spirits*, which are considered as words of the same meaning in the Creed."

As just intimated, the Apostles' Creed, including these words, is in our Catechism, and in the symbols of all the churches of Christendom; the expositions of them, however, are not all alike. "He descended into hell" is explained in our standards and by a marginal note to mean: "He continued in the state of the dead and under the power of death until the third day." And the answer to the fiftieth question, larger Catechism, says, "This is the meaning of the words, He descended into hell." The third Article of the Church of England, which is the same in the Episcopal Church of this country, is in these words: "As Christ died for us, and was buried; so also it is believed that He went down into hell."

This Article, in the time of King Edward VI., was much fuller than it is now. These words were added to it: "That the body of Christ lay in the grave until His resurrection; but His spirit, which he gave up, was with the spirits which were detained in prison, or in hell, and preached to them, as the place in St. Peter testifieth." This was in A. D. 1552, in the seventh year of the reign of King Edward VI. But ten years after, in the synod under Queen Elizabeth, the Article was adopted as it now stands. As expressed in King Edward's day it was determinate in its meaning, but as now used it is wholly indefinite, and very free and general, and may mean almost any thing.

Perhaps it is asked, why were these words inserted, or why are they retained in the Creed?

The reasons why, or the object in view for inserting them, I think may be briefly stated in this way.

1. It was felt to be a necessity to state something concerning our Lord's place of existence and actions during the time that transpired between His burial and His resurrection. The words incorporated into the Creed were regarded as the best form of expressing what was thought to have been the universal or almost universal belief of the Fathers; and yet, as there was a want of certainty as to the meaning of the terms, or as to the doctrine intended to be expressed by them, the Article was left liable to a very general interpretation, just as it was in England under Elizabeth. The leading minds of Christendom could agree on the form of words as a whole, but could not and did not agree in the details, or reasons given for believing it. This is seen in the history of the great Council of Nice. See our Appendix.

2. It seemed necessary to be thus full and comprehensive in declaring the true faith concerning our Lord's death and burial, in order to meet, deny, and refute the extraordinary conceits and false doctrines of those who from the times of the Apostles themselves had denied our Lord's human nature. It is well known that spurious gospels filled Christendom through all the early centuries of the Church; and strange as it may seem, yet it is believed to be true, that in the first ages of the Christian Church it was not our Lord's Divinity, so much as his real proper humanity, that was the subject of the chief controversies. It was not the reality of his miracles that was denied, so much as the source of the power by which He wrought them.

3. I understand, therefore, that this Article was intended to mean that Christ fulfilled all the conditions of his covenant in taking our place and dying for us. It is not so much the design of the Article to explain what those conditions are, or what they required of Him, as it is to declare that He did faithfully and fully comply with all his engagements, whatever they may have been. The words, "He descended into hell," as used by the Fathers generally, and in the Creed, I understand, therefore, to mean, that He underwent whatever was predicable of man's dissolution—whatever was true of any man as to the absolute separation of his soul from the body, and the independent existence of the soul when out of the body, was true as to the separation of the soul of Christ from his body.

When Adam our progenitor died, his body was buried; so when Christ died, his body was buried. When Adam died his soul went to God; and when Christ died his soul went to God. But as Christ conquers death and sin, and gains a complete victory over Satan, so Christ's body does not see corruption, as Adam's did, nor does his soul remain in the invisible world without his body, as ours do, waiting for the resurrection of the last day. Our Lord Christ fulfilled the twofold conditions required in man's dying, and then resumed his proper and true character by rising from the dead to die no more—rising before his body could see corruption.

II. Having thus briefly taken an historic view of the Article, let us now investigate, a little after the same manner, the history and meaning of the terms used. The word *hell*, in the English version of our Creed, corresponds to *Inferi* or *inferna* in Latin, *Hades* in Greek, and *Sheol* in Hebrew. I do not say it is proper to use these words always as interchangeable. I do not say they are always synonymous, or that there is no shade of difference in their meaning, according to their respective derivations, nor that these terms, in their respective languages, have not undergone considerable changes, meaning sometimes, and in some places, something a little different from what they meant at other times, and in other places. This is true of many words in all languages. It must be true of all languages having words that can be used to convey sense at all. Still, we may venture to say there is a remarkable correspondence between the Hebrew Sheol, the Greek Hades, the Latin-Greek *Inferi*, and our English or Saxon Hell, both in their etymologies and history. *Sheol* is believed to come from *Shaal*, "to ask, seek," especially in reference to finding a place, or ascertaining the nature of a thing—meaning, it is out of the way, and to find it and see it, one must seek for it. The Greek *Hades* is from *a*, which is privative—a negative, meaning *not*, and ιδειν, to see—*not to see*—"the unseen"—"that which is invisible"—and was used among them for the

abode, receptacle, or mansion of the dead, and changing what the religious opinions of the two nations requires to be changed. Where the Hebrews used *Sheol*, the Greeks used *Hades*. *Inferna, Inferi*, is Latin, borrowed from the Greeks, having the same general meaning—*the unseen*—and applied by the Romans to those beneath the earth, the manes, or spirits of the dead. And our English word *Hell* is from the Saxon *hel-an*, to hide, or to cover, having the same root as *holl*, a cavern or a *hole*, and as *Hel-yer*, a roofer, one that covers, and hence also that which is covered—the thing or the place that is covered. In some parts of England to this day the slating or tiling of the covers of their houses are called their *hel-ings*.*
There is, then, a remarkable similarity in the etymological meaning of the words *Sheol, Hades, Inferni*, and *Hell*, as seen in the roots from which they are derived. They all agree in signifying hidden, covered, unseen, secret, invisible. And the correspondence between these terms, historically examined, is quite as remarkable, and the more remarkable because the Hebrew, Greek, and Latin are now dead languages. Concerning *Sheol*, I design to speak in another place. And as we have no use for the Vulgate in this discussion, I say nothing further of the Latin *Inferi*. But it is well to remember that the Septuagint, the Greek version of the Bible, generally uses *Hades* as equivalent to *Sheol*. It is found eleven times, if I am not mistaken, in the Greek Testament, signifying not the past simply, perhaps never, but a dark place, invisible, what is covered, unknown, or known vaguely—a darkness, a place in which one cannot see for the want of light—especially the unknown future state, including the grave, which is the abode of the dead. In the 2d chapter of Acts, *Hades*

---

* See Dr. A. Clarke on Matthew xi. 23. Bishop Harold Browne, also, on this particular.

is the translation of *Sheol* from the 16th Psalm, and in the places where it is found in the book of Revelation, it is connected with death, and the result of death, namely, the *grave*. And in the glorious passage: *O grave, where is thy victory*, the original of Paul is *Hades*.

In considering historically the word *Hades* among the Greeks, we find them using it for the grave, and also for the place to which the spirits or manes of the dead went after their burial. Their belief was, like that of the Egyptians, that the unburied were detained on the Styx; while the buried passed over and mingled with the souls of men detained there in a state separate from their bodies. *Hades* was in fact represented by the Greeks as the Deity who presided over these realms, comprising both the happy fields of Elysium and the gloomy realms of Tartarus. Every one who is familiar with classic authors knows that the souls of the good were in Elysium, while such wicked spirits as Ixion, Tantalus, and the Danaids were grievously tormented in Tartarus. So the Odyssey and Æneid everywhere. Quotations are unnecessary.

And so the Hebrew *Sheol* was applied to the whole region below the surface of the earth, extending downwards indefinitely or inconceivably, and meaning a vast extension, ill-defined, dark, desolate, and dungeon-like, and called *a pit*, a deep pit, or covered place, *an abyss, the darkness, the depths of the earth*. Thus Jonah (ii. 2) says: "Out of the belly of hell cried I, and thou heardest my voice." Here hell in Hebrew is *Sheol*, and the Prophet must have meant out of the whale's stomach, at the bottom of the sea. He was out of human sight, in a terrible place, and in a fearful condition. And not to dwell on other places, take Ps. 16th, ver. 10: *For Thou wilt not leave my soul in hell*, which is explained according to Hebrew idiom by the corresponding clause : *neither wilt thou suffer thine Holy One to see corruption.* That is, thou wilt not leave me under the power of death ; and Ps. cxli. 7 : "Our bones are scattered at the mouth of the grave"—Sheol ; and also xlix. 14 : "Like sheep, they are laid in the grave"—Sheol. That is, says, *Witsius*, they die like sheep, which are not usually buried, and which surely do not penetrate into the hell of the lost, or into what is called a *Limbus*. And Hezekiah and Jacob both use Sheol for the grave. Is. xxxviii. 10 ; Gen. xxxvii. 35. "I said, in the cutting off of my days, I shall go to the gates of the grave"—Sheol. "I will go down into the grave—Sheol—to my son mourning." Clearly meaning the state of the dead—to be among the dead—equivalent to *gathered to one's fathers.* According to this usage, and the old Hebrew idiom, if we wished to say Christ was buried, and was, while He remained in the grave, and in the state of the dead, in the same condition as the Patriarchs and Prophets were when they died, we could not use more appropriate words than *He descended into Sheol, Hades.* And St. Peter in his discourse on the day of Pentecost quotes from the 16th Psalm, and uses *Hades* for *Sheol,* where it must be admitted the meaning is the state or condition of departed spirits—the invisible world where the dead are. True, Hades among the Greeks was a very comprehensive word. It comprised the place, condition, and state both of the wicked and of the good. It included *Tartarus* for the wicked, and *Elysium* for the good. Our Lord, in Matt. xi. 23, says : "And thou, Capernaum, which art exalted unto heaven, shalt be brought down to hell." Here hell is in opposition to heaven, and both are used figuratively. Great privileges enjoyed but abused lead to utter desolation, and irretrievable ruin. In this text the original word for hell is *Hades.*

And in Rev. i. 18: "I am He that liveth, and was dead; and, behold, I am alive for evermore, Amen; and have the keys of hell and of death." Here hell is Hades—and means not the place of departed spirits, but the *grave*, in a general sense. And in vi. 8: "And his name that sat on him was death, and hell followed with him." Here Hades is hell—clearly meaning the *grave*, the state of the dead, into which the slain entered. And xx. 13, 14: "And the sea gave up the dead which were in it; and death and hell delivered up the dead which were in them; and they were judged every man according to their works. And death and hell were cast into the lake of fire. This is the second death." Here it is clear that *death* is personified, and represented as the keeper or jailer of the dead, and *Hades* is the general name for the place of the spirits of the dead. The *sea* and *death* have the bodies of the dead, and *Hades* holds their souls, and both give up their wards, and the bodies and souls are united, and enter upon their eternal and unchangeable destiny, after the general resurrection and the judgment of the great day. And as to St. Peter's quotation of the 16th Psalm, it is to be observed that he applies these words, with his own peculiar energy and directness of purpose, in such a way as to prove the resurrection of Christ, by showing that they were not, and could not be true when applied to King David, but that they were emphatically and undeniably true when applied to Jesus; for that "his soul was not left in Hades, nor did his flesh see corruption," where it is plain he means that David's soul did remain in Hades, and his flesh did see corruption. David was not himself the Messiah; but as Christ fulfilled these requirements, He was the Messiah. And here *soul* being for *person*, and Hades for the grave, the last clause is explanatory of the first, in the sense I have attached to the words of the Creed. And the point of the argument lies clearly in the miracle of the resurrection, which is true, because our Lord's soul, his perfect human nature, did not remain in the grave, and under the power of death, and consequently his body did not see corruption. As He is the *second* Adam, the Lord from heaven, who died for us, meeting the curse of temporal death on the first Adam, so his body and his soul passed into and through the same state that our souls and bodies do when we die—changing what is to be changed, because He was the immaculately Holy Son of God. Our bodies see corruption, our souls do not come back and reanimate our bodies. They remain in the spirit-world. But Christ rose from the dead, having his perfect human nature, both body and soul, in union with Divinity.

Whatever, then, may be the derivation of the word Sheol, or however varied its signification, all agree that it is used in the Sacred Scriptures for the state and abode of the dead, and hence that it means the grave in which the body rests, and the invisible world to which our souls go when they leave the body in death. The poetical description of the gates of death implies that it is something more than the grave. It is true, there are other Hebrew words for the grave, and for pit, corruption, and burying, and sepulchre; but still it is true, that in many passages Sheol must mean the grave, the invisible world, the state and abode of the dead, as a state and a place distinguished from the present life. Any Hebrew Concordance or Dictionary will assist the reader to the places.

On the whole, it seems to me the Creed must be taken either figuratively to mean, that Christ endured in his soul, while still in the body, the agonies of hell; or that the words, *He descended into hell*, must mean that his body was buried, and his soul went to God, so that He completed his work for us by dying just as we do. The *first* of these views just named, the figurative or metaphorical interpretation of the Article, is adopted by the great Witsius, and many others.

According to this view the meaning is, that not only was the body of Christ given up for our redemption, but that His soul suffered the tortures of condemned and ruined men. This view is taken by the authors of the *Heidelberg Catechism*, in answer to 44th Question, where it is said the words, "He descended into hell, are added, that in my greatest temptations I may be assured and wholly comfort myself in this, that my Lord Jesus Christ, by his inexpressible anguish, pains, terrors, and hellish agonies, in which He was plunged during all his sufferings, but especially on the cross, hath delivered me from the anguish and torments of hell."

This was the exposition of the Reformers generally. *Calvin* says, that our Lord's descent to hell means not his going to the place of spirits, but His suffering upon earth, in Gethsemane and on the cross, all the torments of hell and the sufferings of damned souls. And it is thought it was owing to the growing popularity of Calvin's views in England, during Elizabeth's reign, that the Article put forth in King Edward's reign suffered the change we have already referred to. But although this is the view of Calvin and a great many of the Reformers, I am not satisfied that it is the meaning of the Creed, or according to the Word of God. Those who hold this view do not agree in telling us what Christ did suffer. They tell us He suffered the extreme wrath of God, or the very torments of hell in his soul, and some of them that his soul actually went to *Gehenna*, the place of the damned, and suffered there its extreme torments. This view I cannot receive for before our Lord could actually suffer the torments of lost souls, He must feel the consciousness of personal guilt and degradation, as well as the superadded wrath of God. As I understand the Word of God, this consciousness of degradation—this feeling of personal guilt—is the essence of the fire unquenchable, the life of the worm that dieth not. Now, as a lamb at the temple bore the sins of the people, so Christ bore our sins. But was the lamb guilty of sin? No. The lamb bore the curse of sin, endured the wrath of God as to the penalty it met; but there was no transfer of personal guilt to the lamb. In fact, the lamb was not punished at all. The lamb was sacrificed. So Christ suffered, but He was not punished. He endured the wrath of God due to our guilt, not due to himself. It was our debt, not His own, which He paid. He died as our substitute and in our place, but, according to our view of the atonement, it was impossible for Christ to suffer the actual torments of hell, or to endure in his person the agonies of lost souls in Gehenna. Perhaps we may say He suffered the equivalent of them for his people, but not the actual torments of the lost; for the torments of the damned consist—

1. In a consciousness of *personal guilt*—a feeling that they themselves deserve all that is inflicted on them, both as to degradation and suffering. This our Lord could never experience. There was not and could not be any transfer of personal guilt to Him, but only the transfer of obligation to pay a debt or endure a penalty.

2. The torments of hell comprise utter despair. Doleful region; no hope ever enters there! This cannot be said of our Lord's sufferings.

3. Hell is total separation from God, without any glimpse of his favor. Now, as it is impossible to apply

these things to Christ, I do not believe that the great men who explain the Creed as teaching metaphorically that Christ endured the torments of hell for the elect, are correct. If the time allowed it, much more might be said on this point; but this must suffice, at least for the present. [See Pearson and Lightfoot on this point.]

The other view to which I alluded a few minutes since, and which is the one I adopt, namely, that Christ died and was buried, and his soul went to God, and that this is simply all the Creed means and all that the Scriptures teach, is sustained, I think, very satisfactorily, and in this way:

1. There is no passage of Holy Scripture that teaches, when properly explained, that Christ either endured the actual torments of hell, or locally descended to the place of damned souls. This statement I am obliged for the present to assume, but if the Lord be pleased to give us his assistance, I will try to prove it in the next Discourse.

2. It has been proved that the descent into hell is not found as a separate, distinct Article in any of the earlier Creeds. It is not in any copy or draught of the Apostles' Creed in use in the Eastern or the Roman churches for at least four hundred years after Christ. It is not in the Creed of Irenæus, nor of Tertullian, Origen, or Cyprian. It is not in the Nicene Creed adopted in A. D. 325, nor in the version of the Nicene Creed used by the Fathers of Constantinople. The words of the Nicene Creed are: "He suffered and was buried, and the third day He rose again." But in the Creed called the Creed of Athanasius, of the year A. D. 333, eight years later, we read: "Who suffered for our sins, *descended into hell*, rose again the third day." Here observe that

was buried is omitted, and *descended into hell* is used in its place, clearly showing that these phrases were then supposed to be synonymous. How the doctrine that Christ descended into hell, in the sense of the Church of Rome, ever got into the Apostles' Creed, nobody knows, but certainly it was not there before the fifth century, and possibly not until long after. We have the opinion of Erasmus, that it was not formally adopted till long after.

It is to be remembered here, that almost, perhaps, all of the old creeds that recognize the descent into hell in any way, explain it as meaning the same thing as *He was buried*. The creeds that contain these words, "He descended into hell," omit the words, "He was buried;" while those that have the words, "He was buried," omit the other words, "He descended into hell." It is fairly concluded, therefore, that the one phrase was equal in meaning to the other, and varied merely as a matter of taste. "The churches of the East originally understood by Christ's descent into hell, just what the churches of the West called his burial."*

The only difference, according to the view I have, between the phrases: "Christ was buried," and, "Christ descended into hell," when properly understood, is this: The latter words have a wider meaning, and are to be referred partly to his body and partly to his soul; whereas the words *was buried* are limited to the body, and do not go beyond the grave. And this is the main reason for retaining the words in the Creed, as we now have it. The expressions used are emphatic as to the reality of our Lord's death and burial. They affirm that his death was a real human death. His soul was

---

* Vossius.

separated from his body, just as our soul is at death, and his body was buried, and his soul went to God, and remained with Him until the morning of the third day, and then returned and resumed his body. And all this is for our comfort, and the assurance of complete redemption. Let us repeat. Our view (1.) is according to the draughts or versions of all the known creeds of the Churches for four or five hundred years after Christ. (2.) In itself it is true, and contains nothing but the truth: namely, that Christ's body was buried, and his soul went immediately at death to God. And, allow me to say, (3.) That, while this view can be shown to be in harmony with the Word of God, and the analogy of our holy Faith, that the other, and all other interpretations, as far as I am able to comprehend them, *break down*—utterly break down, when tested by common sense, reason, and the Bible. And, (4.) It may be important, in view of the historic sketch we have taken of the terms used in the Creed, to observe distinctly, that words change their meaning, even in the same language, in passing from one generation to another, and are even shaded or modified by their adjuncts in the same age and country. There are many instances of this in our own language. Take a single example. *Knave* originally meant a boy, a young man, then a servant, and now a *rogue*. It is now always used in a bad sense, yet there was a time when it was used precisely as we use the word *servant*. The words of our translation, "Paul, a servant of the Lord," in old versions is, "I, Paul, a *knave* of the Lord." A similar change has come over the word *hell*. It has been shown that it corresponds in its original signification to *Inferni*, *Hades*, and *Sheol*, and like them has passed through several modifications, until now its common literal signification is the place of the damned—the home of Satan, and the central seat of his empire. It does not seem to us that the Creed meant to say, or that the Scriptures allow us to believe, that Jesus Christ, at his death, went to Satan's home. The word "hell" in the Creed is, then, to be understood in its historic sense, and not as now popularly applied. The original Saxon, we are told, meant to hide, and then the place where a thing was hidden, a hole, a cavern, and hence the common idea of hell even now is associated with a pit, a hole, a gloomy cavern.

Thus we have "hell's gate," "hell's mouth," and the like popular expressions. The word, therefore, means both the *place* of the dead and the place of the punishment of the wicked. The primary idea was the place of the dead, in a very general sense, the unseen, unknown "bourne" beneath the earth, or in the invisible state, from which "no traveller returns" to give us a description of it. The Hebrews had two words for which our translators have used but one. For *Gehenna* and *Sheol* our translators used the same word, *hell*, which, when it is the translation of *Gehenna*, is to be taken in its secondary sense of the place of the future eternal punishment of the wicked; but when our translators used *hell* for *Sheol*, then it means the region beneath the ground, the grave, the place of the dead, the unseen world, which is the primary sense of the word. We must not, therefore, confound *Sheol* and *Hades* and *Hell* in the sense of the grave, the unseen world, with *Gehenna*, or the place and condition of lost souls. I do not, indeed, regard the doctrine of a future state, or of the future and eternal punishment of the wicked, as depending essentially upon the critical examination of words; but still it is fair and proper to observe, that we do not depend upon the use of the terms "Sheol" and "Hades" by the sacred writers for our knowledge of the nature and intensity or duration of the punishment of the ungodly after death. The awful realities awaiting impenitent, unbelieving souls at death are spoken of in God's Word in terms of no doubtful meaning, and are proved and explained by the Bible as a whole. And, (5.) That the soul is separate, and different from the body, and at death leaves the body altogether, but still exists, and does not go to sleep or sink into an unconscious state. It returns to God who gave it, in just as literal a sense as the body returns to dust whence it was taken. And the state of happiness succeeding immediately after death to the souls of the pious is called Paradise, which is heaven, or at least a part of heaven, and is the same thing as a being present with the Lord; while the souls of the wicked go at death into torment, which is hell—but neither the wicked nor the pious receive their final and full reward until the resurrection and the general judgment, when the soul is united to the body. I believe, therefore, in an intermediate state—not as a half-way stopping-place between heaven and hell—not as a *Limbus Patrum*, or Purgatory, out of which souls may be delivered by masses, or the intercession of saints and angels; but as the first degrees of glory or of perdition, which are as it were preparatory to the final consummation of bliss or misery to be assigned to each one at the last day according to their works, whether they be good or evil. The Paradise which our Lord promised the penitent on the cross was a place of bliss; it was the place to which His own soul went, according to His commitment of it to God His Father. It was heaven—the same kind of a heaven Abraham was in when he took Lazarus into his bosom. And so the rich man opened his eyes in hell; but it does not follow from this that a deeper hell was not still in reservation for the lost, after the general judgment, and greater and higher degrees of glory in heaven for Lazarus, and for the penitent, and for all the pious dead after the general resurrection.

Rejecting as I do the idea of an intermediate state, as a kind of Purgatory, and not being satisfied with the metaphorical interpretation offered by the Reformers, but explaining the words, *He descended into hell*, as substantially synonymous with, *and He was buried*, it may be properly asked, What then became of our Lord's soul during the time that passed between His death and His resurrection? It might be quite a sufficient answer to this question to ask another: Where was the soul of the son of the widow of Nain, or of Lazarus of Bethany, during the time between their dying and their restoration to life? And I have no answer to give to this question as to the young man of Nain or as to Lazarus, for the Word of God does not furnish us any information on the subject. But as to our Lord's soul we may safely say: It was with God all this time. His soul returned to God, according to His dying commendation of it to God his Father, and with him was the penitent thief, to whom He had promised Paradise the very same day they were crucified. Our Lord went immediately to heaven when He gave up the ghost. The next day was the holy Sabbath, and so, speaking with reverence, He spent it with His Father resting in heaven, after completing His great redemption work, as His Father did after the work of creation. And so, after the rest of the Sabbath, He descended on the morning of the first day of the week, which we now call the Lord's day, from heaven into Sheol, that is, into the tomb of Joseph of Arimathea—early in the morning, not to remain there under the power of death, and in the state and abode of the dead, but to take up His dead body, and come forth as the conqueror of sin, death, hell, and the grave.

Truly thus was it impossible for Him whom God hath raised up, having loosed the pains of death, to be holden any longer in the grave. Thus He ascended upon high, leading captivity captive.

> "Now empty are the courts of death,
> And crushed thy sting, despair;
> And roses bloom in the desert tomb,
> For Jesus hath been there.
>
> "And He hath tamed the strength of hell,
> And dragged him through the sky;
> And captive behind his chariot wheel
> He hath bound captivity."*

Christ's work for his people is indeed complete. He exhausted the curse, and for the soul that believes in Him there remains no more hell—for there is no more guilt. There is no condemnation to them that are in Christ Jesus. He follows us into the regions of the dead, and bursts asunder the bars of death, and opens the door for a glorious resurrection, when our vile bodies shall be fashioned like unto his own glorified and ascended body. And not only so, but thus are we called to follow Him to heaven. First at death our soul is to be commended to His God and our God, to His Father and our Father—and the body to the grave, to rest in hope, until He calls us to arise and see Him in the full glory of his kingdom.

Almighty God, enable us by Thy grace to cast away the works of darkness and put on the armor of light, that in the day when Thy Son, our Lord Jesus Christ, shall come with great power and glory, to judge both the quick and the dead, we may rise to the life immortal, through Him who liveth and reigneth with Thee and the Holy Ghost, now and ever. Amen.

---

* Heber's Easter Hymn.

X.

"HELL" NOT GEHENNA NOR PURGATORY.

"For thou wilt not leave my soul in hell: neither wilt thou suffer thine Holy One to see corruption."—PSALM xvi. 10.

ACCORDING to the division of the Creed which I am following, the whole of the Fifth Article is: "He descended into hell; the third day He rose again from the dead." At present I am engaged only on the first clause of this Article: "He descended into hell."

Last Sabbath evening, in order to be as concise and as clear as the nature of the discussion of such an Article as this admits, I proposed the following method: namely,

I. To offer you a short history of the clause—*He descended into hell*, as it lies in our Creed.

II. Ascertain historically and from the Scriptures the meaning of the words, *descended into hell*. And,

III. I proposed to examine briefly the passages of Scripture which it is alleged teach the local descent of Christ's soul into hell, and which are thus made to support the *modern* doctrine of Purgatory. The first and second heads I presented as well as I could last Sabbath evening. The third and last one remains for our present attempt. That is, it is my purpose now, with God's assistance, to show that the words, *He descended into hell*, as they lie in our Creed, do not mean Gehenna or Purgatory in any sense, and that the passages of Holy Scripture generally brought forward in proof of such an interpretation of the Creed, do not teach or favor it, nor allow any such doctrine to be preached as a part of the Faith once delivered to the saints.

It has been shown, I hope satisfactorily, that the words *Sheol*, *Hades*, *inferi*, *inferna*, and our Saxon word *hell*, bear a remarkable correspondence with each other, both as to their etymological meaning and as to the changes and applications they have undergone. They are terms so vague and extensive that they are found comprehending the invisible world, wherever and whatever it is, or is supposed to be—the *state* of the dead—the *place* of spirits separated from their bodies, both good and bad—and often simply the grave. Also it is to be noted that these words, as is usually the case in the primitive state of a language, and perhaps especially so in the Oriental languages, have passed from their primary to a secondary sense. This is emphatically the case with our word *hell*. It has now a determinate meaning. Now it means the place of the future and eternal punishment of the wicked; but its original meaning was any thing covered—a hole, a pit, an abyss, the invisible. It is also true with these terms, as with others, that they are used in a figurative or metaphorical sense.

Again, although the *descent of Christ into hell* is not formally stated anywhere in the Scriptures, nor found as a distinct Article in any copy or draught of the Apostles' Creed, or of any ancient Creed, public or private, for about four hundred years after Christ, yet it was held as an Article of Faith, in some sense, by almost all the Fathers. And Augustine boldly says, "None but an infidel would deny the descent of Christ into hell."

There was, undoubtedly, a general opinion among the ancients, both heathen and Christian, that the souls of men descended at death into what they called the infernal regions, not meaning the hell of the damned, but the state or receptacle of spirits separated from their bodies, which was supposed to be beneath the earth. Here they thought the soul was detained—left to wander about in vast undefined regions. Some of the Fathers and theological writers of former ages have maintained that this was the meaning of these words in the Creed, which, however, I think is a mistake. Old *Tertullian* says that Christ descended into hell that He might satisfy the conditions of mortality, and complete the form of human death in the shades below.* As I understand him, he means precisely what I suppose our Creed means—namely, that the body and the soul of Christ were reduced by death to the precise condition that marks the natural dissolution of every other man.† Seeing, then, that such Fathers as Tertullian and Augustine, and the Church of the earliest ages, generally understood the sixteenth Psalm, quoted by Peter in the second chapter of the Acts of the Apostles and portions of Colossians and Ephesians, and of first Peter, to mean that in some sense Christ did descend into hell, it is important and necessary for us to examine these several places of Holy Scripture, and ascertain, as clearly as we can, what they do really mean. They are: Ps. xvi. 10, quoted in Acts ii. 27; Eph. iv. 8–10; 1 Pet. iii. 18–20.

---

* See Browne and Pearson. † See Harvey, vol. 1, p. 337.

As far as my present investigations are concerned, the main interpretations of those passages of Scripture may be classed in the following order: I. The Fathers and Schoolmen, at least many of them, used the words of the Creed or their equivalent, *descendit ad inferna*, as expressing what they understood these passages to mean, without affixing any clear or definite meaning to the phrase, every one having his own interpretation.

II. The Roman Church and some others teach that Christ descended literally and locally to hell; that is, to some part of it; at least, to the part they call *Limbus Patrum*—alleged to be on the confines of the place of torment; and that He delivered from this Limbus Patrum the souls of the Patriarchs especially, and of good men who had died but were still not fit to go to heaven till He rescued them. There is great diversity of opinion, however, about Christ's descent into hell, and great latitude as to the doctrine of Purgatory, among those who believe in it. Even in the Church of Rome it was not formally affirmed till the Council of Florence, in 1439. The Primitive Church knew nothing of it, nor of the *descent of Christ into hell*, if these words mean any thing more than Christ's death and burial, as I have endeavored to explain them in the last discourse. The general idea among the Fathers and the Schoolmen of Hades and Sheol was that they meant the state of the dead, including the place of their existence, both of the good and bad, comprising Elysium and Tartarus, Paradise and Gehenna, and at least that the godly were not perfectly happy till the resurrection of their bodies. Even those who have taught that Christ by preaching to the spirits in prison delivered them from hell, do not hold that all sorts of bad people are thus to be saved. They tell us some are so bad they go to hell at once, and for them there is no hope. Others dying who are not bad enough to go to hell, and yet not good enough to go to heaven, are sent to Purgatory, and there their sins are scoured away by fire and torment, provided money enough is paid to priests for singing dirges and saying masses. If there is not much money paid, it takes hundreds of years to get out of Purgatory; but such is the power of the Church keys in the hands of his Holiness the Pope, that prayers, masses, and dirges, well paid for, are supposed to shorten greatly the time. It is perfectly consistent with this view of Purgatory, for rich men to bestow vast sums of money on monasteries, chapels, cathedrals, and schools, on condition that the priests say so many masses and prayers to deliver their souls as soon as possible from the fires of Purgatory. But does the Creed mean this? Is there such a doctrine taught or allowed to be believed by the Word of God? I think not. That a higher degree of glory, a more perfect state of holiness and happiness is in reserve for God's people in the ages to come—after Christ's second coming, or after the general judgment—is the common belief of Christendom. We have Origen, Lactantius, Hilary, Ambrose, Augustine, and others, in proof that the souls of the pious dead are at least in some measure held back from perfect glory—such a fulness of glory as is to be given to them at the resurrection.* This I can believe, if by it we are to understand that believers at death are happy, and do immediately pass to glory, so that, being absent from the body, they are present with the Lord; and provided also that it allows of different degrees in glory, and ever increasing weight of glory, especially at the resurrection of the body, and also different degrees of punishment for the ungodly. But if these Fathers are to be interpreted so as

---

* Quotations are in Browne, pp. 81, 82.

to mean that the state of the souls of the pious dead is a Purgatory, as explained by the Church of Rome, then I cannot believe them. Nor can I receive the opinion of Durandus, that all the texts produced to prove the descent of Christ into hell and Purgatory simply mean that a virtual influence from Christ's death was exerted on the souls of the dead, and thus the words, *He descended into hell*, are to be taken figuratively, and mean that the benefits of His redemption are extended to the regions of perdition.

III. Witsius, Calvin, and the Reformers generally taught that the words, *He descended into hell*, were to be interpreted figuratively, or as a metaphor, and were exhausted in the agonies of our Lord's soul while in the body. This has been shown to be altogether inadmissible.

IV. Bishop Pearson and some others hold the doctrine that Christ literally went to hell—to Gehenna—and passed through the regions of lost souls, and devils damned, literally, for the purpose of showing that He really was a conqueror, and that His people have nothing to fear from hell or the devil. This view, also, I am obliged to reject. But another, and, as I think, the true view of this whole subject, is,

V. That the Creed, the best Fathers, and the Word of God all agree in teaching as an Article of Christian faith, that by our Lord's death, burial, and descent to Hades, we are to understand that, as the second Adam, he met the death penalty incurred by the first Adam, both as to his "true body" and "rational soul:" that is, in every sense, whatever is predicable of man's dissolution in consequence of Adam's sin, was true as to the real separation of the soul of Christ from his body. His body was buried and his soul went to God just as the body of any other mortal man returns at death to dust, and his soul to God who gave it. But as Christ conquers sin, death, and the grave, so His body and soul remain in Sheol, Hades, Inferni, Hell, only as long as Jonah was in the whale—that is, his body did not see corruption, nor did his soul remain with God, waiting the general resurrection. The only difference between the death of the Lord Jesus in these particulars, and the death of a believer, lies in this: *His* body is taken up again by his soul before it decays—*our* bodies remain till the resurrection. His soul remained only one day and two nights with God his Father in Paradise, which is heaven, till it came back to reanimate his body, but the souls of believers remain with God, waiting the resurrection of the last day.

This view seems to me to harmonize every text of holy Scripture that refers to the subject at all, and to be true in itself and consistent with reason and common sense. I quite agree, however, with the very learned and excellent Dr. Lightfoot, when he says: "There is not an Article in our Christian faith that still hath more need of explication to bring it to common reason or the analogy of faith than this one." The wording of this part of the Article is so obscure and harsh, that I could wish it were modified. For to think of the soul of our Saviour, in any sense, in the same place with Judas Iscariot who betrayed Him, is to my mind exceedingly repulsive. To think that He who had by his death purchased heaven for others, should himself, after death, literally and locally descend into the place of the damned, I cannot believe.

I. All the symbolical books of the Churches of the Reformation as well as the Creed of the Church of Rome acknowledge the truth of the proposition as it lies in our Creed—that *Christ descended into hell.* The only question, then, is, in what sense are these words to be understood, and, when thus understood, is the doctrine so stated according to the Word of God? In the minds of most of our writers who defend a literal, local descent of Christ's soul into hell, the principal text is the one read out of the sixteenth Psalm: "For David speaketh," &c. [See Acts ii. 25-27, with 31-36 verses.]

Here observe, that having repeated the text from the Psalmist, the Apostle applies it to Jesus of Nazareth, to prove that He is Christ the promised Messiah: "He David, being a Prophet, and seeing this before, spake of the resurrection of Christ, that his soul was not left in hell, neither did his flesh see corruption." The way this passage is made to teach the doctrine that Christ descended into hell is this: If the soul of Christ were not left in hell at his resurrection, then his soul was in hell before his resurrection: but it was not there before his death; therefore upon or after his death, and before his resurrection, the soul of Christ descended into hell.* But if we can show that the passage, as we have it in the Psalms and in the discourse of St. Peter, does not admit of such an interpretation as this, then of course it does not prove this doctrine. The interpretation under review requires that *hell* should mean the place, at least some part of the world of woe, where the spirits of men separated from their bodies at death are detained, and undergo more or less torment; but I have shown that Sheol or Hades here means the grave, or the unseen world, and not the place of future punishment at all. Again, to make this interpretation true, it must be shown that the word *soul* as used by the Psalmist signifies the *human soul* of Christ in distinction from his body, and as it was while wholly

---

* See Pearson, p. 338.

separate from his dead body. But this cannot be proven from the Psalms nor the Acts. The Hebrew word for soul in this place is *nephesh*, which does not mean the spirit, the immortal, thinking part of man. Its primary sense is "breath," "life," whether of man or beast—*a living creature*, whether rational or irrational. So the word is used in Gen. i. 20, 21 and ii. 7, and its corresponding word in Greek in Acts and in 1 Cor. xv. 45. In process of time the same word came to signify the body of a man or of a beast, and even the corpse after the life had left it. Thus, Numbers xix. 11 : " He that toucheth the *dead body* of any man shall be unclean seven days." "Whosoever toucheth the *dead body* of any man that is dead." " If one that is unclean by a *dead body*." In each of these passages, and there are many more, the Hebrew for *dead body* is nephesh—the very word used for soul in this Psalm. There are two other texts where this word is so emphatic that I wish to quote them. They are these: " All the days that he separate himself to the Lord, he shall come at no dead body"—*nephesh*. Numbers vi. 6. And in Lev. xix. 28: " Ye shall not make any cuttings in your flesh for the dead "—*nephesh*. Again, the word soul means *person*. "Whosoever hath killed any soul," that is, any person. " Let *me* die the death of the righteous." In Hebrew it is, Let my soul. "Let me die"—Hebrew, let my soul " die with the Philistines." In these and such places, soul means the person, the man himself. In Amos vi. 8 : " The LORD GOD hath sworn by himself," Hebrew, *be-nephesho*—by his soul, that is, by himself, by his own being, existence, there being no one greater. And every one acquainted with classical authors remembers that the Greek equivalent is used with quite as much latitude, meaning the body, and the body and the soul, *the person*. If I say not a soul was present, do I not mean not a person was present? Even in our own language, soul is not limited to the thinking, immortal part of man, but is synonymous with person. See Psalm xi. 1; xxxv. 3, 7; Job ix. 21. Observe the Apostle's words: "For David speaketh concerning him." [25, 27 verse]. Here *my flesh*, that is, my body, my dead body, as distinguished from the *living soul, shall rest in hope*. "Because Thou wilt not leave my soul"—ME—my person, my humanity, comprising both my true body and reasonable soul, under the power of death in the grave. "Neither wilt thou suffer thine Holy One"—Me—Myself—"to see corruption." *To see corruption* is to undergo corruption, as to *see death is to die*, undergo death. Believers in general are saved from the perpetual dominion of death, but Christ was saved even from the first approach of putrefaction.

"Thou wilt not leave my dead body in the grave"—Beza, and also the Geneva Bible.—Thou wilt not resign, abandon, give me, *myself*, over to the dominion of the grave. The *Holy One* cannot mean the dead body separate from the soul; and yet it means just what my soul means in the other phrase, where *my soul* is an oriental way of using the emphatic personal pronoun *myself*. The essential meaning certainly is: "Thou wilt not leave my soul and body separate."

If I am not mistaken, I have made the point that our scholars admit that the word used by the Psalmist for soul does sometimes mean the body, even the body of a dead man, a corpse—such a body as a Nazarite was forbidden to touch, and which no one could touch, according to the law of Moses, without being rendered unclean. And in this place it means *me, myself*.

As I understand the two clauses of the Psalm to mean essentially the same thing, soul cannot here be limited to the body as separated from the immortal spiritual part which we call the soul, but must be taken here for the person of man, consisting of both soul and body. That it is so to be understood, in this and many other places, many of our scholars admit.

A second point here to be noted is, that the word "hell" in our translation is used in this place in its old wide sense—the unseen world, containing the grave for the body, and the existence of the soul separate from the body.

Thus, then, if the soul of Christ means Christ himself, is an emphatic oriental way of saying *me*—meaning his entirety as a man, his "true body" and "rational soul;" and if *hell* here means the state of the dead, including the *grave* for the body and the return of the soul to God, then the meaning is plain and eminently Scriptural.

Dr. Barrow, indeed, contends that *Sheol, Hades,* and *Inferna,* in the sense of the Creed, has no application to the state of the soul at all. His argument is to the effect that the Old Testament does not speak of the soul of man going down into any such a state or place as is denominated *Sheol,* but thus represents the body, while the soul returns, going up to God who gave it. The bodies of men naturally return to dust, fall into the dust of death, descend into the bosom of the grave, and are therefore said to descend. But the souls of the righteous are in the hands of God, not in Sheol. Now it is certainly true that the Hebrew idea was that the soul went *upward,* not *downward,* consequently did not go into Sheol, in the sense of Purgatory or *Limbus Patrum.* One of the things that distinguishes the soul of man, in Bible language, from the spirit of a beast, is that it *goes up.* Enoch and Elijah were taken up. The souls of the righteous are always supposed to ascend, to *go up* to the society of the heavenly Jerusalem. Again, it may fairly be asked, if Sheol signifies the state or place of the soul, how are we to understand such expressions as these, namely: "The grave (*Sheol*) cannot praise thee, death cannot celebrate thee; they that *go down* into the pit cannot hope for thy truth. In death there is no remembrance of thee. In the grave (*Sheol*) who shall give thee thanks? There is no work, nor service, nor knowledge, nor wisdom, in the grave (*Sheol*) whither thou goest." All these expressions are easily understood if *Sheol* means the place to which the body is consigned at death; but they are not true if applied to the state of departed souls.

It is, however, true, that in the times of the New Testament the Jews adopted the heathen idea of Hades, and seem to have supposed it meant the place of punishment for the souls of the wicked, or at least the invisible world into which the soul passes when it leaves the body, just as some Christians have adopted the idea of Purgatory, from the heathen.

Now, if we take the words, *He descended into hell*, in the sense of the grave, or in the still more general sense of into the state of the invisible world into which the dead pass, then the meaning of the Creed is certainly a correct one. The meaning, then, is just as it was often expressed in some of the old Creeds, an expletive of the word *buried*, or as standing in the place of *was buried*. The meaning, then, is, our Lord passed into the state of death—that happened to him which happened to Jacob and the pious prophets and kings of Israel—namely, His soul went to God, to whom He committed it when He gave up the ghost, and his body was laid in the tomb. This meaning meets the requirements of every text of Holy Scripture concerning the Messiah, and is sustained by all the passages in the New Testament descriptive of his burial and resurrection. In 1 Cor. xv. 1-4, you remember Paul says, as if he intended an exhaustive enumeration of points of doctrine to be believed on this subject, "I delivered unto you first, that Christ died according to the Scriptures, and that he was buried, and that he rose again the third day." Here note, he mentions only his death, burial, and resurrection. If, then, by *He descended into hell*, any thing else or any thing more is meant than what his death and burial comprehend, would not the Apostle have specified it also? If, between his burial and his resurrection, our Lord had performed any such work as going down to Gehenna, or delivering the patriarchs from the torments of Purgatory, would he not have here enumerated it as among his memorable exploits?

Again, suppose that *Hades* is to be taken in its Greek meaning, and not strictly in the sense of Sheol, as in the earlier Hebrew, still there is this difficulty—the indefiniteness of the term. It may mean the place of damned spirits, shut up in despair, or it may mean the place common to all souls, both good and bad, miserable and blessed. But against this view is the text from Revelation, where Death and hell (Hades) were cast into the lake of fire. Now it cannot be true that Paradise, the good part of Hades, was cast into the lake of fire, which is the second death. And, besides, if this is true, then that part of Hades, which is *Elysium*, Paradise, as opposed to Tartarus, is below us—beneath our feet—under the earth. Who believes that? Does not Paul clearly intimate that the third heaven is Paradise? At least, I cannot believe, from all I have yet seen, that the place destined to receive the souls of God's people is in the darksome bowels of the earth. I conclude, therefore, that Sheol, Hades, Hell, in the sense of the Creed, is not to be applied to the place or state of the soul at all, but to that of the body. It means either the grave, or, more generally, the invisible world into which the dead pass when the soul leaves the body. In this sense, *descending* means falling from life and the descent of the body to the tomb. And the word hell is used in its broad sense of *Sheol*, meaning that his body was laid in the grave, the common receptacle for the bodies of all Adam's race, and his soul went to God, as do the souls of all God's children at death.

If the word *Sheol*, translated *hell*, means here the grave in its wide sense, as it does in other places, including the state or condition of men after death, and during the separation of the soul from the body; the prophecy of the Psalmist would then run in this style: "Thou shalt not leave my soul in hell"—that is, thou shalt not suffer ME to remain under the power of death and in the common state of the dead, whose bodies see corruption, and whose souls are without their bodies until the general resurrection. This interpretation makes the Creed mean: that Christ was crucified unto death, was actually dead, and was buried, and He descended into hell:—that is, His death and burial were accompanied with and realized the twofold conditions of the death penalty resting on Adam and his posterity as to both his soul and his body. His body was laid in the grave, and so far was committed dust to dust, and his soul returned to God His Father—He went unto the dead, He was as the pious dead are, He remained in the state of death as other men do. The only difference here to be noted between his death and burial and that of one of his followers lies in this: namely, His body remains only a short time in the grave. It did not, could not see corruption. As He finished His work as representative sufferer on the Cross, and as His body in itself, like His soul, was without sin, so it could not see corruption. And therefore His soul returned from heaven on the morning of the third day after His burial, whereas our bodies see corruption, and our souls are with God without their bodies until the resurrection. "For the further assurance of His death, and glory of His resurrection, as likewise to commend the grave to us, as now a very sweet resting-place, He hath warmed the cold bed of the grave to a Christian, that he need not fear to lie down in it, nor doubt that he shall rise again, as we know, and are after to hear, that Jesus did Himself"—*Leighton*. There is then nothing here about Christ going to Gehenna, nor in favor of a heathen Purgatory.

II. But perhaps no place of Holy Scripture has been more abused by perversion than Eph. iv. 8–10, which is this:

"Wherefore He saith, When he ascended up on high, he led captivity captive, and gave gifts unto men.

"Now that he ascended, what is it but that he also descended first into the lower parts of the earth?

"He that descended is the same also that ascended up far above all heavens, that he might fill all things."

Now it is admitted many of the ancient Fathers understood these words of the Apostle to mean that *Christ descended into hell*, although it is not clear what they understood hell to mean. Perhaps generally, however, by hell they meant the *lowest parts of the earth*, supposing that hell was in the centre of it, or at least inside of our earth, and so they conceited the Apostle meant.

Confessedly this is a passage of some difficulty, but I hope to give you a fair and clear view of it. What, then, is the Apostle's object? Answer. He is exhorting believers to walk worthy of their vocation, which they were to do by showing themselves obedient to all the commands of Christ. And as a motive urging them so to do, he reminds them of the variety of gifts and offices conferred on them as members of the Church of Christ. And speaking of the gifts of Christ to his people brings to His mind one of the Psalms (lxviii. 18), that speaks of Messiah as a military conqueror, and this suggests to his mind a beautiful analogy. The Psalm probably was primarily used for the removal of the tabernacle, but is here applied by the Apostle to the glorious ascension of Christ after His resurrection from the dead.

1. *When he ascended up on high*, alluding to a Roman triumphal procession, when the conqueror was placed in an elevated car or chariot.

2. *He led captivity captive.* Conquered kings and generals were usually bound behind the triumphal car, to grace the procession.

3. *And gave gifts unto men.* The triumphing conqueror among the Romans was wont to throw money and bread among the crowd—*even to the rebellious*—that is, to those who had fought against him. For it belongs to the hero to be generous.

The next verses (9 and 10) are parenthetical, and applied positively by the Apostle to our Lord. Where,

1. Observe, He who descended and ascended is the same, and is the Messiah.

2. Ascending implies descending.

3. And this descending is his humiliation, in contrast with his exaltation after his death. And,

4. *The contrast* so tersely presented does not say or intimate, or even allow the idea of his descent into Gehenna. His ascent was not from Gehenna, nor from Hades. He who ascended *so high* is the same who had descended *so low*, but this descent is most remarkable in view of the glory He left when He emptied himself of it to become a man. His abasement is unparalleled; so also is His exaltation. His humiliation was down to the lowest parts of the earth; His exaltation "far above all heavens." And the purpose,

5. Is "that He might fill all things." Be head over all to his Church—the sole, Supreme, only Head. Fountain to Jews and Gentiles—filling His Church with gifts and graces. Hence it follows,

6. "And he gave some, Apostles; and some, prophets; and some, evangelists; and some, pastors and teachers.

"For the perfecting of the saints, for the work of the ministry, for the edifying of the body of Christ:

"Till we all come in the unity of the faith, and of the knowledge of the Son of God, unto a perfect man, unto the measure of the stature of the fulness of Christ:

"That we henceforth be no more children, tossed to and fro, and carried about with every wind of doctrine, by the sleight of men, and cunning craftiness, whereby they lie in wait to deceive."

Descended must be understood in a literal or metaphorical sense. The metaphorical sense is easy enough, if we apply it in general to our Lord's humiliation, which includes all His sufferings both of body and soul. But if *descended* is taken literally for a local descent, it requires limitations and must be guarded. Taking *Sheol, Hades, hell* in a general sense for the receptacle of the dead, both the grave and the future state of the dead, then we can see that *descended* was used specially in regard to the body, and means that it was laid in the grave—*descended* to the tomb and to the dust of death. Thus Jacob in his bitter wailing said, *I will go down,* descend *unto the grave,* Sheol—the common grave, the house appointed for all living, *unto my son mourning.* Now what did Jacob mean? Unquestionably, as I think, he meant, I shall die; my body will descend into the grave, dust to dust, whence it was taken, just as the body of my son has already done, and my soul will return to God who gave it, just as the soul of my son Joseph has done. He meant that whatever had happened to his son Joseph, both as to his body and to his soul when he died, would soon happen to him. When our Lord said: "No man hath ascended up to heaven, but he that descended from heaven" (Jo. iii. 13), He did not mean that He had descended or would descend into the place where the souls of the dead were detained separate from their bodies, nor to the place where the souls of men are tormented. He meant that He had come from heaven into this world. Nor is it probable the Apostle meant any thing more than just what our Lord meant—namely, the Incarnation, His descent from His Father's bosom to the womb of the Blessed Virgin, and to the sufferings of human life—the lower parts of the earth—in opposition to the heights of heaven. As when our Saviour said: "Ye are from beneath. I am from above: ye are of this world. I am not of this world;" and the phrase, "I will shew wonders in heaven above and signs in the earth beneath,"—the meaning is, this world which is below and heaven is above. This portion of Holy Scripture does not teach that Christ descended into any such a place as Purgatory, or Limbus, or Gehenna, when His body was laid in Joseph's tomb. For,

1. It is not proven, nor can it be proved, that the descent of which the Apostle is speaking was performed *after* his death at all. The contrary is strongly implied.

2. It is not proved, and cannot be proved, that the Apostle means the place of departed souls in any sense by the words *the lowest parts of the earth*. When Paul says, Christ descended into *the lower parts of the earth*, what does he mean? Does this mean any thing more than the whole state of Christ's humiliation? In his mind, according to Hebrew ideas, the universe was divided into two parts: the *upper*, which is heaven; and the *lower*, which is the earth. When Christ therefore came forth from the Father out of heaven, to be born of a woman, He descended into the lower parts of the earth—by clothing himself with human flesh. The Psalmist uses the words "lowest parts of the earth" metaphorically for the womb. "Thou hast covered me in my mother's womb. My substance was not hid from Thee, when I was made in secret, and curiously wrought in the lowest parts of the earth." Ps. cxxxix. 13, 15. "The lowest parts of the earth," then, may denote the earth itself, as opposed to the highest, which is heaven, and also those parts of it which are lower than others, and less known, obscure and hidden: and thus came to signify the place of burial. Thus in Ezekiel: "When I shall bring thee down with them that descend into the pit, with the people of old time, and shall set thee in the low parts of the earth." Again: "They are all delivered unto death, in the midst of the children of men, to the nether parts of the earth, with them that go down to the pit." Chrysostom calls death, *the lower parts of the earth*. Those that are buried are therefore said to be under the earth. *Theophylact* has briefly given the sense, saying: "It is manifest that He who was above, not only descended

into the earth, when He became incarnate ; but also into Hades when He died "—that is, He was buried. Even hell is used in the same sense—as opposed to heaven both in situation, dimension, and character. Thus Job says, when speaking of the unsearchableness of the Divine perfections: "It is high as heaven, what canst thou do? Deeper than hell, what canst thou know?" And *Amos* says: "Though they dig into hell, thence shall mine hand take them ; though they climb up into heaven, thence will I bring them down."

III. And now, as to the only other text I have time to notice, 1 Peter iii. 18-20, which is as follows: "For Christ also hath once suffered for sins, the just for the unjust, that he might bring us to God, being put to death in the flesh, but quickened by the Spirit : By which also he went and preached unto the spirits in prison ; Which sometime were disobedient, when once the long-suffering of God waited in the days of Noah, while the ark was a preparing, wherein few, that is, eight souls, were saved by water." This text the Article of the Church of England, by the Synod of Edward VI., claims as authority for believing that Christ's soul went to hell and preached to the spirits there. But I must say I do not think it admits of any such an interpretation. Even Augustine says that the difficulties of interpreting this place as many of the Fathers did, so as to make it support the actual descent of Christ's soul into hell, are so many and so great that he was ready to give it up ; and, in fact, he did at last declare that St. Peter's words did not belong to the doctrine of Christ's descent into hell.* In order to make this text prove that Christ descended into hell, it is

---

* The original is in Pearson on the Creed, p. 338. And the texts just commented on, see the Commentators generally.

necessary to show, (1.) that the spirit here spoken of is the *soul of Christ;* (2) that the time when he preached to the spirits in prison, referred to by the Apostle, was *after* his death, and *before* his resurrection. But neither of these conditions is possible. They are not in the text. The spirit here spoken of is not the soul of Christ, but the Holy Spirit, or the power of His Divinity. Let us look at this passage carefully. The Apostle's object is to exhort believers to suffer persecution patiently, and be ready always to give a reason for the hope that is in them, and to preserve a good conscience, although they suffered for righteousness' sake. [See the verses going before.] And to strengthen them, the Apostle presents the example of *Christ* himself also, Who hath once suffered (18–20 verses). It seems to me the only possible inference here is, as Christ suffered and yet conquered, so be of good cheer, you shall conquer also. The only points to be made emphatic in support of my views are,

1. Christ was put to death *in the flesh*—that is, in human nature.

2. *But was quickened by the Spirit*—which does not mean his human soul, but the Holy Spirit, the same by whom He was conceived ; and,

3. *By which* Spirit (19 ver.), He went and preached— that is, by the ministry of Noah, one hundred and twenty years—*unto the spirits in prison.* The only meaning of this passage, in the light of Revelation and common sense, is, that Jesus Christ, by his Holy Spirit, inspired Noah, and preached by Noah to the disobedient antediluvians, who are and were, when Peter wrote, in the prison of

hell—the place of lost souls.* In confirmation of this view,

1. Noah is expressly called in Scripture a preacher of righteousness.

2. The Apostle tells us elsewhere that the Spirit that was in the Patriarchs and Prophets of the Old Testament was the Spirit of Christ.

3. The inhabitants of the old world were disobedient, as here described, and were cut off for their sins. They were warned and called to repentance. And,

4. For this very purpose, the Apostle makes emphatic the preaching of Christ to them by Noah—to prove that they were without excuse. True, it had been said, "My Spirit shall not always strive with man." But God's Spirit—the Holy Spirit—the very same by whom Christ was conceived, and by which he was raised from the dead—did strive with them in the days of Noah, but they are now, says he, in prison, for they were *disobedient*, impenitent. They would not repent.

The place, honestly and thoroughly examined, then, is not to be interpreted figuratively—*spirits in prison* are not Gentiles and Jews in this world in the bonds of iniquity, and under the power of Satan; they are the poor lost souls of the old world who rejected the preaching of Noah. Nor does the place furnish a syllable of proof that Christ suffered himself the torments of Gehenna, either in his soul before he died, or when he died, or that his soul went to Gehenna before his burial and his resurrection, or that He preached the Gospel to souls in *Limbus*

---

* So Hammond, Barrow, Pearson, and a great many of the most learned and best authors.

Patrum, and took thence the Patriarchs and Prophets with him to Paradise. The great Calmet, a Roman Catholic, and a believer in Purgatory, frankly admits this text does not admit such a meaning, nor teach this doctrine.

It should be here remembered, that the opinion that Christ's soul went to hell to preach to the souls of men there, in order to save them by applying unto them the benefits of his death, is not to be taken as teaching universal salvation to all the lost. This is not the sense in which this doctrine was generally applied. This is not the meaning of Purgatory; although by *hell*, *Hades*, and *Inferni*, the Fathers who held this view understood the common receptacle of the souls of all men, both good and bad, yet it was not to the souls of the wicked that Christ preached, but to the souls of the Patriarchs, Prophets, and of the people of God. And as those who believed in a Saviour to come were kept out of heaven and shut up in Purgatory till He came, so, since his death, those who believe in Him as having come—as having already and actually suffered under Pontius Pilate, must also go to Purgatory. Certainly, this is a most gloomy, uncomfortable doctrine, and in my humble judgment altogether contrary to the Word of God. Nor can I believe this is the meaning of the Creed; nor do I believe that Christ ever preached in any such a place as hell, in the meaning of this interpretation:

1. Because the texts of the sacred writers produced as proofs do not admit of such an interpretation as favors this opinion.

2. The whole idea of Purgatory is borrowed from the Apocrypha and a corruption of heathen superstition.

3. The doctrine itself that Christ went to hell to preach the Gospel is false, and inconsistent with the nature of

the Gospel itself. The time does not allow me to dwell on this. But surely it is admitted: 1. That the souls of Noah and of the Patriarchs are not the *disobedient* spirits Peter tells us were in prison. Noah, and the Patriarchs and Prophets, are remarkable for their *obedience*—faith prompt, implicit. They were blessed with Divine favor before their death. They received their reward.

2. If faith in a Messiah to come was not sufficient, we have no reason to believe that faith in Jesus as the Messiah who has come is any more efficacious.

3. If preaching on earth is not effectual, we see no reason why it should be after death. If the living hear not Moses and the Prophets, neither would they be persuaded though one arose from the dead. And when dead, neither would they be persuaded if Christ and his Apostles were sent unto them.

4. In the nature of things, probation, trial, free agency, implies retribution, an end of the trial.

5. The Word of God everywhere teaches that it is grace, not sufferings—not the sufferings of the creature, but grace, that purifies, and saves.

6. We are not to expect deliverance from hell, because the Word of God teaches that the punishment of the wicked is without an end. The certainty of the future punishment of the wicked is as clearly and distinctly and earnestly taught in the Bible as is the happiness of the righteous. And that there is a place for the punishment of the incorrigibly wicked is as positively taught in the Bible as that there is a place for the dwelling of the godly; and the duration of the punishment of the wicked in the place of

future torment is described by the very same terms that are used to express the duration of the happiness of the pious. If the Word of God does not authorize and require our belief in a place of torment for those who disobey the Gospel, then it is impossible for us to prove from it that there is any such a place as heaven.

It seems proper to turn again for a few moments here to the opinion of Pearson. He says the word *Hades* in the Creed may be taken in its general sense for the state of the dead, or as meaning nothing more than that Christ was literally and truly buried; and yet he contends that the meaning of the Article on this subject, according to the Church of England, is, that Jesus went through the regions of sorrow and of hell in order to prove to us that we who believe in Him are delivered from the consequences of sin, so that we have nothing to fear from hell or the power of Satan.

As to this opinion, that Christ went to hell, not to suffer its torments, nor to preach to the spirits there in prison, but to triumph over Satan and all the powers of hell in their own dominions, and to show thus to His people that they have nothing to fear from hell and the grave, nor from the devil and his angels, let us remark:

1. It is true that Christ, having spoiled principalities and powers, did make a show of them openly, triumphing over them, and that when He ascended up on high, He led captivity captive, and gave gifts unto men. And it is true that believers are more than conquerors over sin and death, and hell and the grave, through Him that loved them, and died for them. But—

2. It is also true that this triumph is everywhere in the Scriptures ascribed to the death of Christ—not to his

descending into hell, but to *His Cross* and resurrection from the dead. There is not a single text or passage of the sacred writers that tells us that Christ descended into hell to triumph there over the devil. All those places which have been produced in favor of any such an opinion, we have found, when properly understood, wholly opposed to any such meaning. *Leading captivity captive* belongs to Christ's ascent, not to his descent. The spoiling of principalities and powers was on Calvary, and the fastening of the handwriting of ordinances was to the Cross, and the making a public show of his trophies—all refers to his death on the Cross. His triumphal arch is erected on Calvary, not in hell. His triumphal procession is not through the infernal region, but from the grave on earth to heaven. None of his glorious achievements are ascribed to his descent into hell. All is ascribed to his death and resurrection.

"—The Incarnate LORD,
Once bleeding, now triumphant for my sake,
I mark him, how, by seraph hosts adored,
He to earth's lowest cares is still awake.

"The sun and every vassal star,
All space beyond the soar of angel wings,
Wait on His word; and yet he stays his car
For every sigh a contrite suppliant brings.

"He listens to the silent tear
For all the anthems of the boundless sky—
And shall our dreams of music bar our ear
To His soul-piercing voice, forever nigh?

"Nay, gracious Saviour—but as now
Our thoughts have traced thee to thy glory-throne,
So help us evermore with thee to bow—
Where human sorrow breathes her lowly moan."*

---

* Keble.

The essential meaning of the Article is given in the marginal reading of the Catechism: "He continued in the state of the dead, and under the power of death, until the third day."

The words, "He descended into hell," mean that the soul of Christ was really separated from his body, and his body, being truly a dead body, was laid in the tomb. This was necessary, that as our Surety, the second Adam, He might undergo the condition of death—of the death penalty pronounced upon Adam—might be truly man in death as He was when living. He was born as other men are born. He lived and died, physically, as other men die. He appeared in this world in the similitude of sinful flesh, and went out of this world into the other and future world in the same similitude. He died from the same causes that produce death in any other man. He suffered, he bled, he cried out, he thirsted, he gave up the ghost as any other man. His body was as lifeless, as dead, as the body of the penitent thief at his side, when taken down from the cross. His body was laid in the grave in the ordinary way, and his soul went to God who gave it, just as the soul of Abraham did when he gave up the ghost. Christ's soul went to God according to his own wish and direction, when He commended it to his Father, and the soul of the penitent went with him. But as his conception was not like that of any other man, as He was conceived by the Holy Ghost, so He was the *Holy One*, and his body could not see corruption. The death penalty had exhausted itself when He gave up the ghost. But remember, my dear hearers, that He who thus suffered was the God-man, the Mediator, and that we have in all His sufferings and in all His triumphs a deep personal concern. For,

I. When He emptied himself of his glory—to descend to the womb of a woman, to the lowest parts of the earth —to engage in the great work His Father sent him to do in his state of humiliation—then He entered the palace of the strong man armed, namely, the devil, the enemy of God and man, but being stronger than the devil, He took from him all his armor in which he trusted, and divided his spoils—took from his list of charges against us, the long, heavy indictment against us, and the mortgage bond he held upon our souls for the heavy debts we are under, and He nailed the handwriting of ordinances that condemned us to his own cross, and satisfied Divine Justice by the sacrifice of himself, so that through the blood of the everlasting covenant, we who believe in Him shall be more than conquerors over sin and death, hell and the grave.

II. Behold, then, how much He loved us! How closely are we united to Him! He bore our iniquities, that we might be partakers of His heavenly glory. Are you then afflicted? Do you suffer hours of terrible darkness, when Satan seems almost to get possession of you, and you feel as if surely God has forgotten to be gracious? Then remember your dear Saviour's agonizing prayer: "O my Father, if it be possible, let this cup pass from me: nevertheless, not as I will, but as Thou wilt." And a few moments afterwards He prayed again, saying: "O my Father, if this cup may not pass away from me except I drink it, Thy will be done." And as it was not possible for it to pass away, so He drank it. But hark! what a piercing cry is this! "My God, my God, why hast thou forsaken me?" And Jesus, when he had thus cried, gave up the ghost.

III. My dear brethren, there is no enemy before us

that Christ has not already met and already defeated before us and for us, and so signally defeated that all His followers are sure to be more than conquerors in every conflict to which they are called on their way to His heavenly kingdom. Light shall surely arise after darkness. After the storm there is the happy haven into which we are certain to make a glorious entrance with all sails spread.

Are you not, then, willing to endure a little as soldiers of the Lord Jesus? Are you not willing to be conformed to Him in suffering, as you hope to be like Him in glory? For if we suffer with Him, we shall reign with Him. And since He drank the bitter cup of suffering, that the cup of grace might be offered to us, surely we should submit to the chastisements of His love; they are to strengthen our holy desires—try our devout affections and exercise our labor of love.

Dear friend, have you seen the Son of God in tears? Have you seen His bloody sweat? Have you heard His piercing cry when He died drinking the dregs of the cup of Divine wrath, and have you never in remembrance of Him taken your place at the Lord's Supper? He died for you—died to open to you the gate of heaven. Why then are you not converted and saved? Though indeed Christ were born a thousand times in Bethlehem, and crucified again on Calvary, and not born in thee, thou art eternally lost.

O, Almighty God, most gracious and merciful, raise up, we humbly pray Thee, thy power, and come among us, and create us anew in Christ Jesus, and with great might succor, strengthen, and help us by Thy grace; and whereas through our many sins, and shortcomings, and wickedness, we are sore let and hindered in running the race that is set before us; O, be graciously pleased, in thy sovereign mercy, speedily to help and deliver us, through the sacrifice and satisfaction of Thy Dear Son, our Lord, to whom, with Thee, and the Holy Ghost, be honor and glory, world without end. Amen.

XI.

CHRIST ROSE THE THIRD DAY.

"That like as Christ was raised up from the dead by the glory of the Father, even so we also should walk in newness of life."—ROM. vi. 4.

"Say not in thine heart, Who shall ascend into Heaven? (that is, to bring Christ down from above:) Or, Who shall descend into the deep? (that is, to bring up Christ again from the dead.) But what saith it? The word is nigh thee, even in thy mouth, and in thy heart: that is, the word of faith which we preach; that if thou shalt confess with thy mouth the Lord Jesus, and shalt believe in thine heart that God hath raised him from the dead, thou shalt be saved. For with the heart man believeth unto righteousness; and with the mouth confession is made unto salvation."—ROM. x. 6–10.

"For I delivered unto you first of all that which I also received, how that Christ died for our sins according to the Scriptures; and that he was buried, and that he rose again the third day according to the Scriptures," &c.—1 COR. xv. 3, 4.

So prominent is the fact of our Lord's resurrection in the preaching of the Apostles on the day of Pentecost and ever afterwards, as well as in some of their Epistles, that the truth of all we are taught in the New Testament concerning Christ depends on the fact of his resurrection. It is necessary to the proof of the Divinity of his person, the genuineness of his mission, the efficacy of his atonement, and the eternal life of his people. When Philip preached Jesus from Isaiah to the Ethiopian, he told him that the condition on which he might be baptized and saved was: "If thou believest with all thine heart." And the Ethiopian answered: "I believe that Jesus Christ is the Son of God." That is, he believed all that Philip had preached to him concerning the life, Messiahship, death, resurrection, and ascension of Jesus. That is, he preached as Paul preached, saying, "If thou shalt confess with thy mouth the Lord Jesus, and believe in thine heart that God hath raised him from the dead, thou shalt be saved." And so also Paul, in his discourse in the synagogue at Antioch (Acts xiii.), boldly declares that the voices of the Prophets read every Sabbath were fulfilled in the things which the Jewish rulers and people, with the Gentiles, did unto Jesus, and that Moses, David, and all their sacred writers had foretold the sufferings and death of the Messiah, just such sufferings, and just such a death and burial and resurrection as the admitted facts of the day declared to have been accomplished in Jesus of Nazareth, and that, therefore, He was the true Messiah of God. Nothing can excel the point and power of the Apostle's argument in this case. It is precisely the argument used by Peter on the day of Pentecost.

And it may be well here to observe, that whatever disputes have been carried on about the other Articles of our Creed by the Fathers and the Schoolmen, and by the theologians of the Reformation, they have almost universally agreed about this one. Among them all, it has been recognized as the corner-stone of the Church of God, without which it would fall to the ground, "the pillar of Christianity itself." Its nature, and the consequences inevitably flowing from it, if true, are of such importance that it is an essential, fundamental Article of our holy faith. The Apostle, in 1 Cor. xv., shows conclusively, that if Christ did not rise again the third day from the dead, according to the Scriptures, then we have no

Church, no Gospel, and Christianity itself is nothing. "And our preaching is vain, and your faith is also vain. Yea, and we are found false witnesses of God; because we have testified of God that He raised up Christ; whom He raised not up, if so be that the dead rise not. For if the dead rise not, then is not Christ raised; and if Christ be not raised, your faith is vain; ye are yet in your sins. But now is Christ risen from the dead, and become the first-fruits of them that slept. For since by man came death, by man came also the resurrection of the dead."

In the light of so many clear passages of Holy Scripture that assert, imply, or allude to the resurrection of Jesus, it is astonishing that any one claiming to be a Christian at all should deny it, or have any cavils about this Article of our Creed; and yet, according to the public journals, an assembly or synod of Protestant divines and laymen in Europe have passed solemn resolutions by a large majority vote, within the last few months, to the effect that we have no satisfactory and consistent account of the resurrection of the Lord Jesus.* In fact, the direct and inevitable tendency of all those theological speculations that throw doubts on the inspired authority of God's Word, and do not recognize the death of Christ as an atonement or vicarious sacrifice for sin, and do not receive the doctrine of justification by faith and salvation by free grace, is to ignore or set aside the doctrine of Christ's resurrection. It is of great importance, there-

---

* This Synod met in Nismes, France, in the summer of 1866. I refer to the proceedings as published at the time from memory, and simply as an illustration of the signs of apostasy in our day. I feel very confident that my allusion is fully supported by the published notices of the meeting. It is, however, exceedingly gratifying to know that Guizot, Pressensé, and others of like views, are making their influence felt in France in favor of the old faith of the Reformed French Church.

fore, to find an Article of our holy faith setting forth so clearly and firmly the fact that in all ages, from the time of the crucifixion and resurrection of Jesus, it has been most surely believed that "the third day He rose again from the dead." Such testimony from the voice of the holy apostolic universal Church is a safeguard for those who love the truth as it is in Jesus. According to the Scriptures, the Church on earth is God's witness to testify concerning the Lord Jesus, His Holy Anointed One, and is especially set forth in the world to bear witness of His resurrection from the dead. Thus, in choosing Matthias, it is said: "Wherefore of these men, which have companied with us all the time that the Lord Jesus went in and out among us, must one be ordained to be *a witness with us of his resurrection.*" And accordingly God did pre-design witnesses for this purpose—such persons as were best fitted to give the proper testimony—persons well qualified to know and state the truth, and sufficient in number to establish a fact by law. They were so well acquainted with our Lord's person before his death, and admitted to such familiar intercourse with him after his resurrection, that it is impossible for them to have been themselves deceived. Nor are we able to discover any possible motive they could have had to deceive others. And besides the many separate, distinct appearances of our Lord to different parties, at different times and under different circumstances, and for the space of forty days, we have the testimony of above five hundred eye-witnesses that He did appear alive in his human body after his resurrection, and gave them such tokens and signs of the identity of the body in which He appeared to them with the body in which He was crucified, that they did firmly believe in the reality of his resurrection; and He the more convinced them of this by continuing with them and speaking to them many things concerning the kingdom of God. And as we do not see how it was possible for so many eye-witnesses to be deceived, or to desire to deceive others, so we are not able to conceive how it was possible for them to have succeeded in deceiving themselves or the world in such a matter of fact as this, if they had been wicked and reckless enough to have tried to do so.

In the two Discourses already delivered on the fifth Article of our Creed, it was my object to show in what sense our Lord *descended into hell*, and that whatever Gehenna or Purgatory may or may not be, our Creed knows nothing of them. As I am now travelling on the line of the Apostles' Creed, I do not wish to be turned aside to other discussions, however important they may be. The other clause of the fifth Article is: "*The third day He rose again from the dead.*" This is a distinct, positive proposition, and I propose, with God's assistance, the following method: namely,

FIRST. A brief history of the Article, and some exposition of its main particulars. And the

SECOND Discourse, for next Sabbath evening, if the Lord be pleased to grant us his blessing, will be a brief historical demonstration of the truth of our Lord's resurrection.

I. HISTORICALLY, we find this Article in all the ancient creeds just as it stands in the Apostles' Creed, coming after our Lord's burial or descent into hell, and followed by his ascension, sitting at the right hand of the Father Almighty, and coming to judgment. There are no essential variations in its wording—no variations at all except as to some small matters of mere taste as to the use or omission of "again," or "from the dead," some considering these words as implied in *He rose*, and not necessary to the meaning. This Article was inserted in the symbols of the Church's faith in ancient times, and preserved with fidelity just as we have it; *first*, because it is stated with singular emphasis by the Apostles; and, *secondly*, because it was a proper denial of many foolish and wicked conceits that were taught by false teachers even in Apostolic times. For we learn from *Paul* to Timothy that there were false teachers in his day who said "the resurrection was already past." 2 Tim. ii. 18. And from 1 Cor. xv. 12, that there were some who said "there is no resurrection of the dead." The Sadducees, who denied a future state, and denied all resurrection, did not of course admit the resurrection of Christ. The Essenes, who seem to have been quite a large sect in the first centuries of our era, believed in the immortality of the soul, but denied the resurrection of the body. Then, of course, Simon Magus, the Docetæ, and all the errorists of those days who denied the real and proper humanity of our Lord Jesus, denied also the reality of his resurrection and ascension. Augustine tells us, that the Cerinthians held that Jesus, whom they took to be a mere man, had not risen, but was yet to rise. Apelles, a disciple of Marcion, held that when Christ came from heaven, He formed for himself as He descended an airy and sidereal flesh, but when He arose and ascended into heaven, He restored this body to its pristine elements, which being thus dispersed, His spirit alone returned to heaven.*

It does not seem to me necessary, or for our edification, to have at present any further details concerning the fables and conceits of many men who have tried to be wise above what is written in the Word of God for our

---

* Browne, p. 99, and our Appendix.

instruction concerning the resurrection of Christ. Quite enough has been said to show that the strong language of the Article in the Church of England, and in our Confession of Faith, and in our Catechism, and in the Catechism of Heidelberg, is justified, and was no doubt designed to oppose the exaggerated opinions that were advanced on the one hand by those who taught that our Lord's body after his ascension had ceased to be human, by being transubstantiated into his Divinity; and to oppose also, on the other hand, the absurd views entertained by all those who denied the verity of his essential humanity.

The words of our standards on this point are: "On the third day He arose from the dead, with the same body in which he suffered; with which also He ascended into heaven, and there sitteth at the right hand of the Father, making intercession."—*Conf. Faith*, Chap. viii. sec. 4. And the Fourth Article, Church of England, says, "Christ did truly rise again from death, and took again his body, with flesh, bones, and all things appertaining to the perfection of a Man's nature, wherewith He ascended into heaven, and there sitteth until He return to judge all men at the last day." The same doctrines are taught in the symbols or formularies of the faith of the Christian world; but perhaps nowhere set forth with more clearness and emphasis than in the questions 51 and 52 of the Larger Catechism, with their answers, which are as follows:

Q. 51. What was the estate of Christ's exaltation?

A. The estate of Christ's exaltation comprehendeth his resurrection, ascension, sitting at the right hand of the Father, and his coming again to judge the world.

Q. 52. How was Christ exalted in his resurrection?

A. Christ was exalted in his resurrection, in that, not having seen corruption in death (of which it was not possible for him to be held), and having the very same body in which he suffered, with the essential properties thereof (but without mortality and other common infirmities belonging to this life), really united to his soul, he rose again from the dead the third day by his own power; whereby he declared himself to be the Son of God, to have satisfied Divine Justice, to have vanquished death and him that had the power of it, and to be Lord of quick and dead. All which he did as a public person, the Head of his Church, for their justification, quickening in grace, support against enemies, and to assure them of their resurrection from the dead at the last day.

In the proposition of the Creed: THE THIRD DAY HE ROSE AGAIN FROM THE DEAD, there are three particulars to be noticed:

I. The simple statement of the fact itself, *He rose again.*

II. "He rose again from *the dead.*" And,

III. He rose again from the dead *the third day.*

The thing affirmed is the resurrection of Christ,—the action itself. *He rose again.* This part of our subject may be dealt with in this way: namely, *First*, show from the Hebrew Scriptures that the ancient Jewish Church believed that the Messiah was to rise from the dead; and, *Secondly*, show from the New Testament that Jesus of Nazareth did rise from the dead just as it was promised and foretold the Messiah should do; and, therefore, we believe this Article is true, and that Jesus is the true and only Messiah. This is the line of argument offered by Bishop Pearson.

I. It is directly and repeatedly declared by the Apostles, as well as by our Saviour himself, that his sufferings and resurrection were *according to the Scriptures.* Paul asserts, in one of the places cited in the beginning of this Discourse, that he constantly preached that Jesus rose again from the dead the *third day, according to the Scriptures.* And our Lord himself, in his discoursing with the two disciples on the road to Emmaus, after they had recited to him the things which had just come to pass in Jerusalem; namely, that Jesus of Nazareth, a Prophet mighty in deed and word before God and all the people, had been delivered by the chief priests and rulers to be condemned to death, and that He had actually been crucified, and besides all this, to-day, said they, is the third day since these things were done. Yea, and certain women also of our company made us astonished which were early at the sepulchre; and when they found not his body, they came, saying, that they had also seen a vision of angels, which said that He was alive. And certain of them which were with us went to the sepulchre, and found it even so as the women had said; but Him they saw not. Then said Jesus unto them, O fools and slow of heart to believe *all that the prophets have spoken:* Ought not Christ (who is the Messiah) to have suffered these things, and to enter into his glory? And beginning at Moses and all the Prophets, he expounded unto them in all the Scriptures the things concerning himself. And afterwards, late in the evening, after long communing with them, when, as they say themselves, their hearts were burning within them, *unconsciously* testifying of Jesus while He talked with them, and while He opened to them the Scriptures—for all this time " their eyes were holden that they should not know him"—but when it was towards evening, "he opened their eyes and they knew him; and he vanished out of their sight. And they rose up the same hour and returned to Jerusalem, and found the eleven gathered together, and them that were with them, *Saying, the Lord is risen indeed and hath appeared to Simon.*"

Observe here, 1. That the Jews then had and acknowledged as their Holy Scriptures the very same books that we have, and spoke of them as consisting of the same divisions that we recognize. Our Saviour speaks of "Moses and *all* the Prophets, and expounded, unto them in *all* the Scriptures." And in the verses following, when He appeared to the disciples and did eat a piece of broiled fish and honeycomb, He said unto them, These are the words which I spake unto you while I was yet with you, that *all things must be fulfilled which were written in the law of Moses, and in the Prophets, and in the Psalms, concerning me.*

2. It was then admitted by the Jewish Church that their Scriptures did promise and speak of a Messiah to come. When these two disciples had recited the facts of the sufferings, death, and resurrection of Jesus of Nazareth, our Lord immediately replied that these were the very things their own prophets had spoken concerning the Messiah. *Ought not Christ*—which you know is the Greek for Messiah—ought not this Jesus of Nazareth, who claimed to be the Messiah, and who was as you believe the Messiah—who should have redeemed Israel; I say, if Jesus of whom you speak was indeed the Redeemer of Israel, as you once hoped he was, *ought* He not, according to your Prophets, to have suffered precisely these things and to enter into His glory? And then to prove this, "*beginning at Moses and all the Prophets,* He

expounded unto them in all the Scriptures the things concerning himself." And,

3. On the very same point, and at the same time, as a proof also that Jesus had foretold his sufferings and resurrection to his disciples, observe what He says to them when He appeared to them after his resurrection, and when they were so terrified and affrighted, and supposed that they had seen a spirit, that in order to calm their troubled hearts, and give them the strongest assurance that it was He himself, their own real and true Lord and Master, that He said: "Behold my hands and my feet, that it is I myself. Handle me, and see; for a spirit hath not flesh and bones as ye see me have. And when He had thus spoken, He shewed them His hands and His feet. And then they gave Him a piece of a broiled fish and of an honeycomb, and He took it and did eat before them. And He said unto them, *These are the words which I spake unto you, while I was yet with you, that all things must be fulfilled, which were written in the law (that is, in the five books of Moses), and in the Prophets, and in the Psalms, concerning me.*" These are the words, said Jesus, that is, the things that have come to pass in these days here in Jerusalem, and about which you are so much concerned, and which are just the things I was in the habit of talking to you about. I taught them to you out of your own Scriptures. They are the things concerning me which you should believe. And "then opened He their understanding, that they might understand the Scriptures. And He said unto them, Thus it is written, and thus it behoved Christ to suffer, and to rise from the dead the third day: and that repentance and remission of sins should be preached in his name among all nations, beginning at Jerusalem. And ye are witnesses of these things." Luke xxiv.

So clearly do the Hebrew Scriptures speak of a suffering Messiah as well as of a glorious and conquering and reigning and exalted Messiah, that modern Jewish doctors have held that there were to be *two* Messiahs: one to fulfil the prophecies concerning the suffering Messiah, whose earthly sorrows were to end in a bloody death; and the other to fulfil the predictions concerning a Messiah who was to conquer and reign as the Son of David, and restore their nation to the golden age and land of their fathers.* It is not necessary to spend a breath in proving that the Scriptures know nothing of *two* Messiahs. There is but one Mediator between God and men. Nor can it need illustration in such a presence as this, that both classes of the Hebrew texts concerning the Messiah who was to come—both those that foretell his sufferings and the glory that should follow, as Moses and Elias did on the mount of transfiguration, are fulfilled in Jesus of Nazareth. The things foretold as to happen to the Messiah, are the very things which did happen to Jesus of Nazareth. The predictions of a suffering Messiah were fulfilled in his state of humiliation, and the predictions of a conquering, exalted, and reigning Messiah are fulfilled in his state of exaltation. "For Him hath God exalted with his right hand to be a Prince and a Saviour." But I have not time, nor do I think it necessary, to enter further upon details to prove that the Jewish Church believed in a Messiah who was to rise from the dead. For all those places in the Psalms and in the Prophets that speak of his sufferings and death, and then of his glory, and of his kingdom, involve the necessity of his resurrection from the dead. According also to the types, as well as to fulfil the prophetic oracles, the Messiah

---

* Pacatumque regot, patriis virtutibus, orbem. See Vth Discourse.

promised to the Jewish Church was to rise from the dead. And now, *secondly*, that Jesus of Nazareth did rise from the dead the third day, as our Article affirms, and just as it was promised in the Old Testament Scriptures the Messiah should do, I have need only to point you to the history of the event itself in the Gospels, and the repeated declarations and allusions to it by the Apostles in their discourses and Epistles. But just here I only wish to say on this point, that if the proofs of the resurrection of Jesus Christ are not sufficient to establish its truth, then no matter of fact on earth can be established by testimony. As a "sturdy" old author says—to refuse the proof we have of the resurrection of Jesus, "is in effect to decline all proof by testimony, to renounce all certainty in human affairs, to remove all grounds of proceeding securely in any business or administration of justice, to impeach all history of fabulousness, to charge all mankind with insufficiency of perception, or extreme infidelity, and to thrust God away from bearing credible attestation in any case."*

II. The second particular which I am to notice is that "HE ROSE AGAIN FROM THE DEAD." The subject of this affirmation, *He*, is Jesus Christ, who "suffered under Pontius Pilate, was crucified, dead and buried: He descended into hell. The third day he rose again from the dead." And still more, it is of his human nature this affirmation is made. As to his Divinity, no accession of glory is predicable. God is the highest, and cannot ascend. He is always the ever blessed and unchangeable in all His perfections. The words, "He rose again from the dead"—imply, 1. That He was really dead. This

---

* Quoted from Barrow in Bethune, vol. i. p. 436.

has been proved beyond the possibility of doubt. His friends, his enemies, the Roman guard, Pilate and the centurion, have all given their testimony that his death was real. The piercing of his side by the soldier's spear itself was enough to make sure of his death. 2. He was also actually buried—laid in the new tomb of Joseph of Arimathea, in a garden. Although He was so soon to rise again, yet He was honored with a solemn funeral, and His burial was according to the Scriptures, and the marks of honor bestowed upon Him at His funeral completed the evidences that in His state of humiliation he met all the requirements of the promised Messiah. He was not carried from his own house to his tomb, but from a Roman cross, by a small but honorable and select train, who were unable from the shortness of the time to prepare His body as they wished for His burial. It was not the burial of an earthly conqueror, but of the Prince of Life, who even then held in his hands the keys of death and hell. The rent veil, the opened graves, and the earthquake after the darkened sun, attested that it was God's own Son that was laid in the tomb. His body was not enclosed in a coffin of wood or iron, as with us, but was laid in a recess or niche—on a kind of shelf somewhat like a vault in our house of reception for dead bodies, except that it was the side and not the head that was toward the open court. Nor was there any wall, door, or slab to fill the mouth of the vault or recess where the body was laid. To fully understand the passages of the Gospel narratives of the burial and resurrection of our Lord, we must remember some minute matters concerning Jewish sepulchres. They differed in several particulars from our ordinary graveyards. The sepulchres of wealthy Jews were made out of caverns in the rocks. Sometimes a natural cave was selected, and cut and changed to their taste. Others cut their tombs out of the living rock—this was the way Joseph's tomb was made. It was *hewn out of a rock*. There was then no possible outlet from it, or way to get into it but by the door. Let this be noted. It was hewn out of the solid, living limestone rock. Ordinarily the entrance into such a sepulchre was first a descent into an open area, or kind of court, the covering of which was the living rock itself, and then, if you looked around on each side, you would see a recess some six feet or more lower than the area in which you are standing. And these recesses also had cavities or niches of their own, in which the dead bodies were laid. Of course their sepulchres were not always precisely of the same shape or size. This is a description of an ordinary one, such as might have belonged to a man of wealth, like Joseph of Arimathea. Usually there were places in such a tomb for twelve or fifteen bodies, or more if the family was very large. There is no difficulty then in our record, which speaks of John and Peter having entered into the sepulchre where our Lord was laid, "and, stooping down, looked into the place," the niche below the entrance area, where the body of our dear Lord had been laid. But while the rest are standing in the area, and looking down into the receptacles where the dead bodies were to be placed, Peter, true to his nature, actually descends, and goes to the very recess whence the dead body of Jesus had just risen. [See Lightfoot and Witsius.]

Five circumstances are to be noted in the narrative. (1.) Our Lord's tomb was not in the family vault of Joseph the carpenter of Nazareth, but the sepulchre of Joseph of Arimathea. Our Lord was not born in a house belonging to his reputed father, nor was He buried in a tomb that was his own. He was born and lived among the poor, but had his tomb with the rich; for the Scriptures cannot be broken. He lived in other mens' houses, and his body was embalmed at the expense of his friends, and then laid to rest in another man's tomb. (2.) It was a tomb *hewn out of the rock*. There were no concealed passages in the earth, through which the body could have been removed. (3.) It was a *new tomb*—one in which no man had ever been laid. Joseph belonged to a provincial town. His father was not buried in Jerusalem. But he, having risen to distinction, being now a member of the Sanhedrim, and residing in Jerusalem, has prepared himself a tomb. And Providence so orders all this that no suspicion could arise about the identity of our Lord's person when He arose from the dead, or any one be able to say that it was some other person who had risen in his place, or that he had arisen by virtue of having touched the bones of some old prophet who had been buried there before him, after the example of the case spoken of in 2 Kings xiii. 21. (4.) It was a new tomb *in a garden*—which, among the Jews, was often the case. You remember our Lord's last passion of the bloody sweat began in a garden—so his humiliation was concluded in a garden, and thence He rose to glory. The sepulchre, says *Burkitt*, was in a garden, to expiate Adam's sin committed in a garden ; as by the sin of the first Adam we were driven out of Paradise, the garden of delights and heaven-like pleasures ; so by the sufferings of the second Adam, the Lord from heaven, our Mediator, who lay buried in a garden, we may hope to gain a joyful entrance into the Heavenly Paradise itself. And well may we ask, where else could He have been buried with more propriety than in a garden, who, like Aaron's rod, was to bud forth again on the third day, and to whose death, burial, and resurrection it is owing that our bodies shall again, like reviving grass, come forth from the earth? So Witsius. (5.) Our Lord's tomb was near the place of the crucifixion, in the immediate neighborhood of the place of the punishment of convicted persons, so that he did indeed make his grave with the wicked—that is, surrounded by them and among them, though not of them. The words, therefore: "*He rose again from the dead,*" are emphatic—they do not mean that He had risen once before, and that this was the second time He rose from the dead. They are intended to express that it was He himself who rose—the very same soul and body—the same soul that he committed to God when He gave up the ghost on the cross—entered again into the very same body that had hung on the cross, and had been embalmed and laid in Joseph's new tomb; that his reasonable soul and true body were actually united again. The saints who rose out of their graves at his resurrection received new bodies, for their old ones had decayed; but our Lord's body did not see corruption. His body was truly dead. His soul was altogether and completely out of his body. The separation between his body and soul was as complete as between the body and soul of a believer now at death; but there was no dissolution of his body in the sense of decay, or of the separation of its constituent elements. His body was saved from the first or faintest approach of putrefaction. For as Christ was conceived by the Holy Spirit, and suffered only in so far as He was our Surety, and as the work of atonement was completed when the sacrifice was made, and He himself said, "It is finished, and gave up the ghost;" so it was not possible for His body to be holden in the grave so as to see corruption. There was none of Adam's sin resting on it, nor was the guilt of any actual transgression found in all His life. He was holy, harmless, the innocent Son of God. The honor of his burial, after his death, with the rich, is ascribed by the Prophet to his immaculate character: "Because he had done no violence, neither was any deceit in his mouth." Isa. liii. 9. There were causes proper and natural to retard the work of corruption, such as the embalming with the precious spices, but doubtless as far as necessary it was the effect of miraculous or supernatural power. For in addition to the reason just intimated, that as his sufferings were now at an end—the penalty ceasing with his death—and as he knew no sin, neither original nor actual; so there was nothing in His body that corruption could seize on. And besides, it was necessary also that His body should not see corruption, by being turned into dust, so that its identity might be so clearly seen that no doubt could be raised on that point.

III. The third particular affirmed is that He rose the *third day*, on which I need not dwell long. In Matt. xii. 40, our Lord said to the Scribes and Pharisees, who demanded of Him a sign, that no sign should be given to them "but the sign of the Prophet Jonas; For as Jonas was three days and three nights in the whale's belly; so shall the Son of Man be three days and three nights in the heart of the earth." Here it is to be observed,

1. The history of Jonas was then known to the Jews.

2. It was received by them as a true history. Our Lord appeals to it as both genuine and authentic. And,

3. The Prophet Jonas was in this matter a type of our Lord's burial and resurrection.*

Now three days and nights, according to Hebrew reckoning, means any part of two days having two nights and one whole day between them. This mode of compu-

---

* See VIIIth Discourse.

ting time prevails still in the East. When travelling in Bible Lands, I was frequently put in quarantine for three days and nights, as at Hebron and Smyrna—the meaning of which was, that I was hurried off to the quarantine grounds just before sunset, kept there the following night, next day, and the following night, and then next morning at sunrise discharged, as having fulfilled my quarantine of three days and three nights, not forgetting the *backshish*. That this is the true view of the Jewish mode of computing time is seen conclusively in the circumcision of a child, which you know was to be on the eighth day, but any unexpired portion of the day of the child's birth, however short, was reckoned as one of the entire days, and circumcision was performed on the eighth day, that is, upon the day week from birth—the eight days including the first and the last. Bishop Pearson illustrates the Hebrew usage by the third day ague, which is so called, though there be but one day's intermission between the paroxysms thereof, and hence, to make it *tertian*, the first and third days are both included in the computation. There are instances in the Bible also in which it is clearly seen that eight days mean only six full days, counting the fragment of the day at the beginning of the reckoning and the fragment of the day at its close, which, being held as two days, make the eight. In our Lord's resurrection the facts are thus: He was crucified and buried on the *day of preparation for* the Jewish Paschal Sabbath, which is our Friday. His body was laid in a tomb before sunset on Friday, which was counted by the Jews as one day. He remained in the tomb that night and all the following day and night, which was the Jewish Sabbath, and answers to our Saturday. Then early the next day, which was the first day of the Jewish week, and answers to our Lord's day, He rose again from the dead.

And thus were fulfilled the Scriptures and His own promise kept. The third day, on which He rose, is our Sabbath. The learned Witsius adds here, and elaborates it with his usual eloquence, that our Lord's resurrection was in the Spring of the year, which he considers an emblem. This is an accommodation I do not fancy.

IF, THEN, it is still asked, Why did our Lord continue three days, and but three days, according to Jewish reckoning, in the grave? Our answer is,

1. So much depended upon His resurrection, that sufficient space between His death and resurrection was given, that every reasonable and proper proof might be furnished of the reality of His death.

2. But he did not continue under the power of death any longer, because this third day was the time required by the types and our Lord's own prediction for him to rise. The proof, moreover, of His resurrection was more easy and determinate then than it could have been if the time of rising had been prolonged.

And now from this brief review of the Article from a historic point of view, I ask, have we not proofs quite sufficient to demonstrate the truth of this Article, as far as the nature of such a subject admits of demonstration? *First.* We hold that the resurrection of Jesus is an Article of Faith resting upon testimony *purely historical.* Nor is there any defect in the evidence. There is no broken link in the chain. The Scriptures at once and boldly remove the objection that such a thing as the resurrection of the human body is impossible, by ascribing it in our Lord's case, and in every case, directly to the power of God. St. Paul introduces his argument about the resurrection of the human body by declaring that God gives to every seed its own body. So also is the resurrection of the dead. There is no antecedent presumption that can make the resurrection of the body incredible. For as a simple act of Almighty power, the resurrection, to say the least of it, is in no way more marvellous or more to be cavilled at than the creation of man at first. Besides, except among the Sadducees, the Jews cherished a traditional faith in the doctrine of the resurrection from the dead in order to the highest happiness of the future state. It is clearly demonstrated in our Lord's discourse with the Sadducees on this subject that the resurrection of the dead was an Article of faith in the Jewish Church. "But as touching the resurrection of the dead, have ye not read that which was spoken unto you by God, saying, I am the God of Abraham, and the God of Isaac, and the God of Jacob? God is not the God of the dead, but of the living."

And in his preaching before Agrippa, you remember Paul appeals boldly to the king's reason on the subject: "Why should it be thought a thing incredible with you that God should raise the dead?" And again, when preaching at Thessalonica, in the Jewish synagogue, on the Sabbath days, he *reasoned* with the people out of the Scriptures, opening and alleging that Christ must needs have suffered and risen again from the dead; and that this Jesus, whom he preached unto them, is the Christ, the promised Messiah. And then on Mars' hill he preached to the Athenians, reasoning from the works of creation, and the admitted sayings of their own poets, that the only true God was Jehovah, the Creator of all things, and that He was to be worshipped, and not images of gold and silver or stone, graven by art and man's device. And that He now commandeth all men everywhere to repent. BECAUSE he hath appointed a day in which He will judge the world in righteousness by that man whom He hath ordained; whereof He hath given assurance unto all men, in that He hath raised him from the dead. Acts xvii. 2, 3, and 30, 31. Here the Apostle plainly sets forth that the raising of Jesus from the dead is the most persuasive and convincing of all arguments for the truth of his Messiahship that could be used. We see our Lord's humiliation in his birth and the circumstances of his life, and in his sufferings and death, and we see the favor of God demonstrated in his resurrection. "For though He was crucified out of weakness, yet He liveth by the power of God." His resurrection was a miracle of the greatest power. It is recorded out of *Pliny* that he reckoned two things impossible, even to God himself; namely, *to endow mortals with eternity, and to recall the dead to life.** And yet in our Lord's resurrection we have both these impossibilities realized, and so realized that Jesus is the life and the resurrection, and by his Gospel life and immortality are brought to light. In raising our Saviour to life, God the Father declared his special love to Him, his approbation of His work as Mediator, and acceptance of it as completely meeting all his demands. It is in this sense St. Paul explains the Psalm concerning the Messiah: This day have I begotten thee. That is, this day was He declared to be the Son of God by the resurrection from the dead.

Secondly. Our Lord himself distinctly told his disciples that He must rise again the third day after his death. He made repeated declarations of this kind, and so widely was the fact known that He had given such assurance to his friends, that his enemies did all in their

---

* Mortales æternitate donare et revocare defunctos.

power to frustrate any collusory attempt on the part of His followers to give the semblance of verification to his words—to the fact that he had announced in the early part of his ministry, in figurative language, saying, "Destroy this temple, and in three days I will raise it up;" but the Evangelist adds, "This he spake of the temple of his body." And if his friends forgot this, his enemies did not. They made it a matter of accusation against him before Caiaphas, and taunted him with it as He hung bleeding on the cross, while, as it appears from their conduct after his death, they knew perfectly well they were perverting his words, and accusing him of saying what he had never meant. Oh, with what a fiendish hypocrisy did they come to the Roman governor, asking for a guard to be placed over the sepulchre; "for we remember," said they, "that that deceiver said, while he was yet alive, After three days I will rise again. Command, therefore, that the sepulchre be made sure until the third day." And accordingly a guard was set, and the tomb was sealed.

I have only time to add, that we do not believe that our Lord's body was absorbed into his Divinity, or that it was changed into a spirit; but that it remained truly a human body; yet it was divested of all that was mortal or corruptible—of all that was attached to it in consequence of his taking our place to die in our stead. As He lived in the similitude of sinful flesh—in our nature, when He lived—subject to our earthly accidents, as hunger, thirst, sleep, work, pain, and death; so He lives after the spirit, that is, in the similitude of the spiritual body, when He was taken up from the earth in the body with which he was raised from the dead—which body* is

---

* This is the sense of a passage quoted by Browne, p. 101, from Theophylact.

incorruptible, unchangeable, and is the model after which our bodies are to be fashioned in the resurrection. As the union between the Divinity and the humanity of Christ was not dissolved by death, nor by his burial, so neither is the union between believers and Christ dissolved by death. As Christ's body rested in hope in the grave, so the believer hath hope in his death. How sweet are the lines of a Christian poet,* in view of death, saying :

> "Hide me in my Saviour's grave
> Till thy wrath is all o'erpast—
> Summoned to my heavenly home,
> Then I shall with joy reply,
> Answering to thy call, *I come*,
> Gladly get me up and die ;
> Made, and bought by grace divine,
> Thine I am, forever thine."

Yes, *forever thine*, for Christ both died and rose from the dead as a public person, the Head of his Church, for the justification of His people, their "quickening in grace, support against enemies, and to assure them of their resurrection from the dead at the last day." He could say, and no one else could have so said: *I am the resurrection and the life. He that believeth in me, though he were dead, yet shall he live. And whosoever liveth and believeth in me, shall never die.* Our Lord's resurrection is the seal and pledge and model of our resurrection. Now is Christ risen from the dead, and become the first fruits—which are a pledge of a full and glorious harvest —the first fruits of them that slept. For as Christ is risen, so them also that sleep in Jesus will God bring with Him. The Head living in glory, the members must

---

* Rev. C. Wesley.

be there also. Because I live, said the blessed Saviour, ye shall live also, and where I am, there shall ye be also. Blessed be God, our life is hid with Christ in God, "and when Christ, who is our life, shall appear, then shall we also appear with Him in glory." "Forever blessed be the God and Father of our Lord and Saviour Jesus Christ, who according to his abundant mercy hath begotten us again unto a lively hope by the resurrection of Christ from the dead to an inheritance incorruptible, undefiled, reserved in heaven for those who are kept by the power of God through faith unto salvation." Amen.

XII.

THE RESURRECTION HISTORICALLY DEMONSTRATED.

"For I delivered unto you first of all— * * And that He was buried, and that He rose again the third day according to the Scriptures."—1 COR. xv. 3, 4.

IN the Discourse last Sabbath evening, I offered you, *First*, some brief remarks on the importance of this Article of our Creed—showing that it was the key-stone, without which the whole arch must fall to the ground. *Secondly*. I explained the history of the Article and the reasons for adopting its phraseology. *Thirdly*. The main particulars of the Article—namely, He *rose*, He rose *again*, and He rose again the *third day*, were explained. It was found: *First*. That the Jewish Church believed in a Messiah who was to suffer and die, and to rise from the dead. *Secondly*. It was also found that *Jesus of Nazareth* suffered and died, was buried and rose from the dead, precisely as the promised Messiah of the Jewish Church was to do; and our conclusion—and certainly it seems to us a fair and an inevitable conclusion—is, that Jesus is the true and only Messiah. It is my purpose now, with God's blessing, to offer you—

I. A summary of the evidence on which we believe this Article—that Christ rose from the dead the third day according to the Scriptures.

II. The Effects or Benefits resulting from His resurrection.

I. A summary of the evidence in behalf of the truth of our Lord's resurrection. And on this head we may remark, that our Lord's resurrection from the dead is not absurd or incredible in itself. In the history of his life and death, as well as in the whole history of the Jewish Church before his mysterious Incarnation, and in the history and existence of the Christian Church at this very hour, we have very strong presumptive proof of the truth of his resurrection from the dead, just as it lies before us in the Evangelical Memoirs, and in the Discourses and Epistles of his Apostles. All cavils about the resurrection of Christ, as to its impossibility, are silenced at once by resolving it into the power of Divinity. St. Paul boldly meets this objection in regard to the resurrection of believers by his argument from the growth of plants from seed. He declares, you remember, that "*that* which thou sowest is not quickened, except it die. And that which thou sowest, thou sowest not that body that shall be, but bare grain, it may chance of wheat, or of some other grain: But God giveth it a body as it hath pleased him, and to every seed his own body. So also is the resurrection of the dead." God giveth to every one his own body. Nor is there any antecedent presumption why the raising of the body is more incredible than its original creation. The same Almighty power that created man at first out of the dust of the ground, can raise his body in the resurrection. And besides, it is certainly a presumptive argument of no small force to look at the consequences. For such is the relation of the fact of Christ's resurrection to Christian doctrines, that it is their only support, and the foundation of Christian faith. It is the key-stone of the arch. If Christ is not risen from the dead, "Christianity is the most consummate imposture" that the world has ever seen. But if Christianity is the result of a base conspiracy, how can we account for its fruits in the world? What consistent, intelligible account does any one give of the ordinances, institutions, and effects of Christianity, who denies the resurrection of Jesus? The Lord's Day, the existence of the Church itself, proves the truth of our Lord's resurrection. This doctrine must be true, or we must abandon every thing that belongs to the Gospel. All our hope of salvation depends on the truth of what the Apostles preached, and the Creed of the Church has always declared, that Jesus Christ rose from the dead the third day. If Christ be not risen, our preaching is indeed foolishness, and your faith is vain; ye are yet in your sins, and we are all false witnesses. And they also which are fallen asleep in Christ are all perished. But now is Christ risen from the dead, and ever lives and reigns as an Almighty Saviour. And "if thou shalt confess with thy mouth the Lord Jesus, and shalt believe in thine heart that God hath raised him from the dead, thou shalt be saved."

II. In the second place, we do not rest our belief on presumptive proof alone. We have abounding *positive evidence of the truth of this great fact*, which is as strong as the nature of the case admits. And as a specimen of this kind of evidence, may I ask you to read, *first*, an account of our Lord's death and burial, as in John xx. 38-42, compared with what the other Evangelists say on the same points—as in Matthew xxvii. 57-66; Mark xvi. 1-7. And, *secondly*, the narrative of our sacred writers concerning his resurrection, especially in Matthew xxviii. 1-15. Also Luke xxiii. 55, 56; xxiv. 1-9. John xxi. 1-10.

First, then, may I not ask any one who reads this account of our Lord's death and burial and resurrection: Is there not in it internal evidence that it is a simple, staightforward, natural account of just what eye-witnesses saw, heard, and believed? Is there in any part of these records any particle of evidence against the honesty of the writers? Is there, in regard to any particular, the slightest or smallest sign of a made-up story? Do not "Fictions usually go naked of circumstances?" The events described in them are said to have happened "once upon a time;" but the narrators do not tell us when, nor where, nor how; or, if they do profess to give us such details, it is done in such a way that we can never find the place nor identify the parties, nor get a solid foundation for the things stated as facts. Whereas our sacred writers have, each in his own way, given a simple and direct and independent narrative of the resurrection of Jesus from the dead. No one of them ever seems to think that any account of it was to be written, or had been written, different from his own, or that any other view could be taken of it than the one he presents. And hence, although at first there may seem to be such omissions or additions as to amount to discrepancies in their accounts, yet when the Evangelists are fairly examined, there is no contradiction between them, and that which at first seemed to be against them, turns out, in fact, in favor of their intelligence and honesty as witnesses. Each one is an original, independent picture from his own point of view. And both the fact itself of our Lord's resurrection, and of the preaching and recording it as a fact, were so arranged as to make the time suitable, and in every way best calculated to give strength to the truth of the facts stated. Our Lord was long enough in the tomb to prove that there was no delusion as to the fact of his being really dead. He was so long in the tomb that no ordinary or natural cause could by any possibility bring him forth alive. And yet his resurrection was not delayed until he was forgotten. He rose from the dead while yet his features were fresh, vivid in the memories of friends and foes—even his wounds fresh—and while the feelings of both friends and enemies were greatly excited, and while the whole conversation in many a circle and through many warm discussions must have still occupied the time and thoughts of the Jewish rulers as well as of Jesus' late followers—He rose while both friends and foes were keenly alive to the scenes of his death. And yet, strange as it may seem, his enemies were more observant of what He had said about his rising from the dead than his friends were. It is strange that his disciples were so stupid or forgetful as not to keep in mind his promise that He would rise the third day from the dead. Still, it was so ordered as to fulfil the Scriptures, and make the proofs of the fact of his resurrection as strong as they could be.

In the early part of his public ministry, our Lord had said, speaking of his body: "Destroy this temple, and in three days I will raise it up again." You remember the Jews perverted his meaning, and made these words the ground of a charge against him before Caiaphas that he was the enemy of the Jews, and desired to destroy their beautiful temple, and overthrow their worship and polity; and yet, after his crucifixion, they understand the words literally, and do every thing they could to prevent their coming to pass. And again, our Lord declared no sign from heaven should be given to that generation, in regard to his Messiahship, except that of Jonah the Prophet, for "as Jonas was three days and nights in the whale's belly, so must the Son of Man be three days and nights in the heart of the earth." And still again, immediately after our Lord had instituted the

Holy Supper, He said unto his disciples: "All ye shall be offended because of me this night; for it is written, I will smite the Shepherd, and the sheep of the flock shall be scattered abroad. But after I am risen again, I will go before you into Galilee." Matt. xxvi. 31, 32.

It is certainly wonderful, how many Scriptures were fulfilled in our Lord's sufferings and death, and that the events, moreover, by which they were fulfilled were the free acts of parties wholly unconscious of these outstanding prophecies, or at least without any idea or wish to bring about their fulfilment in Jesus of Nazareth. Little did the Jews design, by arresting Jesus and delivering him to Pilate—to be mocked, to be condemned—his garments parted—to be crucified, and pierced, and then to be buried just as he was buried, to prove that in all and each and every one of these particulars God was ordering the exact fulfilment of the prophecies and types concerning the promised Messiah, and that by their fulfilment in Jesus, it was to be demonstrated that He was the Messiah, God's own Son, our Redeemer.

Again: *Secondly*. Our records clearly authorize us to take up another line of argument in support, historically, of the truth of our Lord's resurrection, namely, from the conduct of the Jewish rulers, as it lies in the history before us. If they had designed to make themselves *unconscious witnesses* to the truth of our Lord's resurrection, the chief priests and rulers of the Jews could not have done better than they did. For observe, when they heard all that had been done on the morning of the resurrection at the tomb of Joseph of Arimathea, they immediately summoned the assembly, and took counsel, and resolved to bribe the soldiers to make a false statement, saying, "Say ye, His disciples came by night and stole him away while we slept." Read here the account from Matt. xxviii. 11-15. Perhaps this idle story is not worthy of credit. It scarcely deserves serious consideration; yet you will not fail to observe the sepulchre is under guard, a Roman guard—κουστωδια—which usually consisted of sixty soldiers. How many were detailed for this service we do not know, but the circumstances justify us in concluding it was quite a strong guard. Was it, then, probable that all such a guard would fall asleep at once, and that, too, when death was the penalty for sleeping on guard? Besides, if they were all asleep, how did they know the disciples had stolen away the body, and if they were not asleep, why did they not make resistance, and prevent the body being removed? And how could the breaking of the great seal and the removal of the body have been effected without making such a noise as to rouse the sleeping guard? Or, how was it to be made credible that a few unarmed men and women could have overcome, in any way, a Roman guard, and carry away the body? The disciples were not thinking of any such a thing. They had forsaken their Lord and fled, and were so broken in spirit and without hope, that they were still in an upper chamber, "with closed doors for fear of the Jews." And besides, it is marvellous that such a handful of men could have supposed they could effectually conceal the stolen body, if they had succeeded in getting possession of it. If they had stolen it, where did they hide it? Why were they not compelled to produce it? Why did not the Sanhedrim have them all arrested? Why did not Pilate order the arrest of the guard that had so failed to do their duty? The history, it is true, is not full on all these points. But it is quite fair to ask, why was not the missing body sought for? Why was it not produced? The burial linen was left in the tomb—was found neatly folded up. There was no hurry or fright in the coming out of the tomb. No human eye saw Jesus rise out of the tomb, but the evidence that He had risen is positive.

The earthquake and the angels have so completely overcome the guard that they neither see nor do any thing until some time has elapsed; then some of them go into the city and report, and the Jewish rulers *invent* this idle tale to account for the disappearance of Jesus' body. If there was any shadow of truth in their invention, why did not Pilate charge the disciples with the offence? Or why did they not fly to the rocky shores of the Lake of Galilee, to Herod's jurisdiction? Why were they never taxed with this charge afterwards? The infatuation and want of common forethought in the Jewish council when they put their money into the hands, and their falsehoods into the mouths of the Roman soldiers, really become strong evidences against themselves, and proofs for the truth of our Lord's resurrection.

The following lines from an old Latin poet are worthy of being preserved. The argument may be better than the poetry, but still it is not without merit:

> " Speak, ruthless keeper; answer, guard profane;
> Your words, I'll show, are wholly false and vain.
> If fast asleep, as you presume to say,
> Within the grave immur'd, our Jesus lay,
> Till stolen from the tomb by daring hands,
> Unawed by terror of the Roman bands,
> Whose are these clothes, that in the grave remain,
> The charge of which two angels don't disdain?
> Can you suppose the thief would long delay,
> In judging which might seem the quicker way—
> To unbind the clothes, and strip the body bare,
> Or seize the sacred corpse without such care?
> If thieves make haste, and not one moment lose,
> What man of sense or reason can refuse,

<blockquote>
That, in its linen wrapt, 'tis fully proved,
CHRIST's stolen body must have been removed?"*
</blockquote>

Thirdly. Let us attend to *the declaration of the angel to the women at the sepulchre.* You remember these women designed to make our Lord's embalming more perfect than they had done, for the want of time on the evening after the crucifixion. They came to the sepulchre early in the morning, prepared with spices. And they said among themselves as they were coming, Who shall roll us away the stone and open the door of the sepulchre ? And behold, there was a great earthquake. (Read here Matt. xxviii. 2-8, &c.)

They did not know of the Roman guard and the sealing of the great stone at the door of the sepulchre. These things had been done after they left, and at the request of the Jewish rulers. These pious women had no thought that Jesus had risen, nor, at that time, was there any such expectation among his friends. They came prepared, after having rested over their Sabbath, according to the commandment, to anoint and embalm his dead body in a more perfect manner than they had been able to do when it was laid in the tomb. You remember it was the tomb of a rich member of the Jewish Sanhedrim — that it was a new tomb, in which no man had ever been laid—that it was hewn out of the solid limestone rock on the hill-side of the garden—there was no passage into it or out of it except by the door, which was closed with an immense hewn stone that rolled into the opening on a grooved runner—a heavy hewn stone door that was easily rolled into its place for shutting the door, because for that purpose the

---

* Quoted from SEDULIUS in Witsius, vol. ii. p. 177, where the Latin may be seen.

groove was on an inclined plane, the descent of which aided the pushing up and closing the door, but of course to roll or push it back so as to open the door would require greater strength. These doors were so arranged that while one man could shut them, it would take full half a dozen men to open them. Nor was the sealing of the stone an unheard of or unusual thing. We read of the same thing in Daniel's life, when he was cast into the lion's den by the king of Persia. In such cases the door was sealed either by closing the two faces together and placing the wax on them, or by sealing the ends of cords that were used in tying the stone in its place, as the ends of cords are sealed over packages by our express companies, or for custom-house purposes. In the case before us there was less trouble, because the great stone was really a door worked in grooves and could therefore be easily sealed. The seal used was no doubt Pilate's official seal, or that of the city of Jerusalem.

Fourthly. Observe the manner of our Lord's resurrection.

All the incidents attending the rising of our Lord on the third morning must be studied, in order to realize the simplicity and the awful grandeur of the scene. 1. There was a great earthquake.

2. A glorious retinue of angels descended and went into the tomb, and sat watching where the body of Jesus had lain.

3. Our risen Lord left his sepulchre vestments in the tomb: "The linen clothes and the napkin wrapped together in a place by itself," intimating that henceforth He should have no need of funeral garments or adornments, because He rose to die no more, but to put

immortality on his human nature, and assure his people of eternal glory with him in his heavenly home.

4. The angels declared to the women that Jesus was risen as He had foretold to them, and was going into Galilee to meet his disciples, as He had promised them. And here we should keep in mind who these women were. They were his friends; they could not be mistaken as to his identity. There are various conjectures and in some cases conflicting opinions concerning the different Marys spoken of in the Gospels, and in some instances it is difficult to distinguish them. All that is important, however, we can know. It is probable they were all together at our Lord's funeral, and at the sepulchre on the morning of his resurrection. There are at least *four Marys* in the Gospels: 1. Mary, the Blessed Virgin, who was the mother of our Lord. 2. Mary Salome, who was her sister, and wife of Cleophas. 3. Mary Magdalene, that is, Mary of Magdala. And, 4. Mary sister of Martha and Lazarus of Bethany. Note the piety as well as courage of these women. They were ardently desirous of completing their pious work on our Lord's dead body, but they did not forget the duties of the Sabbath. They waited till the Sabbath was past. They did not fulfil one commandment by violating another. Nor are we without some useful reflections on the communication of the news of our Lord's resurrection to such women first of all. 1. Has not God a right to reveal himself to whom He pleases? 2. Is it not agreeable to his method of making known his glory to employ weak and feeble instruments to bring about great results, for the purpose of showing clearly that the efficiency and the glory are to be ascribed to himself, and not to the agent employed? The treasure of Gospel grace is committed to *earthen* vessels, that the excellency of the power may be of God,

and not of man. 3. There was a fitness in rewarding these pious, zealous, and holy women with the first intelligence of their Lord's resurrection. They were more faithful, and attached, and courageous to our Lord than the Apostles themselves; therefore, as Burkitt says, our Lord sent them as Apostles to the Apostles. When all the disciples forsook him and fled, they followed Jesus to the cross, and followed his body to the tomb, and are the first to visit it after the Sabbath, and are the first to hear of his resurrection.

Note also the circumstances of the resurrection. When our Lord died there was an earthquake, and the sun was veiled; so at his resurrection there is another earthquake, as if to show that all nature sympathized with its Creator, the God-man, in his great work of redeeming the world. And an angel comes from heaven to open his prison-door. The descent of such an officer from the court of heaven was a proof that the Eternal Throne was now begirt with the bow of Peace. Justice was satisfied. The prisoner was to be discharged. And besides, it would seem fit for angels to assist at the resurrection of our Lord. An angel first made known his conception, and declared his birth. As angels had been his companions and comforters in the temptation, and in many a severe conflict with the devil and the powers of darkness, and had witnessed his agony in the garden, it was well for angels to witness his resurrection. He could indeed have raised himself, and have rolled away the great stone, and have put to flight the Roman guard, or have restrained them from touching him as He walked out and away. But it is ever agreeable to the plan of Sovereign Grace to employ creatures as agents, both men and angels, and even the lower creation, when the Divine glory can be better presented to our comprehension by so doing. And besides, as an angel had foretold his conception, first proclaimed his advent, and now rolled away the stone, and first preached his resurrection, and bore him company in his ascension to heaven; so when he comes to judgment He shall be revealed from heaven with his mighty angels. Note also how emphatic is the angel's declaration to the women. *He is not here.* His body is no longer where you laid it. Death has lost its prey, and the grave has lost her guest. Do not doubt. *Come, see the place where the Lord lay.* He appealed to their senses. *Come,* see for yourselves. His body is not here. Here are the grave-clothes, but He is indeed risen, as He said He would do, and He goeth before his disciples into Galilee to meet them there, as He promised them. For we must remember that it is constantly repeated, according to our authorities, that all his sufferings, and every thing about his death and his rising the third day from the dead—all was *according to the Scriptures*, and according to his own predictions and promises to his disciples. Nor can I help thinking that any one who thoughtfully reads the history of our Lord's death and resurrection, will be impressed with the fact that there was an overruling Providence directly employed in making the evidences of the reality of his death so plain that no doubt could remain on that point; then also in making sure of the sepulchre, to prevent our Saviour's resurrection, or even the semblance of a verification of his words about his rising again from the dead. Every thing the Jewish rulers and the Roman governor did to prevent our Lord's resurrection only made it more certain and palpable. And thus were his enemies made witnesses for the truth. The providence of God so overruled the circumstances of our Lord's burial as to avoid the possibility of deception. Though his friends obtain leave to embalm and bury his body after the manner of the Jews, yet as soon as this is done they go away home to keep the Sabbath, and then his enemies obtain a guard of Roman soldiers to act as sentinels in keeping the body. His friends, His enemies, the centurion, Pilate, and the soldiers, all agree in declaring he was really dead. His funeral is public, and distinguished from the burial of the malefactors that were crucified with him. And then, after He was buried alone by himself, the place was made as secure as possible, and put under the care of a Roman guard, expressly to prevent his body from being removed; and thus the precaution of his enemies becomes the means of furnishing the most striking proof that his death and resurrection were awful and yet most glorious realities.

The point in hand is on this wise: Jesus often foretold his death and resurrection. He was really dead. Every precaution was taken to prevent the removal of His body by stealth. Yet on the third day the body is missing, and was never seen again as a dead body. Thus far friends and foes are agreed. Now there are two explanations offered for the missing of the body. *First.* The angels, the women, and our Lord's disciples affirmed that He was alive—that He had risen from the dead, and that his resurrection was proof that He was the Son of God, the Messiah, as He had claimed to be. *Secondly.* The Jewish rulers, as soon as they hear a report of what has occurred, invent the tale that while the Roman guard was asleep his disciples came and stole away his body, and hired the Roman soldiers to adopt and affirm this story as their explanation for the missing of the body. But the story of the Jewish rulers is not worthy of belief. 1. For it supposes a guard of sixty Roman soldiers all sound asleep at once—although it is known the punishment for sleeping while on guard was death. 2. The disciples were few, unarmed, and in every way despondent.

3. Nor could they have concealed the body, if they had obtained it. And, 4. Neither the Sanhedrim nor Pilate ever charged the disciples with this offence, or made any effort to produce the body. Here is the empty sepulchre, the grave-clothes, but where is the body?

On the other hand, the account given by our Evangelists is the true one, because it is supported by testimony *angelic*, *human*, and *divine*—by testimony unimpeachable by reason, common sense, or legal rules of evidence.

1. It is presumed to be true, because, the whole case being considered, there is nothing absurd or incredible in the history.

2. It explains how it happened that the soldiers did not see Jesus when He rose. They had been prostrated by an earthquake, and were so affrighted or fainting they could not see him.

3. Then the angels declare Jesus was risen—the women saw Him, and the disciples affirmed that He was alive. Nor could they be deceived. Nor could an increase of the number of witnesses add any thing to the validity of their testimony. Nor is it possible to conceive of any motives that could have induced them, as men of common sense, to adopt as true what they knew was false. They were persecuted, and almost all of them put to death, for believing and declaring that Jesus was risen from the dead, and was alive, and was both Lord and Christ. They gained no pleasure of a worldly nature; no wealth or rank, or any such thing, by affirming the resurrection of Jesus. Rather, they endured every species of trial and toil on land and sea, going everywhere to declare that Jesus was the Messiah, and proved what they said by showing that He had risen from the dead according to the

Scriptures. And they were believed at the time by thousands in Jerusalem and wherever they went preaching.

The proof of our Lord's resurrection, then, is *two-fold*. It rests upon sufficient testimony, and it is confirmed by miracles, and is theologically demonstrated by all the arguments and reasons for the truth of Christianity. The witnesses are the Jewish priests and rulers, the heathen guard, the two angels at the sépulchre, and the numerous parties to whom Jesus showed himself alive after His resurrection, and with some of whom He remained for forty days, giving them every opportunity, by free, familiar social intercourse, to satisfy themselves as to his identity. There are recorded eleven different times, when, on eleven different occasions, and in different places, our Lord appeared alive after his resurrection to his friends, not always the same friends, but to parties of them differently composed every time.

These parties were his Apostles, friends, and a great multitude of above five hundred brethren at once. The number of such witnesses is then more than sufficient. And they were qualified by their intelligence and moral character to give evidence. There is not a syllable known or even offered as to their characters, on which their veracity can be impeached in any respectable court on earth. They were in such a situation and temper as to be very slow in believing themselves. They were incredulous to a fault; and yet their unbelief should make us more ready to believe what they reported. Clearly, as it seems to us now, our Lord had foretold to them that He would rise from the dead; yet so blind were they on this subject, and so little were they expecting Jesus to rise from the dead, that when the women reported what the angel had told them at the sepulchre, *their words seemed to the disciples as idle tales, and they believed them not.* And at a later period, and after they had received more information touching the matter, and had conversed more about it, and when Jesus appeared in their midst, then they were terrified as if they had seen a spirit. This does not look as if they were too ready to receive the report of his resurrection as worthy of credit. And, you remember, Thomas was so determined in his unbelief, that "unless he saw in his hands the prints of the nails, and put his finger into the print of the nails, and thrust his hand into his side, he would not believe." And yet our Lord was pleased to indulge him—to take him upon his own conditions, and to give him the demonstration he required.

Nor is there a single moral blot on their characters by which to discredit the testimony of our Lord's disciples. No instance of dishonesty or any want of integrity was ever brought to light by the magistrates or ecclesiastical bodies before whom they were examined and gave their testimony. They were called fools and fanatics, and reviled as the offscouring of the world, not for crimes or vices they had committed, but for believing the Gospel of the Cross. There was no possibility that they could have been deceived. "We have not," says the Apostle Peter, "followed cunningly devised fables, when we made known unto you the power and coming of our Lord Jesus Christ, but were eye-witnesses of His Majesty." Nor was there any motive for them to deceive others. There were no worldly gains or honors to be obtained by professing to believe in the resurrection of One who had been crucified, and whose Gospel promised no earthly kingdom. To profess the faith of Jesus' followers, then, was to submit to persecution of every kind from both Jews and Gentiles, and often to endure death on the cross or in the amphitheatre, or in dungeons or on the block. Nor were they martyrs for mere opinions, but to facts which as eye-witnesses they could not deny. And among these witnesses we should remember that even Judas is to be numbered. He declared, throwing down the cursed money which he had received for his treachery, "I have betrayed innocent blood"—meaning, that Jesus was truly what He said He was, the Son of God; and that all He said of himself is true. And so also Nicodemus and Joseph of Arimathea, both members of the great Hebrew Senate, men of culture, rank, and wealth. They honored him dead more than they had ever had courage to do while He was alive; and rejoiced no doubt in His resurrection. And then we must not forget the testimony of that fierce, persecuting Pharisee, Saul of Tarsus, who, as Paul the Apostle, exposed himself to all sorts of dangers, gave up all his expectations of worldly honor and fame, and devoted his life to preaching Jesus and the resurrection, and laid his head under Cæsar's bloody axe as a martyr to the faith.

Again, all those texts of Holy Scripture that speak of Christ's ascension and of His coming to judge the world imply the truth of His resurrection. A remarkable incident is recorded concerning the death of Stephen, who, in the presence of his enraged enemies, as they were heaping stones upon him, said: *Behold I see the heavens opened, and the Son of Man*—THE SON OF MAN—Jesus in his human nature, *standing on the right hand of God.* Remember, in coming to your verdict, that Jesus was dead—that He was laid in the tomb—that it was sealed and guarded. Remember, it is now empty. His dead body was never produced after it was laid in the new tomb of Joseph of Arimathea. Remember the angelic testimony—the divine demonstration in the earthquake, and in the resurrection of many of the saints that slept.

Take into account the *number* and *character* of the witnesses—the *places* where they gave their positive evidence in behalf of the resurrection of Jesus—and that their arguments were never refuted—no other explanation was ever offered to account for the missing body except the clumsy falsehood of the Jewish rulers—that no contradictory testimony was ever offered—no cross, questioning before the magistrates ever put them to shame or weakened their evidence—nor did any torturing or cruel kind of death ever wring from them any recantation. Remember too the *time* when they gave this evidence. It was in Jerusalem, and immediately after the resurrection took place; and that they continued ever afterwards, wherever they went, till death closed their labors, to give their testimony to these facts. The truth of our Lord's resurrection may be shown from miracles, concerning which we may truly say: *If we receive the witness of men*—in this case it is in fact the witness of both angels and men—*the witness of God is greater.* If then the human testimony, the historic proof of the truth of our Lord's resurrection, is of such a character that it cannot be impeached, or shown to be unworthy of credit by any respectable court having jurisdiction of historic verities, how shall we escape from the seal which God himself has been pleased to set to this truth? It is not needful for me to say that I refer to the descent of the Holy Spirit on the day of Pentecost, and to the miracles wrought by the Apostles in the name of the Lord Jesus, as well as to all the miracles of Christ himself before his death, and the attestations from heaven at His baptism, and on the mount of transfiguration, and then His ascension, and in a word the success of His Gospel and the present existence of His Church, and the influence of Christianity upon mankind, past and present. You remember the Apostles, on the day of Pentecost and afterwards, boldly declared that their power to work miracles and to preach the Gospel was from the Holy Ghost, which was given as a proof that Jesus was Christ, and had died and risen from the dead, as they constantly alleged. "With great power gave the Apostles witness of the resurrection of the Lord Jesus." Acts iv. 33. "We are," said they, "his witnesses of these things, and so is also the Holy Ghost, whom God hath given to them that obey Him." Acts v. 32. It is to be remembered that this point is made distinct and clear by the declaration, that "the Holy Ghost was not yet given, because that Jesus was not glorified." And our Lord himself promised to send the Holy Ghost as a comforter and companion to his disciples after his ascension. And in giving his last command to go into all the world and preach the Gospel, it is said, and "these signs shall follow them that believe"—during the apostolic age—"in my name shall they cast out devils; they shall speak with new tongues, they shall take up serpents, and if they drink any deadly thing, it shall not hurt them." These signs are the miracles ordained to give proof of His resurrection, as a cardinal doctrine in planting the churches and establishing His kingdom in the world. This argument comprises every conversion to Christianity that has taken place—every poor sinner that has been pardoned and saved by the Gospel is a witness for the resurrection of our Lord Jesus.

II. But I must hasten through the *second* and last part of this discourse: *What are the Benefits or Reasons for Christ's resurrection?* I answer, they are two-fold: FIRST, as to Himself; and *secondly*, as to His people. By his rising from the dead He declared himself to be the Son of God—proved that He had satisfied Divine Justice, vanquished death and him that had the power of death, that is, the devil, and that He was Lord of quick and dead. "For to this end Christ both died, and rose, and revived, that He might be Lord both of the dead and living." Rom. xiv. 9.

There was a necessity, then, for the human body of our Lord to be raised from the dead. It illustrated the Dignity of his person, and showed his enemies and his friends that He who suffered under Pontius Pilate was crucified, dead and buried, was God's well-beloved Son, and accepted in heaven above as the only Mediator between God and men.

The Reasons for, or the Necessity of, our Lord's rising from the dead might be shown in this way. 1. To fulfil the divine oracles and types concerning the promised Messiah. 2. Hereby it was clearly proved that He was the Son of God in the sense He had claimed to be, and that He had completed the work He came to do. CHRIST, says the Apostle, "was raised up from the dead by the glory of the Father," which means not merely *to* the glory of the Father, or for the Father's glory, but by the glory of the Father displayed in His Son, owning Him as His Son, showing that Jesus was not guilty of blasphemy in claiming to be the Son of God. His resurrection was a perfect demonstration that He had fully satisfied Divine Justice—paid the whole debt laid to his account for us—and had conquered death, hell, and sin, and was now Lord and Christ.

If our Lord had continued under the power of death, it would have argued that the satisfaction He had rendered by his obedience and the sacrifice of himself was not sufficient, and that the end designed by him in his sufferings and death had not been attained. But as the Justice of God was fully satisfied. it was not possible for our Saviour to be held any longer as a prisoner. His release was demanded by Justice, as well as to accomplish the promise and purposes of God previously revealed concerning the Messiah, in the types and prophecies of the Old Testament. He is the first-begotten of the Dead, and the Prince of the kings of the earth. He alone can say: "I am He that was dead and am alive forever more, and have the keys of hell and of death."

> "Hail, purest victim Heaven could find,
>   The powers of hell to overthrow!
> Who didst the chains of Death destroy;
>   Who dost the prize of Life bestow.
>
> "Hail, victor Christ! Hail, risen King!
>   To Thee alone belongs the crown;
> Who hast the heavenly gates unbarred,
>   And dragged the Prince of Darkness down.
>
> "O Jesus! from the death of sin
>   Keep us, we pray; so shalt Thou be
> The everlasting Paschal joy
>   Of all the souls new-born in Thee."—*Breviary*.

SECONDLY. "*What doth the resurrection of Christ profit us?*

"*Ans. First,* by His resurrection, He hath overcome death that He might make us partakers of that righteousness which He had purchased for us by His death; *secondly,* we are also by His power raised up to a new life; and *lastly,* the resurrection of Christ is a sure pledge of our blessed resurrection."—*Heidelberg Catechism.*

He rose from the dead as "a Public Person, the Head of His Church, for the justification of his people, their quickening in grace, support against enemies, and to assure them of their resurrection from the dead at the last day." [See *Ans. to* 52d *Question, Larger Catechism.*]

1. *Then our Justification.*

"He was delivered for our offences, and was raised again for our justification." "Justified in the Spirit"—proving that Divine Justice was satisfied, and consequently all who are in Christ are also justified. "Who then shall lay any thing to the charge of God's elect? It is God that justifieth, who is he that condemneth; It is Christ that died, yea rather that is risen again." Since God hath acknowledged that His Justice is satisfied by the resurrection of Christ—for that is the discharge of our Surety from prison—then all further prosecution is arrested.

2. Through Christ's resurrection we have *sanctification*—"Ye are risen with him through the faith of the operation of God, who hath raised him from the dead." Believers therefore are risen with Christ as well as justified in Him. They are said by the Apostle to be planted together with him in the likeness of his resurrection, that, as Christ was raised up from the dead by the glory of the Father, even so they also should walk in newness of life. This is what Paul means by knowing the power of his resurrection, and being made conformable to his death. When our Lord came forth from the grave, He was both a living soul, like the first Adam, and He was also a quickening Spirit. He had life for his people as well as for himself. Not merely that He was to ascend and reign in glory, but that He might live by His Spirit in believers. As the Head, He sends life through all his members. He is their life. As we are by nature dead in trespasses and in sins, so we must be quickened and raised by His Spirit to newness of life; our hearts must be created anew, and our affections set on things above. And if when we were enemies, we were reconciled to God

by the death of his Son; much more, being reconciled, we shall be saved by his life. That is, by his resurrection and life as Lord and Christ. It is thus that we are regenerated unto a lively hope of an inheritance uncorruptible and undefiled, reserved in the heavens for us.

3. *The glorification of believers* follows their justification and sanctification. This Paul declares positively in Rom. viii. 30. "Moreover," says he, "whom He did predestinate, them He also called, and whom He called; them He also justified; and whom He justified, them He also *glorified.*" Nor could it be otherwise, as He is the first-fruits of them that sleep in Him. He is the first-born brother; believers are joint-heirs with Him. If by his resurrection, He is declared God's own Son, and receives his title to life and immortality, then are his people partakers with Him of the same inheritance. He is the beginning, the first-born from the dead, among many brethren. CHRIST the first-fruits; afterwards, they that are Christ's at his coming. As Christ is the Head, and his people are the members, they cannot be separated. "The body shall follow the head." Because I live, ye shall live also; and where I am, there shall ye be also. For as in Adam all die, even so in Christ shall all his people be made alive. If the spirit of him that raised up Jesus from the dead, dwell in you, He that raised up Christ from the dead, shall also quicken your mortal bodies by his Spirit that dwelleth in you. His rising from the dead is an earnest that we shall rise also. Our Lord's resurrection demonstrates the validity of all his promises, and the truth of all He has taught concerning a future state. This is an illustration in his own person that He is the resurrection and the life; and that His Gospel does bring life and immortality to light. Thus Paul says before Agrippa and Festus, that "having

obtained help of God, I continue unto this day, witnessing both to small and great, saying none other things than those which the Prophets and Moses did say should come: that Christ should suffer, and that he should be the first that should rise from the dead, and should shew light unto the people and to the Gentiles." Acts xxvi. 22, 23.

He is, therefore, the *pledge and pattern* of our resurrection. If we are planted together with him in the likeness of his death, we shall be also planted together with him in the likeness of his resurrection. As we have borne the image of the earthy—that is, of Adam—so we shall also bear the image of the heavenly—that is, of Christ, knowing that He who raised our Lord shall raise us by His power, and our vile bodies shall be fashioned like unto His own glorious body; that He who raised the Lord Jesus, shall also raise us by Jesus. And as Christ rose to eternal life, heavenly, holy, and blest, so shall his people live with him in glory, where sin and sorrow, pain and death, can never again reach them. And, dear brethren, as Christ rose from the dead by the glory of the Father, so ought we to be dead to sin, but alive unto God, and to walk in newness of life, in the hope of the resurrection unto eternal life in glory. Amen.

XIII.

CHRIST ASCENDED INTO HEAVEN.

"And it came to pass, while he blessed them, he was parted from them, and carried up into heaven."—LUKE xxiv. 51, with MARK xvi. 19, and ACTS i. 1-12.

THIS Article, like the one on the Resurrection of Christ, is a simple question of fact supported by testimony and by theological argumentation. It implies the truth of Christianity, and Christianity involves its truth as an essential part of itself. The same line of historic evidence and of theological reasoning that proves the truth of our Lord's resurrection, proves also his Ascension. Still, I am quite willing this Article should rest on an independent investigation, and on its own evidence, in the light of this nineteenth century.

In the early ages of the Church, the Ascension and Assumption of Christ meant the same thing, and, like the solemn days of the Nativity and the Passion, the feast of the Ascension was kept as a great day. Chrysostom calls the feast of the Assumption an illustrious and refulgent day, and describes our Lord's exaltation as the grand proof of God's reconciliation to sinners. Our Lord's emphatic words to Mary, after his resurrection, "Touch me not, for I am not yet ascended to my Father: but go to my brethren, and say unto them, I ascend unto my Father and your Father, and to my God and your God," are especially worthy of attention. Here our risen Saviour expressly declares that He would ascend to his Father, and it is clearly implied that something of peculiar importance was involved in his ascension. And this inference is abundantly borne out by history. It is in evidence that it was not until after Jesus was glorified, by ascending into heaven, that the Holy Spirit was given with such marvellous and unparalleled power. The festival of the ancient Cappadocian Christians in commemoration of Christ's ascension, was not an unmeaning one. This festival they called *Episozomene*, because they observed it as a proof that on this day our salvation was perfected, JESUS CHRIST having finished the great mission He came to fulfil on earth, and having returned to heaven. In our Lord's resurrection from the dead, we see Him receiving from the High Court of Heaven and the hand of Eternal Justice his discharge from prison in full for the payment of the debt He had assumed for us; and in his Ascension, we see the Father recalling him, as an ambassador who has fully succeeded in accomplishing his mission in a foreign country is called home to his native land to enjoy the honors and fruits of his labors.

The ceremonies of Ascension Day in Papal churches are somewhat after this style: After the Gospel, the Paschal taper is put out, to denote that on this day our Saviour left the earth and returned to heaven. Flowers, images, and relics are then heaped upon the altar. The priests are robed in white. On this day the Pope used to curse all heretics, and pronounce his blessings on the faithful. It is still one of the three solemn days on which his Holiness pronounces blessings, but the cursing is now confined to Holy Thursday. The old and the Eastern churches make a much greater display of ceremony on this day than is known among us. At one time, in many of the ancient churches, it was usual to represent Christ's Ascension by drawing up an image of him to the roof of the church edifice, and then cast down an image of Satan, in flames, to represent his falling like lightning from heaven before our Lord. Nor are there wanting historic evidences that the most ridiculous pageantry was often resorted to in the early ages of the Church in celebrating this day. Ceremonies that we regard as nothing but a wicked travesty—a blasphemous commemoration of one of the greatest events in the history of our redemption. For ages, also, Christians used to travel into the Holy Land to adore the footprints of Jesus' feet where He last stood, and from whence He ascended into heaven, just as they do now to kiss the marble tomb that represents the place of his burial, and to witness the lights that are kindled on Ascension Day in the Church of the Ascension on the Mount of Olives, which are so many and so brilliant that it looks as if the whole of the sacred mount was on fire. Such historic traditions concerning such an event are only valuable, however, as presumptive evidence of the truth of the fact commemorated. It is, accordingly, an undisputed fact that Christians have always contemplated our Lord's ascension with the most profound satisfaction. Poetry and painting have vied with each other in celebrating this event in our Lord's history as the most perfect triumph of His humanity over every adverse power.

The only variation I find in this Article: "He ascended into heaven, and sitteth on the right hand of God the Father Almighty," is, that in some of the ancient Creeds the name of God and the attribute Almighty are omitted. In such copies as I refer to, the Article reads in this way:

"He ascended into heaven, sitteth at the right hand of the Father." The sense is the same. The only part of the Article I design to consider this evening is the first part: "He ascended into heaven."

The history of our Lord's ascension is given in Mark xvi. 19; Luke xxiv. 51, and in Acts i. 1-12. In this history you see,—

I. We have *the place* from which He ascended. It is nothing to my purpose to prove or disprove that the church or mosque on the Mount of Olives marks the exact spot from which our Lord ascended; yet I have so much reverence for what is called the *religio loci*, that I could not enter that church, and climb to its summit, and then look up into the clouds that hung over the whole region, without feeling that I was indeed looking on the very pathway my Saviour had used when He ascended into heaven. It will not be understood, however, that I receive as true the foolish stories found in the legends of saints, and the traditions of the Church of Rome, about the building of the splendid chapel by the Empress Helena on the place whence Christ ascended to heaven— that miracles were wrought to protect the dust that last received the prints of our Lord's sacred feet—that the marks of his feet are still there to be seen—and that it was found impossible, as Jerome reports, to cover and arch over the summit of the building, and that hence it was circular, leaving an open dome, where the Lord's body had passed, and that thus the passage-way along which our Lord's body went, in his ascension from earth to heaven, still continues open. It is of no consequence to me, as a traveller, to be shown the marks of footsteps that are said to be the prints of our Lord's foot, either on the earth or on the rock, nor is it of the least concern to me which has the best claims to the oldest foot-marks, the monks or the Mohammedans, for both claim the original stone on which our Lord's foot last rested at the moment when He began his ascent; but it is of importance to me that it is historically true, that the Empress built a chapel on the Mount of Olives, and such a chapel stands there to this day as a monument of the truth of the faith of the Church on this subject, nor is there any shadow of doubt but this Church of the Ascension, if not covering the precise spot, still overlooks the real spot and the whole surroundings of the glorious Ascension.* And I candidly admit I do not envy any one who is such a skeptic that he is not in sympathy with the poet who says:

> "I cannot look above and see
>   Yon high-piled pillowy mass
> Of evening clouds, so swimmingly,
>   In gold and purple pass,
> And think not, Lord, how Thou wast seen
>   On Israel's desert way
> Before them, in thy shadowy screen
>   Pavilioned all the day!
>
> "Or, of those robes of gorgeous hue
>   Which the Redeemer wore,
> When, ravished from his followers' view,
>   Aloft his flight he bore,
> When lifted, as on mighty wing,
>   He curtained his ascent,
> And wrapt in clouds, went triumphing
>   Above the firmament.
>
> "Is it a trail of that same pall
>   Of many-colored dyes,
> That high above, o'ermantling all,
>   Hangs midway down the skies—

---

* This subject is quite fully presented by Witsius and Lightfoot, and often commented on by modern travellers.

>   Or borders of those sweeping folds
>   Which shall be all unfurled
>   About the Saviour, when He holds
>   His judgment on the world?
>
> "For in like manner as He went,—
>   My soul, hast thou forgot?—
>   Shall be his terrible descent,
>   When man expecteth not!
>   Strength, Son of Man, against that hour,
>   Be to our spirits given,
>   When Thou shalt come again with power,
>   Upon the clouds of heaven."—WILLIAM CROSWELL.

There may be a thousand lying traditions uttered by the guides of the Holy places, but when I tread the soil of Olivet, I am sure I tread "where His blessings were heard, and His lessons were taught." I am sure that I am treading on the place whence "His humanity, clothed in the brightness of God," ascended into heaven, to show me the way and teach me how to follow Him. I know perfectly well that on these hills, which I see around the Holy City, Jesus toiled; from these still gushing fountains, I know He drank when weary and thirsty. And the same airs are blowing on me "which breathed on his blessed brow." But, my brother, complain not, if with untravelled eyes you are seeking to follow Jesus. For even—

> "If my feet may not tread where He stood,
> Nor my ears hear the dashing of Galilee's flood,
> Nor my eyes see the Cross which He bowed Him to bear,
> Nor my knees press Gethsemane's garden of prayer—
> Yet, loved of Thy Father, Thy Spirit is near
> To the meek and the lowly and penitent here:
> And the voice of Thy love is the same even now,
> As at Bethany's tomb, or on Olivet's brow."—H. H. MILLMAN.

Witsius thinks Christ chose to ascend from Olivet,

(1.) Because, as it was the place of his great suffering and bloody sweat, so it was proper to exhibit in the same place his glorious ascent, as a Conqueror, to heaven. (2.) That from the very spot where He had struggled with the infernal hosts, He might ascend to the highest heavens with trophies of their complete and final overthrow. The scene of conflict was the scene of victory.

Note the two statements before us: "And He led them out as far as to Bethany." Luke. "And they returned to Jerusalem from the mount called Olivet," after witnessing his ascension. These are not contradictory. You know the Mount of Olives and Bethany are places very dear to our Lord. They lie on the same side of Jerusalem. The name Bethany was applied both to the city and district in which it was situate. And in going to Bethany, the way was by or over the Mount of Olives. "He led them out as far as to Bethany," therefore means, He led them along the usual road towards Bethany, which winds round the Mount of Olives, until he came to the spot where *the district*, that is, the township of Bethany began, and in which was the city of Bethany, and which was also in view from the spot where He blessed them, and from which he ascended. And hence the statement, that after the ascension the disciples returned to Jerusalem from the mount called Olivet, is strictly correct. It is a simple and natural description of the journey and of *the place*. He ascended *not from the town of Bethany*, but from the *district of Bethany*, lying on the side of Olivet next to and overlooking the town of Bethany.

II. We have *the time*. "Until the day in which He was taken up," being seen of his Apostles and friends *for forty days* after his resurrection. During these forty days our Lord had appeared many times to his disciples, and spoke many things to them pertaining to the kingdom of God. Perhaps it was for the purpose of giving them such instruction, extending through such a length of time, that they might have more clear and distinct views, and be the better able to understand him, and to satisfy themselves of the reality of all they were called to testify about, that the interval of forty days was allowed to pass before He ascended. I do not know why just *forty days*, and no more and no less, were the determinate number. You know, however, that this is a favorite Bible number. Moses was just so long on Mount Sinai. Elijah travelled forty days in the strength of the food he received under the juniper-tree in the wilderness of Beersheba, until he reached Horeb, where Jehovah's still small voice had more effect upon him than the earthquake. And Jesus fasted forty days in the wilderness. And so also it is to be noted, as parallel, that it was forty days from his birth to his presentation in the temple. Let us now attend to

III. The FACT ITSELF. "He was parted from them, and carried up into heaven." "And when He had spoken these things, while they beheld, He was taken up; and a cloud received him out of their sight. And while they looked steadfastly toward heaven as He went up, behold, two men [that is, angels], stood by them in white apparel, which also said, Ye men of Galilee, why stand ye gazing up into heaven? This same Jesus which is taken up from you into heaven, shall so come in like manner as ye have seen him go into heaven."

You may remember that an Apostle says, "Now, he that descended is the same that ascended." This is different from the case of Moses in the mount; he had to ascend before he could descend. But Christ descended first, and took upon himself in his descent our nature, and then in it He ascended. It is He, the God-man, the person Jesus Christ, who ascended into heaven. Our Lord's ascension is, therefore, the second step of his exaltation. By his ascension is meant that on the fortieth day after his resurrection, and in the full view of his disciples, in clear daylight, He went up in his body from the earth into heaven—ascending from the side of the Mount of Olives overlooking Bethany, and that He ascended truly into heaven, passing through air and visible clouds into the highest heaven, and that his human body is there to remain in glory till He comes to judge the world.

The FACT ITSELF of our Lord's ascension is as clearly affirmed as terms can do it. It was not a vision, nor a mere appearance, but a reality. Christ Jesus was visibly elevated to heaven. It was the perfect man Christ Jesus that ascended. The ascension, however, is predicable, strictly speaking, only of his humanity. The Godhead is omnipresent, but the human nature of Jesus Christ is not ubiquitous.* It was the same body that " was dead and buried," that arose and ascended. "This man, after he had offered one sacrifice for sins, forever sat down at the right hand of God," Heb. x. 12. Many texts of Scripture might be quoted as to the fact that it was his *human body* the Apostles saw ascend, but I give you here only one, and that one especially for the purpose of showing that his body *glorified* is the pattern and earnest of our own glorification. Paul expressly tells us that as in this life, while living in this world, we are after the likeness of the first Adam, so in the resurrection we shall have the

---

* The doctrine of transubstantiation or of consubstantiation cannot be true. For Christ's body remains in heaven. It is only his Divinity, his Spirit, that is everywhere with his people. See this point well but briefly argued in Bethune, vol. i p. 459.

image of Christ the second Adam, the Lord from heaven our Redeemer. "For our conversation is in heaven; from whence also we look for the Saviour, the Lord Jesus Christ: Who shall change our vile body, that it may be fashioned like unto His glorious body, according to the working whereby He is able even to subdue all things unto himself." Phil. iii. 20, 21.

Here it is clearly taught: (1.) That our lives and conduct are to be heaven-ward. For (2.) Our Saviour is in heaven, and that His body is glorified in heaven. And (3.) He is coming again to perfect his work of redemption in us, by changing our vile bodies into the likeness of his glorious body. And this He will do by his mighty power in subduing and overcoming all things for his own glory.

THE PROOFS of our Lord's ascension need not be dwelt upon. The method used to prove upon evidence His resurrection might be repeated in support of the fact of His ascension. Thus, we could show from the types and prophetic oracles of the old Jewish Church that the promised Messiah was to ascend into heaven; and then we can prove that Jesus of Nazareth did really and truly ascend into heaven, and therefore we believe this Article to be true, and that Jesus is the true and only Messiah.

The high priest, under the law, is understood to have been a type of the Messiah, and his going into the Holy of Holies once a year is considered typically to represent Christ ascending into heaven. Such an application of this type to the Messiah has been generally admitted even by Jewish commentators. And then, prophetically, we might refer to passages out of the Psalms, especially from the sixty-eighth, which Paul expressly quotes, and applies not to Joshua, David, or any of the Prophets, but to

Christ: "Thou hast ascended up on high; Thou hast led captivity captive, Thou hast received gifts for men." And so, on the other hand, we have the authority of the New Testament for believing that Jesus Christ did really and truly ascend into heaven, just as the Jewish Church believed the Messiah was to ascend. There is no more figure of speech nor metaphor used in describing his ascension than in describing his birth—which is in no sense metaphorical, but literal and true. Jesus of Nazareth was literally and truly "conceived of the Holy Ghost," and took unto himself of the Virgin Mary "a true body," with "a rational soul," and literally and truly did He die and rise again, and ascend into heaven. All this we do most firmly believe, 1. Because the disciples saw him ascend. 2. Two angels declared that he had thus ascended. 3. Jesus said He would ascend. 4. Stephen and Paul, and John the Evangelist, saw him in his ascended state. 5. His ascension was demonstrated by the descent of the Holy Spirit; by the miracles of the Apostles, the fruits of their labors, and the spread of the Gospel to this day. Every thing that proves the reality of the Christian religion is an evidence of the truth of Christ's ascension. And 6. The destruction of Jerusalem, the end of the Hebrew polity, the ceasing of Hebrew sacrifices in the overthrow of the temple, are standing proofs that He was the Son of God; and that as He said, He would ascend again to His Father, so He undoubtedly fulfilled his own words, and thus is it proved that He is the true and only Messiah, the Saviour of sinners.

IV. In the fourth place, *what are we to believe as to the nature and properties of the body in which Christ appeared after his resurrection, and which He took with him when He ascended into heaven?* The best answer we can give to this question is found in the answers of the Larger Catechism to the 52d and 53d questions, and in the fourth Article of the Church of England, all of which let us read.

Q. 52. How was Christ exalted in his resurrection?

A. Christ was exalted in his resurrection, in that, not having seen corruption in death, of which it was not possible for him to be held, and having the very same body in which he suffered, with the essential properties thereof, but without mortality and other common infirmities belonging to this life, really united to his soul, he rose again from the dead the third day by his power, whereby he declared himself to be the Son of God, to have satisfied Divine Justice, to have vanquished death, and him that had the power of it, and to be Lord of quick and dead: all which He did as a public person, the Head of his Church, for their justification, quickening in grace, support against enemies, and to assure them of their resurrection from the dead at the last day.

Q. 53. How was Christ exalted in his ascension?

A. Christ was exalted in his ascension, in that having, after his resurrection, often appeared unto, and conversed with his Apostles, speaking to them of the things pertaining to the kingdom of God, and giving them commission to preach the Gospel to all nations; forty days after his resurrection, he, in our nature, and as our head, triumphing over enemies, visibly went up into the highest heavens, there to receive gifts for men, to raise up our affections thither, and to prepare a place for us, where himself is, and shall continue till his second coming at the end of the world.

The Article of the Church of England says: "Christ

did truly rise again from death, and took again his body, with flesh, bones, and all things appertaining to the perfection of man's nature, wherewith He ascended into heaven." Some have objected to these statements because it is said they are contradicted by the Apostle's denominating the body of the believer, in the resurrection, "*a spiritual body.*" But the objection is not well put. For we do not exactly or fully know what a spiritual body is. "A spiritual body," however, is clearly material, and is called "spiritual" only because it is refined from all earthly elements. Our Lord's body after his resurrection was the same body that was buried, but without any of the liabilities or infirmities of this life—such as belong to mortal bodies. Moreover, according to St. Paul's reasoning, it was essentially the same body—or there was no resurrection at all. That which is sown is altered in shape, and yet that which is sown is the same for substance that is raised. In a modified sense, the body of Christ as He rose from the dead was material, and so continues to be. It was endowed with the same senses that it had before his death, and these senses were exercised in the same manner, although doubtless capable, humanly speaking, of a much greater degree of action and of higher perfection. The Fathers of the Church understood the Scriptures on this point just as we do. Ignatius says, Christ was in the flesh, that is, in perfect humanity, *after his resurrection.* And Irenæus says, Jesus Christ was received into heaven after his resurrection in his flesh. And another says: "If any one shall not acknowledge that Christ is set down at the right hand of the Father, in *the same flesh* which He took here, let him be anathema." And so another: "He ascended into heaven, not divesting himself of his holy body, but uniting it to a spiritual one," which is explained by Augustine by saying, that all the difficulty about our

Lord's taking his human, that is, his earthly body, into heaven, is removed by understanding what is said in Scripture: "It is sown a natural body, it is raised a spiritual body."

As the heresies in primitive times denied the reality of our Lord's human nature, and taught that he had a body only in appearance, and that when His Divinity left his body, it dissolved into air; or, as some of them said, his body ascended no farther than the sun, in which it was deposited; so it was proper and necessary for the Faith of the Church to be expressed in such terms as would clearly teach that His body was a true and proper human body; and that it was with the very same body in which He lived and suffered, and was crucified, and which was buried in Joseph's new tomb, in which no other body had ever been laid, that He ascended into heaven. Accordingly our records say that He actually ascended—ascended in clear daylight, in full view of all the disciples, in the same body in which He was when He talked with them, ate with them, and had kept company with some of them for forty days after his resurrection. He blessed the disciples, and ascended, and was parted from them. While they were standing looking on He went up through the atmosphere. *How* his body thus ascended without wings I am not informed; but you remember the Angel Jehovah, who appeared to Manoah, and who was no other than Jesus Christ, did the same thing. This angel appeared in the shape, size, and dress of a pious prophet. But when the flame of Manoah's altar of sacrifice went up toward heaven from off the altar, then the angel of the Lord ascended in the flame of the altar. Judges xiii. Nor is there any difficulty here that is not removed the moment we remember that He possessed absolute Divinity as well as true humanity. The power of the Godhead within himself was quite sufficient to raise himself aloft, or to command legions of angels, invisible to human eyes, to form a glory-cloud with their wings, and bear Him up to heaven. The words descriptive of the manner of his ascending are peculiar and suggestive. "Until the day in which He *was taken up*," intimating that He was lifted up as into a chariot of triumph by legions of invisible angels, and borne aloft through the air into heaven. And this very properly brings me, in the next place, to inquire :

V. *By what cause or immediate agency did our Lord rise from the dead and ascend into heaven?* Who raised Jesus from the dead and exalted Him into heaven? The Agent, or immediate efficient cause of his exaltation, is certainly no other than the power of Godhead— certainly could be no other than "that Divinity common to the three Persons not divided in nature, power, and operation ;"* whence it is attributed most commonly to God the Father, who in the order of nature and in all common operations precedes. Sometimes it is ascribed to his own power—the Son laid down his life and took it up again. Sometimes, also, our Lord's resurrection is attributed to the Holy Spirit, by whom He was filled at his baptism, and by whom He cast out devils and wrought his miracles, and so also performed this, the greatest of all his miracles, raising himself from the dead. [See Rom. viii. 11.] Observe, it is an undoubted fact, that, according to the Scriptures, our Lord's resurrection from the dead is ascribed to the Father, to himself, and to the Holy Spirit. Thus St. Paul in several places ascribes the raising of Christ from the dead to God the

---

* The learned Dr. Barrow.

Father. He says in 1 Tim. iv. 13, that it is a part of the Divine glory, that He who quickeneth all things raised up the Lord Jesus. And so St. Peter, on the day of Pentecost, says, "This Jesus hath God raised up." And St. Paul again, as if he could not find words, but labored to express his thoughts, speaks of the "exceeding greatness of his power which he wrought in Christ when he raised him from the dead." "He was raised up from the dead by the glory of the Father." And yet Jesus himself declared he would raise himself up; and so also his resurrection is ascribed to the Holy Spirit—"*quickened by the Spirit*"—"He was declared to be the Son of God with power, according to the Spirit of holiness, by the resurrection from the dead." Observe especially the positive language of Peter in Acts v. 30, 31: "The God of our fathers raised up Jesus, whom ye slew and hanged on a tree. Him hath God exalted with his right hand to be a Prince and a Saviour, for to give repentance to Israel and forgiveness of sins. And we are his witnesses of these things." And again, in another place, he said, "Ye killed the Prince of Life, whom God hath raised from the dead, whereof we are witnesses." And then, when speaking of the lame man healed at the Temple gate, he says, "Be it known unto you all, and to all the people of Israel, that by the name of Jesus Christ of Nazareth, whom ye crucified, *whom God raised from the dead*, even by Him doth this man stand here before you whole." Many passages of Holy Scripture ascribe our Lord's exaltation to God the Father, showing that "the God of our Lord Jesus Christ, the Father of glory," has shown unto us the wonders of redemption, and "what is the exceeding greatness of his power to usward who believe, according to the working of his mighty power, which He wrought in Christ when He raised him from the dead, and set him at his own right hand in the heavenly places." Eph. i. 17–23.

And so also there are many places in the New Testament where our Lord's resurrection and ascension to the glory of the Father are ascribed to himself. In John x. 17; ii. 19; v. 26. As where He says, "Destroy this temple," meaning his body, "and in three days I will raise it up." *I will.* "Therefore doth my Father love me, because I lay down my life that I might take it again. No man taketh it from me, but I lay it down of myself. I have power to lay it down, and I have power to take it again. This commandment have I received of my Father. And as the Father hath life in Himself, so hath He given to the Son to have life in himself." And his promises were often made in his own name, and to the effect that He would rise again from the dead after He should be crucified.

And so also the same life-giving power which belongs to the Father and to the Son, belongs also to the Holy Spirit. The same power, honor, and homage is ascribed to the Three persons of the Godhead. And as Jesus Christ was conceived by the power of the Holy Spirit in the womb of the Virgin Mary, so His body was quickened and raised by the same Holy Spirit. How then are we to understand these texts of Holy Scripture? I answer, they are all harmonized by receiving the doctrine of the Catechism, that "there is but one only, the living and true God." And that "there are three persons in the Godhead; the Father, the Son, and the Holy Ghost; and these three are one God, the same in substance, equal in power and glory." Clearly there is no other explanation than this: the same Divine Essence is common to the Three persons in the Godhead.

VI. *Why, then, did Christ ascend into heaven?*

The REASONS why Christ ascended into heaven are plain. 1. It was to fulfil the types and prophecies concerning the Messiah. 2. It was necessary to fulfil his own words, in which He had foretold this of himself. John vi. 62; xx. 17.

3. That He might thus appear as a Priest in the presence of God for us.

4. That He might take upon himself more openly and exercise more fully his kingly office; and,

5. Give perfect assurance to his followers that his promises of life everlasting and of the resurrection of their bodies were to be faithfully and literally kept.

By believing this Article, therefore, our faith is confirmed in Jesus Christ as God's only Son, our Lord and Saviour. And our Hope is also strengthened, and our affections are to be set on things above where Christ is. "For where our treasure is, there will our hearts be also." "If I be lifted up from the earth, I will draw all men unto me."

VII. Then, in the last place, let us consider THE BENEFITS we derive from the ascension of our Lord into heaven. For as our Mediator He ascended for his people as well as for himself. His ascension proves his work of atonement finished and accepted, and that He has completely triumphed over all his enemies. The *Heidelberg Catechism* asks: "Of what advantage to us is Christ's ascension into heaven? Ans. *First.* That he is our advocate in the presence of his Father in heaven; *Secondly.* That we have *our flesh* in heaven, as a sure pledge that he, as the Head, will also take up to himself, us, his members; *Thirdly.* That He sends us his Spirit as an earnest by whose power we seek the things which are above, where Christ sitteth on the right hand of God, and not things on earth."

1. As our ADVOCATE with the Father, He intercedes for the pardon of our sins, for the acceptance of our persons and services. He offers up our prayers and praises, pleading for their acceptance because of his own merits, and our complete salvation for his sake. "He ever liveth to make intercession for us." "If any man sin, we have an Advocate with the Father, Jesus Christ the Righteous; and He is the propitiation for our sins. Him hath God exalted as a Prince and a Saviour to give repentance unto Israel and remission of sins."

> "O Christ! the beauty of the angel worlds!
> Of man the Saviour and Redeemer blest!
> Grant us one day to mount the path of light,
> And in thy glory rest."

2. He ascended into heaven to take possession of it, and to reside there, as to His humanity, in our name and behalf and in our nature. As Head of His Church, He sits on the throne of dominion, overruling all things for the Church, which is His body. And as He is there in our nature, His glorified body is a pledge that where the Head is the members must be also. As Enoch, under the patriarchal dispensation, was translated to heaven as a pledge of a future state and the resurrection of the body; and Elijah under the dispensation of the Law and the Prophets, so Jesus Christ rose from the dead, and in His true body ascended from earth to heaven, as a pledge,

earnest, and proof of the resurrection of His people and their ascension to eternal glory.

There is a sense also in which our Saviour went to heaven to prepare a place for us; to prepare mansions in His Father's house for his followers, where is fulness of joy, and at whose right hand are pleasures for evermore. He is therefore our forerunner, who has gone to prepare for our reception and entertainment in the heavenly world. It is His declared will that where He is, there we shall be also, that we may be partakers of his glory. Well may it be said, we have a double assurance of heaven: since our flesh is there as a pledge, and the Holy Spirit is in our souls as an earnest.

Again: 3. Our Lord tells us himself that it was necessary for Him to return to the Father, *to send the Holy Spirit to dwell in His Church on earth.* "Nevertheless I tell you the truth: it is expedient for you that I go away; for if I go not away, the Comforter will not come unto you; but if I depart, I will send him unto you." And when "He, the Spirit of Truth, is come, He will guide you into all truth—He shall glorify me: for he shall receive of mine, and shall shew it unto you." And again, in John vii. 39, it is said, "the Holy Spirit was not yet given, because that Jesus was not yet glorified." This clearly means that the Holy Spirit was not yet poured out in the manner and measure that God did intend to bestow it upon his Church, because Jesus was not yet actually received into glory. It was God's purpose, therefore, to send the Holy Spirit more abundantly, as on the day of Pentecost, into his people, as a distinguishing sign of Christ's ascension. And accordingly, just before He ascended, He told his disciples to tarry in the city of Jerusalem until they should be endued with power from on high. "For behold, I send the promise of my Father upon you. And He led them out as far as to Bethany; and he lifted up his hands, and blessed them. And it came to pass, while He blessed them, He was parted from them, and carried up into heaven. And they worshipped him, and returned to Jerusalem with great joy; and were continually in the temple, praising and blessing God." Luke xxiv. 49-53.

It is not for us to explain why it is that it has pleased Infinite Wisdom to bestow the gifts and graces of the Divine Spirit upon the Church, for the enlightening, sanctifying, and saving of His people, as a reward for the obedience of His Son, and as a proof of his ascension, but it is in this manner the Scriptures set these things before us. The Apostle expressly declares that all the gifts and graces bestowed on the Church for the perfecting of the saints is according to the measure of the gift of Christ after His ascension up on high. "And because He was obedient to death, therefore did God exalt him; for the suffering of death, we see Jesus crowned with glory and honor." It is thus He sees the travail of his soul and is satisfied. And herein also lies our encouragement. We cannot distrust his promises to give us comfort in affliction, strength in weakness, and complete deliverance from all our enemies, for He is exalted to reign over all things for His Church. He is exalted as our Advocate. He is our friend at court, to receive and hand in our petitions, indorsed by his recommendation. Wherefore we may come boldly to the Throne of Grace, that we may receive mercy, and grace to help in time of need.

Grant, we beseech Thee, Almighty God, that like as we do believe Thy only-begotten Son, our Lord Jesus Christ, to have ascended into the heavens, so we may also, in heart and mind, thither ascend, and with Him continually dwell, who liveth and reigneth with Thee and the Holy Ghost, one God, world without end. Amen.

XIV.

"AND SITTETH ON THE RIGHT HAND OF GOD."

"Therefore, being by the right hand of God exalted, and having received of the Father the promise of the Holy Ghost, He hath shed forth this, which ye now see and hear."—ACTS ii. 33.

"Looking unto Jesus, * * * and is set down at the right hand of the throne of God."—HEB. xii. 2.

"The God of our fathers raised up Jesus, whom ye slew and hanged on a tree. Him hath God exalted with his right hand to be a Prince and a Saviour, for to give repentance to Israel, and forgiveness of sins."—ACTS v. 30, 31, with EPH. i. 20–23, inclusive.

IN the Discourse last Sabbath evening on the sixth Article of our Creed, which is in these words: "He ascended into heaven, and sitteth on the right hand of God the Father Almighty," I desired you to consider it as divided into two parts: *First*. Our Lord's ascension. *Secondly*. His position—"sitteth on the right hand of God the Father Almighty." The *first* part was the subject of the last Discourse, in which I spoke of the history of the Article, how it has been regarded by the Church, and how the festival of Ascension Day has been observed. I endeavored to explain the fact of the ascension of our Lord, its *nature, manner, truth* and *certainty, necessity* and *advantages*. The proofs of the fact were named, and the nature and properties of the body in which Christ ascended were found to constitute the *spiritual body* of St. Paul, which he declares is the body of believers in the resurrection. The body in which Christ ascended into heaven, and which is still in heaven, according to our standards, and of the Orthodox Church throughout the world, is "the very same body in which he suffered, with the essential properties thereof," "with flesh, bones, and all things appertaining to the perfection of man's nature," "but without mortality and other common infirmities belonging to this life." When our Lord rose from the dead, He took again the same body in which He lived, suffered, and died, and in this same body He ascended into heaven. This body had the same senses that belonged to it before death, and they were capable of the same, and even of a greater perfection of their functions, as it was now a spiritual body— that is, a purified, a heavenly body. This was the doctrine of the best, and, in fact, of almost all the Fathers.

It will be remembered, also, that in the history of the ascension of our Lord, *two places* are distinctly specified —the place from which He ascended, and the place to which He ascended. He ascended from the side of Mount Olivet, which lies towards the town of Bethany, and on the border of the district or township of Bethany; and "He ascended *into heaven*," where He "sitteth on the right hand of God the Father Almighty." It is of the position, posture, or "the session" of our Lord's human nature in heaven that I am to speak this evening. And the order I propose is—

I. The fact itself, as stated in the Holy Scriptures.

II. Some explanation of the terms or phrases, "into heaven," and "sitteth at the right hand of God the Father."

III. Some reasons for Christ's "session" on God's right hand in heaven.

I. The fact itself. The learned and eloquent *Witsius* introduces his dissertation on Christ's sitting at the right hand of God the Father in the following style : Whoever loves Christ in sincerity, cannot fail, on many accounts, to take pleasure in meditating on that unbounded glory, to which the Father has been pleased to exalt him. No spectacle can be more excellent, more splendid, or more delightful in the esteem of believers, than that to which they are invited in the Song of Solomon: "Go forth, O ye daughters of Zion, and behold King Solomon with the crown wherewith his mother crowned him, in the day of his espousals, and in the day of the gladness of his heart." According to his method of interpreting Scripture, which is still followed by many good men, King Solomon here is the Lord Jesus; the day of his espousals is the Gospel dispensation, which is the day of the gladness of his heart. And the putting of the crown upon his head denotes the great glory of his kingdom by the conversion of souls, as on the day of Pentecost and in the spread of the Gospel. I do not altogether adopt this typical illustration, but still the application is beautiful. And we can all pray that the daughters of Zion, true believers in Jesus, may come in great crowds from all parts of the world to behold His crown.

As to the fact: "and sitteth on the right hand of God, the Father Almighty." *First.* The Scriptures speak as plainly and as positively as they can. Mark says, "He was received up into heaven, and sat on the right hand of God." And this was the fulfilment of our Lord's own words to the priest, who asked him, "Art thou the Christ, the Son of the Blessed? and Jesus said, I am: and ye shall see the Son of Man sitting on the right hand of power, and coming in the clouds of heaven." Mark xvi. 19; xiv. 62. The same is found in Matt. xxvi. 64. And in Luke xx. 42, our Lord quotes the 110th Psalm, 1, and applies it to himself. See verses 41-44.

And before the council of the elders and chief priests, when they demanded to know whether He were the Christ or not, He said, Hereafter shall the Son of Man sit on the right hand of the power of God, and by this He meant He was the Son of God. Luke xxii. 69, 70. And Acts ii. 34-36. Peter, preaching by the power of the Holy Spirit, applies the 110th Psalm, 1, to Jesus. In Rom. viii. 34: "Who is he that condemneth? It is Christ that died, yea rather, that is risen again, who is even at the right hand of God, who also maketh intercession for us."

"If ye then be risen with Christ, seek those things which are above, where Christ sitteth on the right hand of God." Col. iii. 1. " By the resurrection of Jesus Christ, who is gone into heaven, and is on the right hand of God ; angels, and authorities, and powers, being made subject unto him." 1 Pet. iii. 22, with Hebrews i. 3 and 13.

And Heb. viii. 1: "We have such an high priest, who is set on the right hand of the throne of the Majesty in the heavens." Now there can be no denial but that these texts refer to Jesus Christ.

And *Secondly*. As the largest portion of the Apostles' Creed is composed of terms, words, and statements designed to embody and set forth the true faith concerning our *Lord Jesus*, so these statements are meant to deny and refute heresies that disturbed the faithful followers of Jesus even in the early ages of the Church. Many erroneous and blasphemous doctrines were taught, and foolish conceits indulged, even in the days of the Apostles, by Judaizing and philosophical teachers, concerning the *human nature* of our Lord. His DIVINITY was admitted, but his humanity denied. Hence, the Creed was intended to affirm that his human nature was perfect —that though conceived by the Holy Ghost in the womb of the Virgin Mary, yet He was truly born of her, taking a true body from her substance, and having a reasonable soul—and that it was this perfect human body that was really crucified, dead and buried, and rose again and ascended into heaven, and sitteth still at the right hand of the Throne of God. And thus the Creed denies the doctrine of the heretics who said that His body was not real, but only, assumed, and also the doctrine of those who said that when His Divinity left his body it dissolved into air, or, as some of them have said, his body ascended only as far as the sun, in which it was deposited. On the contrary, the true faith of the Church, and which is certainly according to the Holy Scriptures, is : that Christ took his body, the very same body that was laid in Joseph's new tomb, and which was a perfect human body, but free from all sin, and hence could not see corruption in the grave, and with this body came forth from the sepulchre, and in it appeared alive after his resurrection for forty days, and in the same body ascended into heaven, where He sitteth at the right hand of God.

II. The words *into heaven* and *sitteth* imply clearly that Heaven is a *place* as well as *a state*. *Into heaven* indicates the place to which our Lord ascended. Heaven, in ordinary language, the immediate presence of God—the place of purity and happiness where God's greatest favor is enjoyed. The Jews used the term for heaven, however, in a more general sense. The clouds are called "the clouds of heaven," that is, of the first heaven. And

Paul speaks of being caught up into the *third* heaven, and sometimes we hear of the *seventh* heaven, and the heaven of heavens, and in Hebrews vii. 26, it is said: "And he must needs pass through the heavens, because He was made higher than the heavens." And again, Eph. iv. 10: "For He that descended is the same also that ascended up far above all heavens." And in Heb. ix. 12, 24, we are expressly told that Christ our High Priest entered into that within the veil—"into the holy place, even into heaven itself to appear in the presence of God." This is the place called the heaven of heavens. And by ascending into heaven, our Lord fulfilled his words to his disciples when He said: "What and if ye shall see the Son of Man ascend up where He was before." Now as the Son of God came from the Father Almighty, it was not strange that He should return to Him—to the place where He was before his actual incarnation; but it is a wonderful display of his sovereign love, that He should take our nature from the grave, and in it ascend to the heaven of heavens—that His body which was taken out of the substance of the Blessed Virgin, and which was a true human body—with flesh and blood, and bones, like ours—that He should take this body to the right hand of Infinite Majesty, to be seated above angels, and archangels, and principalities, and powers: this is what he meant when He spoke to his disciples about going up to where He was before. Bishop Pearson speaks of the Heaven of the Creed into which Jesus ascended, in this way: "Whatsoever heaven," says he, "then, is higher than all the rest which are called heavens; whatsoever sanctuary is holier than all which are called holies; whatsoever place is of greatest dignity in all those courts above, into that place did He ascend, where in the splendor of his Deity he was, before he took upon him our humanity." p. 400.

It may not be out of place here to remark, that the late eminent and scholarly Sir William Rowan Hamilton, of Dublin, attempted to illustrate from our Lord's ascension the vastness of our universe, and the consequent glory of our Lord as Head over all to His Church. It is certainly a very ingenious attempt to elucidate one of the grandest questions of our faith. His theory is this. As God is everywhere present, the ascension is predicable only of our Lord's body, which is certainly correct. Then a local translation of Christ's body implies a *change of place*, and a change of place requires *time;* and as we have already attempted to show, this must also be true. For even a *spiritual body* is material, and cannot be ubiquitous, nor pass without a period of time from one place to another. But what has all this to do with our Lord's ascending into heaven? Well, let us see. (1.) The ascension was *gradual.* While our Lord was blessing his disciples, He was parted from them. A cloud received him, and as they stood gazing up towards heaven, he disappeared far up, passing still upwards through the air. His ascension did occupy time. It was not instantaneous. (2.) Is it not reasonable, then, to suppose that still more time was occupied in the ascending of his body, after the disciples lost sight of him? The cloud that received Him out of their sight was not the heaven where Jesus sitteth at the right hand of God. Some period of time must have elapsed between his disappearing in the cloud over the Mount of Olives, and his taking his seat at His Father's right hand. *But how long was this period?* I cannot decide. May we say it was ten days? Did it take the human body of our blessed Lord *ten* days to ascend into the heaven which is *far above all heavens?* If so, then how mighty, how vast is our Father's house! No eye, no telescope has pierced through the awful interspace. Light itself may not yet have been able to come from thence to us. And who can tell but such an effluence of light from the Eternal Throne is to burst upon us when the new heavens and the new earth are to appear? I do not say, brethren, this is to be an Article of Faith. I do not venture to say that Christ's body was ten days in ascending into heaven. Reason has nothing to say on this point. It is a matter of Revelation, and revelation leaves us with a record that only suggests. And the suggestion lies in this way: *First.* According to the Scriptures, our Lord's ascension was to be *before* the descent of the Holy Spirit on the day of Pentecost. The Scriptures fully authorize us to say that the gifts of the Holy Spirit are ascribed to Christ's ascension as a completed act. *Secondly.* The descent of the Holy Spirit, being purely Divine, Spiritual, cannot be measured by time. *Thirdly.* As our Lord's ascension into heaven is alluded to in the Scriptures in such close connection with the descent of the Holy Spirit, may we not say, that as soon as Jesus took his seat on the right hand of God, then the Holy Spirit fell upon the Apostles? May not the finished work of ascending up on high have been *instantly* followed by the wonderful outpouring of the Spirit on the day of Pentecost? And we know that Pentecost was ten days after the Ascension. May not the transit of our Lord from the cloud over Bethany to the Throne have been but one continued passage, in long triumphal pomp, through Powers and Principalities made subject to him? May not the only-begotten Son have then been set forth by proclamation and investiture, while the Universe beheld its God, and all the angels worshipped him?* And would not this view harmonize with the 110th Psalm, and the application

---

* See North British Review, Sept. 1866, p. 37.

of it to Christ by the Apostles? Was it not thus the everlasting gates lifted up their heads, that the King of Glory might return to his Throne? This view is not contrary to Scripture or the articulated faith of the people of God, as far as I know. And it certainly opens up grand conceptions of the glory of Christ, as well as of the mighty vastness of our Father's House, in which are many mansions.

Although there are but few themes, if indeed there are any, in the whole range of theological contemplation, more noble than this one—very few more sublime and profitable for devout reflections—yet it is a subject of considerable difficulty, and of much controversy among learned men, both ancient and modern. It is the more important, therefore, that in our remarks we should endeavor to keep the facts as stated in the Holy Scriptures distinctly before us, and try to know the meaning of the terms in which these facts are set forth.

I do not understand that the Creed or the Word of God teaches, that Christ's sitting at the right hand of God means that He is not equal to the Father. I do not see that the learned controversies that have been carried on about the place of honor among the ancients, or with the Romans, have any thing to do with this point. Whether with the Romans the highest place of honor was at the right hand or at the left one, has nothing to do with this Article. All we need to know is, that the Bible speaks of the practice of the Hebrews. In the Epistle to the Hebrews, we have the expressions, "the right hand of the Majesty," and "the right hand of the Throne of the Majesty," and "the right hand of the Throne of God," clearly intimating that this was the place of honor. Accordingly, we find in the 80th Psalm, 17, that the man whom

God loves and honors is *the man of his right hand*. And Solomon says: "A wise man's heart is at his right hand; but a fool's heart is at his left." The meaning of this is, that *right-hand things* are wise, useful, excellent, good; and left-hand things are just the contrary. In Joseph's placing of his sons to receive his father's blessing, we find the elder on Jacob's right hand, as the place of the highest honor. And Job complains of the want of respect among the young men of his day for the aged, by saying that things had come to such a pass, that even the lads, the youth not of age, assumed to take their places at his right hand. And our Lord himself declares that at the last day, His people will be set on his right hand, as a token of his approbation and of the honors to be done to them; but the wicked on his left, in testimony of their disgrace. The sacred writers certainly refer to the custom of the Hebrews, and mean by the right hand, the place of highest honor—denoting dignity equal to that of the Father. *Chrysostom* says: "If inferiority had been intended, the Scriptures would have placed our Lord on the left hand of the Throne." And *Theophylact* says: "*Christ* sitteth on the right hand, and on high; in order to show that He is equal in dignity to the Father." And another old writer says: "The Father offers Christ his Son an exalted place by himself on his Throne; and, for the purpose of doing him honor, he has set him in an everlasting seat at his right hand."*

Is Christ, then, greater than the Father? So some Socinians have charged us with holding. They say it must be so, if our views of the dignity of sitting at the right hand of the Father Almighty are correct. But the Apostle takes an entirely different view: "When all

---

* Quoted from Witsius, vol. ii. p. 242.

things are put under Him, it is manifest that He is excepted, who did put all things under Him." 1 Cor. xv. 27. It is clear therefore that sitting at the right hand of the Throne of God does not mean superiority, but only that He is equal, not inferior. The Father is considered as sitting in the midst of the throne, and our Lord as Mediator is next in dignity. Nor are you to suppose that the seat on the left of the throne must always be filled with some other person who is inferior. When King Solomon desired to show that there was no one whom he would honor more than his mother Bathsheba, he placed her on his right hand, whereas if he had placed her at his left side, leaving the seat at his right side, vacant, it would still have implied there was some one to be preferred to his mother, although not then actually occupying the seat of dignity. The representation of the Persons of the Godhead as occupying a throne refers to the administration of the Mediatorial kingdom of our Lord Jesus. And his Session at the right hand is a metaphor, signifying that He occupies the place of honor, of power, and of joy. And so also,

The term *sitteth* on the right hand of God the Father Almighty in heaven is metaphorical, not expressive of literal posture, but implying dignity, sovereignty, repose, continuance, and the exercise of supreme judgment and authority. Our learned men have shown that it denotes, *first, honor.* Servants stand, but the master sits. Angels stand around the Throne ; but Daniel says, "I beheld till the thrones were cast down, and the Ancient of days *did sit.*" And in showing Christ's superiority to angels, the Apostle asks : "To which of the angels said He at any time, Sit thou on my right hand ?"

Secondly. It expresses *judicial and royal authority.* "Ye also shall sit upon twelve thrones, judging the twelve tribes of Israel." Matt. xix. 28. And it was predicted of the Messiah that He shall bear the glory, and shall sit and rule upon his Throne. "In mercy shall the Throne be established, and He shall sit upon it." Zech. vi. 13. Isa. xvi. 5.

Thirdly. Sitteth at the right hand of God denotes *rest* and long continuance in dignity. It refers to the glorious rest which the Redeemer enjoys. "*Sit* thou at my right hand, until I make thine enemies thy footstool." Ps. cx. 1. "For He must reign till He hath put all enemies under His feet." 1 Cor. xv. 25.

We must not think, however, that our Lord's *sitting* is inconsistent with Stephen's vision of him "*standing* at the right hand of God." Here the word does not denote posture of the body so much as his perfect readiness to receive the martyr's soul. Sitting expresses his glorious rest and authority; and standing declares his readiness to protect his servant. Thus Gregory the Great says: "We must consider what is intended by Mark's expression, 'He sat on the right hand of God,' and by Stephen's saying, 'I see the heavens opened, and the Son of Man standing on the right hand of God.' Why does Mark affirm that He *sits*, while Stephen avers that he saw Him standing? But know, brethren, that it belongs to a judge to sit; to a warrior, or helper, to stand. Since, therefore, our Redeemer, being exalted to heaven, even now exercises universal judgment, and will come at last as the Judge of all, Mark describes Him as *sitting* after He was received up; for, in consequence of the glory of His ascension, He will appear as Judge at the end of the world. Stephen, engaged in the labors of the contest, beheld him whom he regarded as his helper in a *standing* posture; because He fought for him, and supported him by his grace from heaven, that He might obtain the victory over the perverseness of His persecutors on earth."*

The meaning, then, of the words : "And sitteth on the right hand of God the Father Almighty," is that Christ in his person and in his kingly office occupies the highest glory. This is the crowning part of His exaltation. Even on earth He was transfigured, as an illustration of the glory that was in him, but then veiled, and in his resurrection He came forth from the dead to an immortal state, and in his ascension "He was received up into heaven and sat on the right hand of God." This glory is peculiar to Christ. "He set him at his own right hand in the heavenly places, far above all principalities, and power, and might, and dominion, and every name that is named, not only in this world, but also in that which is to come: and hath put all things under His feet, and gave Him to be the Head over all things to the Church, which is His body, the fulness of Him that filleth all in all." Eph. i. 20, 23. From this passage of the Apostle it is clear that Christ is above all prophets, teachers, and legislators of past ages, and of the present and of all future ages of the Church. Men and angels, however glorious in his service, are under Him. So it was with Moses and the Prophets, and so it was with his own Apostles, and so in all ages to come, Christ is far higher than all the angels. No creature is associated with Him in his dominion. He is the sole, Supreme, only "Head over all things to the Church, which is his body, the fulness of Him that filleth all in all."

But it is said, believers have the promise of reigning

---

* Quoted out of Witsius, vol. ii. pp. 248, 249.

with Him, of sitting on thrones, standing at his right hand, and the Apostles are to sit on thrones with Him, judging the twelve tribes of Israel. Now, I apprehend that these and all such expressions are figurative. They mean identity of will and communion with Him. They approve of and rejoice in His government and in His glory, as if it were their own. When it is said believers are "partakers of the Divine nature," the meaning is not that they become infinite as God is infinite. The only sense possible to such a phrase is that they are partakers of Divine things, not in degree and quality, but in *kind*—they are assimilated in a small degree to His likeness.

The words, then, "sat down at the right hand of the Throne of God," express the glory of our Lord, which is common to Him and the Father and the Holy Spirit; and they set forth at the same time the peculiar glory which, according to the mystery of the Trinity of Persons in the Godhead, is to be ascribed to the person and offices of Christ as Mediator. We do not read anywhere in the Bible that the Holy Spirit sits at the right hand of God. Nor do we read of the Holy Spirit being born of a woman, or sent into the world to suffer and die. As it was the Son of God, the person Christ Jesus, who fills the office of Mediator, so the glory of that office belongs only to Him. He therefore sits at the right hand of the Throne. You have observed, doubtless, that the term HOLY is an eminent specialty of the third person of the ineffable Trinity. Why is this? Not because the third person is more holy than the first or the second; but simply, because it is the divine economy that the third person shall operate on the human heart, and make it holy by applying to it the benefits purchased by the death of Christ. And hence the third person is called the Holy Ghost, or the Holy Spirit, because it is his office to make men holy. And as Christ is the Mediator between God and men, so his person and offices are peculiarly glorified by his ascending into heaven and sitting at the right hand of the Throne of God. His own glorified body is there in the glory which, as God's own Son, he had with the Father before the world was. And in respect to his office, He fills it by sitting at the right hand of God the Father—that is, He is reigning, ruling, ministering, and governing all things for his Church. As Peter said: "Therefore, let all the house of Israel know assuredly that God hath made that same Jesus, whom ye have crucified, both Lord and Christ." "Being by the right hand of God exalted."

III. In the third place, let us inquire, WHY is Christ thus sat down at the right hand of the Throne of God in heaven?

1. To show the glory of God the Father. "God hath highly exalted him," Phil. ii. 9. In his resurrection from the dead, our Lord received his discharge for the full payment of the debt He assumed for us; and in his ascension the Father recalls him, as an ambassador who has accomplished his mission in a foreign country is called home to his native land to enjoy the honors and fruits of his labors. As God's only Son, He has essentially a kingdom and glory, but it is in his mediatorial or personal kingdom as God-man that we see him sitting at the Father's right hand. In his humiliation, he emptied himself of his glory, took on himself our nature. In his exaltation He takes human nature with him to his eternal glory, and in it is exalted, that in all things He might have the pre-eminence. For He is the Head of the body, the Church, who is the beginning, the first-born from the dead.

"Who, being in the form of God, thought it not robbery to be equal with God:

"But made himself of no reputation, and took upon him the form of a servant, and was made in the likeness of men:

"And being found in fashion as a man, he humbled himself, and became obedient unto death, even the death of the cross.

"Wherefore God also hath highly exalted him, and given him a name which is above every name:

"That at the name of Jesus every knee should bow, of things in heaven, and things in earth, and things under the earth:

"And that every tongue should confess that Jesus Christ is Lord, to the glory of God the Father." Phil. ii. 6–11.

In the work of redemption Christ glorifies the truth, holiness, justice, and mercy of God. The Father is glorified in the Son.

2. One part of His office as our High Priest is to appear before God to *make intercession for us.* You remember that when Solomon had caused his mother to be seated at his right hand, he assured her that none of her requests should be denied. But how much more may we rely on the interceding requests of Jesus sitting at the right hand of the Throne of God? He upholdeth all things by the word of his power, and having made an atonement by the sacrifice of himself to satisfy Divine Justice, He then sat down at the right hand of the Majesty on high, to make intercession for us. "For Christ is entered into heaven itself, now to appear in the pres-

ence of God for us." Heb. ix. 24. "But this man, after he had offered one sacrifice for sins, forever sat down at the right hand of God. From henceforth expecting till his enemies be made his footstool." Heb. x. 12, 13.

3. Again, *Christ is thus exalted at the right hand of God to protect His Church and vindicate His people, and complete their salvation.* The Father gave him to be the Head over all things to the Church. He is a King who rules in the midst of his enemies. He will maintain the right of His people, and powerfully defend their cause against all their enemies; for their enemies are His enemies.

4. And is there no terror in the consideration of this Article to the ungodly? Who is this that is seated in glory ineffable at the right hand of the Throne of God? Is it not He whom the Jews rejected, saying: "We will not have this man to reign over us?" But He does not now wear the mock robe of royalty, but is clothed with the majesty of the Eternal Throne. The sceptre in his hand is no reed, but the rod of His Power, with which He keeps the universe in awe. Vain are the efforts of men and devils to keep Christ from reigning. "He that sitteth in the heavens shall laugh; the Lord shall have them in derision." In spite of the feeble rage of the ungodly, and the fury of demons, our Jesus reigns still, and shall reign forever. He shall put down all rule, all authority and power, and bring every thing into subjection. And with Him His Church is exalted and reigns in spite of all her foes.

> "Superior to their rage in every form,
> Treads on the clouds, contemns the bursting storm;
> Hears tempests rush, and dreadful thunders roll,
> With smiling count'nance, with undaunted soul."

Let the potsherd of the earth strive with the potsherds of the earth, but woe unto him that striveth with his Maker. However rich or powerful his adversaries may be, Jehovah will break them in pieces like a potter's vessel. He will beat them like dust before the wind, and reduce them to powder like the mire of the streets. "Serve the Lord with fear, and rejoice with trembling. Kiss the Son, lest He be angry, and ye perish from the way, when his wrath is kindled but a little."

Are you indeed, my dear brethren, subjects of such a King? Are you followers of the Lord Jesus? With what fervor, then, should you adore Him! How earnestly should you serve Him! What is there on earth, among all its joys, honors, or pursuits to be compared to the riches of the glory of the inheritance of His saints? Are you, then, living for His glory? Are you praying and laboring that His kingdom may come? Are you toiling in anticipation of that unfading crown of glory which He will put on your heads, and which is to encircle them forever? May you be faithful unto death, and enter into life eternal. Amen.

XV.

CHRIST COMING TO THE LAST JUDGMENT.

"Which also said, Ye men of Galilee, why stand ye gazing up into heaven? this same Jesus, which is taken up from you into heaven, shall so come in like manner as ye have seen him go into heaven."—ACTS i. 11.

"But I would not have you to be ignorant, brethren, concerning them which are asleep, that ye sorrow not, even as others which have no hope. For if we believe that Jesus died and rose again, even so them also which sleep in Jesus will God bring with him. For this we say unto you by the word of the Lord, that we which are alive and remain unto the coming of the Lord shall not prevent them which are asleep. For the Lord himself shall descend from heaven with a shout, with the voice of the archangel, and with the trump of God: and the dead in Christ shall rise first: then we which are live and remain shall be caught up together with them in the clouds, to meet the Lord in the air: and so shall we ever be with the Lord. Wherefore, comfort one another with these words."—1 THESS. iv. 13-18.

LAST Sabbath evening we saw God's only Son, our Lord Jesus, sitting on the right hand of God the Father Almighty, as Lord and Christ, exalted with the right hand of God to be a Prince and a Saviour, on the throne above all angels, principalities, and powers of the present age, and of all ages to come, Ruler and Judge Supreme over all things to His Church. We have now to consider the *seventh* Article of our Creed, which embodies the declaration of the two angels to the disciples as they witnessed our Lord's ascension. The words of the Creed are: "From thence He shall come to judge the quick and the dead;" or, as it is expressed in the fourth Article of the Church of England: "And there sitteth until He return to judge all men at the last day." Our subject, then, is CHRIST COMING TO SIT IN THE JUDGMENT OF QUICK AND DEAD AT THE LAST DAY. And may the spirit of Almighty wisdom and grace assist us to make a profitable use of this doctrine.

This is the last of those particular characters ascribed in the Creed to our Lord Jesus. The whole of the Article, if fully expressed, would read in this way: "And I believe in Jesus Christ his only Son, our Lord, who was conceived by the Holy Ghost, born of the Virgin Mary, suffered under Pontius Pilate, was crucified, dead and buried: and I believe that He descended into hell, and that He rose again the third day from the dead, and that He ascended into heaven, and there sitteth on the right hand of God the Father Almighty; and I believe that our Lord Jesus Christ, who now sitteth in his perfect human nature on the right hand of God, shall come 'with glory' to judge the quick and the dead; and that 'his kingdom shall have no end.'" You see, brethren, how large a portion of the Creed is employed in expressing what we are to believe concerning the Lord Jesus. If the Creed be printed in fourteen lines, nine of the fourteen are required to express our belief in Jesus; and of course the same proportion will obtain in whatever sized type it may be printed. This may remind us that our faith in Jesus is to be regarded as of special consequence, both as to our own souls and as to our influence on others.

The points of this Article are four in number: *First*. That Christ shall come again, that is, to this world. *Second*. That He shall come from the highest heaven into which He ascended when He left this world. *Third.* The end of his coming is to *judge;* and, *Fourthly.* The objects or persons to be judged are *the quick and the dead.* The Article relates to Christ in His person and office as Mediator and King, and implies the presence of the same human body in which He ascended. It declares His *coming, the place* from which He shall come, *the end* of his coming, and the *parties* to be judged by him. There is no essential variation in the old copies or draughts of this Article of the Creed. In some of them it is read *from thence,* and in some *from whence,* and in some simply, *He will come,* and in some *from thence* or *from whence He shall come* is all left out, and we have only : *He shall judge the quick and the dead.*

The other words, however, when omitted are left out not because they are not supposed to be true, but because they are thought to be unnecessary, being implied in the other clause. For if Christ is to judge the quick and the dead, it is implied He will come again from heaven to this world. In choosing words to constitute an articulated faith, it is better, however, not to leave any thing to be implied that can by any possibility be misconstrued. The Article, therefore, is to be received as we have it. Nor are the reasons for our holding it as a part of our faith essentially different from those that caused it at first to be adopted. In the early ages of Christianity, the chief difficulties in the Church as to Articles of Faith related to our Lord's human nature. And hence the fulness and earnestness of the large part of the Creed that speaks of Christ. The same teachers and sects for the most part who held erroneous views concerning our Lord's human nature, also denied a future judgment. The bearing of the ancient Creeds is very clear on the Incarnation. And in them the sitting of Jesus on the right hand of God in his human nature is connected immediately with his coming from thence to judge the world. This was designed to condemn the idea of Sabellius, that the Son was merely an emanation from the Father, without personal subsistence, put forth for a time and then reabsorbed when his mission was achieved. Particularly was this the purpose of the clause added in the Nicene Creed: "And whose kingdom shall have no end." When the work of redeeming our race is complete, the exercise of the Redeemer's office will cease, but not his kingdom of glory, for from all eternity the decree had gone forth in behalf of God's own Son, "Thy throne, O God, is forever and ever." For when the kingdoms of this world become the kingdoms of the Lord and of his Christ, He shall reign forever and ever.

Some, as the Manicheans, it is believed denied both the resurrection and the future judgment. The Marcionites and other Gnostics also denied the future general judgment, on the ground that God was so full of grace and mercy, that there was no necessity for the general judgment, for God regarded all human actions with indifference. Men were insignificant in his sight. Now even a limited acquaintance with the literature of our day is quite sufficient to show that similar views are prevalent among us. The Swedenborgians, after their founder, generally hold that the passages of Scripture which speak of the judgment day are not to be literally interpreted, but are used as metaphors or figures of speech. The idea of Swedenborg probably was, that men are a kind of waif, subject to two opposite influences, one from God and good spirits, and the other from evil angels, and as they yielded to one or the other, the soul was good and rose, or was bad and fell. Consequently heaven and hell are not to be regarded as places, or as the result of a Divine appointment, but as the necessary conditions or *status* of the man himself, according as he is good or evil.* Another reason for the use of this Article was to express the faith of the Church in the *continuance* of our Lord's kingdom, and the eternity of the union between his Divinity and humanity—two perfect natures in one person forever. *Origen* taught that the kingdom of Christ, after many ages, should end. And *Marcellus* of Ancyra thought that the office of King was committed temporarily to our Lord, and consequently that his kingly office would cease and his human nature come to nothing. On the other hand, the Scriptures teach that His kingdom shall have no end. The present forms of His kingdom of power and of grace will cease, but the kingdom of his glory shall have no end. It shall last forever. *This Article therefore teaches the eternity of the mysterious Incarnation.* It asserts that Christ as man shall reign forever. On this point we may well adopt the words of *Chrysostom*, saying: "We wonder at the awful and ineffable nature of this mystery. Our Lord put on our flesh, not to lay it aside again, but to have it ever with Himself. He inhabits his human tabernacle forever. Otherwise He would not have deemed it worthy of the royal Throne, nor would He have been adored, wearing it, by all the heavenly host of angels, archangels, thrones, dominions, principalities, and powers."†

There are two additions in the Nicene Creed as adopted by the Fathers of Constantinople, namely, the words "with glory:" "and he shall come again *with glory*, to judge both the quick and the dead:" and also the words:

---

* See Bishop Browne, p. 101. † Forbes, 250.

"whose kingdom shall have no end." The texts of Holy Scripture brought forward in the preceding Discourses in proof of our Lord's ascension, and sitting on the right hand of God as Christ in human nature,* all imply the doctrine that Christ will come to judge the world. Several of them expressly affirm it. *Paul*, in his celebrated discourse on Mars hill, declares, that "God now commandeth all men everywhere to repent: Because he hath *appointed* a day in which He will judge the world in righteousness by that man whom He hath *ordained*, whereof he hath given assurance unto all men, in that He hath raised him from the dead." Acts. xvii. 30. It will not then seem out of place, or useless, I hope, to have alluded thus briefly to the crude conceits and unscriptural opinions that are denied and refuted in the Creed, for by so doing we see how error has promoted truth. If such errors had not arisen, we should not have had such accurate statements of the truth in the early formulas of the Church. When dangers were discovered, then the Church was obliged to define and protect the truth as it is in Jesus. And it is wonderful to see how the three great Creeds— the Apostles' Creed, the Nicene, and the Athanasian, are devoted to the full and accurate statement of what was believed concerning the two natures of Christ, God and man, intimately united, yet not confounded, and to remain "in two distinct natures, but one person forever." —*Catechism.* Athanasius, in A. D. 365, declares that all the Churches in the world, whether in Europe, Asia, or Africa, approved of the Nicene faith, except a few persons who followed Arius.† The great value of these old Creeds consists in the way they guard and set forth

---

* Deus et Homo unus est Christus.—*Athanasian Creed.*
† See his Epist. ad Jovian, tom. 1, p. 246.

the doctrine of the Trinity and of the Incarnation. The ancient subtleties and monstrous errors of the early ages may not be revived again, but doctrines quite as blasphemous and damaging are held and taught among us. In fact, on this subject it is particularly to be noted, that there is but little that is *new*.

The departures from the faith of God's elect that grieve us now are for the most part similar to, or identical with, those that tried the Church in past ages, even from the days of the Apostles themselves. And a knowledge of these facts should strengthen our faith and comfort us, for they prove that there has always been a faithful body of believers, who have held to the truth essentially as it is in Jesus. And if the errors and awful apostasies and moral degeneracy of past ages have not destroyed the Kingdom of God, we need not fear that the gates of hell will prevail against it now. The existence of the Church of Christ, with the purity and power that it now has, in the midst of and in spite of the corruption, apostasy, and unfaithfulness of its members, is a strong argument for the Divinity of the Gospel.

It is not without special significance that the Apostle, in the Epistle to the Hebrews, speaks of the necessity of considering the doctrine of Eternal Judgment as among the first and great principles of the doctrines of Christ. Therefore, leaving the principles of the doctrines of Christ, let us go on unto perfection; "not laying again the foundation of repentance from dead works, and of faith toward God, of the doctrine of baptisms, and of laying on of hands, and of resurrection of the dead, and of eternal judgment." Heb. vi. 1, 2.

Here it is clearly seen : 1. That the Apostle thought there were signs of departing from the faith of the Gospel in fundamental doctrines even in his day, and hence his exhortation not to fail or go back from the doctrine of Christ.

2. *Eternal judgment* is one of the fundamental doctrines which the ungodly in his day denied, as also in our times, and as, in fact, they are always desirous of denying and getting rid of.

3. It is well to observe here also the connection in which this doctrine is spoken of—"and of the resurrection of the dead, and of eternal judgment."—And

4. This doctrine of *eternal judgment* is here enumerated among the fundamental principles which lie at the very foundation of all godliness—"the foundation of repentance from dead works, and of faith toward God."

According to the standards of our holy religion, we do most certainly believe that

"I. The bodies of men, after death, return to dust, and see corruption; but their souls (which neither die nor sleep), having an immortal subsistence, immediately return to God who gave them. The souls of the righteous, being then made perfect in holiness, are received into the highest heavens, where they behold the face of God in light and glory, waiting for the full redemption of their bodies; and the souls of the wicked are cast into hell, where they remain in torments and utter darkness, reserved to the judgment of the great day. Besides these two places for souls separated from their bodies, the Scripture acknowledgeth none.

"II. At the last day, such as are found alive shall not die, but be changed: and all the dead shall be raised up with the self-same bodies, and none other, although with different qualities, which shall be united again to their souls forever.

"III. The bodies of the unjust shall, by the power of Christ, be raised to dishonor; the bodies of the just, by his Spirit, unto honor and be made conformable to his own glorious body."

And the next *chapter* "*of the last judgment,*" says:

"I. God hath appointed a day, wherein he will judge the world in righteousness by Jesus Christ, to whom all power and judgment is given of the Father. In which day, not only the apostate angels shall be judged, but likewise all persons that have lived upon earth shall appear before the tribunal of Christ, to give an account of their thoughts, words, and deeds; and to receive according to what they have done in the body, whether good or evil.

"II. The end of God's appointing this day is for the manifestation of the glory of his mercy in the eternal salvation of the elect; and of his justice in the damnation of the reprobate, who are wicked and disobedient. For then shall the righteous go into everlasting life, and receive that fulness of joy and refreshing which shall come from the presence of the Lord: but the wicked, who know not God, and obey not the Gospel of Jesus Christ, shall be cast into eternal torments, and be punished with everlasting destruction from the presence of the Lord, and from the glory of his power.

"III. As Christ would have us to be certainly persuaded that there shall be a day of judgment, both to deter all men from sin, and for the greater consolation of the godly in their adversity : so will he have that day unknown to men, that they may shake off all carnal security, and be always watchful, because they know not at what hour the Lord will come, and may be ever prepared to say, Come, Lord Jesus, come quickly. Amen." [Chapters xxxii. and xxxiii. of *Confession of Faith.*]

By the day of the future general judgment is understood the important day which is the last day of the present economy, or dispensation of grace, the day when the eternal state of all men will be unchangeably fixed. It is the day on which Christ shall come to judge the quick and the dead, and we believe in this doctrine of our holy faith, not only because we are personally concerned in it, but also because it is the last act of the Mediatorial reign of Christ, "the brightest manifestation of his divine glory, the anchor of Christian hope, a powerful antidote against carnal security, a check to raging lusts, and an incentive to conscientious piety."—*Witsius.*

I. In the order I propose to follow, our first inquiry is as to the PLACE where CHRIST is to judge the world. "From thence He shall come." But to what place will He come?

WHERE is this general judgment to take place? The general Scriptural designation is, in the air or in the clouds. 1 Thess. iv. 16; Matt. xxiv. 30.

1. Perhaps this is the best place, in order to fill the Apostle's declaration that every eye shall see him. As if the clouds were to form a vast amphitheatre for this day, "the day for which all other days were made."

2. It is a favorite scriptural representation to speak of the clouds as God's chariot, or as his royal Throne. The law was given in clouds. The Son of God dwelt in the

pillar of cloud by day, and unveiled enough of his glory by night to make it a pillar of fire. He ascended in a cloud, and He will come again in like manner.

Those who are not content with a cloud-formed amphitheatre for the scene of the judgment, in a general way, have endeavored to prove that the words of the two angels to the disciples, on the Mount of Olives, when the Saviour ascended into heaven, mean that He is to come in the *same place*—that all men are to be assembled for the last judgment in the Valley of Jehoshaphat, which lies below the Mount of Olives, from which our Lord ascended.

It is alleged that Christ should display the Majesty of his glory in view of Calvary, where He suffered the ignominy of the Cross, and that He should judge where He himself was judged. This idea is held by many, in both Papal and Protestant churches. Even Mohammedans have adopted the idea also, that the scene of the last judgment is to be over Jerusalem. There are many conceits about this, as well as about the holy city itself, that I do not think worthy of formal statement or refutation. I do not think the words of the angels, on any fair rule of interpretation, can be applied to the *place*, but to the *manner* of Christ's coming. Nor is it at all clear from the best interpretation we can get of Joel's prophecy, which is generally applied to this subject, that he had any such meaning in his mind. On the contrary, it is clear that Joel is not speaking of the last judgment at all, but of a day of vengeance on Messiah's enemies previous to it. Our conclusion therefore is, that the place will be in the air or on the earth, then a part of the new heavens and new earth. To fix the place, however, is of little consequence. For the fact that God has appointed such a general judgment, according to the Bible, is certain, and it will be *righteous, universal, decisive,* and *eternal* as to its consequences.

II. Our second inquiry is as to THE TIME when Christ is to come to judge the quick and the dead.

1. God has fixed a day—a certain, determinate day—by which we are to understand a fixed period, without determining how many hours are to be occupied with the proceedings.

2. The precise period in the chronicles or epochs of time when this day shall be is not revealed to us. And as we understand our Lord, we are even forbidden to exercise our curiosity about it. The angels of heaven do not know when it is to be. Paul could not write about it. Even the inspired Apostles, who were guided to write on other subjects by the Holy Spirit, were left in darkness as to the time of our Lord's appearing to judge the world. It is not strange, then, if men will indulge their own inventions on such a subject, that they shall write many absurd and wicked follies about it. God has concealed it from us to try our faith and obedience, and teach us to watch and be always ready.

3. It is called the *last day* of the world. It will be preceded by the resurrection of the dead. It is always spoken of in such a way as to imply, even when it is not so expressed in words, the resurrection of the dead and the end of the present economy, and the beginning of the eternal and unchangeable state of all men of Adam's race. The term *last day* does not of necessity imply the annihilation of our solar system or of our solar globe itself. Time may go on. The planets still occupy their orbits. This globe, being purified as by fire, may be the abode of happy beings forever. But the last day means the end of the

present dispensation—the winding up of the Mediatorial economy in regard to our race. It is nonsense, however, for unbelievers to argue that the Scriptures teach the literal consuming and end of the world by fire, and then to argue that the Scriptures are in error, for that science—astronomy and geology, for instance—teach us there can be no such thing; for we have the most palpable evidence of fearful convulsions having taken place in our planet already, and that we embody within ourselves elements quite sufficient to rend us all to pieces, and to burn us to cinders. We know, astronomically, that other bodies in the solar system have been torn to pieces. Why may not the earth in like manner be multiplied into a small system of asteroids? There is nothing in true science, as yet developed, to contradict the sacred writers, even if they taught that this earth is to be literally consumed by fire. Many learned and able theologians so understand the Word of God. But this is a point, like the duration of our present dispensation, that does not seem to us to be revealed. I find nothing in the Bible that authorizes us to say *when* the end of the world is to be, nor any thing that requires us to believe that the end of the world literally means the destruction of our solar system. On the contrary, all that I understand by it is its purification.

III. In the third place, who is to preside in the judgment of the world? "From thence HE shall come to judge the quick and the dead."

1. The Scriptures teach that the Triune God will be the Judge of all men. *Solomon* says, "Know thou, that for all these things GOD will bring thee into judgment," and "GOD will bring every work into judgment." The Apostle *Paul* also speaks of the "day of wrath and revelation of the righteous judgment of GOD," and of "GOD the

Judge of all." These texts represent God as the Creator, Lawgiver, and Supreme Governor of the Universe, and as having, therefore, the power and the right, and in fact being under obligations to take cognizance of the actions of his creatures, who are his subjects, and to reward or punish them according to their conduct, rendering to every man according to his deeds done in the body, whether good or bad.

2. It is, however, clearly revealed in the Scriptures, that it is the settled economy between the Persons of the Godhead, that Messiah, who is the God-man, the Mediator between God and men, is to be the Judge. This is a part of the official duty of the Messiah promised to the Jewish Church. The pious Israelites looked for a Messiah who is described as "judging and seeking judgment, and hasting righteousness." As the anointed King over Zion, we may apply to him the words of the Prophet: "The LORD is our Judge, the LORD is our Lawgiver, the LORD is our King: He will save us." Isa. xxxiii. 22. Nor is it without good reasons that the Chaldee paraphrast renders the 72d Psalm with direct reference to Christ: "Give the King thy judgments, O God, and thy righteousness unto the King's Son." That is, according to the Chaldee comment, to King Messiah, who is King David's Son. Nor should it be forgotten that literally in the history of our Lord's trial, we have the exact fulfilment of the prophecy of Micah, v. 1: "They shall smite the Judge of Israel with a rod upon the cheek."

And our Lord spoke plainly on this subject: "The Father judgeth no man, but hath committed all judgment to the Son." John v. 22; Matt. xxv., xxvi.; Acts xvii. 31; Rom. ii. 16; Rev. xx. 12.

You observe ~~St. Paul says~~, God has appointed a day

to judge the world, and He hath ordained that the judgment shall be by that man Christ Jesus; and *Peter* says, God hath commanded us to preach unto the people, and to testify that it is He, which was ordained of God to be the judge of quick and dead. And accordingly it is declared in another place of Holy Scripture, that it is before the judgment seat of CHRIST that we must all appear. 2. Cor. v. 10.

"He shall come as a Judge, who once stood before the Judge. He shall come in that form in which He was judged, that they may see Him who pierced him, and that they who received Him not may then know Him."*

3. It is true also that our Saviour said, according to the passage in John viii. 15—50: "I judge no man: and there is one that seeketh and judgeth, that is the Father."

But a little candor and reflection will relieve these places from any contradiction. The meaning is: 1. That the Father judgeth no man in a visible form. The embodiment of the Godhead is in the Second Person, as developed or manifested to man. 2. The meaning is, there is a perfect harmony and oneness of mind between the Father and the Son. The judgment is not held separately by either. And, 3. The meaning is, that as the work of redemption has been executed by God's Son— as He is the Mediator—as He was born of a woman, suffered under Pontius Pilate, was crucified, dead and buried, rose again from the dead, and ascended into heaven, and sitteth on the right hand of God, to reign as King and Head over all things to His Church, so it is a part of his kingly office to preside in the general judgment. This is the meaning of the Apostle's words, when

---

* Augustine.

he declares that God will judge the world in righteousness by that man whom He had ordained. Acts xvii. 31. "And God shall judge the secrets of men by Jesus Christ." Rom. ii. 16.

When therefore we hear our Lord saying, "I judge no man," the meaning is, I am not sent as Moses was. I have not come as a minister of wrath to condemn the world. "God sent not His Son into the world to condemn the world, but that the world through Him might be saved." John iii. 17.

Clearly also our Lord means, that He will not judge separately from the Father. "And yet," says He, "if I judge, my judgment is true, for I am not alone, but I and the Father that sent me." "The Son is come in the name of the Father, nor can He do any thing of himself, but what He seeth the Father do." "I do nothing of myself; but as my Father hath taught me, I speak these things." John viii. 28. "And hath given Him authority to execute judgment also, because He is the Son of Man." John v. 27.

The reasoning of *Augustine*, in his sixty-fourth sermon on these passages, and in explanation of the economy of the judgment by the Son, is very much to my mind. It is to this effect. That as the Son of God became the Son of Man, and by His humiliation, obedience, and sufferings in human nature, and by His sacrifice of himself satisfied Divine Justice, so that we may be reconciled to God, so it is eminently proper for Him as Mediatorial King to judge and punish the enemies of His kingdom. And as He submitted to be judged and pronounced guilty and was put to death by men, so it is expedient that his judges should be judged and their sentences reversed. "He who stood under a judge will sit as Judge." "He who was himself falsely pronounced guilty, will condemn the truly guilty." It is as the Son of Man, to judge the quick and the dead, that He will appear *visibly* in the clouds, and every eye shall see Him, and they also which pierced Him. Rev. i, 7. In saying therefore that "the Father judgeth no man, but hath committed all judgment unto the Son; that all men should honor the Son, even as they honor the Father," the meaning is that the Father and the Son are equal, and that in the judgment of the quick and the dead no one will see the Father; but all shall see the Son, because He is also the Son of Man, so that the wicked may see their Judge. "It is right that they who are to be judged should see their Judge."* But oh! who can support the dreadful presence of God, or who may stand in His sight? Who can endure to hear the voice at which the earth melteth, and at whose reproofs the pillars of heaven tremble—that awful majesty before which the seraphim hide their faces? Is it not then a proof of the condescension and mercy of God, that the judgment of quick and dead is assigned to the Son of Man?

He shall come to judge—He who came once before in our nature—He who was conceived by the power of the Holy Ghost in the womb of the Virgin Mary, and born of her—He who suffered so deeply for us, who died to redeem us: He shall come in glory to judge the quick and the dead.

In holding that Jesus Christ, visible as the God-man, is the Supreme Judge of all men and angels, we are not to be understood as separating his Divine from his human

---

* Rectum erat ut judicandi viderent Judicem. See also Augustin de Trini. lib. 1. cap. 13.

nature. His majesty, power, wisdom, and glory will then manifest his Eternal Divinity, but his acts in judging will be visible by his human form. Consequently He is the Judge in his own right, and not by a merely delegated authority. The *will* as well as *the Deity* of Christ is the same as the will and Deity of the Father. The exercise of the Divine perfections, therefore, in judging the world, is by the authority of the ineffable Godhead. Isaiah, speaking in the name of Jehovah, says: "I have sworn by myself; the word is gone out of my mouth in righteousness, and shall not return; that unto me every knee shall bow, every tongue shall swear." Isa. xlv. 23. And yet we find St. Paul applying these very words to our Lord Jesus. As Judge, therefore, the Son of God appears in his own right and by his own authority, but makes himself manifest as the Son of Man.

Thus it is plain that the quick and the dead are to be judged by the Lord Jesus. He has the original, absolute right to be judge, because as God He is the Creator of all things, and, as Supreme Lord and King over the universe, all things are governed by him. It belongs to Him therefore to institute an inquiry as to the way his laws have been observed,—to reward service performed, and punish disobedience. If this is not to be done, then, so far as His government is concerned, there is no difference between the good and the bad. But we know there is a difference. Virtue is in part its own reward, but only in part: vice is in part its own punishment, but only in part. There must, therefore, be a final adjustment. The uneven scores that run on so long here must be compared and put together, and perfect justice rendered. Hence, there must be an account given of the talents bestowed upon us, and the opportunities granted to us for doing good and getting good. This is everywhere taught or implied in the Word of God. And as our Saviour is thus qualified by his attributes to be the final judge of men and angels, so also is He placed in the proper position by his office as both Lord and Christ. He sits on the right hand of the Throne of God as King over all things for his Church. He is therefore the judge by his Father's appointment. The Apostles expressly declared He is *ordained* by God the Father for this very office. Nor are there wanting even to our limited apprehensions important reasons why the Father assigned the final judgment to the Son. Does it not prove that God condescended thus to show us his goodness? There must be a strict and impartial judgment, says God, but let my creatures see there is no vindictiveness in it. Let the administration of it be attempered by putting it into the hands of my Son, who is also the Son of Man. Surely his worst enemies cannot complain that He is their judge when they remember that He is the very same who prayed for them when He was dying, and who shed his blood to redeem sinners. Nor will His followers fear to meet him face to face, when they call to mind that He is their brother, that He sits in judgment in their own nature, and remember how meek and lowly, merciful and full of pity He was, and that they are to meet him clothed in the robes He has put on them, redeemed and washed from sin in his blood. And besides, how better could God the Father show his creatures the greatness of his Justice than by exalting to the Judgment Throne Him who, out of regard for his Eternal Rectitude, obeyed his will and offered himself a sacrifice to satisfy Divine Justice? Who better deserves this crown, or can so worthily hold the sceptre, than He who willingly submitted to the scourge and the mockery of royalty, and bore the Cross? And how awfully will it aggravate our guilt to be condemned by a Judge so mild, just, and gentle? How can we stand before Him and answer for having violated laws so righteous and good—for having neglected and despised blessings and mercies so numerous, great, and long continued, and so well devised to bring us to repentance! How can we stand before such a Judge, and answer Him for having rejected so many calls and so many gracious offers of his pardoning mercy; for defeating so perseveringly his serious purposes of mercy towards us; for having forfeited his favor and incurred his displeasure by sinning against our own souls, and for having abused His great love!

When one looks at the world it may well be asked, do any of us really believe this Article? Even if we admit the vague idea of future retribution, do we bring home to ourselves the awful strictness with which the proceedings of the judgment-day will be carried on? There may be a kind of general mute acquiescence that the balance will be adjusted at last between good and evil, and the good will be somewhat rewarded and the bad in some measure punished; and even this vague, unsatisfactory conviction causes great uneasiness when some great crime has been committed, or when death knocks at the door. But this is far below the proper and scriptural view of the awful judgment to come which should dwell upon our minds. We need both the prohibitions of conscience, supported by the sanctions of Eternal Justice, and the stimulus of faith to enable us to maintain our Christian character. No point is more emphatically pressed in Holy Scripture than the certainty and strictness of the details of the coming judgment. "And I saw the dead, small and great, stand before God; and the books were opened, and another book was opened, which is the Book of Life; and the dead were judged out of those things which were written in the books according to their works. And the sea gave up the dead which were in it; and death and hell [that is, the grave and the whole region of the departed,]—delivered up the dead which were in them; and they were judged every man according to their works. And death and hell were cast into the lake of fire. This is the second death. And whosoever was not found written in the Book of Life was cast into the lake of fire." Rev. xx. 12–15.

1. In conclusion, as an unbelieving heart is one of the greatest curses which can come upon a man, so a real belief in the last judgment is a great grace from God. For promoting zeal and piety, the saintly Basil has well said concerning the future judgment: "Blessed is that soul, which day and night hath no other care than how, in the great day, when every creature shall stand around the Judge to give an account of their works, she shall be able to relate her life. For whosoever continually places that day and that hour before his eyes, and ever thinks of his defence at that most just tribunal, is likely to commit no sin, or at least very few." And so also *Chrysostom* says: "Let us ever be saying to ourselves and to others, there is a resurrection, and a terrible judgment awaiting us."

2. *The sincere belief* of this Article would powerfully reconcile us to submit to the dispensations of Divine Providence. All earthly prosperity and adversity is rapidly passing away, and we are hastening to the Judgment-seat. Surely then we are not to repine at the Providence of God as exercised toward us or our fellow-men.

3. It should also keep us from judging *rashly* concerning our fellow-men. God has not appointed us to sit in judgment over them, nor has He trusted to our hands the avenging sword of Justice. "Who art thou

that judgest another man's servant? To his own master he standeth or falleth. Yea, he shall be holden up, for God is able to make him stand. So every one of us shall give account of himself to God." Rom. xiv. 4-12.

Is it possible for us, my dear brethren, to think of any subject that can be compared in importance with this one? It is said of a distinguished name, expressive of a *noble life*, that he lived and acted as God's steward over an immense estate, doing good with all his revenues and maintaining a cheerful and happy state of mind under a life-long deformity, which deprived him of most of the pleasures and pursuits of other men, *because he felt every day that he might die to-morrow.**

How should it influence our words and our conduct, if we could, in a proper way, realize that we must hereafter certainly render a strict account of all our actions—that all our doings must undergo a strict scrutiny before Him who searcheth the heart and trieth the reins of the children of men! And how careful should we be of the entries now made in the records which are to be produced in that day, since every one is to be judged and rewarded and punished according to the deeds done in the body, whether they be good or bad! It is with the greatest propriety, then, that the Apostle speaks of the doctrine of eternal judgment as a fundamental principle of our holy religion, necessary to be believed, in order to repentance from dead works and faith toward God. It is impossible to conceive of a sharper "spur"† to the doing of good, or to devise a stronger "curb" from doing ill, than the real belief that we must appear before the awful and impartial Judgment-seat of Christ.

---

* "A Noble Life," by Miss Muloch.   † See Dr. Barrow on the Creed, p. 457.

4. And so on the other hand, if we are ourselves dealt unjustly by; if we are misunderstood and wickedly misrepresented; if we are subjected unjustly to reproach, scorn, persecution, even unto death, then let us remember there is One who knoweth all these things, and He will appear for the innocent at last and vindicate the honor of His laws. God shall bring forth thy righteousness as the light, and thy judgments as the noonday. The Apostle, in view of this final settlement, and with a good conscience, could say: With me it is a very small thing that I should be judged of you, or in man's judgment. Ps. xxxvii. 6; 1 Cor. iv. 3.

5. Nor can I conceive of a more powerful stimulus to beget in us *sincerity*, than the profound conviction that God will judge us—not by our professions or pretensions, promises or appearances, but according to our individual realities—according to the deeds done in the body. Not only our words and actions, but our motives, designs, feelings, the most inward recesses of our hearts, where are the seeds of things, the germs of moral character which no human laws can reach, will then be brought to light. Every thought that rises in the mind, as well as every word that passeth out of our mouth, as well as every deed that our hands have performed, will then be judged. And since we know that this awful judgment awaits us—but when we may be called to meet it we know not—then surely we should watch and be diligent. What manner of persons ought we to be in all holy conversation and godliness, looking for and hastening unto the coming of the day of God? Notice how the blessed Apostle stirred himself up, and reminded his beloved Timothy of the awards of the eternal judgment: "I charge thee therefore before God, and the Lord Jesus Christ, who shall judge the quick and the dead at his

appearing and his kingdom. For I am now ready to be offered, and the time of my departure is at hand. I have fought a good fight, I have finished my course, I have kept the faith: henceforth there is laid up for me a crown of righteousness, which the Lord, the righteous Judge, shall give me at that day: and not to me only, but unto all them also that love his appearing." 2 Tim. iv. 1-8. Let us, then, by the grace of God, which appeareth to all men, deny ourselves—deny all ungodliness, worldly lusts, and live soberly, righteously, and piously in this present world, in the blessed hope of the appearance of the great God, even our Saviour Jesus Christ, to whom with the Father, through the eternal Spirit, be equal and eternal praises. Amen.

XVI.

CHRIST JUDGING THE WORLD.

"Because he hath appointed a day, in the which he will judge the world in righteousness, by that man whom he hath ordained : whereof he hath given assurance unto all men, in that he hath raised Him from the dead."—ACTS xvii. 31.

1. IN the Discourse last Sabbath evening, the doctrine of our Creed concerning CHRIST coming to judge the world was stated, and a brief history of the Article was given, and some reasons were offered, why it was adopted as an exponent of the Faith of the ancient churches, and why it should be retained and believed in, just as we have it.

2. Your attention was directed to the PLACE where and to the time when the general judgment was to be held. The place, we thought, was the air of the new earth ; the time not known, because not revealed to us nor to the angels.

3. It was *shown*, however, that the fact was certain, and that *Jesus Christ* was to be the Judge—that according to the Scriptures it was the solemn appointment of the Father Almighty that his only Son our Lord Jesus CHRIST, in His human nature, should be the Judge—in the same perfect human nature in which he ascended into heaven

after His resurrection, and in which He now sitteth on the right hand of the Throne of God in heaven, shall He come visibly with power and great glory to judge the world.

Among the particulars yet to be considered on this Article, let us now proceed—

I. To consider, *why God hath appointed a day of general judgment.*

And 1. That God has appointed such a day is as clearly and as positively affirmed in the Word of God as language can express it. Matt. x. 15; xii. 36; xxv.; Ecc. xi. 9; Acts xvii. 31; Heb. ix. 22; 2 Pet. ii. 9; iii. 7; 1 John. iv. 17; Jude; 2 Thess. i. 7–10; iv. 14–18; Heb. vi. 1, 2; 2 Cor. v. 10; Rom. xiv. 10, 11; Jo. v. 22; Rev. xx. 12.

2. *The resurrection of Christ is a proof that He is to come again to judge the world.*

A few texts on this point at present, as Acts xvii. 31; and Rom. xiv. 9, 12, are deemed quite sufficient. "Because God hath appointed a day, in the which he will judge the world in righteousness, by that man whom He hath ordained; whereof He hath given assurance unto all men, *in that He hath raised him from the dead.*" "For to this end Christ both died, and rose, and revived, that He might be Lord both of the dead and the living. For we shall all stand before the Judgment-seat of Christ. So then every one of us shall give account of himself to God." It is usual in the sacred writers to connect the resurrection of the dead with the *eternal judgment,* as in the Epistle to the Hebrews, vi. 1, 2. For the most part the same texts of Holy Scripture that prove our Lord's resurrection, ascension, and sitting on the right hand of God, also speak of his coming again to judge the world; and when in any of these proof texts

His second coming is not spoken of in express terms, it is always clearly implied. "THIS SAME JESUS," say the angels to the disciples, "which is taken up from you into heaven, shall so come in like manner as ye have seen him go into heaven." Acts i. 11. "For if we believe that Jesus died and rose again, even so, them also which sleep in Jesus will God bring with him. For the Lord Himself shall descend from heaven—and the dead in Christ shall rise first." 1 Thess. iv. 14–18. "And to you who are troubled rest with us, when the Lord Jesus shall be revealed from heaven with His mighty angels, in flaming fire taking vengeance on them that know not God, and that obey not the Gospel of our Lord Jesus Christ." 2 Thess. i. 7, 8.

It is in evidence then that God has appointed a *determinate* day for the judgment of the world in righteousness by Jesus Christ, as the Creed affirms. This Article then denies and refutes on Scriptural authority the opinion or surmise of those who hold that there is no fixed day for a general judgment. It is a notorious fact not only that there were ancient heretics who denied any resurrection from the dead, or any determinate general judgment of mankind ; but there are now certain teachers who either altogether avoid committing themselves on the subject, or who hold the opinion that by the term *day*, in regard to the last judgment, we are to understand simply that as the present season of grace is sometimes called the sinner's day, or the day of God's long-suffering and patience towards us, so when the Gospel dispensation ceases, and there is an end of its shining light, during which sinners were called to repentance, then comes what is called the *last day*, for then the Judgment will commence, but that we cannot fix any definite idea to the term *day* as used in reference to it. On the contrary, the Creed implies what the Scriptures declare, that God has appointed a day for the judgment of the world in righteousness by our Lord Jesus Christ, who shall come from heaven for that purpose. [See *Confession of Faith*, chaps. xxxii. and xxxiii., quoted in previous chapter.]

3. Again : *Such are the relations between God as Creator, Supreme Lawgiver, and Universal Governor, that His Justice requires an open and final adjustment of the affairs of His Universe.* Speaking with reverence, He is bound by his Eternal Justice to be faithful to himself, to his laws, and to all the virtuous beings in all his universe—to vindicate his moral government by rewarding the obedient and punishing the disobedient, and thus show that there is a difference between those that serve Him, and those that serve Him not. If the Supreme Being does not take notice of His creatures, and reward the obedient and punish the disobedient, then this world is indeed a poor melancholy atom, and we are orphans in the vastness of a creation that has no Creator. If Epicurus is right, that there is no notice taken of human conduct by the Supreme Being, then what becomes of God's Justice? But we know that some visitations of vengeance have fallen upon mankind. And if so, must there not be equal justice done to all? For if the inequalities of this life are not put to right in the world to come, it is impossible for God's creatures to see His Justice, or to know that there is in fact any difference between doing well or doing evil. To deny the future judgment is to destroy the foundation of all morality.

Even among the heathen, we find from the remotest antiquity some dark notions about a future judgment— some "few sparkles of light in their consciences" about a future state or of a judgment to come. Both philosophers and poets in Greece and Rome wrote about it. Plato and the Platonists, and Cicero and Virgil abound with references to a future trial and rewards and punishments to come from a final adjustment of the contest now carried on between good and evil. Man's moral nature is so strongly impressed with the idea of some future state, and of some final result as to the contest between good and evil, that all nations and ages have in some way expressed their belief on the subject. All lands have temples and worshippers, and all zones have altars and sacrifices. The savage tribes of the wilderness, the hierophants of Egypt, the schools of Rome, the sages of the Academy, and the wise men of the East, have all, though in different ways, confessed their conviction as to the reality of moral evil, and the necessity of some future retribution. Now whence this moral sense, and this idea of a future judgment? Is it innate? If so, whence does it come, but from the Creator? Is it learned from tradition or acquired by reason? Whence its *universality* unless it is divinely inspired? But although all ages have felt painful convictions on these subjects, yet none knew how to escape from the wrath to come. For the two thousand years intervening between Noah and the coming of Christ, God left the world to prove to itself that by its own wisdom it could not find Him out nor deliver itself from the power of evil. The very idea of our accountability after death for the actions of this life involves the day of future retribution.

And although it is not possible to analyze these notions of the heathens, and say exactly how much they received from others, or how much they have discovered by the mere light of nature, or how much they owe to the dim and scattered glimmerings of divine truth revealed to the Hebrews, yet enough is clearly seen to show that there is a wide-spread and deeply painful consciousness that something is needed to break down the reign of evil; and that, as an actor in the old French revolution said, if there is no God, we must make one, for the world cannot be governed without a God. Human society cannot continue to exist, if all idea of a future state and accountability for our conduct after death were lifted off the heart of man. Moral responsibility is necessary to break or to endure the reign of moral evil.

The heathen, especially *Plutarch* and *Cicero*, have written largely concerning the necessity of a judgment to come. And the Sacred Scriptures clearly and fully confirm what natural religion, or perhaps we should rather say, what common sense, reason, and the Providence and attributes of God require, that there should be a future general judgment.

Nor is it unworthy of notice, as *Witsius* argues, that we have precedents in sacred history that should be received as proofs and warnings of the judgment to come. We read in the Bible of *four* public and universal judgments upon our race. *First*, in Paradise, when we were all represented in Adam; *second*, on the world before the flood; *third*, on the nations in the plains of Shinar, at the tower of Babel. And the *fourth* is the last judgment.

The wisest heathen have been found, like the royal Psalmist before he went to the sanctuary of God, and learned their dreadful end, stumbling at the prosperity of the wicked in this world. From this unequal, unfinished state of things two opposite conclusions have been drawn: namely, that the Supreme Being is totally indifferent to human actions, and consequently there is no final judgment-day for rectifying the miseries of this life. Every thing is left to chance or blind fate. This is too monstrous to need refutation. The other view is that the miseries of this life, in which the most pious and good, and in every way some of the best men on earth are deeply involved, and pass out of this world without any redress, imperatively call for a future judgment. The moral proof, then, of a future judgment is derived both from within ourselves, and from the works of creation and Providence,—from conscience in us, and from evidences of design in the works and government of God. The whole constitution of the universe, and the whole framework of human society, are witnesses for its necessity. The testimony of the moral sense is universal and strong. Nor are there wanting evidences of design in the works of the Creator, which lead us irresistibly to the conclusion that the *unfinished problems* of his Providence in this world must be completed in the world to come. We cannot believe they are dropped and abandoned. On the contrary, all we know of the wisdom of God constrains us to believe that He has secured a perpetual identity to all His moral creatures, and guaranteed that this life of man shall so far lap over and impress itself on the life to come, that this world is only the sowing, and futurity is the harvest. The natural world unquestionably demonstrates the perfect wisdom, Almighty power, and Supreme goodness of the Creator. Is it reasonable, then, to suppose that His moral government is less perfect? In the light of reason and common sense, does induction teach us there is a God, who is all wise, all powerful, and supremely good? And is it not, then, a legitimate conclusion that there is a final Judgment-seat, when and where the apparently inconsistent dispensations of His moral government over the universe will be cleared up? For if this life is really nothing but a life of trial, to be succeeded by a final retribution, then we are sure the goodness, truth, and justice of God will be vindicated in the moral world quite as clearly as his glorious perfections are seen in the natural world. Some things are clear, even now. For example, there are some cases just such as we have referred to. Cunning gains over honest simplicity. The truth is, that though *honesty is upon the whole the best policy*, yet there are cases whose sequel we do not see, and hence, as far as this world is concerned, there are exceptions to this great maxim. No one is prepared to say there are not individual cases that are exceptions to this rule, if this life is the whole of human existence. For it is certainly the testimony of human experience that many things here are *unfinished*. Many cases are adjourned to a heavenly tribunal, where, from the character of God, we look for a perfect vindication of innocence, and of all his ways towards his creatures, in the punishment of wrong-doing and the reward of well-doing. If, in the checkered events of human life, we see men of integrity made the victims of the snares and evil deeds of the artful, who receive a temporal reward; and if we find the godly suffering from sickness and other visitations of Divine Providence, is it not evident that this is not the end?—these cases are adjourned to the eternal world. It is quite true also that sometimes God lays his hand upon transgressors, so that He may be known on the earth by the judgment which He executes upon them. And are these any thing but preludes or pledges of that awful judgment which is to come? Proofs that we must leave many things, sadly unfinished as they are, without seeing the reasons, to the judgment of the last day, being perfectly sure there is One above us who sees all, and who renders to every man according to the deeds done in the body—according to his works.

4. Let me call your attention now, in the next place,

to something in regard to the *circumstances* and *manner* of the proceedings of the Judgment-day which may be clearly learned from the Scriptures. The Lord Jesus shall come in his human nature from his throne at the right hand of God, from heaven, and He shall come *visibly* in the clouds of heaven, and with power and great glory. Innumerable hosts of holy angels will appear with him. Matt. xxiv. 30; 2 Thess. i. 7.

His coming is to be *sudden*,—as it was in the days of Noah and of Sodom and Gomorrah. This proves that the world will then be very much as it is now—that His coming will be unexpected—that it will be sudden—in a moment, in the twinkling of an eye, the archangel's voice shall shake all the earth, and rouse the dead out of their sleep.

> "Lo! on a narrow neck of land,
> 'Twixt two unbounded seas I stand,
> Yet how insensible!
> A point of time, a moment's space,
> Removes me to that heavenly place,
> Or shuts me up in hell.
>
> "O God! my inmost soul convert,
> And deeply on my thoughtful heart
> Eternal things impress.
> Give me to feel their solemn weight,
> And save me ere it be too late;
> Wake me to righteousness."—*Wesley.*

The manner in which the sacred writers speak of our Lord's coming to judge the world impresses us with the great solemnity, glory, and magnificence of the event. He once came in meekness and humility to teach us how great was his love for us, and to show us our duty. He shall come again in his glory, and His holy angels with him, in terrible majesty, to teach us that every creature is subject to Him.

In Heb. xii. 26, the Apostle seems to have in his mind a contrast between the glory of the giving of the law at Mount Sinai and the glory of the eternal judgment, when Christ shall judge the world according to that law "whose voice then shook the earth; but now He hath promised, saying: Yet once more I shake not the earth only, but also heaven."

Our Lord expressly declares, in Luke ix. 26, that He would come to this world again after his sufferings and death, and come in His own glory, and in the glory of His Father, and in the glory of the holy angels. The same is substantially, and almost in the same words, to be found in many other places.

The splendor of the Divine Majesty will be made manifest: "When the Son of Man shall come in his glory, and all the holy angels with him, then shall He sit upon the throne of his glory." Matt. xxv. 31. "Hereafter shall ye see the Son of Man sitting on the right hand of power, and coming in the clouds of heaven." "All the tribes of the earth shall *see* the Son of Man coming in the clouds of heaven, with power and great glory." Matt. xxiv. 30, and xxvi. 64.

According to the Scriptures also, the magnificence of this day is to be ushered in with *the trump of God*, by which the dead are to be raised. "For the LORD himself shall descend from heaven with a shout (1 Thess. iv. 16), with the voice of the archangel." That is, with authority to enforce obedience from all angels, powers, and authorities—for all are put under Him who is the Head over all things to His Church.

But how are we to understand these words, *with a shout, with the voice of an archangel, and with the trump of God?* Are they to be taken in a literal sense? Why not? Is there any reason for departing from the literal meaning? Was there not a literal sounding of the trumpet *exceeding loud* at the giving of the law? Why was not this intended to be a model for the Judgment-day? And is not this view supported by the use of trumpets in executing the Divine judgments upon Jericho? It may be *metaphorical*, however, so far as the instrument is concerned. It may be that the voice that is to call the world to judgment and wake the dead, will be composed of thunder such as those heard when God spoke in the hearing of the people at Mount Sinai. Perhaps it will be an articulated voice formed by the angel hosts in the air, so in harmony as to produce a sound loud enough to fill the whole earth, and yet as if the utterance of but one trumpet, and that as soon as the attention of quick and dead is secured, from the same hosts will be heard the summons of the parable of the virgins: "Behold, the Bridegroom cometh; go ye out to meet him."

All that need be insisted on is, that Christ's command to bring the quick and the dead to judgment will be effectual. It will gather them before him. And as the sound of a trumpet by one who blows it well is loud, penetrating far and wide; so Christ's call to judgment will reach every cavern and receptacle of the dead on the mountains and on the plains, and under the seas. And as the phraseology of the sacred writers is Jewish, it is not strange they should represent the gathering of mankind to be judged, as if called by a trumpet, as the Israelites were accustomed to be assembled on festival days, or for other solemn purposes.

Again, an immense retinue of angels are also mentioned in several places by the inspired writers, as contributing to the glory of Christ when He shall come to judge the world. So our Lord says himself: "When the Son of Man shall come in glory, and all the holy angels with Him, then shall He sit upon the Throne of his glory." And *Enoch*, the seventh from Adam, prophesied, saying, "Behold, the Lord cometh with ten thousand of his saints," and *Paul* says the Lord Jesus shall be revealed from heaven "with his mighty angels."

Nor are the angels to be mere idle spectators. They are to be employed in assembling the vast multitudes. "He shall send His angels with a great sound of a trumpet, and they shall gather together his elect from the four winds, from one end of heaven to the other." "And the angels shall come forth and sever the wicked from the righteous, as the goats are separated from the sheep. For the Son of Man shall send forth his angels, and they shall gather out of His Kingdom all things that offend, and them which do iniquity, and shall cast them into a furnace of fire." Angels are employed as his ministers now, and assist His people, and carry home their souls when they leave their bodies, and will aid in taking them through the air to meet their Lord, and in punishing the incorrigibly wicked.

It may be asked, in what sense then are saints to judge the world, and even angels, according to St. Paul's words in 1 Cor. vi. 2, 3? I answer, in precisely the same sense that the Apostles and believers are promised to sit on thrones with Christ, or to reign with Him: namely, their will is in perfect harmony with His. They approve of his decisions. And their justification and example, as sinners saved, is a just condemnation of those who have rejected Christ. No importance is to be attached to the fact that historically believers became magistrates in the Roman empire, or may be such now, as an interpretation of this passage. Nor do I think it exhausted by simply saying that believers judge the world and angels in Christ as their Head. This is true; but a specialty is attached to the fact that their individual wills are in perfect submission and in sweet harmony with the mind of Christ. They rejoice therefore with approbation in all his ways. It may also be true that the term judge is here to be taken in the sense of *govern*, and that saints are to exercise authority under Christ in the new heavens and the new earth.

5. We have come now to the PARTIES TO BE JUDGED. "From thence He shall come to judge the quick and the dead." God hath appointed a day in the which He will judge *the world* by Jesus Christ.

Both persons and their works must pass the Judgment-seat of Christ—those who may be living, the quick, and all who have died—both good and bad—and all evil spirits. 2 Pet. ii. 4; Jude 6.

To judge the quick and the dead, that is, the world, or rather the moral agents that are in it, or have belonged to it. Those are dead who are said to have fallen *asleep;* and those who are living at that time, who, in contradistinction to the dead who are asleep, are denominated *the quick,* the living. The terms the *quick and the dead* are co-extensive with the whole of our race. The dead are to be raised, and the living to be changed, for in every case corruption must put on incorruption and mortality must put on immortality.

The *quick and dead* does not mean, as some say, *the bodies* and *the souls* of men, nor *the good and the bad,* but those who are alive at the moment of the judgment, and all the dead from the beginning of Adam's race. The similes used of the flood and of the overthrow of the cities of the plain imply clearly that the world shall be going on just as it is now. It shall be peopled, and there will be good and bad, and those alive shall be caught up quick to judgment, undergoing a change equivalent to death, for the purpose of putting off mortality and putting on immortality. The Son of Man shall come as a thief in the night. St. Peter declares, in the very words of the Creed, that God ordained Jesus Christ to judge the quick and the dead; and so does St. Paul: "I charge thee therefore before God and the Lord Jesus Christ, who shall judge the quick and the dead at his appearing and his kingdom." And Peter in another place says: "Who shall render an account to Him that is ready to judge the quick and dead;" and Paul in another place, that He may be Lord both of the dead and living.*

From which Scriptures it is clear *the quick and the dead* means all men; and that some shall be living when the Judge shall come, but that the living and the previous dead shall together and at the same time be the subjects of the last judgment. Thus we are told in 1 Thess. iv. 15, that we which live—who shall be alive—remaining on the earth when the Lord shall come, shall not prevent them which are asleep. We shall not, indeed, all fall asleep—all shall not die, or be found dead, when the day of the great judgment comes, but we, that is, the human beings then alive, shall be changed in a moment, in the twinkling of an eye. 1 Cor. xv. 51.

That all must be judged is according then to both reason and Scripture. All are creatures. All are therefore accountable in the measure the Creator has imposed obligations upon them. As it is appointed unto all men once to die, so after death is the judgment for all men. And so also says St. John: "I saw the dead—all the dead

---

* Acts x. 42; 2 Tim. iv. 1; 1 Pet. iv. 5; Rom. xiv. 9.

—small and great, stand before God, and the dead were judged out of the things written in the books, according to their works." All will be there, every one—the rich and the poor, the master and the servant, the mightiest and the lowest, the learned and the ignorant—all, without any exception and without any partiality, must appear before the Judgment-seat of Christ and undergo this trial, and receive sentence according to the deeds done in the body. The last judgment is to be universal. No one, not you nor I can escape it. We shall certainly stand before the Judgment-seat of Christ. He shall come to judge *the quick and the dead.*

But whether good angels are to be judged or not, all men, both good and bad, must appear before the Judgment-seat of Christ. So the Scriptures positively affirm. 2 Cor. v. 10, and Jude 14; Rom. xiv. 10–12; Acts x. 42.; 2 Tim. iv. 1.

Collective terms are used, and classes specified by the sacred writers, in such a way as to show conclusively that all men must be judged. It could not be otherwise; for all are creatures, all have sinned; their outstanding unsettled accounts must be adjusted, so that it may appear that God is indeed just when He judgeth, and righteous when He condemneth. If any were rejected or overlooked, there would be no guarantee for justice.

6. *What is to be judged?* Thoughts, words, and deeds. The sacred writers specify idle and hard speeches, that is, arrogant and cruel expressions against our fellow-men as well as against God.

And are the sins of the godly now to be exposed as well as the sins of the wicked? Much is said on both sides of this question. That they will be published is argued—

First. From the fact that the Scriptures speak in a general way of the works of all men, good as well as bad, coming before God in the judgment.

Secondly. Impartial justice would seem to require both sides of a case, what is against as well as what is for the parties to be judged. The sins from which they are saved, if seen, would show the greatness of their salvation and render the condemnation of the ungodly more fully justifiable, if it could need it.

Thirdly. The memory of the sins of the godly is perpetuated in the sacred records: Why may they not be mentioned again and for the last time at the judgment?

Fourthly. The Grace of God in their salvation, and the Justice of God in the punishment of the incorrigibly impenitent, would be more palpably displayed by bringing their sins to light than by keeping them in darkness. Nor is it possible not to see that the idea of publishing their sins at the last day is a stimulus to watchfulness against committing sin, whereas the contrary doctrine would lead to carnal security.

On the other side, it is said:

1. The Scriptures do not anywhere affirm positively that the evil doings of saints will then be made public.

2. The promise of God on the contrary is, that He will remember no more our sins, but will cast them into the depths of the sea. And it is asked, if God has removed our sins out of his sight, why will He allow them to be exposed to the gaze of angels and men, our former friends and enemies? If they have once been buried, why bring them from the depths of the ocean before the vast assembly of the universe?

3. It is said again, Christ is our advocate, our propitiation, the mercy-seat which covers our sins: He will not expose the short-comings of his clients, nor allow the covering of the mercy-seat to be lifted to discover our sins which are under it.

4. It is alleged also that as we are to be judged by the Gospel, and not by the Law, therefore our sins will not be published, for the Gospel has forever pardoned them. And *finally*, it is said, the sins of believers will not be made known to the universe on the day of judgment, for such an exposé would overwhelm them with shame, whereas the Church is to be presented at that time to the Father holy, without blemish, not having spot or wrinkle or any such thing. While so much may be said on both sides, and many of our ablest theologians have confessed themselves unable to come to a decision, it does not become me to dogmatize at all; but I cannot help inclining to the first view: namely, that such a recognition, at least of the sins of Christ's people, will then be manifested as shall exalt the exceeding greatness of His Grace. The texts just quoted on the other side are capable of a clear explanation without proving the points they are quoted for.

The time admonishes me that I must close this discourse. In doing which, allow me two remarks. I. While angels and men shall be spectators of the judgment, they will also *all be interested in its awful scenes*. Holy angels assist and approve. And every man and every evil spirit will both feel in himself, even in his own condemnation, the justice and the goodness of God, and see the same in the judgment of others. The uttered and executed sentences of the last day will be exactly according to what every one has read beforehand in his own conscience, and has been reading all the time from his death till the judgment in his own heart. The decisions of the last day will be as it were transcripts from the consciences of the parties judged. Men are happy or miserable immediately after death, but their case is not fully made up, for all their works are not then matured. Some men's sins are open and go beforehand to judgment, but other men's sins follow after them. This is clearly taught by our Lord in one of his parables, in the anxiety of the rich man about the coming of his brothers to the same place of torment with himself. And also in the voice from heaven, saying, "Blessed are the dead which die in the Lord from henceforth; yea, saith the spirit, that they may rest from their labors; and their works do follow them."

There are many fearful cases that cannot be fully made up for judgment till the last day itself. Their records are not complete. There remains a reckoning to come after death for those sins to which men are accessories, though committed long after they have themselves left this scene of action. A man's influence is immortal. The sins of ill-educated children are to be laid to the account, in some measure, at least, of their parents; and so the influence of teachers on their pupils, of the heads of business houses over the young people in their employ; and, in short, of all the corruption and evil that has or may result from the example one sets, or the opinions and doctrines one publishes. The harvest that a bad book or fiendish print may reap for the garner of the authors and publishers at the last day, it is beyond the power of any mortal tongue or pen to describe. Beware of your influence upon others.

II. My second and last remark is, that *the Bible view of the day of future and final retribution proves the necessity of regeneration and sanctification by the Holy*

Spirit. According to the Scriptures, so minute and exact are the records for the Judgment-day, that our thoughts and words, as well as deeds, are to be scrupulously examined. We are then to answer for the meanest as well as for the loftiest of our thoughts; and so awfully thorough and just will the scrutiny of the last day be, that with an unerring hand all the threads of the intents of our heart will be traced out, and all the complications of the web of life will be unravelled, from the beginning to the end. It may be that comparatively our world is as a grain of sand on the shores of eternity, yet we know that God hath prepared his Throne in the heavens and that His Kingdom ruleth over all. We know that the hairs of our head are numbered—that a sparrow cannot fall to the ground without the knowledge of our heavenly Father. The very same reasons and arguments and convictions on the human heart, and testimonies of Holy Scripture, therefore, which establish the existence of God and of his moral government over the world, prove at the same time that all the complications implied in the holding of a general judgment are clear as day to God's all-seeing eye, and quite as easily held in his Eternal Mind and Omnipotent Hand as the minute and exact and vastly complicated works of creation and Providence. And if the All-wise and All-powerful has made every atom of the material universe subject to His laws, which is certainly true, why is He not as supreme over the intellect and the moral feelings? If the Almighty has arranged for weighing and adjusting every particle of matter, and does actually control it, is He not quite as able to weigh and balance every principle of the heart, that has been called into play, through every day and hour and moment of our lives? He knoweth our frame: He knoweth that we are but dust. *We must then be born again.* We must be created anew in Christ Jesus. We must be restored to the image in which we were created, and this work can only be done by God's own Spirit. We cannot stand in judgment and answer for our thoughts, no more than for our words and deeds, without the new creating and cleansing power of the Holy Ghost. Our prayer should therefore continually be: "Create in me a clean heart, O God; and renew a right spirit within me."

The carnal mind is at enmity with God. The great object, therefore, to be kept in view by us all the time is, that we may be clothed with the righteousness of Christ, to find mercy of the Lord through the propitiation that is made for our sins—to bring into captivity every thought to the obedience of Christ, that we may be conformed more and more to the pattern of Him who is the brightness of the Father's glory and the express image of his person. And may God grant unto us grace, that at the general resurrection in the last day, we may be found acceptable in His sight, and receive the blessing which His well-beloved Son, our Lord, shall then pronounce on all who love and fear Him, saying: "Come, ye blessed of my Father, receive the kingdom prepared for you from the beginning of the world." Grant this, we beseech Thee, O merciful Father, through Jesus Christ our Mediator and Redeemer. Amen.

XVII.

RULES OF CHRIST'S FINAL JUDGMENT.

"And I saw a great white throne, and him that sat on it, from whose face the earth and the heaven fled away; and there was no place for them.

"And I saw the dead, small and great, stand before God; and the books were opened: and another book was opened, which is the book of life: and the dead were judged out of those things which were written in the books, according to their works."—REV. xx. 11, 12.

In some measure you have in your minds from the preceding Discourses the *history* of the Article of our Creed, which is in these words: "From thence He shall come to judge the quick and the dead." You have learned something of the *reasons* why it was adopted by the ancient churches, and why we should retain and believe it just as it is. *The place* and *the time* of the general Judgment have been spoken of. It has been found that JESUS CHRIST in his perfect human nature is to appear visibly in the clouds of heaven with his holy angels, with power and great glory, as the Judge of quick and dead. *Reasons* also have been given why God hath appointed a day in which to judge the world in righteousness by the Lord Jesus Christ. *The ends* to be accomplished by the general judgment, speaking with reverence, seem to be worthy of the Creator and of his works and ways. *The manner* of conducting the assembly of *quick and dead*, which terms are co-extensive with all the moral agents that have been on our globe, at least all of our race and all evil spirits, has impressed us, I hope, with the *solemnity, glory, and magnificence of the event*. It only remains, according to our method, to speak of the RULES OF PROCEEDING according to which the last judgment is to be held, and sentence pronounced and executed, and to make a few reflections on the awful scene. And if I am not very much mistaken, all attempts at rhetoric or impassioned oratory are wholly out of place when directed toward such a subject as this. I am aware that ORATIONS by one of the greatest Christian orators, and one of the most remarkable men of modern times, were delivered and published on the "Judgment to Come," and that much art and oratorical machinery has been used by great French preachers, and perhaps by others, in preaching on the awful Judgment-day of Almighty God; still I cannot help thinking it is misplaced. The fact, the simple fact itself that there is *a judgment to come*—a day appointed by our Maker in the which He will judge the world in righteousness by our Lord Jesus Christ, and that when He comes to judge the quick and the dead, we must every one appear before him, and stand at his Judgment-seat, this fact itself is more awfully eloquent than any declamation can make it. On such a theme, the best possible effort is to get the simple, awful subject into the mind and upon the heart, as nearly as possible in the way it is presented to us by the inspired writers themselves. The text is a palpable allusion, if not to the passages themselves, yet certainly to the same customs, and employs the same imagery, that we have in Matthew xxv. and Daniel vii. 9, 10.

1. Note the utter destruction of the kingdom of Satan,

the complete overthrow of the powers of darkness (Rev. xx. 9 and 10), which comes before the last judgment.

2. Here is a description of the Day of Judgment. And truly may we say, with the pious *Matthew Henry*, as we read it: "The Lord help us firmly to believe this doctrine of the judgment to come." "And I saw," says the Apostle, "a great white throne." The same our Lord speaks of, saying: "When the Son of Man shall come in his glory, and all the holy angels with him, then shall He sit upon the throne of his glory." The same that Daniel saw: "I beheld, till the thrones were cast down, and the Ancient of days did sit, whose garment was white as snow, and the hair of his head like the pure wool; his throne was like the fiery flame, and his wheels as burning fire. A fiery stream issued and came forth from before him; thousands ministered unto him, and ten thousand times ten thousand stood before him; the judgment was set, and the books were opened. And I saw in the night visions, and behold, one like the Son of Man came with the clouds of heaven, and came to the Ancient of days." vii. 9-13.

I do not say that the events referred to by Daniel are identical with the event described in Matt. xxv. 31-46, and in the text. Nor is there any direct connection between them in point of time, or as of cause and effect, that I am aware of. But the imagery is essentially the same. And no one should press the figures used beyond what the nature of the scene fully justifies. Reference is had in the mind, in all these passages, to oriental customs. The Rabbins were constantly in the habit of speaking of the opening of the books before the Throne of Judgment, as if allegations were then to be made out of the records, the indictment read and proof submitted, after the manner of human courts, or as in the calling and sitting of a grand judicial convention or Sanhedrim.

A *great* throne here means a very *high* throne; and *white*, that is, shining, refulgent, intimates its purity, equity, justice, righteousness. The great white throne is the Throne of His glory.

And him that sat on it—the Son of Man, the Lord Jesus Christ, but appearing now in such awful majesty, that heaven and earth fled away; and there was found no place for them. As if the sun, moon, and stars grew pale, and were overshadowed by the brightness of his coming; and that He was all in all, the fulness of all. The language does not imply necessarily the annihilation of the material universe, nor the total destruction of our solar system. But it does imply the destruction of all evil, and the impossibility of any escape from the all-seeing eye of the Judge.

And I saw the dead—all the dead, as well as all living, small and great, stand before God. "And before Him shall be gathered all nations;" and all the individuals of all nations and ages. The sea, the land, the grave—"death and hell delivered up the dead which were in them: and they were judged every man according to their works."

"*And the books were opened: and another book was opened, which is the Book of Life: and the dead were judged out of the things which were written in the books, according to their works.*" The imagery here, though taken from human courts of justice, is painfully emphatic and minute. The scene is on this wise. Here is the judgment throne. Here are the laws enacted and promulgated by the All-wise and Almighty Creator. Here are His creatures, and here are the records of their lives, of their thoughts, words, and deeds. It is at once apparent that the acts and characters of the persons to be judged are far from being in conformity with the statutes. *The books are opened;* namely, the records of common sense and reason, proclaiming the propriety, fitness, and prudence of things, all of which shows that the laws of God were reasonable, just, and good, and that there is no valid excuse for having violated them. And the book of providence, common, special, and universal, is opened. And so also are the *books of Divine omniscience*, of *God's remembrance*, and the book of every sinner's own CONSCIENCE. And the Book of Revelation, of nature and of law, natural and revealed, and by all these records the dead are condemned. *But now another book is opened, which is the Book of Life.* No defence is supposed to be made, for the reason that none is possible. No excuse can be offered. All are speechless; even those who are saved are saved by free sovereign grace. They have no claims to plead, but their pardon. The Book of Life, in a strict sense, is opposed to the book of death, the second containing the names of the condemned. It is the record of Christ's people, of those whom the Father gave him; but in a more general sense we may understand by it the whole Revelation of His grace, in which repentance is preached, pardon offered, and eternal life promised, to all who shall believe upon Him.

Thus we see from this brief summary of the proceedings, as set before us in the text, that though the expressions are strongly figurative, and after the style of the Rabbins on Daniel vii., still, awfully grand truths are embodied in the passage. There is a fearful speciality in this trial. All the persons are judged out of those things which were written in the books, according to their works, and the issues of the trial are, that whosoever of all that were judged was not found written in the Book of Life was cast into the lake of fire. The Judge "shall separate them one from another," &c. Read Matt. xxv. 37–46.

Now, *according to their works* does not exclude their faith. For their works are nothing but the fruits of their faith—proofs whether their faith was true or false. It is only by its works that faith can be visibly judged. No one can suppose that repentance, faith, and prayer are excluded altogether out of the account taken of the good works which are acknowledged by the King, when He welcomes the blessed of his Father into the kingdom prepared for them from the foundation of the world.

According to their works implies there are degrees of guilt, and consequently of punishment. Our Lord clearly refers to an appointed day of final judgment in his woes upon Capernaum, Chorazin, and Bethsaida, and that it would be more tolerable in the day of judgment for Tyre and Sidon, and for Sodom and Gomorrah, than for those who had the offer of His mercy, but rejected it. The greatest guilt will rest on them who have had the most light, the greatest gifts and talents, and neglected or abused them the most. Men will be judged according to what they had, whether with one talent, or two, or five, or ten. They will be judged according to the dispensation under which they lived, whether of the Patriarchs, or under Moses or Christ, Socrates or Confucius, and the sentence will be pronounced according to the compliance or non-compliance with the rules of the dispensation under which the persons judged have lived. And as every man's conscience condemns him, so those who have not had the written law of Moses, nor the light of the Gospel, are condemned, not for neglecting or despising what they never had any knowledge of, but for not living according to the light they had. The greatest guilt will therefore rest on those who have the law of nature, the light of tradition, the teachings of conscience, and the revelation of God's will, and the preaching of the Gospel, if their names are not found in the Book of Life. He that believeth not is condemned already—the wrath of God abideth on him that hath not believed on the Son of God.

Allow me to present you here with a paragraph from Dr. *Watts** on this point: "To make this matter yet plainer, and to reconcile the different representations which are given of our justification by faith in this life, and the importance attached to our justification by our words and works at the day of judgment, it must be considered that every Christian who is admitted into heaven, may be said to have a twofold right to it; namely, there is a right of inheritance which is by faith, whereby we are justified, and become the children of God, and joint-heirs with Christ (Gal. iii. 26; Rom. viii. 17); being interested by the free gift of God in the benefit of his Son's purchase, that is, the inheritance of heaven: and there is also a right of congruity or fitness (meetness or preparation for), which arises from actual holiness of life and heart, whereby we are prepared for the actual possession of this inheritance. So an infant may have a right of inheritance to his father's estate by birth or adoption; but he has not the right of congruity, fitness, or qualifications for possessing the estate till he grow up to twenty-one years, or to the age of discretion and capacity to enjoy it, and then he is put into the possession." Now it seems to me this dis-

---

* Watts's Works, vol. iv. p. 39.

tinction is clear and proper. We may be said to be justified by faith and by works, and the one implies the other. It is certainly by faith alone we are justified, and have peace with God through our Lord Jesus Christ; and it is just as certain we must be sanctified, and that every man will be judged according to his works—according to the deeds done in the body.

1. When it is asked, what is to be the rule according to which sentence is to be pronounced upon those who have not had the written Word of God or the preached Gospel of his grace? the answer is, the sentence will in every case be in exact conformity to strict justice. For as many as have sinned without law, shall also perish without law; and as many as have sinned in the law shall be judged by the law. Rom. ii. 5-16. A heathen will not be condemned for rejecting the Gospel, for it was not offered to him. But he will be condemned for what his own heart condemns him, and for not knowing God. Their guilt will lie in this: "Because that which may be known of God is manifest in them, for God hath showed it unto them. For the invisible things of Him from the creation of the world are clearly seen, being understood by the things that are made, even his eternal power and Godhead; so that they are without excuse. Because that when they knew God, they glorified Him not as God, neither were they thankful; but became vain in their imaginations, and their foolish heart was darkened. Who changed the truth of God into a lie, and worshipped and served the creature more than the Creator, who is blessed forever. Amen. For this cause God gave them up unto vile affections. For even their women did change the natural use into that which is against nature. And even as they did not like to retain God in their knowledge, God gave them over to a

reprobate mind, to do those things which are not convenient." Rom. i. 19-28.

2. *The method of the judgment will be according to righteousness.* Judgment will then be laid to the line and righteousness to the plummet. The dead and the living changed will be judged, out of the things written in the books which will then be opened, according to their works. There will be no passion, prejudice, partiality, mistake or error, nor any arbitrary severity. The eternal principles of right will be observed in all the proceedings. The conscience of all moral beings will testify that the world is judged in righteousness. The mercy shown in that day will be through perfect righteousness. God will be faithful to himself, to his laws, and to his Son and to his promises. As Christ is the end of the law for righteousness to every one that believeth, and as there is no condemnation to them that are in Christ Jesus, and as Christ has fulfilled the law, magnified it, and made it honorable, God can now be just and yet justify them that believe. So the sinner who is found penitent and believing, is justified and saved. Divine Justice is satisfied with the sacrifice of Christ, and beams brightly because of the atonement which He made, and the sanctification He has wrought. Sin is punished, but the sinner is saved through the righteousness of Christ. But let us never forget that there is no escape in that day, unless we are pardoned for Christ's sake. We must be sheltered under the covering wings of the Almighty Saviour.

3. *It deserves to be noted, that the pronouncing of the sentence of absolution comes before that of condemnation.* This order of proceeding with the twofold sentence may have been intended to teach us that God delights more in mercy than in wrath—is more ready to forgive than to

condemn. In the mean time, too, every word of approbation towards the godly, uttered in the hearing of the incorrigibly wicked, will add to their anguish.

The approbation of the godly will be wholly of free Grace and according to the riches of Divine Mercy. It is not here required that we prove that salvation is by Grace and not by works. For the works approved of in the day of judgment are not without flaws—stained with numerous blemishes, and if accepted, it is through Grace. Nor would they have ever been undertaken or executed without the mighty working of God's Spirit, nor are they ever spoken of in the Scriptures as having merited the favor of God. The rewards given are all gracious. The reasons for making mention of the services of believers are: *First.* To show that they are believers, and their good works are the evidences of their faith, fruits of the Spirit of God which has been sent forth into their hearts. *Secondly.* To show that they are indeed meet for their inheritance in glory. Their good works prove that they are in union with Christ, and have friendship with God. For they are the fruits of the spirit of adoption given unto them. These good works prove they have sought the Kingdom of God and His righteousness—proofs that they walked by the Spirit and not after the flesh—proofs that as Christ was interceding for them above, so His Spirit dwelt in them and interceded in them in a corresponding work—that as He was preparing a place for them in his Father's house of many mansions, so He was preparing them for their place in glory.

4. You note that the day of the general judgment is made a *distinctive, prominent day in the Holy Scriptures.* "But the day of the Lord will come as a thief in the night," says St. Peter. And so *the coming of our Lord*

is often referred to as a prominent and great event. As it marks the end of time in the sense of merging it into eternity, it is the last day, the day of final, universal judgment, when Christ is to be glorified, and all the attributes of God will be seen to be perfect and glorious. His Justice, Goodness, Mercy, Holiness, Immutability, Omnipotence, Omniscience, and Truth and Grace, will then all be made so manifest, that every intelligent creature will unite in saying: Just and true are all thy ways, Lord God Almighty.

5. In reference to the execution of the sentence:

First. Observe the order is the reverse of that observed in pronouncing it. "And these shall go away into everlasting punishment, but the righteous into life eternal." The pronouncing of. the absolution and welcome of the godly comes before the condemning of the wicked, but the wicked are sent away into everlasting punishment before the righteous go into life eternal. In the execution of the sentence, then, there is a fulfilment of the Scripture, which says: The righteous hath joy and shall increase his joy, "when he seeth the vengeance."

Secondly. To both the righteous and the wicked there is the same fixed, determinate idea of *a place* for them to dwell in or to inhabit—not more so for one than for the other. There is equal positive, absolute certainty of character in the wicked as in the righteous. One goes into life eternal, the other to endure punishment everlasting.

Thirdly. Eternity is equally attributed to the existence and place of the abode of both—not of one more than of the other. The duration of the punishment is expressed by the very same word that expresses the duration of the life of the righteous. The terms used and the justice of

God clearly teach that the same duration, continuance of existence, awaits both the godly and the ungodly.

Fourthly. Nor is the sentence a mere negative one. The mere going away does not exhaust it. The righteous go *into life eternal*—a life that is to be filled with joy and service—with enjoyments which only those who love God can ever know. It is a life of service and of pleasure—a life of knowledge and love ever increasing and never to be diminished or to have an end. The wicked, on the other hand, not only lose all this, but they are driven away from the presence of the glory of God. They lose every thing that makes heaven, and to this are superadded the pains of hell. They go away into everlasting punishment. They depart from the glory of God to the perdition of devils. They depart into everlasting fire, prepared for the devil and his angels. And even if it is admitted, as some say, that this language and similar Scriptural phrases are not to be interpreted in a literal but in a figurative sense, the meaning is essentially the same. Material fire, and a literal pit vomiting forth fire and smoke, is not at all necessary to constitute the eternal hell of the finally and incorrigibly wicked. Material elements in their punishment are not essential. The chief ingredients of their suffering will be within, of the conscience—self-condemned—and upon this the outpouring of the wrath of God Almighty. If the Word of God describes the torments of the lost in the world to come by metaphors and figures of speech, it is because such is the weakness and poverty of language that it is not sufficient for describing the realities in simple words. And if the figures used—which are the most awful that can be found—come short of the things themselves, what must the realities be? Truly it will be an awful thing to fall into the hands of the living God as an unreconciled sinner—as one who has despised so great a salvation!

6. The doctrine of a future general judgment is not to be so understood as to stand in the way of each man passing under a particular and personal judgment, immediately after death. The Bible tells us the soul at death returns to God who gave it, and must then receive evidence of his favor or of his condemnation, and consequently pass at once to a state of happiness which is Paradise or heaven, or into a state of misery, which is hell. This is not the place for me to speak of the latitude with which the terms heaven or hell are used, nor of the degrees, spheres, or mansions there may be in the amplitudes of the world to come. It is perfectly clear, however, from the parable of our Lord about Lazarus and the rich man, that happiness or misery immediately follows death, and also that the state into which men pass at death may be increased in intensity. And our Lord promised the penitent thief on the cross that he should be with Him that day in Paradise. And according to *Peter*, the souls of those who refused to believe Noah's Gospel, were in the prison of hell when he wrote, suffering the vengeance of God. And nothing is plainer in *Paul's* Epistles than that he conceived of but two possible states for believers: namely, *present* in the body in this world, or *absent* from the body and present with the Lord in a state of happiness. But it is not seen how these passages of holy Scripture are in conflict in any way with those that speak of a future general judgment.

It is evident, for two reasons at least, that a general judgment must follow the private sentence that is passed on individuals. *First.* The justice of God must be made manifest to all the universe, in order that He may be adored by His intelligent creatures. It must be seen that

He is just when He judgeth, and righteous when He condemneth. He must *appear* to be, as well as actually be, just, holy, and good. *Secondly.* It is necessary that a future public judgment should follow after the personal judgment has passed, because neither all the penalties of a man's sin, nor all the rewards of his well-doing are rendered up at his death, nor can they be before the general resurrection. This point was considered at some length in the last Discourse.

7. If in the proceedings of the general Judgment, and in many points connected with the events of that day, grave difficulties are suggested, we should remember that we are finite and very feeble, and of very limited understandings—that our globe itself, the theatre of so many events which seem to us so vast, is only a grain of sand of exceedingly small proportions compared with the vastness of the Universe of God. What difficulties are there which Omnipotence and Omniscience cannot remove or overcome as to the *place* of the judgment, the assembling of the parties to be judged, and the examination of the records of guilt, and the pronouncing and execution of the sentences? "GOD will bring to light the hidden things of darkness, and will make manifest the counsels of the hearts of all men." Conscience will then be set free and unmasked. The very elements of nature will give up the echoes of human crime.

8. There is no argument against the minuteness or exactness of the individual judgment and sufferings of the ungodly after the day of the general judgment that does not lie equally against the minuteness of Divine Providence now, and the fact of individual suffering in this world. And as the Providence of God over our world needs no proof from us in this place, and as it is equally

palpable that an awful individuality of suffering is laid, or may be laid upon us in this life, so it is just as palpable the same thing may be done in the Day of Judgment. The scrutiny of that day must be concerning individuals, not as classes, races, or societies, but into their several individualities, and into the thoughts, words and deeds of each one, as if he were the only subject and stood alone before the Judgment-seat. It cannot be otherwise. For as our sins are our own acts, so every soul must then answer for himself to his own master, and bear his own burden, and bear it as if he were absolutely alone. And yet every ungodly man, while he will be condemned by his own conscience, will also be condemned by all other sinners. And every secret sin will then be exposed, and all the ramifications of evil-doing will come home to rest on the head and the heart whence they proceeded.

> Now the books are open spread;
> Now the writing must be read,
> Which condemns the quick and dead;
> Now, before the Judge severe,
> Hidden things must all appear;
> Naught can pass unpunished here."*

Nor will there be any mistakes committed on this day. The judgment will be according to the deeds done in the body, and what these deeds are the books then opened will show, so clearly that there will be no denial or error. No miscalling of names, no perjury, nor false testimony; but every case will be determined according to the books, according to the deeds done in the body, and each one's case separate and distinct from all others, whether the things done be good or bad.

---

* Missal Dies iræ dies illa

By way of reflections, I offer—

I. This thought: *The field of knowledge is indeed wide.* The number of things desirable to be known may be very great, but our happiness may be eternally secured if only a few things were drawn down from our heads into our hearts. How much would our lives be altered, if we did really and truly believe in the great and last Judgment of which we have been speaking! Then how gladly would we hearken to the Gospel's joyful tidings, offering us pardon! How much more seriously would our thoughts be directed to those things that concern the world to come! And if we thus lived under a solemn and ever present sense of infinite realities, then we should feel much less the sorrows of this life. and the noise and vanities of this world would pass as if we heard them not. What is all this world in view of the Judgment-seat! Is it not altogether unworthy of beings as intelligent as we are to allow the speck of time to eclipse eternity—to allow the strife and toil, passion and pleasure of this short life to shut out from our view the awful future? Should we not strive to live as in the light of the Judgment-seat of God, and always in full view of the Cross of his Son?

" Rock of ages, cleft for me,
Let me hide myself in thee:
Let the water and the blood,
From thy wounded side which flowed,
Be of sin the double cure;
Cleanse me from its guilt and power.

" While I draw this fleeting breath,
When my heart-strings break in death,
When I soar to worlds unknown,
See thee on thy judgment-throne,
Rock of ages, cleft for me,
Let me hide myself in thee."

But I must guard you against the presumption that any mere degree of awakened attention to the salvation of your soul in view of these awful scenes will secure your safety. Deep and powerful convictions do not always result in true conversion. There is a kind of repentance which is not unto life, but unto death. Such was the repentance of *Judas* when he came and threw down the thirty pieces of silver, saying, I have betrayed innocent blood, and then went and hanged himself, and went to his own place. You read also of one who trembled as *Paul* reasoned before him of righteousness, temperance, and a judgment to come, but was not converted. *Felix* cried, When I have a more convenient season, I will send for thee. But there is not the slightest evidence that he ever thought the convenient time had come. He had ample opportunity to see the Apostle, and to have learned more about the way to prepare to meet the judgment to come, if he had desired to do so. But he did not avail himself of these opportuities. He escaped from the importunity of his conscience at the time, on the plea of a more convenient season, which he never found. But, dear hearer, what more convenient time can you ever have than the present? To-morrow may not be yours. This very night your soul may be required of you. And if to-morrow does not come to you, the awful day of judgment will surely come. If the more convenient season for you to come to Christ does not come, still it is absolutely certain you must appear before his Judgment-seat. And if the Apostle contemplates the day of the appearing of the Lord Jesus in His Kingdom as the day of his coronation, when he shall receive his crown of righteousness, and so also all who love his appearing, then how awful will be the doom of all hypocrites and unbelievers! If the righteous scarcely be saved, what shall be the end of the ungodly and of all who disobey the Gospel? *He that believeth and is baptized shall be saved: He that believeth not shall be damned.*

II. The consummation of all things belonging to our dynasty, in the way that we understand the Holy Scriptures, is *in perfect harmony with the best views of the heathen*, and is supported by reason, common sense, and tradition. It is in harmony essentially with Rabbinical and Hindoo philosophy, as well as with the teaching of Greek and Roman poets and moralists. According to the Hindoos, the Supreme Deity is the Supreme Pontiff and Judge of the universe. All law, all intelligence, all systems are from Him and accountable to Him. Even the Brahmin is an emanation from Him, bringing to the earth the attributes he possessed in heaven. Now all such ideas imply a final judgment, when the conflict between good and evil must be decided. Is it not reasonable to suppose there is a just end appointed for this contest? For without this eternal judgment, how will the Justice of God ever be made manifest? If men's lots are now diverse, is that difference always according to right? Is there no injustice in the disproportions of this world? Is not Divine Providence a golden chain that hangs between heaven and earth, of which we see at best only a few links, while all the rest are either so far above, towards the end that is attached to the Eternal Throne, that even our faith cannot see them, or they are so deep in the mysteries of Providence that we cannot fathom them: and in the mean time, is it not a precious discipline to wait in hope for the clearing up of all in the Great Day? Is there not a God who is all-wise, almighty, and just? Does not evil now reign? If not triumphant over good, still certainly it has a vast empire. Are there not evil spirits, angels who have fallen from their allegiance in heaven, and some who have kept their places of duty and glory ? Is there to be no final settlement with the wicked angels ? Did not God make man holy, and then, after he sinned and fell, did He not show him mercy, and does He not now offer to restore our race to Paradise again ? But all do not accept this offer. Many live in total ignorance or wicked contempt of it. Must there not be a day for showing the harmony of all God's ways—a day for doing justice to the pure and holy angels and other virtuous beings in the universe, as well as for avenging his saints ?

III. *The Day of Judgment is a clear demonstration of the Supreme Divinity of our Lord Jesus Christ.* Nothing less than the sum of all the Godhead could be equal to the functions of the Judgment-seat. Not only will the duties of that awful day require that all authority and power in heaven and earth should be in his hands, but that He should also have omniscience to search the heart and try the reins of all intelligent beings. And as CHRIST in his own person executes his office as Judge of the quick and the dead, He will show more of the splendor and majesty of God than had ever before been manifested to created beings. The Judge of quick and dead is the Lord Jesus Christ, who is ordained as Mediator, Saviour, Advocate, King, Lord, and Christ. Thus the Apostle declares that God hath given assurance of the judgment of the world in righteousness by Christ, in this, that He hath raised him from the dead, and ordained him to that work, and appointed a day for it. As Christ has redeemed his people, they meet Him on the judgment throne as a friend. But his enemies, who would not that He should reign over them : how will they stand before Him, and answer for rejecting His offers of pardon ? Then will they be speechless and without excuse. The mercies of God and the very blood of the Cross will be awful witnesses against them.

IV. *Such a day must be thought of with very different views and feelings by different kinds of people.* The vast assembly at the Judgment will be divided into two great classes, the righteous and the wicked. The righteous rise to the resurrection of life, and the wicked to the resurrection of shame and everlasting contempt. The righteous will then lift up their heads with joy. Their sorrows are past. Oppressed innocence is now redressed. The Judge on the Throne is their friend. His words are distinct and authoritative. COME, ye blessed of my Father, inherit the kingdom prepared for you from the foundation of the world. Enter now into the joy of your Lord. Here on earth, He said, Come, take up your Cross; deny yourselves; follow me. But now the work is done, the race is run, "the gate is past and heaven is won." And so, on the other hand, how awful the condition of those who are then numbered with his enemies! Every mouth will be stopped, and all will be guilty before God. And the Judge will say, Bring hither these mine enemies, WHO WOULD NOT that I should reign over them, and slay them before me. Cast them into utter darkness, where there shall be weeping and wailing and gnashing of teeth. I called them to come. I besought them to repent and forsake their evil ways. They were warned that sin would bring them to this awful end; but they would not hearken. Now they must reap as they have sown.

V. Since, then, there is a day fixed for the judgment of all men by the Lord Jesus, let the wicked and the profane know that Divine vengeance, though it is slow, does not sleep. The record of every human being is now making up for this awful day. And though we know not the time, we know it will surely come. And whether that day be far remote or near at hand, the day of death cannot be very far from every one of us, and after death we can make no more preparation for the Judgment-seat. As we die, so we appear for judgment. Nor is there any possible escape. No place in which to hide. All nations, small and great, and of all generations are there. The sinner hidden in the centre of the material universe, even if it were piled in ruins upon him, could not escape. The piercing eye and Almighty hand would drag him forth to the Judgment Throne.

VI. And the certainty of a judgment to come should make us more in earnest for the salvation of our fellow-men. Can it be that there is an endless eternity just before us? Is there an endless heaven for the pious and an eternal hell for the ungodly? How then can we rest, or allow ourselves to live so sluggish, so engrossed with the things of this life? Seeing that such awful things are before us, part and parcel of which we must ourselves soon be, what manner of persons ought we to be in all holy conversation and godliness, looking for and hastening unto the coming of the day of God!

VII. The contemplation of the judgment to come should make us more patient in suffering, more content to endure the trials of this life, and teach us to think less of the honors and show and riches and glory of this world. What will all these things be in that eventful day! How then will the unjust, the slanderer, the drunkard, the whoremonger, the liar, the murderer, the profane and the contemner of God, the despiser of the Gospel of Christ appear before God! In that splendid and awful assembly their laughter will be turned into mourning, and their joy into lamentation. But it will be all in vain for them to cry for the rocks and the mountains to fall on them and hide them from the face of the Throne of God and of the Lamb.

There is, then, no need of arguments to prove that it is wisdom to prepare for the judgment. We know we are sinners. We cannot escape death and the Judgment. As sinners out of Christ we cannot abide the day of the revelation of the righteous judgment of Almighty God. Then surely we should now acquaint ourselves with Him, and be at peace.

VIII. *Will there not, then, be many awful changes in human conditions*—many awful disappointments at the Judgment-seat of Christ? We cannot judge of men's condition after death from their condition here. The parable of Lazarus and the rich man is a picture of most striking contrasts. Every thing was reversed. *Here* Lazarus had his evil things: *there* he was comforted. *Here* the rich man had his good things: *there* he was tormented. We cannot, then, always judge of a man's true character from his present circumstances. A man's true character is what he really is in the sight of God. It is the way of his life and of his heart towards his Maker and towards his fellow-men. This is not fully known to any but the All-seeing Eye. But a man's circumstances, his status and condition in this world, are affected by the dispensations of Divine Providence towards him in things material, or of the earth, earthy. And hence worldly prosperity is not always a sure indication that we are in a state of grace, nor is worldly adversity a proof that God does not love us. On the contrary, adversity is more friendly to a heavenly disposition and the laying up of treasures in the skies than prosperity. It is believed that worldly prosperity destroys more happiness, and ruins more immortal souls, than adversity. Chastisements are evidences of our Divine sonship. Whom the Lord loveth He chasteneth. The branches of the true vine are pruned that they may bring forth more fruit. Alas! that many who are first will then be last—first in promise and expectation, in gifts and opportunities—shall then be found rejected, reprobate, lost! To what a height of glory will the meek then be raised up, and to what a depth of woe will many of those who have been so prosperous in this world be then consigned! And, ah! if such disappointments as these were all. But to think of the divisions that will take place in that day between Pastors and their flocks, Sabbath-school teachers and their pupils, parents and their children. Ah! there will be mourning in the judgment, when the wicked go away into everlasting punishment.

Will not the young think on these things? Will not the impenitent consider? How can any of you abide in this awful day! The year is drawing towards its close. You have been often, very often invited to come to Christ and live. And some of you, I see from the almond blossoms on your heads, are already far advanced in the way to the house appointed for all living. Are you ripening for heaven, or are you far down in the broad and crooked way, which leads to destruction? Do you not know that it is appointed unto you once to die and after death the judgment? How do you expect to feel and conduct yourself amid the astonishing scenes just referred to? When you die, you expect to be buried. You do not believe your soul will be in your coffin. Where will it be? Will not your body rise from that grave? Will you not, with these very ears of yours, hear the archangel's trumpet much more distinctly and effectively than you hear my voice? And will not your eyes see the Judge and the great white Throne, and the gathering millions of millions, and the books opened? And then what sentence will you hear? And what will become of you then? Which way will you go from the Judgment?

Will you ascend with the glorious Redeemer to reign with him, or be sent down with evil angels and ungodly men to perdition? And do these things make any impression on you? Does your heart tremble? Then to-day seize the offer of mercy. Cry unto God for pardon. Accept the Gospel's gracious offer. Now Jesus says, Him that cometh unto me I will in nowise cast out.

> "Then grant us, Saviour, so to pass our time trembling here,
> That when upon the clouds of heaven Thy glory shall appear
> Uplifting high our joyful heads, in triumph we may rise,
> And enter, with Thine angel train, Thy palace in the skies."

APPENDIX.

APPENDIX.

"It is better to have no opinion of God at all than such an opinion as is unworthy of Him; for the one is unbelief, the other is contumely."—*Lord Bacon.*

"Surely I had rather a great deal men should say, there was no such man at all as Plutarch, than that they should say, there was one *Plutarch*, who used to eat his children as soon as they were born, as the poets say of Saturn."—*Plutarch.*

It is obvious that many points may be in the mind of a thinking, reading, studious, earnest-hearted pastor, which may give shape and color to the pictures which he draws for his hearers, that it is not expedient to give in detail from the pulpit. My object in this Appendix is to describe briefly the field of thought and critical examination passed over in the preceding Discourses, as seen from the study. It seems to me important for us to know something of the views entertained concerning Christ in the ages immediately following that of the Apostles, and to have in view the lights under which the great Council of Nicæa was held, in A. D. 325; and to examine how far and in what respects the skeptical theories of our schools of modern criticism are the reflection of ancient speculations. By taking such a survey of the field, it will be seen that, after all, the Apostles' Creed is essentially the true voice of the Church of God, and that nothing has been brought to light, either by unbelieving science or disbelieving criticism, that should cause us to discard even the articulated utterances of our faith as to its fundamental doctrines. I propose in this Appendix:—

I. A few remarks on the vital importance of the question that occupies so large a part of our modern philosophical and critical literature.

II. A brief review of some of the opinions advanced concerning Christ, from the days of the Apostles to the Council of Nicæa which are alluded to, denied, and confuted in the Apostles' Creed.

III. The Aspect of Modern Thought concerning Christ, with special reference to the theories of Strauss, Tübingen, and Renan.

And, FINALLY, a few words to theological students and young ministers of the Gospel.

I. *The paramount importance of the question now at issue.*

It is seen from the sayings of Lord Bacon and Plutarch, quoted above, that it has been long and learnedly debated by great men, whether Atheism or Superstition was the greatest evil to mankind. Formerly, it was held by many that even *Atheism* was not worse than gross and unworthy conceptions of God; but now it is generally believed that any kind of religion is better than none at all. It is, however, very far from the truth, that all religions are equally good, or that one kind of religion is for one country and one people, and another for another people. This is old heathenism. It is the doctrine of local national deities and patron saints. It is then of great importance to have clear and correct views of God and of His character and Government. For as the stream cannot rise higher than the fountain, and as the effect is of the same character as its cause; so the sum of perfection proposed as attainable by any religion, is to become like the object of worship. There are many ways in which this point might be historically illustrated. It will suffice, however, for our present purpose, to remark:—

That our apprehension of what God is, and our belief concerning His works and ways, have a very important bearing upon our mental and moral character, and consequently have an essential influence upon our happiness, here and hereafter. *Three* facts from the experience and history of mankind may be referred to in proof of this position. *First.* Our race has and does, and, we may add, ever will, worship something. *Secondly.* Men become like the objects which they worship as gods. *Thirdly.* Man has no means within himself, or within the reach of his own inherent power and wisdom, by which to extricate himself from the evil into which he is introduced when he makes his entrance into this world. And hence we may add, *fourthly*, our race needs Divine help. And this Divine interposition is the Gospel. Our holy religion is from heaven. It is of God, and is made known to us by Revelation. It is the religion of the ETERNAL WORD. I stop not here to inquire into the historic proofs, that man is so constituted that he does and will worship something. Nor is it necessary here to inquire what that something is, nor whether it is a good desired or an evil feared. Nor is it to our purpose to ask how our race comes to possess such a constitution. It is quite enough that the fact lies over the whole territory of human existence and migration. Whether man's moral and religious constitution is born with him, or is deduced from reason or tradition, or is implanted by culture, or is the result of all such agencies, it is not material to our argument. All we now insist upon is, *that man is such a religious being, that he has, and does, and ever will acknowledge and worship something as God.* This is characteristic of all the tribes of our race. It is a religious capacity, a moral sense, a conscience, an apprehension of God and a hereafter, rather than any superiority of physical structure or quantity of brain that distinguishes human beings from lower animals. The cases reported by some travellers, of tribes that have no religious belief at all, are not sufficient to disprove the correctness of this position. A more thorough acquaintance with them has thus far shown that such reports were erroneous. If any such example is really found, it will be an exception, and if the whole history of the case were known, doubtless it could be satisfactorily explained. Among all tribes and nations, and through all ages, there has been found some idea of accountability, of a future state, of a Supreme Being, a God. Wherever our race is found, we are found worshipping something believed to possess attributes of possible good or evil to us. Even if human belief in God is implanted in the soul, and is therefore a native feeling, as we believe, it may be subject to growth and decay, as any other power of the soul, from neglect or the influence of education. Such a belief is potentially inherent in the mind, and is seldom, if ever, so extinguished, that it may not, in favoring circumstances, again revive and exert itself against every attempt made to root it out. The feebleness of the religious sentiment in some races, as is alleged of certain African tribes by recent travellers,* and of the savages of this continent and of the

---

* See Baker's "Albert Nyanza and Sources of the Nile;" and Reade's "Savage Africa," *passim.*

Chinese, only proves that the religious feeling, like the moral feelings, a sense of truth and justice, is susceptible of decay. It is admitted that the conscience may be corrupted, but this abuse of the conscience does not prove that there is no native and universal principle of rectitude. We may admit it, therefore, as a fact, that all men do not seem to have equal religious susceptibilities, or to be equally demonstrative in their feelings towards their Creator. But this does not prove that there are any absolutely without a religious capacity. The idea of a God is an original faculty of the soul, and hence we can adopt the saying of Plutarch: *that the sum of all religion is to be like the God we worship.* It cannot be otherwise. The connection here is that of cause and effect. The character of the object worshipped is regarded as superior. And we naturally desire to be acceptable to the Being we worship as God—that our character may be conformable to His. This is the teaching of our Lord Himself. If we are sincere and consistent, therefore, in our religious views, we will strive to keep the commandments, and acquire the attributes which are according to the will and character of our God. Such views and desires will inevitably produce in us strong aspirations after conformity to the moral character of the object of our worship. We become and are what we supremely admire and adore, as far as creatures can become like their Creator.

All human history is in evidence on this point. The character of every nation and tribe and city has been modified by its religion. Grecian cities and states, and the heathen generally, ancient and modern, are but the counterpart of their gods. There is a correspondence of resemblance between their characters, and their opinions about the attributes and precepts of their gods. *Pope* has well described their objects of worship: "Gods partial, changeful, passionate, unjust, whose attributes were rage, revenge, and lust;" and yet these were precisely the gods whose attributes are reflected historically in their own characters. And after all that can be allowed for their heathen virtues, of patriotism, heroism, and devotion to poetry, philosophy, and the fine arts, the Greeks and Romans exhibit nationalities marked with the traits they ascribed to their gods. And if it were possible to institute such a comparison, the principle here presented applies in our day with more emphasis to the character of Christ than it ever did before. It is only through Christ we can approach God, and be reconciled to him. It is only in Christ God can look upon us with delight. And it is only as we have the Spirit of Christ dwelling in us that we are Christians. And we may add, as we regard Christ so He regards us. We may form some idea, then, of what Christ thinks of us from what we think of Him.

II. *The opinions advanced concerning Christ before the Council of Nicæa, which are denied and confuted in the Apostles' Creed.*

The propriety of the condensed notices here offered arises not only from the vast importance of having correct and clear views concerning Christ, but also because it is hardly to be supposed that the majority of our Sabbath congregations or of general readers are familiar with the literature of theological dogmas, or acquainted with the names and details of Church history. It seems necessary, therefore, here to help our readers to some acquaintance with a few of the most famous Judaizing and philosophizing teachers whose erroneous opinions and conceits are alluded to in the preceding Discourses, and which our Creed was intended to deny and refute by holding forth the true faith of God's people. And perhaps it will save us from some confusion to say at once that Cerinthians, Ebionites, Docetæ, and some other less known sects may all be classed under the general name of Gnostics. By this we do not mean that these sects were perfectly agreed. This was not the fact. Perhaps their only unity was in not believing in Jesus Christ as He is set forth in our received Creed. The name *Gnostics* is from a Greek word signifying knowledge.

It is generally believed that they are referred to in 1 Tim. vi. 20; Col. ii. 8, and 1 John ii. 18. At first they were known as philosophers, or simply followers of Pythagoras and Plato, but in process of time they insisted on interpreting the Holy Scriptures according to their philosophy, and making the Scriptures bend to it. Their doctrines, in some shape or other, cover a wide field, and have prevailed more or less among the educated classes of the world from the beginning of the Christian era to this day; but the main point in the line of this volume is, that they agreed in denying the Divinity of our Lord, his equality with the Father, and for the most part denied his real humanity altogether.

The *Docetæ* also have their name from a Greek word signifying to *seem, imagine*, and thus their very name proclaims their great error. They held that Jesus did not exist in reality at all, but only in appearance, just as the angels who appeared to Abraham; and, as a consequence, they denied that there was any reality in Christ's death and resurrection, and of course, then, there is no redemption by His blood. Some of the Docetæ taught that Jesus had a real angelic substance that was at his death resolved again into ethereal elements, and that therefore what we call his ascension into heaven was simply the returning of the angelic substance that constituted the man Jesus into the *pleroma* of the universe. The rise and history of the Ebionites and their influence on Christianity are points of extended and most critical inquiry in our day. Professor Fisher[*] declares "the Ebionites were degenerate Hebrew Christians." Ebrard[†] thinks they were "Judaizing Unitarian Christians of the humanitarian type." They said Jesus was the Messiah, and was only a man, and that his great mission was to give a new enforcement to the Mosaic law. They were divided into several sects. Bauer of Tübingen has written much and learnedly about the Ebionites, but is not to be relied on for orthodox views. The Ebionites and Cerinthians belong to about the same period of history, that is, some part of the second century. Some of our learned men say they were the ancient Essenes. This is doubtful. They held views widely differing among themselves on many points, but were essentially Gnostics both in philosophy and religion, and agreed in denying our Lord's proper Divinity. Irenæus positively declares that St. John wrote his Gospel expressly to confute the errors of these Gnostic sects, especially of Cerinthus. Michælis, Waterland, and many other first-class authors entertain this opinion very decidedly. *Cerinthus*, it seems, admitted that Jesus had a real human body, but that he was born after the ordinary way, and was therefore nothing but a man, the son of Joseph and Mary; and that he became Christ at his baptism, when an æon descended upon him. This æon, he said, was the first of the seven great æons, but a creature. Christ never was, therefore,

---

[*] Fisher's Supernatural Origin of Christianity, p. 320.
[†] Ebrard's Gospel History, p. 522.

in any true sense, properly God. It is believed that Cerinthus was the first person who taught an earthly millennium, promising a Mohammedan paradise to his followers during that period. Who can tell how much Mohammed borrowed from Cerinthus?

Basilides was a Gnostic belonging to the second century, and thought to have been, as intimated in the foregoing pages, a disciple of Simon Magus. It is believed he studied at Alexandria, but spent his life chiefly in Persia. Like Cerinthus, he held that Jesus was a creature, the eldest of the æons, or the first of the seven æons of God, who took on himself the form or semblance of a man, but did not become a man. He admitted the crucifixion as a reality, but said that the person who was crucified was not Jesus, but Simon the Cyrenian. This view was adopted by Mohammed. Basilides of course, therefore, rejected the doctrine of the Trinity, of the Atonement, and of our Lord's resurrection.

Sabellius was a Greek philosopher of Egypt of the third century. He taught that Jesus and the Holy Spirit were but emanations or functions of God—that it was God who was born of the Virgin Mary, and that, having accomplished the mystery of salvation in the form and work which we ascribe to Jesus, he diffused himself on the Apostles as in the fiery tongues of Pentecost, and was then called the Holy Spirit. According to Sabellius there is but one person in the Godhead, and the term Father, Son, and Holy Spirit signify not persons, but merely offices. One of the favorite illustrations of the Trinity among his followers was the sun representing God as the Father, while the illuminating properties of the sun are the Word, or God the Son, and the warming, creating power of the sun represents the Holy Spirit. Those who do not admit any distinction of persons in the Godhead, and yet believe in the reality of the Incarnation and sufferings of Christ, are known in the history of the Church as *Patripassians*, because they say it was God the Father who suffered as Christ. It is alleged that their founder was a Phrygian philosopher by the name of Praxeas. If he lived, as it is said, in the second century, then Sabellius probably adopted his opinions from him.

It is believed that the real father of Socinians lived about this time, namely, Paul of Samosata, who was Bishop of Antioch, in

Syria, A. D. 262, whose followers are the Paulianists of history. They were strongly condemned by the Council of Nicæa. The distinguishing article of their faith, at least as far as our subject leads us to speak of, seems to have been this: the Son of God and the Holy Spirit exist in God the Father, just as the faculties of reason and activity do in man. Consequently they held that Christ was born a mere man, having been begotten as any other man, and that then the wisdom of the Father descended into Him, and by it He wrought miracles; and that it was only to express this union of the Divine reason or wisdom of the man Jesus that he was allowed to be called God.

Of the Nestorians and Eutychians, as they come after the Council of Nicæa, I need not speak. But our line of investigation requires at this point some notice of Arius and the Council of Nicæa.

The COUNCIL OF NICÆA was held in the city of Nicæa, in Asia Minor, by command of Constantine the Great, then emperor of the world, in A. D. 325. Its title is the "Great and Holy Synod." It is claimed, and not without just grounds, that this synod represented the voice, and the conscience, and the learning and piety of the whole Christian world. It was indeed a very august body, composed of the very choicest ministers of God, from many and distant parts of Europe, Asia, and Africa—men who were earnestly engaged in preaching the Gospel to the heathen, and in strengthening and comforting the scattered flocks of believers. Most of them had endured great hardships in the service of Christ. They professed in the decrees of the Council the faith they had suffered for, and had themselves received at their baptism into Christ; and as they believed this faith came to them on the authority of the Church, and was according to the Sacred Scriptures, so they believed they were setting forth and defending the true faith of the Holy Apostles themselves.

The occasion of the Nicene Council was the Arian controversy, but the influence of that sect was not wholly arrested by the Council. For at least three hundred years it had great influence in Christendom, and succeeded in having power enough to persecute and exile some of the leading members of the Council of Nicæa, that had condemned Arius and his followers. And, although the name *Arianism* has sometimes been laid to rest, the views it symbolizes still live. The Arianism of the seventh century differs from that of the fourth, while that of our day differs from that of all preceding ages. The influence of Arius penetrates and pervades the enclosures guarded by all the three great and ancient creeds much more than is perhaps generally admitted. We have the authority of the *Christian Examiner* for saying that Dr. Bellows, in unfolding the Unitarian idea of Jesus Christ, admits that "There are within the Unitarian ranks all shades of opinion about Jesus Christ, from a Modal or Sabellian Semi-Trinitarianism, through high and low Arianism, Socinianism, Priestleyism, down to pure Humanitarianism and Naturalism. But all these diverse parties do agree in one thing, and that is, in ' DENYING THE PROPER DEITY OF JESUS CHRIST.' "

It cannot then be considered unfair to say that the followers of Arius have "a coat of many colors," that fits easily all sizes. For however much the leading minds among them may differ, they all tend in the same direction. The shades of difference, and the modifications of views concerning Christ, from Cerinthus to Arius, and from Arius to Socinus, and from his day to this, do not essentially change the main points. They all say Christ is not equal with the Father, nor is his death a vicarious sacrifice for sin. The latitude observed in the varying views of those who oppose the doctrines of the orthodox creeds, may be accounted for from the fact, that they do not usually profess to attach importance to a positive articulated creed, although they are fond of dogmatizing; and also to the fact that their watchword is, "A fair stage and no favor!" And perhaps also the excessive *prudence* (shall we call it?) of the founder, the shadow of Arius himself, still rests on his disciples. It is well known that the peculiarities of his dogmas arose originally out of his extreme and subtle and abstract views concerning the terms Father and Son. The difficulty was more in what he would not say, than in what he did say. He would never say *when* it was, but he would say there was a time " when the Son was not," leaving the inevitable inference that the Son was not God, but a creature. "His heresy," says Stanley,* " was the excess of dogmatism founded upon the most abstract words, in the most abstract region of human thought." And is not this truly characteristic of his followers, and similar

---

* Eastern Church, p. 173.

schools of theology, to this day? Arius admitted Christ's personal existence, but said He was only a creature, although an exalted creature. Christ then was not equal with God. And from Simon Magus to this hour, is not this the *res gestæ*, the very substance of the belief, or disbelief, of all who deny the Person, or the Divinity, or the equality of Christ with the Father? It is of but little consequence whether they are known historically as Ebionite Gnostics, Arians, Socinians, Unitarians, Transcendentalists, or followers of the last most popular writers on myths and legends. Nor should it excite any surprise that there should be such a diversity of opinions concerning Christ among the followers of Arius, from his day to our own, for a part of their creed is to have no creed. And as they have nothing to believe, they are consistent in never saying, *Credo*. But does not this imply indifference to the character of Christ, and is not the fruit of such indifference seen in the denial of the Christ of the Apostles' Creed?

It would, however, require more time and space, not to say learning and ability, than I have at command, to attempt an exhaustive review of the influence of the Christology of the ante-Nicene age upon the Rationalism and Unitarianism of our own times. Such a review would, of course, cover the Nicene age itself, at least up to the adoption of the so-called Athanasian Creed, the greatest of all Creeds since the days of the Apostles. The general statement made in the foregoing Discourses, that in the Apostolic age it was not so much our Lord's Divinity as his proper humanity that was the occasion of controversy, must be limited to the Apostles' age, and interpreted in the light of the Christology here briefly presented. And doubtless it was then true, as it is now and always will be, that some of the teachers of heresy were better than their opinions, while some of the confessors of orthodox creeds were not equal to their symbols. It is impossible for us to define, limit, and describe the influence of education. The words of Apostolic faith concerning God and his Son Jesus Christ, often have an influence on the experience and belief and conduct of men after they have formally renounced them. They are not aware of the influence that still overshadows them.

Such conflicting views concerning Christ, however, are no more against His Divinity than erroneous and contradictory opinions concerning the Almighty Creator are against our belief in God. Truth is of God, and is unchangeable and eternal. But the history of Redemption extends through immense periods of time, and embraces communications made to man in different ways and at different times. It requires us to contemplate the Son of God before his Incarnation, and the Son of God in human nature in the world, and the Son of God in human nature having ascended into heaven, where He sitteth at the right hand of God. Our Lord declared himself to be the Son of God. His followers believed in Him as such. And although his adversaries denied Him, they admitted that He claimed to be the Messiah. The only question between his followers and his adversaries, was as to the truth of his claims to be the Son of God. His followers believed; His enemies denied. After his ascension, his followers were so filled with awe for his character and miracles that doubts or difficulties in regard to His Divinity, found no place in their mind. The great question in the Apostles' discourses before the Synagogues and Sanhedrim, was concerning Jesus of Nazareth as the Messiah-Christ of their own Scriptures. This question settled, He was received as the Son of God, which the Jews understood to mean God himself. The great dispute in their day was as to the real and proper humanity of Christ, rather than as to His Divinity. The main points at issue were: Is Jesus of Nazareth the Son of God? Did He assume a human body, or was his body a phantom? Or was He really born of a woman, receiving his body from her? Gradually, however, errorists grew in numbers and increased in courage, as human learning and philosophy gained an ascendency among Christians, until the Person of Christ was not only attacked, but his equality with God denied. When Arius arose the main point was, whether Christ was equal with God, and was God, or was a mere creature.

It should not, however, weigh against the Divine origin of Christianity that it had so soon to pass through such severe doctrinal conflicts; for our Lord taught that the wheat and tares were to grow together till He comes. It is not surprising, therefore, that the great Enemy scarcely waited for Jesus' ascension from the world before he began to sow the tares of false doctrines. Before the Apostles themselves were dead, we find Ebionites, Corinthians, and Gnostics teaching that Jesus was a mere man. And immediately afterwards, in the second century,

Theodotus taught the same doctrine; and thus such errors were kept alive until the peace of the Church seemed to require a general Council, at Nicæa, in order that the voice of the churches might express what the true faith of Christ was, and put to silence errorists, or at least hinder them from leading the unwary astray. Under these circumstances we come to Arius, the most distinguished of those who denied the proper Divinity of our Lord Jesus. "The sting of his heresy," and of his followers, was this: that while they used complimentary terms about the sacred person of Jesus, and pronounced eulogies upon his precepts and character, still their language was so equivocal as always to leave the point of his Divinity in doubt, even when it was not absolutely denied. Even modern Unitarians and Rationalists are not more complimentary, and yet unsettled and equivocal in their style of setting forth the character of Christ. But they all agree with the Arians of past ages in denying our Lord's proper Divinity, and his vicarious sacrifice.

Before leaving the Council of Nicæa, it is desirable to notice, in a few words:—

First. The fact that the emperor of the world, sitting on the throne of the Cæsars, called this Council and presided in it. And this was only a little over three hundred years from the birth of Christ. It is to be remembered, also, that the emperor's great object was to obtain harmony among his bishops and consolidate Christianity, so that he might more efficiently advance it and his empire.

Secondly. The number of its members, and the marks of suffering seen on their persons, which they had borne as witnesses for the truth of Christianity in times of persecution, may well command our attention and veneration. In such an assembly there was doubtless a great diversity of persons and some strongly marked characters. A number of those assembled were young, who had never known persecution. They could barely remember the edict of toleration published in their boyhood. The older and the larger part of the assembly had "lived through the last and worst of the persecutions, and they now came like a regiment out of some frightful siege or battle, decimated and mutilated by the tortures or the hardships they had undergone." Most of the older members of that Council had lost a friend or a brother by persecution for his profession of Christianity. "Many still bore the marks of their sufferings. Some uncovered their sides and backs to show the wounds inflicted by the instruments of torture. On others were the traces of that peculiar cruelty which distinguished the last persecution. The loss of the right eye, or the searing of the sinews of the leg, to prevent their escape from working in the mines. Both at the time and afterwards, it was on their character as an army of confessors and martyrs, quite as much as on their character as an Œcumenical Council, that their authority reposed. In this respect no other Council, could approach them, and in the whole proceedings of the Assembly, the voice of an old confessor was received almost as an oracle."*

Thirdly. We should note the place assigned in this Council to the Word of God, and their testimony concerning it and their own worth. In the twenty-first Article in the Canons of this Council, it is said: "Things ordained as necessary for salvation have neither strength nor authority unless it may be declared that they are taken out of Holy Scripture." And accordingly, after the preliminary discussions had taken place, and every thing was prepared for the opening of the Council by the personal appearance of the emperor, we are then told how they honored the Divine Word. The chamber being a large oblong hall, in the centre of the imperial palace, and the benches being arranged so that the Bishops and their attendants, who were very numerous, were seated according to their dignity; and then, in the centre of the room, on a throne, was placed a copy of the Holy Gospels, as the nearest approach to the presence of Christ himself as presiding in the Council; and near this there was another smaller throne, carved in wood and richly gilt, on which the emperor sat. And according to Wescott,† such honor was usually accorded to the Scriptures in the Councils of those days, at least of those held after the Council of Nicæa. And he is supported by Suicer, and by the picture of the Council at Nicæa.‡ Thus did they teach that the use of creeds or catechisms is to assist us to a form of sound words, so that we may more easily and more fully appre-

---

* Stanley's Eastern Church, p. 186.
† Wescott on the Canon.
‡ Stanley's Eastern Church, p. 212.

hend sound doctrines. We are to believe concerning God and the Holy Trinity what is revealed to us in the Scriptures, and to obey and do just as the Scriptures teach us. As the solar system, in all its awful grandeur, existed before there was a son of Adam to study and map out the heavens, so our holy faith existed before there was a syllable of our Book-Revelation, or any Creed formulated, or system of theology taught, or any Council, Pope, Convocation, or Assembly to pour anathemas on all who cannot pronounce the approved Shibboleths. Nor is it possible for any one Creed, nor for all human Creeds, to circumscribe the Truth and Grace of God. Our faith is larger than Creeds. And may God grant not only that we may steadfastly hold them, but be filled with the Spirit of God, which is the life of religion.

Fourthly. Something as to the use of Creeds may be easily learned from their influence on Christendom. Strauss, in speaking of the Apostles' Creed (§ 142), says: "Along with this popular form of confession of faith in CHRIST, there sprang up at the same time a more precise elaboration, induced by the differences and disputes which were early manifested on isolated points."

Next to the Holy Scriptures, the Christology of the three creeds is to be considered the greatest legacy of doctrinal truth that we have received from past ages. And, all things taken into a fair account, they are remarkable for the clear, simple, and brief manner in which they express the fundamental articles of religion. The Apostles' Creed may be considered the summary of Christian faith before the Council of Nicæa, and the Nicene-Constantinople Creed as the work of its own times, and the so-called Athanasian Creed as the articulated faith of the Catholic Church, from the close of the fourth or middle of the fifth century. The errors aimed at are not always named, but clearly seen in the way the true faith is expressed. These creeds were formed under the light of and with all the advantages of the culture of Greek and Roman literature. No age of the Church had ever been able to employ more cultivated ability for the using of precision and accuracy in terms, than that of the Council of Nicæa and the age of Athanasius. And these creeds were formed to deny and refute the heresies of the Cerinthians, Ebionites, Gnostics, Docetæ, of Basilius and Basilides, and of Apollinaris, and of the Nestorians and Eutychians, and are equally valuable as summaries of sound doctrine, in modern times, for both Protestant and Roman Catholic churches, as against Naturalism, Pantheism, Transcendentalism, or Socinianism, or Unitarianism.

Among the first acts of Queen Elizabeth, with the assent of the English clergy in their convocation, was one to raise the Councils of Nicæa, Constantinople, and Chalcedon, as judges of heresy, to the same level as the High Court of Parliament. And the doctrines of these Councils have been widely received as on a level with the Holy Scriptures themselves, and their decrees made equal to imperial laws. And in the Russian Church, every Article of the Nicene Creed is exhibited by series of pictures, in books, and on the walls of their chapels, for the purpose of making the articles of their faith familiar to the popular mind.* The Nicene Creed is the test of orthodoxy and the bond of faith in all the Eastern Churches. In fact, it is the accepted Creed of the Church Universal; for the Apostles' Creed and the so-called Athanasian Creed have never been incorporated formally into the ritual of the Greek Church.

And not only are such articulated forms of faith bulwarks of Christian doctrine, unless emasculated or corrupted by an alliance with secular power, or prostituted to partisan politics, but they are incorporated into the daily devotional life of the people. The faithful are taught them in their youth, and they are recited at the festivals or sacraments of the Church.

But all these creeds were the work of fallible men, or of councils of fallible men, having the defects of judgment common to other men, and liable to be swayed by just such influences as all other assemblies are subject to, not to say, as history strongly intimates, even more liable to violence than many other kinds of assemblies. In proof of this we may cite the violence of the Council of Constance in the murder of John Huss, and of the second Council of Ephesus in trampling to death the Bishop of Constantinople by his reverence the Bishop of Alexandria; and also the violence and outrageous scenes of the Council of Chalcedon. In the twenty-first Article, already referred to, the Council of Nicæa says:—
" Forasmuch as such Councils are assemblies of men, whereof all

---

* Stanley's Eastern Church, pp. 147–150.

be not governed with the Spirit and Word of God, they may err, and sometimes have erred, even in things pertaining unto God." It is well known that the personal presence of the emperor Constantine scarcely sufficed to keep down violence and preserve order in the august Council of Nicæa. Dean Milman, in his Latin Christianity, and the Great Gregory, have said some exceedingly severe but just things about the prejudice and passion of general councils. Are not all these things written in Eusebius, Mansi, Gibbon, Mosheim, and many others?

Nor, *fifthly*, can any one fail, in turning over the points even of this brief review, to be struck with the identity, the essential sameness of what are now recognized as the true evangelical, orthodox views of Christ, with the opinions of the Church in the early ages; and so, on the other hand, the identity of the views that are now recognized by the great majority of Christians as erroneous, concerning the person of Christ, with those that were condemned as heresies in the early ages by the Church, is no less clear and distinct. Those who now deny the proper Divinity of our Lord, and take away from us his expiatory death, are nothing less than the old Ebionites who have furbished up the soiled armor of the Gnostics.

Nor, *sixthly*, should we overlook the fact, that in the second, third, and fourth centuries, the errors that called out the deliberative utterances of the faithful, were chiefly imported into the Church from ritualism on the one hand, and from philosophy on the other. Judaizers and Greek philosophers, becoming Christian theologians, gained a point from which they sought to ingraft new life upon their systems. Nor did they labor wholly in vain. Christianity did put life into the world as the civilization of Greece and Rome had never been able to do. The Cross rose as the world's luminary over the paling fires of Greek and Roman altars. In the theological errors of the early ages of the Church, we see the dying struggles of the old heathen philosophy.* And this, moreover, is a point that should not pass by us unheeded. The corruptions of the faith and worship of our day are the fruits of the very same things. In the last chapter of the Epistle to the Hebrews we are strongly urged to steadfastness in the

---

* See Hypatia, *passim*. By Rev. C. Kingsley.

faith, because of the fulness and completeness of "Jesus Christ, who is the same yesterday, and to-day, and forever. Be not carried about with divers and strange doctrines." Here, variegated doctrines mean such as blended the law and the Gospel, and required circumcision before baptism and the Lord's Supper, and taught that the way into the Church of Christ was through Judaism. Is not this ritualism? And here, *strange* doctrines mean *foreign* doctrines—doctrines brought from Greek and Roman philosophy, from the Transcendentalists of Greece and the Pantheists of Asia. *Strange doctrines* were such as had not the authority of the Word of God, and were unknown to the Apostles' Creed. What was, is, and that which hath been, is what is to be until the Son of Man is revealed. We must guard against will worship, *variegated* as well as *strange doctrines*, a sensual ritualism and a vain philosophy.

As reference has been made in one or two places in the preceding discourses to the singular confusion of the Koran concerning our Lord, a few facts from the history of Mohammed's education and religious experience are proper, and will, at the same time, be in evidence as to the numerous Apocryphal Gospels that existed in the early ages, which have also already been alluded to. It is plain, from the almost endless legends of Mohammed's life, that his knowledge of the Old Testament and of Christianity was derived from a Syrian or Nestorian monk of Bostra, who was with him in his journeys as a camel-driver. Consequently the local legends of Syrian or Arabian Christians formed the ground-work of Mahomet's knowledge of Christianity. These formed the Christ of the Arabian prophet. The genuine canonical Gospels were almost or altogether unknown to him. But the apocryphal Gospels, which were enshrined in so many of the traditions of the East in his day, were familiar to him, and hence we are at no loss to know how he came to fall into so many errors concerning our Lord. The resemblance and the contrast, the errors and the truth, found in the doctrines and legends of the Koran, are easily traced to the prevailing traditions that were known to Mohammed. Nor is this remark to be limited to the case of Mohammed. The *unbelief* of the West is as philosophically accounted for as the *misbelief* of the East; and both are the fruits of ignorance as to the true character of our Lord, and as to the nature of His kingdom. As we forgive the skeptics of the last century, at least find an excuse for their unbelief, and for their hatred of Christianity, because "they only knew it as represented by the corrupt monarchy and hierarchy of France, so may we still more forgive Mohammed for the inferior place which he assigned amongst the Prophets to Him whom he knew not as the Christ of the Four Evangelists, but as the Christ of the Gospel of the Infancy or of Nicodemus."—*Stanley's Eastern Ch.*, p. 367.

III. *The Aspect of Modern Thought concerning the Christ of the Evangelists.*

God's written Word and the Incarnate WORD are in two respects very much alike. Both are human and divine, and both have met with great opposition and with great success in the world. The Bible is the Word of God in human language. Jesus Christ is God manifest in human nature. The Bible has been more frequently burned, and more severely criticised, and more violently opposed, than any other or than all other books, and still the " words of the LORD are pure words; as silver tried in a furnace of earth, purified seven times;" so the person of our Lord Jesus Christ has been subjected to a more laborious, searching examination, both by friends and enemies, than any other has ever sustained on earth. His character has stood such a test of criticism as no other can possibly bear. Nor do we complain of this. It is a necessary condition of His claims and of human responsibility. Never man spake like Him. Never was there a character like Him upon earth before. Never, neither before nor since His coming, has there been such a kingdom as His set up. It was to be expected, therefore, that His life and the nature of His kingdom would be subjected to the most profound and exhaustive investigations. The fact is now simply on this wise : More than eighteen centuries have passed since Jesus was born, and He is now confessedly *the central figure* in the literary, philosophical, and material progressive history of the world. The intellectual powers and the affections of mankind were never so universally directed towards Him as they are now. Even if we admit that there was in some former periods greater simplicity, or more intensity of faith in particular sections of the Church, or a greater enthusiasm or devotion to His person among the martyrs and confessors, still it is true, there is now more intelligent mind, more learning and intellect, and a greater breadth of interest directed towards Christ than at any former period of the world's history. And even those who deny His miracles and do not look to Him for salvation, admit the dignity and moral purity of the character represented by the name Christ, and vie with one another in rendering Him the highest eulogy. They generally agree in saying that He is a person whom mere human history does not altogether explain—" Unique in the history of the world, beautiful and sublime."—*Renan.*

Nor is it here unworthy of remark, that as each age has its own mission, and makes its own literature, so each age of the Church has had its specialities. In the Apostolic age, for the most part, our Lord's Divinity was regarded by his followers very much in the same light as the existence of God is in the Bible. Formal statements concerning it seemed unnecessary. And the greatest differences of opinion among them, immediately after the Apostles' days, arose about the person of Christ, and chiefly as to the reality of his proper human nature. The canon of Holy Scripture soon excited great attention, but none too much, nor any too soon. For apocryphal writings, claiming to be from inspired Apostles and teachers, were numerous at an early day. And so, also, it became necessary for the doctrine of the Trinity, and the nature of Christ's Kingdom, and the proper sphere of His Church, to be stated and understood. And so in the sixteenth century, the doctrine of justification by faith, the right of private judgment, liberty of conscience, and the authority of the Word of God, excited special attention, and were elaborately set forth. We do not mean that the Articles of Faith alluded to were not known before the times indicated respectively, or that all the deliverances made concerning them are infallibly true, or that their advocates have always been consistent. Far from it. But we do mean that certain views of doctrine, or certain articles of religious faith have at different times commanded attention as specialities. In our day the inspiration of the Scriptures, the historic verity of our Gospels, and pre-eminently the questions, *Who is Christ,* and what is the future of Christianity, are the most prominent.

Christianity is now an acknowledged fact. It is the great force or power of the world in the nineteenth century. It is seen in our arts and laws, and in the administration of justice and of international comity. It must have had a beginning. There was a time when the nations of the world knew nothing of it. But now the great nations of the earth, who wield the elements of power on this globe, all profess to have adopted Christianity as their religion. And the historic evidences for its beginning about eighteen hundred years ago, and of its spreading among the nations, are before us and challenge our scrutiny. What, then, is the origin of this world-admitted fact, that Christianity is now the great power of our globe? Is Christianity the scheme or system of a mere man? Or is it the outgrowth of art and science, or an effect from the mere progress of society? Is it the work of a fanatic or of an impostor, or is it the natural result of the wants of man expressed systematically, but founded upon a myth? Or is it of divine origin? The fact of Christianity implies the existence of Christ as a person, unless his existence is historically disproved. And if the Bible is all nothing but a great parable, or if Jesus was merely a man, though as wise as Socrates, Plato, or Confucius, how has it come to pass that thousands of thousands have adopted His moral lessons, although they differ from those to which they are naturally inclined and educated? And how did it come to pass that His followers admired him so much that they attributed miracles to Him, though, according to our opponents, He never wrought a miracle; that they clothed him with Divinity and believed him to be their long-promised Messiah, though he never in a single instance met their expectations concerning the Messiah, nor in a single known instance did he comply with what they wished him to do if He were the Messiah? It is an old and a common, but still a very true remark, that the establishing of Christianity without miracles—of a religion supernatural, and yet based on an appeal to miracles which were never wrought—would be a far greater wonder than all the Scripture miracles put together.

Given the fact, that a Galilean of obscure birth, without wealth or learning, or political influence, overthrew the religions of the world, and established his own, confessedly the most moral and spiritual the world has ever seen, and that it is now the religion of all the most civilized nations—that the empire of this globe is now in the hands of Christian nations—and where is the explanation, if Jesus is not the Son of God? It was an attempt to answer this question that brought out, a little more than thirty years ago, Strauss's "Life of Jesus." This was a marked era in the history of Christianity—the most marked, in some respects, that had occurred since the Council of Nicæa. Strauss's work is far the ablest of modern times on his side of the question. It "startled the world like a clap of thunder out of a calm sky." As his main force was in pulling down, it was not strange that Christians refused at his summons to abandon their faith in the Christ of the Apostles' Creed, who is the Christ of the Evangelists and of history. It was to be expected they would defend the foundations of their faith. And although it is not our immediate purpose in this place to enter into any investigation concerning the authority of the Gospels, we may be allowed to say that the Christ of the Synoptists is identical with the Christ of John's Gospel; or, in other words, that we have one Gospel in four, and four in one. The life of the God-man is drawn for us by four artists, but it is the same life of the same person. We have four pictures, each original and independent, but all true copies of the same original.

Destructive, however, as Strauss's work was, he has not refrained from it, but in his *new Life of Jesus*, still tells us miracles are absolutely impossible, and our Gospels are therefore mere myths, without any real foundation in history. Substantially, although differing in details, the same result is reached by the learned criticisms of the Tübingen school and the eloquent romancing of Renan's "Life of Jesus." Renan rejects myths only to substitute legends. We shall endeavor elsewhere, as we proceed, to see wherein the strength of these champions of unbelief and disbelief and misbelief lies, and to show that their strength is nothing but weakness. In the mean time, every one who desires it may find a happy solution of the question concerning the time when our Gospels were written, in a small work by Professor Constantine Tischendorf. This pamphlet of M. Tischendorf may well be set against all that MM. Strauss, Bauer, and Renan have said about the age of our Gospels. It shows conclusively, and in a brief way, that our Gospel histories are records most trustworthy, and may be historically traced back to the very times of the Apostles themselves.

The intense interest so widely acknowledged on such subjects is proof that whatever may be the errors of our times, ours is not an age of indifference. The love of many of Christ's people has waxed cold, sad declensions have taken place in many parts of the

Christian Church, and iniquity abounds; still there are a few names, as in Sardis of old, which have not defiled their garments. True faith is yet upon the earth, and in it there *is life for the nations.* Nor is there any other hope for the true reformation of mankind and the world's true progress than the Gospel.

1. Then there is such a thing as faith, belief, which is, in a religious sense, a firm persuasion of the truths of religion; and a believer is one who gives credit to the truth of the Bible as a revelation from God, or, more strictly, one who receives Christ as his Saviour as He is offered in the Gospel. To have true belief, therefore, implies knowledge, and a true assent to it and trust in it. It is plain we cannot believe till we have some knowledge of what is to be believed. We cannot believe in a man of whose existence we have never heard. Correct knowledge, then, is important. For a man may not be a believer in Christianity, simply because he knows nothing of it, as the heathen, or even as some in Christendom, who are in profound ignorance for the want of education.

2. Unbelief is negative. It refuses to admit belief. But it is an act as well as belief.

3. Disbelief is also a refusal to give credit—a denial of belief. It is the act of disbelieving—rejecting evidence offered which belief accepts. It is, therefore, a stronger term than unbelief. A disbeliever, therefore, is one who has some knowledge of Christianity, but rejects its evidences. He has the proofs more or less before him, but incurs the guilt of setting them aside. There is, then, more hope of saving an unbeliever than a disbeliever, for the unbeliever may still be open to light—his want of faith may be owing to his ignorance or stupidity. He may yet be enlightened and convinced; but disbelief has already rejected the light.

4. Misbelief is the belief of falsehood, an erroneous belief. It implies the possibility of an amiable, teachable disposition, but misled. The etymologies of these terms and the lexicons are at hand to verify the importance of distinguishing them. Perhaps all are ready to admit that such distinction is of great use to prevent confusion or injustice in such discussions. At least it is not without design that I use the phrases "unbelieving science" and "disbelieving criticism." *Disbelieving criticism* means that the

proofs of the inspiration of the Scriptures, and for the Divinity of Christ, and the personal immortality of the soul have been weighed like Belshazzar, and found wanting—that they have been examined by competent persons, who had a right to examine them, and that they have done full justice to them in the examination, and have found them defective, not to be believed, and they therefore are rejected. Disbelieving criticism takes from us, therefore, at once our Bible and our Saviour, and leaves us nothing in their place. We are left to grope a while in darkness, and then feel our way down to eternal night. And it is just here, in the very beginning, that Strauss's *myths* and Renan's *legends* break down. For if we have no credible sacred writers there is nothing to discuss. There is no original subject for dissection. Accordingly, Ebrard* asserts that it was not historical discrepancies in the Gospels, but dogmatic doubts about the Divinity of Christ, the reality of His miracles and the fact of His resurrection, which first led the negative critics to dispute the historical character of the four Gospels. That is, they did not like to believe the Articles of the Faith commonly received by Christians, and therefore they went to work to destroy the historic verity of the writers who have given us the life of the Founder of our Faith. *Unbelieving science* does not directly belong to the line of my present discussion; but it may be proper here to say, that it is more modest, but quite as dangerous as disbelieving criticism. It is so diffident that it does not profess to know any thing, not even whether there be a God or no. It scarcely ever names the God of the Bible, as if its reverence for the ineffable name was even greater than that of the pious old Hebrews. And yet it does not deny His existence outright. It is far too prudent for that. It goes to work to show that there is no need of a Creator God—that the universe can be accounted for and taken care of without a God. Forces, laws, *natura naturans*, or at least something of this sort, explains every thing. And then the philosophical maxim is applied, If there is no need of a God, of course there is none. At least, there is no supreme conscious personal intelligence, and hence there is no creation, no revelation, no being for man to pray to, and there is no Saviour. Man, as far as he is any thing, is a "development,"

---

* Gospel History, p. 473.

a "continuity," a "transformation," a "transmigration;" and all this these very scientific men talk about, without telling us how any thing ever came into being at first which has developed and continues in such a marvellous way. If there were half a dozen pairs of Adams and Eves, or if man has developed himself out of an Eastern monkey or an African gorilla, or grew like a tapeworm, whence the originals? The main point, however, in the direction of our argument is this: that this modest, unbelieving science brings out as a result, quite as strongly as disbelieving criticism, the doctrine, that Moses and the Apostles are not to be believed as historic verities. Lamarck, Roca, Huxley, Lyell, Darwin, Nott, Gliddon, and Morton, advance under the garb of science to undermine the foundations of our Faith. Disbelieving criticism, under a legion of banners and with variegated devices, is working for the same result. Rationalists, neologists of all schools, both of ideal and material Pantheism, whether swearing by Comerius, Reimarus, Paulus, Spinoza, Strauss, Channing, Theodore Parker, Colenso, or Renan—all are neither more nor less than the successors of the Ebionites and of the various schools of the Gnostics and Arians of former ages—and if they could all succeed in their attack, they would bury themselves and us in fathomless ruins. Still we plead for free inquiry and perfect religious liberty. It is not according to the spirit of the Gospel to denounce all critical investigations concerning the origin and character of Christianity. Truth never fears scrutiny. The waves of critical unbelieving learning, as they roll over us, may wash away the drift, but the foundation rock will stand.

Our Lord's history is not more sacred than it is intensely human. And if such writers as Renan and the author of *Ecce Homo* arouse the Church to study more carefully the life of our Lord, and bring us into closer sympathy with Him, then they will have done a good work. It is unquestionably true that our great theologians since the Reformation have generally kept us out in the cold, gazing up into heaven upon our risen Lord, having his head encircled with the glory of Eternity, and sitting on the right hand of the Throne of God, until we had almost forgotten that He ever walked the pebbly roads of Judea and Galilee with real human feet, and thirsted at Jacob's well, or wept at the grave of his friend Lazarus. No small part of the power of

Edward Irving and of the late Rev. Mr. Robertson of Brighton, as preachers, lay in the deep sympathy with which they introduced their hearers to the humanity of our Lord. As there is a natural tendency in every mind that is at enmity with God—a lurking disposition to avowed unbelief in every unrenewed heart—it is to be regarded as a favoring Providence that we are continually receiving aid and strength as learning and science advance. The progress of Art does not destroy the sense of the beautiful. Nor has "the advancement of science any more tendency to extirpate religion than it has to extirpate morality."—*Professor Fisher.* The searching criticism and the thorough examination of old manuscripts, and the readings of coins and pillars, and cylinders and bricks, and tombs and palaces, are like so many voices coming to us from the long-buried past to testify to the truth of the Holy Scriptures. It is certainly a remarkable feature in the critical history of our times that a manuscript Bible like that of Tischendorf, from Mount Sinai, and various old versions from distant and different parts of the world, have been found and collated at great expense, and that on every side, from all these sources, the united testimony is a confirmation of our faith in Jesus of Nazareth as the Christ, God's only Son, our Lord.

Our unbelieving physicists, for the most part, are content to leave us without any effort to furnish us with a positive religion. Their mission seems to be to suggest doubt, destroy belief, by intimating insuperable difficulties in the way of our book-Revelation, and against the supernatural origin of Christianity. But our disbelieving critics go further. As they deny the historical character of the Gospels, as they have pulled down, as they think, the superstructure of the generally received faith, so they admit they are under some obligations to build up another; and if they have failed, it is neither for the want of a will, nor for the want of learning and genius, nor yet for the want of a patient endurance of labor and devotion to their self-imposed task. They admit the justness of the demand on our part, that if the Gospels are not genuine and authentic as we receive them, they should tell us whence they are. As an answer to this question, various theories have been propounded. The hypothesis of Strauss, stated in as few words as possible, is this:

1. At the time Jesus lived there was a general expectation of a Messiah. The prevailing idea concerning Him was, that He would be a temporal prince, and deliver the Jews from their political adversaries; and that for this purpose he would work miracles, such as their heroes were said to have done in past ages.

2. Accordingly, Strauss says, it happened that John the Baptist arose at this time, and introduced Jesus of Nazareth, and then disappeared through the tower of Machærus with a headless body to an unlettered and unknown grave, though with an immortal name. Jesus, being baptized by John, gradually awoke to the consciousness that he was the promised Messiah; and that in time He gathered around Him a number of disciples, who admitted His claims.

3. His death, however, was soon brought about by His political enemies, and seemed to frustrate all the hopes of His disciples, until they conceived the idea that if they could prove, from the expectations of the old Jewish Church, that the Messiah was to rise from the dead, and succeed in spreading a report that Jesus had actually risen from the dead, then they supposed their ideas of empire or success in some way might still be realized. This impulse revived and completed their scheme.

4. And accordingly, in process of time, in order to make their pretensions plausible, they invented myths, which grew apace as they were repeated, concerning the supernatural conception, miracles, death, resurrection, and ascension of Jesus; and these embodied myths are our Gospels, which are therefore nothing more, nothing less, than the mere inventions of the unlettered men of Galilee. This is the substance of the celebrated theory of Strauss, to account for the Christ of the Gospels and the Christianity of our day. It is not, however, an original theory with him. His main purpose in constructing his argument on this theory seems to have been, to oppose believers in miracles on the one hand, and to overthrow, on the other, the *natural exposition system* of Paulus, by denying the fact that any such miracles had ever been wrought.

On mere critical and philosophical grounds, we regard this theory as unsatisfactory.

1. *First*, because he does not account for the prevailing expectation of a Messiah to come, of which he speaks. He assumes that there was such a general expectation prevailing at the time when Jesus appeared, but gives no account of its rise. To explain the origin of these expectations and show that they were erroneous seems to us the first thing that Strauss should have attempted. Why does he not tell us how such hopes concerning a Messiah grew out of the Old Testament? If they are not legitimately in the Old Testament, how did they arise? Why did the Jews believe that they were authorized to entertain such hopes at the time when Jesus came, if the writings of the old Jewish Church did not contain prophecies that were calculated to raise such expectations? And if such hopes were well founded, how came they into the Old Testament? and if such expectations are justly founded in the Old Testament, is not the New Testament their actual fulfilment? As a critic and an honest logician, there is no way for Strauss to be consistent but to say outright that the Apostles invented the Gospels, and had genius enough besides to make the Jews believe that their old Scriptures foretold a Messiah, when in fact there was no such prediction in them; and yet to invent such Gospels as our Evangelists have given us, and secure such success for their inventions as the facts of Christianity have been and now are, they must have been themselves as divine as they allege their great Master was. [See Discourse II.]

2. It is equally *a begging of the question* for him to assume that the Gospels are unhistoric, because miracles are impossible. For a writer of such pretensions as Strauss to state his leading proposition in the following way is surprising: Miracles are impossible; therefore the Gospels are unhistoric. That is, we must believe that miracles are impossible, and therefore all histories of miracles are myths; and this is all in order to disprove the genuineness of the Gospels. Now, it is so plain and easily apprehended, that there is a palpable distinction between the genuineness of a book and its authenticity, that I need not dwell on it. A book is authentic when it is true, even if it be anonymous; and it is genuine, whether true or not, when it is written by the author whose name it bears. The Gospels we believe are genuine, and they are authentic. It does not seem to have occurred to Strauss, that the same canon of criticism with which he starts out to examine the Gospels, if applied to Livy or Tacitus, or any ancient

author, would seriously damage them, or utterly destroy their authority. It is well known that Whately, in his historic doubts about Napoleon, and several other authors of similar works, have exposed the sophistry and unreliable character of this species of argumentation.

3. How did it happen, on Strauss's theory, that from the miracle of Cana in Galilee, everybody who knew any thing of the life of Jesus regarded Him as a reformer, a public teacher, and that He really did work miracles, or claimed to do so, in proof of His authority? It is not a sufficient answer to this point to say that Jesus did not always work miracles whenever His enemies demanded them, nor such miracles as they required. It is quite enough for us that they admitted that He claimed to have the power to work miracles, and that He avowed himself that He did work miracles by the finger of God, and that his cotemporaries admitted that He did work miracles. The fact of his performing miracles is admitted by all the ancients who admitted the historic verity of His life at all, although His adversaries explained them in such a way as to take from Him his Divinity and Messiahship. Now, unless Jesus was a deceiver, a lying impostor, He must have wrought miracles, for He says He did. But even our antagonist here is not willing to bring such a charge as this against His character.

4. We do not see how it can be believed that such myths were possible as Strauss supposes. What is a myth, and how was it possible for the world to allow such myths to prevail as true histories? I understand a myth to be a narrative, something like a fable, a parable, or an allegory, differing from these rather in its greater simplicity and want of previous intention, more than in any thing else. The true myth, we are told, is *improvised*, and is without deliberation or "conscious invention." Thus it is alleged arose Greek Mythology. *Vilmar* and *Grote* have written largely and exceedingly well on the origin of myths, and the result of what they have written is, that such myths as our Gospels, if they are myths, could not have arisen in the age of Augustus. It was pre-eminently an age of philosophical inquiry, an age of poets, orators, philosophers—the investigating age of Greek and Roman culture. It was the age of Josephus, Tacitus, Cicero, and Seneca. Certainly there was learning enough, critical acumen enough, and

aversion enough to the doctrines of the Crucified, to have then exposed the deceit and fraud of myths that seriously claimed to be true histories, and to found on the alleged facts of these histories a new religion, and a system of morals superior to any other then known. It certainly was not an era favorable to the rise of myths. Where are any other such myths that can be alleged as characteristic of the Gospel times, or as belonging to any similar age? The late Dr. Arnold, of Rugby, has said somewhere, it is ridiculous and wholly inconsistent, "the idea of men writing mythic histories between the time of Livy and Tacitus, and of St. Paul mistaking such myths for realities." All the myths and legends with which we are acquainted have certainly grown out of a very different state of society from that which we find in the Roman empire under the laws and arms that governed the world when and where Christianity had its birth. Nor does the fact, that many apocryphal Gospels were multiplied in the following ages, make at all against our position. For it can be shown that they arose in ages subsequent to the appearance of the Gospels of our Evangelists, and that they were generally, if not always, the offspring of pious frauds. They were intended to favor sects and parties who held doctrines which were condemned by the majority of believers.

We must press our question, then, What had become of the whole Jewish people and of all their sacred writings, that these myths of the unlearned fishermen of Galilee were not exposed and utterly put to silence? How is it possible that the whole world could have been prevailed upon to admit myths as historic verities, so soon after the time when it was alleged these events, and at the very place where such events as the miracles of the life and resurrection of Jesus, had taken place? Is it possible to believe that such events as the crucifixion and resurrection of Jesus could have been admitted as true by anybody, at the time the Apostles alleged these events as facts, in proof that Jesus was the Messiah, in their public discourses, and at the time when our Gospels were written if everybody knew that in fact they were mere myths? Certainly such myths could not have been promulgated till all the Apostles and all other eye-witnesses of the life of Jesus were dead. But we know and can prove, according to Tischendorf and a host of other very learned and respectable writers, that our Gospels date back to the age which we claim for the

Apostles themselves. Nor can it be unfair here to say, that Renan admits the early date of the evangelical histories, as early at least as the second half of the first century—that is, to about the times of the authors to whom they are attributed. *Vie de Jésus*, pp. xiv., xxxvii. Renan's admissions in regard to the Gospels, especially that of St. John, are quite sufficient for the utter refutation of all Strauss has said against them. If what Renan says of John's Gospel is true, it destroys forever the mythical theory of Strauss. No wonder, therefore, that Renan abandoned myths for legends, although we do not think he has materially benefited his cause by so doing.

We can prove, then, so early a date to the Gospel narratives that sufficient time had not elapsed from the death of Christ to have allowed for the invention and promulgation of such mythical tales as Strauss alleges, nor of such legends as Renan has invented. And if the growing and reception of such myths as true histories during the lifetime of the Apostles is inconceivable, it is equally so at any subsequent period in the face of the Christian Church, and of an intelligent, literary heathen empire, such as that of Rome, in the bosom of which Christianity arose. And here it is necessary to remember, that it has always been fundamental with the Christian Church to believe in the literal truth of the facts narrated in the Gospels, at least concerning the supernatural conception, miracles, and resurrection of Jesus. And which now, in this nineteenth century, requires the most faith; namely, to believe in Jesus Christ according to the Apostles' Creed, as the Christ of the Gospels and the author of the Christianity of history, or to believe that the man Jesus of Nazareth has been made the Christ of history by the mere fancy and enthusiasm of his followers, who ascribed to Him attributes and powers he never had, nor claimed to have—that it was only after the popular mind had become excited as to the exploits of some great personage who was expected to come, that miracles and supernatural events were ever thought of in connection with the name of Jesus?

Strauss's theory requires—

1. To deny, at the beginning of the argument, the genuineness of the Gospel histories—which is a main question in the argument. All the proof, therefore, historical and theological,

which are neither few nor light on the side of the genuineness of the Gospels, are against Strauss.

2. According to Strauss, we must believe that Jesus himself and his disciples believed as true what He and they knew to be false, namely, that he wrought miracles, when he did not do so; nor did He even claim to have ever done so. How, then, could such a belief ever have had a beginning? If the Hebrew prophecies did not properly create such expectations as it was alleged were realized in Jesus when He was set forth as the Messiah, how did these expectations arise? And if Jesus did not actually meet such expectations during his life, how could He himself ever have believed that He was the Messiah? and how could his disciples have deceived themselves so as to impose upon the world as true history what they and everybody knew to be mere myths?

3. To answer this, Strauss requires us to believe, again, that there was an original infant Christian Church *outside* of the apostolical society, that agreed on propagating these myths as true histories—a body of disciples able and willing to be deceived, to deceive themselves knowingly, without the slightest selfish motive that can be discovered, and willing to deceive the world, although in their attempts to do so they were required to endure all manner of persecution, even unto death; and yet they succeeded. But all history is to be set aside if we receive such a view as this. This is, indeed, faith stronger than "Great Heart's." Who were these disciples? Who founded this non-apostolic society? Whence came this body of Christians, outside altogether of apostolic labors? And if such a body of Christians gave utterance to these myths, where were the Apostles that they did not deny them? And who was it that preached these myths to the Gentiles, and how did it come to pass that the preaching of such myths turned the world upside down, and converted Athens, Corinth, and Rome, and made the Cross prevail on "mighty Cæsar's" throne?

4. Again: according to Strauss (for his disbelief makes large demands on our faith), we must believe that the resurrection of Christ is a pure fiction, and yet, at the same time, that the Apostles did all sincerely believe that He had risen from the dead. On no other

hypothesis can their steadfast adherence to the cause of Christ be defended or explained. But if Jesus did arise from the dead, as they believed he did, then He is all we believe Him to be. And we must remember that they adhered to the positive declaration that they knew He had risen from the dead, for they saw Him dead and buried, and then saw Him alive, and for many days, until He ascended into heaven, through poverty and persecution unto death; and most of them died as martyrs, not for a mere opinion, but for believing this as a fact. [See Discourse XI.]

5. If, then, the resurrection of Jesus is an historical fact, and if the circumstances and sayings of His life are historical, why is the mythical theory necessary at all? And if they are not historical, is there any thing that can be received as historical truth? Is there any history that has such a monument for its verity as Christianity to-day is for the truth of the Gospel? And if there is any thing, one single supernatural event, blended with the natural in the history of religion, why not enough of the supernatural to produce miracles, and to give us the realities of the Gospels? If there is any thing supernatural in the history of our universe, even the least thing, we have all we need to be consistent in believing in the supernatural origin of Christianity. I do not see how it is possible to receive the Gospels as mythical tales, or legendary narratives having a foundation in facts, and not acknowledge that there are many things that are perfectly natural bound up with them, and as such true; and if so, why is not the supernatural part of the Gospel history true also?

6. This mythical theory does not account for the supernatural character of our Lord. If this theory is correct, the character, temper, and tone, and motives, and conduct, of the first believers in Christianity are anomalous. There is no possible common sense or reasonable way of explaining their character that is consistent with this mythical theory. And, moreover, if this theory is correct, then the character of our Lord himself is an original conception, coming out of the unaided brain and souls of His Galilean followers; and so also is the description of it an original description, out of the mere human mind of unlearned fishermen, from the little sea of Tiberias. And if this is so, how is it that such a conception, and such a description, have never been produced or found anywhere else? If the Christ of the Gospels is

the mere creation of His disciples, then were they themselves as great as they have made their Lord to be. Without the Christ of the Gospels, we have no adequate cause for the Christianity of these eighteen hundred years. As well, to borrow an illustration from another, say that " the Amazon, rolling its broad stream for thousands of miles, and spreading fertility along its banks, is all owing to a shower of rain one spring morning," as to ascribe Christianity to any mere human origin.

In a word, Strauss requires us to ignore history, reject the faith of Christendom, and mutilate the faculties of the human soul, and mock at the cravings of the human heart and conscience. For if there is nothing supernatural in our holy faith, then we must go to naturalism, transcendentalism, or pantheism for comfort. But alas! it is not there.

We have already alluded to Strauss's new Life of Jesus, which while it is a recast, is also a modification of his previous views in one direction, and a stronger presentation of others in another direction. It is a newly written and entirely a different book from his old work, and, on the whole, perhaps a more dangerous one. It is a most laborious and ingenious attempt to incorporate the latest results of the theological criticism of Germany in such a way as to set them before his countrymen at large. He labors to popularize his views, so as to get them into the minds of the masses. He acknowledges the Tübingen school, under the leadership of Dr. F. C. Bauer, Zeller, and Hilgenfeld, and though not agreeing with all their views, they are all against the Christ of our Creed. The *Westminster Review* pronounces Strauss's last work "the most complete and satisfactory solution of the great religious problems with which it grapples that has ever been produced."

It was doubtless the influence of Tübingen that led Strauss to put forth a restatement of his theory. But we can hardly escape from the feeling, as we see new terms, that they are designed in part to conceal his change of base. Comparatively, the repairing of the defects of the old work by the new one is of little consequence. For it is difficult for us to see how wilfully invented narratives are myths. A mere change of ground, therefore, when the old *animus* remains, is of consequence only as far as it gives us the advantage of position, by exposing his own vacillation and weakness.

The success of this new "Life of Jesus," by Strauss, has not come up, we think, to public expectation. Various reasons are assigned for this: such as,

1. It has not the novelty of his first work.

2. It is alleged that the public mind of Germany is fully inoculated with the virus of his first work, and cannot be impressed with the same virus from his second. The atmosphere is so charged, that it cannot contain any more in solution. Therefore the new work is not sold and circulated as was the first.

3. The continental mind was somewhat preoccupied with Renan. There was not room for even two such Richmonds in the field.

4. Perhaps a greater reason than all these is, that the work itself contains in its own bosom so many contradictions that public confidence in it is destroyed. And this is the more damaging, because Strauss is not in harmony with either Strasbourg, Tübingen, or Renan. And when "doctors disagree, disciples then are free." And,

5. We may add, that it is a great coming down for "the head and front" of critical learning in Europe, as directed to the historical evidences of our Gospels, to appeal from the learned to the popular tribune of unbelief among the uneducated classes. It strikes us as a great mark of weakness for a writer of his pretensions, and on such a subject, to make the unlettered the judge of historical evidences. He seeks to put forth his theory. Then he offers a kind of history of Jesus purged from legend and fable, and then a classified list of myths out of which the legend and history are to be framed. His *via dolorosa* is to get rid of myths by growing legends. Perhaps, after all, the most valuable thing about Strauss's new life of Jesus is that it serves as a kind of barometer, giving us the levity or weight of sentiment among the refined and educated, and yet unbelieving circles of Germany, in regard to the life, miracles, and teachings of Christ.

The main difference between Strauss and Renan, in the line of my present argument, is, that Renan uses the term legend where

Strauss employs myth. He makes the Gospels legendary narratives instead of mythical tales. He says these legendary narratives emanated chiefly from the Apostles themselves, and were largely founded on facts. Thus he admits an important point for us as against Strauss, namely, the early date of the Gospels, and historic verities for a beginning. On both of these points Renan is also at direct issue with Tübingen. But as Renan proceeds with his eloquent romancing, he makes the Evangelists no more than deceived honest chroniclers of legends, just like the chroniclers of the legends of the saints of the mediæval ages. He says it was the blind enthusiasm of His followers that made Jesus himself first think of claiming to be the Messiah, and that, making the claim at first to please them, He gradually fell into the belief that He was what they said He was, and could do what they attributed to him; and that his followers came honestly to believe at last that He was the Messiah, and did really work miracles; but that, in fact, he was only a superior benevolent, good kind of man. And thus the Gospels are, at best, only successful pious frauds, "the spawn of the terrible delusion, that one may lie for God."

Finally, it is plain, the truthfulness, the honesty, the moral excellence of Jesus must stand or fall with his supernatural claims. He could not be deceived. His testimony, therefore, concerning himself must be believed, unless he is a deceiver, an impostor. But such excellence of character as is universally admitted to have belonged to him, could not exist in an impostor. It is impossible for Him, who is the Truth itself, and who lived and died for the Truth, to have put forth claims to be what He knew He was not. He was born and died to bear witness unto the truth. He said He was the Son of God, the promised Messiah, and that whosoever believeth in Him should have everlasting life, and that his body should be raised up at the last day. It is credible, it is the highest reason, to believe just what He taught, and to believe it on his own authority.

Clearly, the result of Renan's admissions and argument is, that we must believe in the miracles of Jesus and his Apostles, or charge Christ and his Apostles with wilful and malicious fraud. "We have either truth or gross cheating. Such is the real alternative, and Renan has thus unintentionally done a service to the

Christian Church, by impaling unbelief upon this dilemma."—
Prof. Fisher.

The foundation of the celebrated Tübingen school, which in some respects is the most formidable attack of our day upon Christianity, is an avowed kind of Pantheism. It is a denial not only of the miracles of the New Testament, but of every thing supernatural. It allows no God but natural causes, and hence a miracle is an absurdity! It is only as pantheists, which is only another name for atheists, that Strauss, Bauer, and Renan can consistently deny the possibility of miracles. The Christless Theism of Theodore Parker and of Miss Cobbe requires pantheism as its last stopping-place. Having, however, already exhausted my space for this Appendix, I must leave the pantheism of Tübingen by recommending Prof. Fisher's "Supernatural Origin of Christianity," and Guizot's last volume, on the "Actual State of Christianity"—a volume which, as a whole, is far from being satisfactory, but the last Meditations on modern speculations we think worthy of attention.

It were easy to show that we cannot rely upon negative criticism for a guide to truth, because it is not agreed among its schools what we are to believe. Their contradictions are endless. They begin their arguments by begging the main question; and besides, they mutilate our faculties and destroy the hope of the human heart. "Le cœur," as Pascal says, "a des raisons que la raison ne connait point." "*The heart has reasons that the reason knows not at all.*"

FINALLY, having briefly reviewed the Christology of the ages of the Church before the Council of Nicæa, and taken a rapid look at the appearance of the speculations of the Modern Schools of disbelieving criticism, it seems proper to drop a few words of exhortation, designed especially for *theological students and young ministers of the Gospel.*

You may remember Fuller's advice about dividing a text or a subject: *What is it? Why is it, and what then?* The Athenians made an application of Demosthenes' *what then*, by rising and rushing out with the cry, "Let us fight Philip."

I. Will you allow me to say, we must learn to take a world-wide view of men and things, and escape from local, sectional, and fanatical prejudices? We must acknowledge the facts of science and history as they are brought to light. We must meet the claims of science and literature with a full measure of justice as to what they really are and have done. We have only to know the certainty of what they teach, and admit what are surely known as facts; and if we have not light from the Bible to explain them, we must wait for it. Our capacities are limited. All things are not for one moment. It has been beautifully said, God waited thousands of years for Newton and Laplace to teach us how to read his laws of Nature, and we read them even now with much stammering. We must wait, but we wait with perfect assurance that there is no contradiction between God's works and laws, in Creation and Revelation.

II. We must strive to acquire the ability to look with calmness and with an unblenching face on all the gathering hosts that appear against us. We must not be dismayed by their numbers, nor by the weight of their armor, nor by the noise of their shoutings. We must be willing to know their strength, conscious that He who is with us is more and mightier than they that are against us. The more intense the darkness, the brighter is the light that is ahead. The darkness of the night serves to bring out the stars. The late Hugh Miller, a great man, but in some respects a dangerous writer, especially for young men, used to give a somewhat humorous description of the strategetical methods of the crab and lobster. His description is in the following style. The crab is always for war. It flares up the moment of attack, goes off in a towering passion, and without discrimination grips at every thing within reach, and holds on to whatever it catches hold of, although it is thereby dragged out of its own hold to destruction. So there are some Christian writers and speakers, that are honest and earnest enough, but like the crab, they are not wise. Impetuosity is their besetting infirmity. But the lobster adopts an entirely different method of defence. If a limb is seized he throws it off—saying, "Take it, take it; only spare my life." But the lobster is apt to overdo his discretion. In a panic he yields limb after limb; as for instance, if you fire a musket over him, he throws off limb after limb, of which afterwards he finds he has great need, both as weapons of defence, and means of locomotion and enjoyment. Now I fancy we have all seen some of these panic lobsters. If only French savans or German rationalists say the chronology of Moses is all wrong; or the "Vestiges of Creation," or some huge volume from Baden Powell or Darwin appear, telling us the Bible is all wrong as to the creation; or of Huxley, Roca, or Lyell, telling us there were human races long before Adam, or that "the grand old gardener and his wife," as the poet laureate calls Adam and Eve, are a male and female gorilla a little more decently moulded; or when a Colenso, a Strauss, or a Renan plunges us all into fable-land, to flounder among myths or be smothered with legends, then, like the lobster, they yield limb by limb until there is nothing left but an awkward carcass, which the "pismires" may crawl out of the sand and devour. We should of course yield what is false, but maintain what is true. We must guard against yielding the key of our position out of courtesy, or by way of showing our confidence in our strength.

But as we hear the trumpet waxing louder and louder, calling our enemies to the assault upon our strong fortress, we are not to quake with fear. Bold and defiant as they form into darkening masses around us, and even after some of our outposts are battered down, and some of our pickets driven in, still are we without fear. For our enemies have yet to learn that Zion's walls are impregnable. It is only false or badly constructed, or unwisely or timidly defended outposts that have been shaken. Let all hell move and come with all its earthly auxiliaries against the Church of King Immanuel, and its gates will remain unshaken. The blasphemous boasting of the Syrian general did not take Jerusalem. The remnants of many a shouting host have reeled back shattered over the bodies of their comrades.

And here seems to us a proper place to say that just now there is a tendency to make altogether too much out of the "Religions before Christ," and the heaven-directed education of the world for His coming; almost, if not altogether as divine and as miraculous a mission being assigned to Greece and Rome; as to Moses and Israel. This is an argument as old as the first centuries, and it is a good one, and is wielded with vigor by *De Pressensé*, and put forth by *Mr. Gladstone* in his farewell literary address in Edinburgh, and also urged with overwhelming eloquence by Strauss, and many others of both the positive and negative schools of criticism. And it is not my purpose to reject this argument, but only to guard against making too much of it. It has great fascination for the young mind. It is true, Christ did come in the fulness of time. The world was prepared for his coming. The Divine plan was all pre-arranged. But it is not true that this preparation does, in the slightest degree, diminish the Divinity of Christ, or account for the origin of our holy faith outside of the Gospel. "The strangely inflammable state of the materials" which took fire at the Incarnation, to borrow a phrase from the *Edinburgh Review*, does not in any way help the negative school of critics. At best, it only throws the Divinity of Christianity a little farther back, where indeed it belongs, for Christ's kingdom is from before the beginning of the world. Whatever the religions before Christ may have been, or whatever preparations were made for the Incarnation, they were a part of the Divine plan for manifesting God in the flesh.

III. We must not allow our adversaries to fight men of straw. We must not allow the abuses of our holy religion to be substituted for the religion itself. True Christianity is something very different from mere theological dogmas, mysticism, or formalism. Political hierarchies, with a dogmatic, narrow, and cruel superstition substituted for the Gospel, have done more harm to true religion than all the infidels that have ever lived. We must not allow our antagonists to make Scripture for us, and then hold us responsible for it; nor allow them to bring out of the Bible what God never put into it; nor allow them to require the Bible to be or to do what its Author never designed it to be or to do. The direct and absolute purpose of Divine Revelation is to set forth the way of salvation for sinners of Adam's race by faith in Jesus Christ.

IV. A first and main position which we must boldly take in this controversy is, *that the facts of Christianity are intact.* It is a positive religion, with its history and its rites, and after all that has been said and done, its main facts have never been overturned. Dean Alford, himself a critic and Christian scholar, has just said that all the critical attacks made upon the verity of the Gospels have failed. Not one of the foundations of our Faith has been shaken. The essential fact is the Person of Christ. And, historically, it remains, after all that has been done, undeniable. Our schools of negative criticism have utterly failed to construct any theory that accounts for Christianity. Strauss and Renan make themselves wings out of myths and legends merely to fly over the main questions. We must insist upon it, the main facts of Christianity are to be received as facts, unless disproved historically upon evidence that is more credible than our Gospels. We must insist upon facts being received, not as opinions, or dogmas, or myths, but just as they really are—facts. Our holy religion acknowledges faith in the heart as a product of enlightenment by the Spirit of God, but it rests fundamentally on historical facts, and boldly appeals to the broadest stratum of human intelligence, to common sense, to the shrewdness of man's unsophisticated sense, and to his whole inner life, for evidences of its truth. Revealed religion neither ignores nor opposes right reason. True faith and true reason are both from God.

It is historically demonstrated that every and all systems of faith and morals that come short of a positive and definite belief in God, and of our personal responsibility to Him, will fail to control the masses of mankind. The old French Revolution is an illuminated picture of wild horses spurning the silken harnessings of philosophical morality; or shall I rather say, of furies gorging on blood, in the broad light of the highest philosophical refinement, in the heart of the most intelligent and polished nation of the world? France, during the reign of Terror, was the focus of all the light that science and art could create. It is amazing that the historian of the French Revolution and of the Life of Oliver Cromwell has not felt the force of this illustration. And strange that Goethe was ignorant of it, and Emerson sees it not. Has any thing, then, been gained by the essayists and social reformers and critics who take away our Lord? Are they able to point to moral results like those accomplished by the Gospel? Have they ever offered such ethics as Christianity teaches, or a system of Faith in any way to be compared with the Creed of the Apostles? After all these critics have destroyed, and all these reformers and all these schools of the Gospel of culture have done, is there a father or a mother in all Christendom who would not prefer their children should learn morals from the New Testament rather than from them, and die in the faith of the Christ of the Apostles than in any other?

V. Allow me to say, that we should guard against underrating the strength of *our antagonists*. It is well, it is right for young men, as they gird on their armor to go forth into the conflict, to feel that they are strong, and that their heart is equal for the fight. Encourage this faith; but at the same time be wary. After more than twenty years' constant conflict with our opponents, and that not always with equal armor, skill, or strength, yet always, I trust, with the victory, through the grace of the God of Jacob, I do earnestly beseech my young brethren not to despise the enemies' forces. The opponents of our holy Faith have learning—some of them true, profound, prodigious, and varied learning, as well as talents, genius, industry, and devotedness to their work. It is amazing to see the vastness of the critical and historical studies and metaphysical theories, and the amount of natural science, that are brought in our day into the question of the Truth of our Gospels, or of the supernatural origin of Christianity.

When you run over even an imperfect list of great writers engaged or lately engaged on this subject, you will not fail to see the justice of this remark. Think of what an amount of intellect, learning, criticism, and study is represented by such names as these: Paulus, Schleiermacher, Spinoza, Kant, the Bauers, Hase, Ewald, Neander, Meyer, Weisse, Ebrard, Gfrözer, Lange, Tholuck, Ullman, Dorner, Riggenback, Auberlein, Olshaussen, Hengstenberg, Bleek, Kostlin, Hilgenfeld, Volkmar, Holtzman, Reuss, Keim, Colani, Scherer, Nicolas, Guizot, Pressensé, and a host of others on the continent alone, not to say any thing of writers quite recent and better known among us belonging to Great Britain and our own country.

We must also remember that however acute, learned, able and eloquent may have been the Apologies of the ancients, and the Defences of Revelation made in former days, they are not the weapons now required. They are valuable storehouses and magazines, but our times require new armor. Strauss, Bauer, and Renan cannot be wisely answered in the same way that our fathers refuted Hobbes, Paine, and the French Encyclopedists.

And again, either from personal conviction or the force of education, or the influence of public opinion, the tone of unbelieving science and of disbelieving criticism, as well as the greatly improved moral character of the champions of unbelief in modern times, require answers of a very different character from those that were deemed efficient in past ages. The great names known in the advanced schools of science and of criticism who are arrayed against the verity of our sacred writers, cannot be answered by the charge of licentiousness or ignorance of the Gospel narratives. It only betrays weakness or rudeness on our part to indulge in raillery or flippant abuse, or to assume that they are ignorant defamers of the truth. We must be careful to do justice to our opponents. We must call no hard names, but refrain from all kinds of persecution for opinion's sake. It is unbecoming and useless to sneer at *Renan*, or rush madly at *Ecce Homo*. Let us rather seek to obtain a more and more thorough knowledge of the text of Holy Scripture in the originals, and a close and still more close personal union with THE ETERNAL WORD.

It were certainly a great gain to truth and godliness, if our scholars and interpreters of Holy Scripture would be content to help us to find out the mind of the Spirit, by opening up to us the meaning of the words and idioms of the original languages of the Scriptures, and not attempt to make Scripture for us, as so many of them do. So many of our learned men go to the Scriptures not to find out what they really teach, but to get arguments to prove or support their own peculiar views, that it seems to us the sons of the prophets should be taught Divinity out of the Hebrew and Greek Scriptures as the main text-books, following their own order and method.

It is related of the very learned and great *Selden*, that when he appeared in Parliament he " was regarded in the light of a valuable piece of national property, like a museum, or great public library, resorted to as a matter of course and a matter of right, in all the numerous cases in which assistance was wanted from any part of the whole compass of legal and historical learning. He appeared in the national council not so much the representative of the contemporary inhabitants of a particular city, as of all the people of past ages." In 1643, he was a member of the famous Assembly of Divines at Westminster, where he silenced and puzzled the great theologians. Sometimes, according to Whitelocke, " when the Divines had cited a text of Scripture to prove their assertion, he would tell them, perhaps in their little pocket Bibles, with gilt leaves, which they would often pull out and read, the translation might be thus, but the Greek or Hebrew signified thus or thus, and so would totally silence them." Never was there an age of the world requiring more mature, solid, and varied learning in the ministry than ours. If possible, we need ministers of the Gospel who should be walking libraries, with hearts in them, and baptized with the Holy Spirit.

VI. We need a more unreserved, full-hearted consecration to God and our work. One of our most amiable and eloquent opponents (Renan) says, a fresh contemplation of the Holy Land is equal to a fifth Gospel. May we not hope that our attempt to present a picture of our dear Lord as he is described by the voice of the Church in all ages, will awaken in us a deeper love for Him and a greater devotedness to His service? *There is life in the Church for the nations*, but it is not the Church itself substituted for Christ. We know that when the Israelites profaned the Ark of the Covenant, and when they made an idol of it, and trusted in it instead of the God of the Ark, they were defeated and slain, and the Ark itself was taken by the Philistines. The power of the Gospel, which was "the power of God" in the earlier ages of Christianity, when it went from the cross to the palace, and ascended the throne of the Cæsars, consisted in the glories of Christ's person, the wonders of His redemption, and the infinite worth of His righteousness and the merits of His precious blood. It was by the preaching of his life, death, resurrection, and ascension, and not by exalting the Church and its sacraments, that the Gospel prevailed at the beginning. And it is in the awakening of the Church to the fact, that Jesus is not acknowledged even in his own House in his true character, that inspires us with hope. When Christians are aroused by unbelieving science and disbelieving criticism and freezing formalism and starving ritualism to say, "Ye have taken away my Lord, and I know not where ye have laid him," then we expect Jesus himself to be revealed.

Brethren, let us try to climb fully up to the Cross as it stands on Calvary, and get a fresh baptism of the warm blood of the Son of God. The world around us is earnestly yearning after progress, but for the most part they are looking in the wrong direction. They are seeking the living among the dead. We are in the midst of mighty longings to break the chains that bind the human mind, nor can this tendency be repressed. These longings and aspirations are as innate as our hopes for immortality. What then shall we do? When the world is crying for bread, shall we offer it a stone? Rather, if need be, let us plunge into the gloomy catacombs, or dwell in caves or in the open fields, or dye the heather with our blood, as our fathers before us have done, in order that we may walk with God as Enoch did. Our times call for men who are near to God, who are baptized into the very life of Christ—men, the springs of whose religious life are deep, who cling with all their hearts to the Lord Jesus—men of courage and devotion like the Jesuit Xavier, or like John Knox, whose prayer, supported by his labors, was, *Lord Jesus, give me Scotland, or I die!* And his prayer prevailed. Men are now called for who are willing to be, to do, and to suffer every thing, out of love to Jesus and the souls of men—to travel, labor, endure hardships, and the perils of the seas and of all lands for His sake, and to consider it an honor to suffer in his cause. We want men who will serve God in every thing, and enjoy God in all things, and endure all things to win souls for Christ.

Let us strive to make our Lord himself our model, and to follow his Apostles as they followed Him. Let us remember that all truth on all subjects was perfectly known to Him, and yet he did not meddle with secular or temporal themes. Although full of the knowledge of every thing beautiful and great in the universe, and possessing an unerring acquaintance with all the relations of society, He would not even settle a dispute between two brothers about an inheritance, because it was a matter provided for by the civil government, and lay outside of the great scheme of redemption, to complete and unfold which was the mission of his life, and the purpose of his death and ascension.

If we could realize more of the spirit of Jerome, who said that he never entered the pulpit but that it seemed to him he heard the trumpet of the judgment-day sounding in his ears, then we should have more correct views of our responsibility as men set to watch for souls. O, if we could but feel that our fellow-men are sinners, and lift ourselves and them off our planet, and look upon ourselves and them as before God, amid the awful scenes of the last day, then we should find no time for any other subject in our pulpits but the way of salvation for sinners through Christ crucified.

There is no need for us to leave the Cross to preach on literary, scientific, economical, and political subjects. There are others quite as able, and in all probability much better prepared to take care of these subjects than we are; and, besides, it belongs to them to do so. These are not the elements of our sacred calling. We are sure to soil our robes, and to put ourselves in a wrong position, and to appear to a disadvantage, whenever we leave the duties to which we are consecrated for lower themes. Our business is to show unto men the way of salvation—to know the Word of God, and cause the people to understand it.

Let us take hold of the Cross of Christ, and lift it up as high as we can, and cry, *Behold the Lamb of God!* Let the world drift as it may in the vast ocean; let speculations and theories run as high as they may, and surge and boil, and roar and whirl around us; we have only one thing to do: to cling to the Cross, and busy ourselves with reading its history, and trying to know its virtues, and make our fellow-men acquainted with them. It is when we are nearest to the Cross of Jesus, and feel His blood to be most precious, and feel ourselves so identified with Him that He seems to be walking with us, as if His heart were throbbing against ours as we are toiling on in the path of duty, that we are the best prepared to represent Him and plead His cause. Let us live in the light of eternity reflected upon us from the Cross. Let us try to get the baptism of the truth and of the blood of expiation warm on our conscience, in view of the account we must give of our stewardship, and then we may hope for power and success.

"UNTO HIM THAT LOVED US, AND WASHED US FROM OUR SINS IN HIS OWN BLOOD, AND HATH MADE US KINGS AND PRIESTS UNTO GOD AND HIS FATHER; TO HIM BE GLORY AND DOMINION FOR EVER AND EVER. *AMEN.*"

CONTENTS TO APPENDIX.

APPENDIX, page 383.

I.

THE VITAL IMPORTANCE OF THE QUESTION NOW AT ISSUE.

PAGE

Reason for this Appendix—*Lord Bacon* and *Plutarch*—Atheism or Superstition—We become like the God we worship sincerely—Religious Belief germinal in the Human Soul—Religious Belief gives distinct Characteristics to a People, as in Greece and Rome........................ 386–389

II.

OPINIONS CONCERNING CHRIST BEFORE THE COUNCIL OF NICÆA.

Gnostics, Docetæ, Ebionites, Cerinthus, Basilides, Sabellius, Patripassians, Paulianists, *Arius.*—COUNCIL OF NICÆA, its Character and Occasion.—Modern Arianism—Dr. Bellows—"A Coat of many Colors"—The Reach of the History of Redemption—The Emperor in the Council—Many of its Members Confessors, who bore Marks on their Persons of their Sufferings from Persecution for their Belief in the Christ of the Apostles—How this Council honored the Word of God—All human Authorities fallible—National Influence of Creeds—Violence of Ecclesiastical Councils—Modern Gnosticism—"Divers and Strange Doctrines"—Mohammed's Religious Education—Eastern *Misbelief.*....................389–402

III.

ASPECT OF MODERN THOUGHT CONCERNING THE CHRIST OF THE EVANGELISTS.

The Written and the Incarnate WORD—Every Age has its Great Questions—Christianity a Great Fact in the Nineteenth Century—Strauss's Attempt to account for it—*Tischendorf's* "Time" of our Gospels—A Survey of the Thought of Christendom—Ours an Age of *Faith, Unbelief, Disbelief,* and *Misbelief*—*Ebrard* on the Critical Schools—Unbelieving Science—We claim Free Inquiry—Disbelieving Criticism—STRAUSS'S Theory analyzed and distinctly stated, and the proper Answer sketched—*Renan's* Legends quite as unphilosophical and unsatisfactory—The *Tübingen* School...402–420

FINALLY—

A FEW EARNEST WORDS TO THEOLOGICAL STUDENTS AND YOUNG MINISTERS OF THE GOSPEL.

Fuller's Division of a Subject—A World-wide View—Courage to look at the Foe—Not allow our Opponents to fight "Men of Straw"—Insist on the Facts of Christianity—Not underrate the Strength of our Adversaries—Great Learning as well as Devotedness required—Unreserved Consecration to our Work—MUST PREACH CHRIST MORE, AND NOTHING BUT CHRIST..420–429

THE END.

www.ingramcontent.com/pod-product-compliance
Lightning Source LLC
Chambersburg PA
CBHW051728300426
44115CB00007B/509